LITERATURE

LITERATURE

An Introduction to Fiction, Poetry, Drama, and Writing

TWELFTH EDITION

X. J. Kennedy

Dana Gioia
University of Southern California

PEARSON

Boston Columbus Indianapolis New York San Francisco Upper Saddle River
Amsterdam Cape Town Dubai London Madrid Milan Munich Paris Montreal Toronto
Delhi Mexico City São Paulo Sydney Hong Kong Seoul Singapore Taipei Tokyo

Vice President and Editor in Chief: Joe Terry
Senior Director of Development: Mary Ellen Curley
Development Editor: Katharine Glynn
Executive Marketing Manager: Joyce Nilsen
Senior Supplements Editor: Donna Campion
Production Manager: Savoula Amanatidis
Project Coordination, Text Design, and Electronic Page Makeup: Cenveo Publisher Services, Nesbitt Graphics, Inc.
Cover Designer/Manager: John Callahan
Cover Image: Sailing at Argenteuil, c.1874 (oil on canvas), Monet, Claude (1840–1926)/Private Collection/The Bridgeman Art Library International
Photo Research: PreMedia Global USA
Senior Manufacturing Buyer: Roy L. Pickering, Jr.
Printer and Binder: RR Donnelley
Cover Printer: Lehigh-Phoenix Color Corporation–Hagerstown

Credits and acknowledgments borrowed from other sources and reproduced, with permission, in this textbook appear on pages 2082–2099.

Cataloging-in-Publication Data on file at the Library of Congress

---

10 9 8 7 6 5 4—DOC—15 14

www.pearsonhighered.com

PEARSON

(Literature)
ISBN-10: 0-205-23038-5; ISBN-13: 978-0-205-23038-9
(Literature Interactive)
ISBN-10: 0-205-23039-3; ISBN-13: 978-0-205-23039-6
(Literature Portable)
ISBN-10: 0-205-22956-5; ISBN-13: 978-0-205-22956-7

CONTENTS

Preface xi
To the Instructor xiv
About the Authors xxiv

WRITING

41 WRITING ABOUT LITERATURE 1887

READ ACTIVELY 1887
Robert Frost, Nothing Gold Can Stay 1888
PLAN YOUR ESSAY 1889
PREWRITING: DISCOVER YOUR IDEAS 1889
Sample Student Prewriting Exercises 1890–1893
DEVELOP A LITERARY ARGUMENT 1893
CHECKLIST: Developing an Argument 1895
WRITE A ROUGH DRAFT 1895
Sample Student Paper, Rough Draft 1896
REVISE YOUR DRAFT 1898
CHECKLIST: Revising Your Draft 1901
FINAL ADVICE ON REWRITING 1902
Sample Student Paper, Revised Draft 1903
DOCUMENT SOURCES TO AVOID PLAGIARISM 1905
THE FORM OF YOUR FINISHED PAPER 1906
SPELL-CHECK AND GRAMMAR-CHECK PROGRAMS 1906
Anonymous (after a poem by Jerrold H. Zar), A Little Poem Regarding Computer Spell Checkers 1907

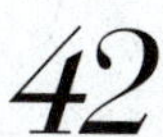

42 WRITING ABOUT A STORY 1908

READ ACTIVELY 1908
THINK ABOUT THE STORY 1910

PREWRITING: DISCOVER YOUR IDEAS 1910

Sample Student Prewriting Exercises 1910–1912

WRITE A ROUGH DRAFT 1913

CHECKLIST: Writing a Rough Draft 1914

REVISE YOUR DRAFT 1914

CHECKLIST: Revising Your Draft 1915

WHAT'S YOUR PURPOSE? COMMON APPROACHES TO WRITING ABOUT FICTION 1915

Explication 1916
Sample Student Paper, Explication 1917

Analysis 1919
Sample Student Paper, Analysis 1920

The Card Report 1922
Sample Student Card Report 1923

Comparison and Contrast 1924
Sample Student Paper, Comparison and Contrast 1926

Response Paper 1928
Sample Student Response Paper 1929

TOPICS FOR WRITING 1931

43 WRITING ABOUT A POEM 1933

READ ACTIVELY 1933

Robert Frost, Design 1934

THINK ABOUT THE POEM 1935

PREWRITING: DISCOVER YOUR IDEAS 1935

Sample Student Prewriting Exercises 1936–1938

WRITE A ROUGH DRAFT 1938

CHECKLIST: Writing a Rough Draft 1939

REVISE YOUR DRAFT 1939

CHECKLIST: Revising Your Draft 1941

COMMON APPROACHES TO WRITING ABOUT POETRY 1941

Explication 1941
Sample Student Paper, Explication 1942

A Critic's Explication of Frost's "Design" 1944

Analysis 1945
Sample Student Paper, Analysis 1946

Comparison and Contrast 1947

Abbie Huston Evans, Wing-Spread 1948
Sample Student Paper, Comparison and Contrast 1948

HOW TO QUOTE A POEM 1950

TOPICS FOR WRITING 1952
Robert Frost, In White 1953

WRITING ABOUT A PLAY 1955

READ CRITICALLY 1955

COMMON APPROACHES TO WRITING ABOUT DRAMA 1956
Explication 1957
Analysis 1957
Comparison and Contrast 1957
Card Report 1957
Sample Student Card Report 1959
A Drama Review 1960
Sample Student Drama Review 1962

HOW TO QUOTE A PLAY 1963

TOPICS FOR WRITING 1964

45 WRITING A RESEARCH PAPER 1966

BROWSE THE RESEARCH 1966

CHOOSE A TOPIC 1967

BEGIN YOUR RESEARCH 1967
Print Resources 1967
Online Databases 1968
Reliable Web Sources 1968
CHECKLIST: Finding Reliable Sources 1969
Visual Images 1969
CHECKLIST: Using Visual Images 1970

EVALUATE YOUR SOURCES 1971
Print Resources 1971
Web Resources 1971
CHECKLIST: Evaluating Your Sources 1972

ORGANIZE YOUR RESEARCH 1972

REFINE YOUR THESIS 1975

ORGANIZE YOUR PAPER 1975

WRITE AND REVISE 1975

MAINTAIN ACADEMIC INTEGRITY 1976

ACKNOWLEDGE ALL SOURCES 1976

Using Quotations 1977

Citing Ideas 1977

DOCUMENT SOURCES USING MLA STYLE 1978

List of Sources 1978

Parenthetical References 1978

Works-Cited List 1979

Citing Print Sources in MLA Style 1980

Citing Web Sources in MLA Style 1981

Sample List of Works Cited 1982

ENDNOTES AND FOOTNOTES 1983

SAMPLE STUDENT RESEARCH PAPER 1984

Sample Student Research Paper, Kafka's Greatness (*See Chapter 8, page 350*)

CONCLUDING THOUGHTS 1984

REFERENCE GUIDE FOR MLA CITATIONS 1985

46 WRITING AS DISCOVERY *Keeping a Journal* 1991

THE REWARDS OF KEEPING A JOURNAL 1991

SAMPLE JOURNAL ENTRY 1993

Sample Student Journal 1993

47 WRITING AN ESSAY EXAM 1995

CHECKLIST: Taking an Essay Exam 1999

PRACTICE ESSAY EXAM 1999

Toni Cade Bambara, The Lesson 2000

48 CRITICAL APPROACHES TO LITERATURE 2006

FORMALIST CRITICISM 2007

Cleanth Brooks, The Formalist Critic 2007

Michael Clark, Light and Darkness in "Sonny's Blues" 2008

Robert Langbaum, On Robert Browning's "My Last Duchess" 2009

BIOGRAPHICAL CRITICISM 2011

Leslie Fiedler, The Relationship of Poet and Poem 2012
Brett C. Millier, On Elizabeth Bishop's "One Art" 2013
Emily Toth, The Source for Alcée Laballière in "The Storm" 2014

HISTORICAL CRITICISM 2015

Hugh Kenner, Imagism 2016
Seamus Deane, Joyce's Vision of Dublin 2017
Kathryn Lee Seidel, The Economics of Zora Neale Hurston's "Sweat" 2019

PSYCHOLOGICAL CRITICISM 2021

Sigmund Freud, The Nature of Dreams 2022
Gretchen Schulz and R. J. R. Rockwood, Fairy Tale Motifs in "Where Are You Going, Where Have You Been?" 2022
Harold Bloom, Poetic Influence 2024

MYTHOLOGICAL CRITICISM 2025

Carl Jung, The Collective Unconscious and Archetypes 2025
Northrop Frye, Mythic Archetypes 2026
Edmond Volpe, Myth in Faulkner's "Barn Burning" 2027

SOCIOLOGICAL CRITICISM 2029

Georg Lukacs, Content Determines Form 2030
Daniel P. Watkins, Money and Labor in "The Rocking-Horse Winner" 2030
Alfred Kazin, Walt Whitman and Abraham Lincoln 2032

GENDER CRITICISM 2033

Elaine Showalter, Toward a Feminist Poetics 2033
Nina Pelikan Straus, Transformations in *The Metamorphosis* 2034
Richard R. Bozorth, "Tell Me the Truth About Love" 2035

READER-RESPONSE CRITICISM 2036

Stanley Fish, An Eskimo "A Rose for Emily" 2037
Robert Scholes, "How Do We Make a Poem?" 2038
Michael J. Colacurcio, The End of Young Goodman Brown 2040

DECONSTRUCTIONIST CRITICISM 2041

Roland Barthes, The Death of the Author 2042
Barbara Johnson, Rigorous Unreliability 2042
Geoffrey Hartman, On Wordsworth's "A Slumber Did My Spirit Seal" 2043

CULTURAL STUDIES 2045

Vincent B. Leitch, Poststructuralist Cultural Critique 2046
Mark Bauerlein, What Is Cultural Studies? 2047

Camille Paglia, A Reading of William Blake's "The Chimney Sweeper" 2049

TERMS FOR REVIEW 2051

GLOSSARY OF LITERARY TERMS 2052

Literary Credits 2082

Photo Credits 2098

Index of Major Themes 2100

Index of First Lines of Poetry 2107

Index of Authors and Titles 2112

Index of Literary Terms 2131

PREFACE

Literature, Twelfth Edition—the book in your hands—is really four interlocking volumes sharing one cover. Each of the first three sections is devoted to one of the major literary forms—fiction, poetry, and drama. The fourth section is a comprehensive introduction to critical writing. All together, the book is an attempt to provide the college student with a reasonably compact introduction to the study and appreciation of stories, poems, and plays—as well as practical advice on the sort of writing expected in a college English course.

We assume that appreciation begins in delighted attention to words on a page. Speed reading has its uses; but at times, as Robert Frost said, the person who reads for speed "misses the best part of what a good writer puts into it." Close reading, then, is essential. Still, we do not believe that close reading tells us everything, that it is wrong to read a literary work by any light except that of the work itself. At times we suggest different approaches such as referring to the facts of an author's life, looking for myth, or seeing the conventions that typify a kind of writing—noticing, for instance, that an old mansion, cobwebbed and creaking, is the setting for a Gothic horror story.

Although we cannot help having a few convictions about the meanings of stories, poems, and plays, we have tried to step back and give you room to make up your own mind. Here and there, in the wording of a question, our opinions may occasionally stick out. If you should notice any, please feel free to ignore them. Be assured that no one interpretation, laid down by authority, is the only right one for any work of literature. Trust your own interpretation—provided that in making it you have looked clearly and carefully at the evidence.

Reading literature often will provide you with a reason to write. Following the fiction, poetry, and drama sections, there are several chapters that give the student writer some practical advice. It will guide you, step by step, in finding a topic, planning an essay, writing, revising, and putting your paper into finished form. Further, you will find there specific help in writing about fiction, poetry, and drama. There are also short features at the end of most chapters that provide help and perspective on writing about literature. In a few places we have even offered some suggestions about writing your own stories or poems—in case reading the selections in this book inspires you to try your hand at imaginative writing.

A WORD ABOUT CAREERS

Most students agree that to read celebrated writers such as William Faulkner, Emily Dickinson, and William Shakespeare is probably good for the spirit. Most students even take some pleasure in the experience. But many, not planning to teach English and impatient to begin some other career, wonder if the study of literature, however enjoyable, isn't a waste of time—or at least, an annoying obstacle.

This objection may seem reasonable at first glance, but it rests on a shaky assumption. Success in a career does not depend merely on learning the specialized information and skills required to join a profession. In most careers, according to one senior business executive, people often fail not because they don't understand their jobs, but because they don't understand their co-workers, their clients, or their customers. They don't ever see the world from another person's point of view. Their problem is a failure of imagination.

To leap over the wall of self and to look through another's eyes is valuable experience that literature offers. If you are lucky, you may never meet (or have to do business with) anyone exactly like Mrs. Turpin in the story "Revelation," and yet you will learn much about the kind of person she is from Flannery O'Connor's fictional portrait of her. What is it like to be black, a white may wonder? James Baldwin, Gwendolyn Brooks, Rita Dove, Langston Hughes, Zora Neale Hurston, Alice Walker, August Wilson, and others have knowledge to impart. What is it like to be a woman? If a man would like to learn, let him read (for a start) Sandra Cisneros, Kate Chopin, Susan Glaspell, Alice Munro, Sylvia Plath, Katherine Anne Porter, Flannery O'Connor, Adrienne Rich, and Amy Tan, and perhaps, too, Henrik Ibsen's *A Doll's House* and John Steinbeck's "The Chrysanthemums."

Plodding single-mindedly toward careers, some people are like horses wearing blinders. For many, the goals look fixed and predictable. Competent nurses, accountants, and dental technicians seem always in demand. Others may find that in our society some careers, like waves in the sea, will rise or fall unexpectedly. Think how many professions we now take for granted, which a few years ago didn't even exist: genetic engineering, energy conservation, digital editing, and website design. Others that once looked like lifetime meal tickets have been cut back and nearly ruined: shoe repairing, commercial fishing, railroading.

In a perpetually changing society, it may be risky to lock yourself on one track to a career, refusing to consider any other. "We are moving," writes John Naisbitt in *Megatrends*, a study of our changing society, "from the specialist, soon obsolete, to the generalist who can adapt." Perhaps the greatest opportunity in your whole life lies in a career that has yet to be invented. If you do change your career as you go along, you will be like most people. According to a U.S. Bureau of Labor Statistics survey conducted in September 2010, the average American holds over eleven jobs between the ages of 18 and 44—often completely changing his or her basic occupation. When for some unforeseen reason you have to make such a change, basic skills—and a knowledge of humanity—may be your most valuable credentials.

Literature has much practical knowledge to offer you. An art of words, it can help you become more sensitive to language—both your own and other people's. It can make you aware of the difference between the word that is exactly right and the word that is merely good enough—Mark Twain calls it "the difference between the lightning and the lightning-bug." Read a fine work of literature alertly, and some of its writer's sensitivity to words may grow on you. A Supreme Court Justice, John Paul Stevens, once remarked that the best preparation for law school is to study poetry. Why? George D. Gopen, an English professor with a law degree, says it may be because "no other discipline so closely replicates the central question asked in the study of legal thinking: Here is a text; in how many ways can it have meaning?"

Many careers today, besides law, call for close reading and clear writing—as well as careful listening and thoughtful speech. Lately, college placement directors have reported more demand for graduates who are good readers and writers. The reason is evident: Employers need people who can handle words. In a survey conducted by Cornell University, business executives were asked to rank in importance the traits they look for when hiring. Leadership was first, but skill in writing and speaking came in fourth, ahead of both managerial and analytical skills. Times change, but to think cogently and to express yourself well will always be the abilities the world needs.

KEY LITERARY TERMS

Every discipline has its own terminology. This book introduces a large range of critical terms that may help you in both your reading and writing. When these important words and phrases are first defined, they are printed in **boldface**. If you find a critical term anywhere in this book you don't know or don't recall (for example, what is a *carpe diem* poem or a *dramatic question*?), just check the Index of Literary Terms in the back of the book, and you'll see the page where the term is discussed; or look it up in the Glossary of Literary Terms, also at the back of the book.

TEXTS AND DATES

Every effort has been made to supply each selection in its most accurate text and (where necessary) in a lively, faithful translation. For the reader who wishes to know when a work was written, at the right of each title appears the date of its first publication in book form. Parentheses around a date indicate the work's date of composition or first magazine publication, given when it was composed much earlier than when it was first published in book form.

But enough housekeeping—let's enjoy ourselves and read some unforgettable stories, poems, and plays.

X. J. K. AND D. G.

TO THE INSTRUCTOR

Literature is a book with two major goals. First, it introduces college students to the appreciation and experience of literature in its major forms. Second, the book tries to develop the student's ability to think critically and communicate effectively through writing.

Both editors of this volume are writers. We believe that textbooks should be not only informative and accurate but also lively, accessible, and engaging. In education, it never hurts to have a little fun. Our intent has always been to write a book that students will read eagerly and enjoy.

WHAT'S NEW TO THIS EDITION?

- **Eleven new stories**—including Isabel Allende's "The Judge's Wife," David Leavitt's "A Place I've Never Been," Eudora Welty's "A Worn Path," Daniel Orozco's "Orientation," Anne Tyler's "Teenage Wasteland," Ray Bradbury's now-classic "A Sound of Thunder," and ZZ Packer's "Brownies," as well as new fables by Aesop and Bidpai.
- **New casebook on Edgar Allan Poe's fiction**—featuring three of Poe's most popular stories ("The Tell-Tale Heart," "The Cask of Amontillado," and "The Fall of the House of Usher"), excerpts from his critical writing, interesting illustrations, plus insightful and accessible prose excerpts by Poe scholars.
- **Sixty-five new poems**—ranging from classic selections by John Keats, Emily Dickinson, Gwendolyn Brooks, Jorge Luis Borges, Robert Hayden, Antonio Machado, H.D., Robinson Jeffers, and William Shakespeare to fresh contemporary works by Kay Ryan, Rafael Campo, Harryette Mullen, Derek Walcott, Lorna Dee Cervantes, Carolyn Kizer, Amit Majmudar, Katha Pollitt, Brian Turner, and Julie Sheehan.
- **Four new one-act plays**—providing greater flexibility in studying diverse contemporary trends in a crowded curriculum. The new works include two short comedies, David Ives's *Sure Thing* and Jane Martin's *Beauty*, as well as Milcha Sanchez-Scott's *The Cuban Swimmer* and Edward Bok Lee's experimental *El Santo Americano*.
- **New audio version of *Trifles***—specially created for this edition by the celebrated L.A. Theatre Works. To help students less familiar with the experience of live theater, we offer this new audio production of Susan Glaspell's *Trifles* (featured in our introductory "Reading a Play" chapter). This play is introduced with commentary by Dana Gioia and is available for students to download in *MyLiteratureLab*.
- **New writing assignments**—new writing ideas have been introduced in many chapters.
- **Updated MLA coverage**—our concise Reference Guide for MLA Citations has been updated and expanded to reflect the latest MLA guidelines and illustrate a greater variety of online sources.

Overall, we have tried to create a book to help readers develop sensitivity to language, culture, and identity, to lead them beyond the boundaries of their own selves, and to see the world through the eyes of others. This book is built on the assumption that great literature can enrich and enlarge the lives it touches.

KEY FEATURES

We have revised this edition of *Literature* with the simple aim of introducing useful new features and selections without losing the best-liked material. We have been guided in this effort by scores of instructors and students who use the book in their classrooms. Teaching is a kind of conversation between instructor and student and between reader and text. By revising *Literature*, we try to help keep this conversation fresh by mixing the classic with the new and the familiar with the unexpected.

- **Wide variety of popular and provocative stories, poems, plays, and critical prose**—offers traditional favorites with exciting and sometimes surprising contemporary selections.
    - **67 stories, 11 new selections**—diverse and exciting stories from authors new and old from around the globe.
    - **452 poems, 65 new selections**—great poems, familiar and less well known, mixing classic favorites with engaging contemporary work from a wonderful range of poets.
    - **17 plays, 4 new selections**—a rich array of drama from classical Greek tragedy to Shakespeare to contemporary work by August Wilson and Anna Deavere Smith.
    - **149 critical prose pieces, 19 new selections**—extensive selections help students think about different approaches to reading, interpreting, and writing about literature.
- **"Talking with Writers"**—Exclusive conversations between Dana Gioia and celebrated fiction writer Amy Tan, former U.S. Poet Laureate Kay Ryan, and contemporary playwright David Ives offer students an insider's look into the importance of literature and reading in the lives of three modern masters.
- **Nine casebooks on major authors and literary masterpieces**—provide students with a variety of material, including biographies, photographs, critical commentaries, and author statements, to begin an in-depth study of writers and works frequently used for critical analyses or research papers.
    - Edgar Allan Poe
    - Flannery O'Connor
    - Emily Dickinson
    - Langston Hughes
    - Sophocles
    - William Shakespeare
    - Charlotte Perkins Gilman's "The Yellow Wallpaper"
    - Alice Walker's "Everyday Use"
    - T. S. Eliot's "The Love Song of J. Alfred Prufrock"
- **Chapters on Latin American Fiction and Poetry in Spanish**—present some of the finest authors of the region, including Sor Juana, Jorge Luis Borges, Octavio Paz, Gabriel García Márquez, and Isabel Allende. These important and unique chapters will not only broaden most students' knowledge of world literature but

will also recognize the richness of Spanish language fiction and poetry in the literature of the Americas—a very relevant subject in today's multicultural classrooms. The bilingual selections in poetry will also allow your Spanish-speaking students a chance to bring their native language into their coursework.

- **Shakespeare, richly illustrated**—production photos of every major scene and character make Shakespeare more accessible to students who have never seen a live production, helping them to visualize the play's action (as well as break up the long blocks of print to make the play's text less intimidating).
  - **Three plays by Shakespeare—*Othello, Hamlet,* and A *Midsummer Night's Dream***—in an illustrated format featuring dozens of production photos.
  - **"Picturing Shakespeare" photo montages**—offer students a pictorial introduction to each Shakespeare play with a visual preview of the key scenes and characters.
- **Audio version of Susan Glaspell's *Trifles***—specially created for this book.
- **Terms for Review at the end of every major chapter**—provides students a simple study guide to go over key concepts and terms in each chapter.
- **Writing Effectively feature in every major chapter** of Fiction, Poetry, and Drama has four elements designed to make the writing process easier, clearer, and less intimidating:
  - **Writers on Writing** personalizes the composition process
  - **Thinking About** ________ discusses the specific topic of the chapter
  - **Checklist** provides a step-by-step approach to composition and critical thinking
  - **Writing Assignment** plus **More Topics for Writing** provide a rich source of ideas for writing a paper.
- **Writing About Literature**—eight full writing chapters provide comprehensive coverage of the composition and research process, in general and by genre. All chapters have been edited for increased clarity and accessibility. Our chief aim has been to make the information and structure of the writing chapters more visual for today's Internet-oriented students. (We strive to simplify the text but not to dumb it down. Clarity and concision are never out of place in a textbook, but condescension is fatal.)
- **Student writing**—sixteen sample papers by students with annotations, prewriting exercises and rough drafts, plus a journal entry, provide credible examples of how to write about literature. Includes many samples of student work-in-progress that illustrate the writing process, including a step-by-step presentation of the development of a topic, idea generation, and the formulation of a strong thesis and argument. Samples include several types of papers:
  - Argument papers
  - Explication papers
  - Analysis papers
  - Comparison and contrast papers
  - Response paper
  - Research paper
- **Updated MLA guidelines**—provide students source citation requirements from the seventh edition of the MLA *Handbook* and incorporates them in all sample student papers.
- **Accessible, easy-to-use format**—section titles and subtitles help web-oriented students navigate easily from topic to topic in every chapter. Additionally, all chapters have been reviewed and updated to include relevant cultural references.

- **Critical Approaches to Literature, a chapter with 30 prose selections**—provides depth and flexibility for instructors who prefer to incorporate literary theory and criticism into their introductory courses. Includes three pieces for every major critical school, carefully chosen both to illustrate the major theoretical approaches and to be accessible to beginning students, focusing on literary works found in the present edition (including examinations of work by Zora Neale Hurston and Franz Kafka, a piece by Camille Paglia on William Blake as well as a piece in gender theory by Richard Bozorth that provides a gay reading of Auden's "Funeral Blues").
- **Glossary of Literary Terms**—Over 350 terms defined, including those highlighted in boldface throughout the text as well as other important terms. Provides clear and accurate definitions, usually with cross references to related terms.

OTHER EDITIONS AVAILABLE

Compact Edition

There is also the Seventh Compact Edition of *Literature: An Introduction to Fiction, Poetry, Drama, and Writing* in paperback, for instructors who find the full edition "too much book." Although this compact version offers a slightly abridged table of contents, it still covers the complete range of topics presented in the full edition. Both the full text and the compact edition are available in interactive editions.

Backpack Edition

There is an even more compact edition of this book, which we have titled *Backpack Literature*, Fourth Edition, in honor of the heavy textbook loads many students must carry from class to class. This much briefer anthology contains only the most essential selections and writing apparatus, and it is published in a smaller format to create a more travel-friendly book.

Interactive Editions

Both *Compact*, Seventh Edition, and *Literature*, Twelfth Edition, are published as interactive editions and come with access to *MyLiteratureLab.com* (as described in the following section) for instructors who want to incorporate media into their class.

Portable Edition

This edition provides all the content of the hardcover text in four lightweight paperback volumes—*Fiction*, *Poetry*, *Drama*, and *Writing*—packed in a slipcase.

Fiction and Poetry Available Separately

Instructors who wish to use only the fiction section or only the poetry section of this book are directed to *An Introduction to Fiction*, Eleventh Edition, and *An Introduction to Poetry*, Thirteenth Edition. Each book has writing chapters applicable to its subject, as well as the chapters "Writing a Research Paper" and "Critical Approaches to Literature."

RESOURCES FOR STUDENTS AND INSTRUCTORS

For Students

MyLiteratureLab.com

MyLiteratureLab is a state-of-the-art, web-based, interactive learning system for use in literature courses, either as a media supplement, or as a management system to completely administer a course online. It provides a wealth of resources geared to meet the diverse teaching and learning needs of today's instructors and students. *MyLiteratureLab* adds a new dimension to the study of literature with Longman Lectures—evocative, richly illustrated audio readings along with advice on how to read, interpret, and write about literary works from our roster of Longman authors (including X. J. Kennedy). This powerful program also features an eAnthology with 200 additional selections, feature-length films from Films for the Humanities and Sciences, a composing space with a "Writer's Toolkit," Interactive Readings with clickable prompts, "Writers on Writing" (video interviews with distinguished authors that inspire students to explore their creativity), grammar diagnostics, which produce personalized study plans, sample student papers, Literature Timelines, Avoiding Plagiarism, and more.

Audio Production of Trifles

So many students today have limited experience attending live theater that we felt it would be useful to offer a complete audio version of our opening play, Susan Glaspell's *Trifles*, which we use to teach the elements of drama. The audio version was produced especially for this edition by the celebrated L.A. Theatre Works for students to download in *MyLiteratureLab*. It includes an introduction and commentary by Dana Gioia.

Handbook of Literary Terms

Handbook of Literary Terms by X. J. Kennedy, Dana Gioia, and Mark Bauerlein is a user-friendly primer of over 350 critical terms brought to life with literary examples, pronunciation guides, and scholarly yet accessible explanations. Aimed at undergraduates getting their first taste of serious literary study, the volume will help students engage with the humanities canon and become critical readers and writers ready to experience the insights and joys of great fiction, poetry, and drama.

Responding to Literature: A Writer's Journal

This journal provides students with their own personal space for writing and is available at no additional cost when packaged with this anthology. Helpful writing prompts for responding to fiction, poetry, and drama are also included.

Evaluating Plays on Film and Video

This guide walks students through the process of analyzing and writing about plays on film, whether in a short review or a longer essay. It covers each stage of the process, from preparing and analyzing material through writing the piece. The four appendixes include writing and editing tips and a glossary of film terms. The final section of the guide offers worksheets to help students organize their notes and thoughts before they begin writing.

Evaluating a Performance

Perfect for the student assigned to review a local production, this supplement offers students a convenient place to record their evaluations and is available at no additional cost when packaged with this anthology. Useful tips and suggestions of things to consider when evaluating a production are included.

For Instructors

Instructor's Manual

A separate *Instructor's Manual* is available to instructors. If you have never seen our *Instructor's Manual* before, don't prejudge it. We actually write much of the manual ourselves, and we work hard to make it as interesting, lively, and informed as is the parent text. It offers commentary and teaching ideas for every selection in the book. It also contains additional commentary, debate, qualifications and information—including scores of classroom ideas—from over 100 teachers and authors. As you will see, our *Instructor's Manual* is no ordinary supplement.

Penguin Discount Paperback Program

In cooperation with Penguin Group USA, Pearson is proud to offer a variety of Penguin paperbacks, such as Tennessee Williams's *A Streetcar Named Desire*, George Orwell's *Animal Farm*, and Charlotte Brontë's *Jane Eyre*, at a significant discount—almost sixty percent off the retail price—when packaged with any Pearson title. To review the list of titles available, visit the Pearson Penguin Group USA website at *www.pearsonhighered.com/penguin*.

Video Program

For qualified adopters, an impressive selection of videos is available to enrich students' experience of literature. The videos include selections from William Shakespeare, Sylvia Plath, Ezra Pound, and Alice Walker. Contact your Pearson sales representative to see if you qualify.

Teaching Literature Online

Concise and practical, *Teaching Literature Online* provides instructors with strategies and advice for incorporating elements of computer technology into the literature classroom. Offering a range of information and examples, this manual provides ideas and activities for enhancing literature courses with the help of technology.

The Longman Electronic Testbank for Literature

This electronic testbank features various objective questions on major works of fiction, short fiction, poetry, and drama. It's available as a download from the Instructor Resource Center located at *www.pearsonhighered.com*.

CONTACT US

For examination copies of any of these books, videos, and programs, contact your Pearson sales representative, or write to Literature Marketing Manager, Pearson Higher Education, 51 Madison Avenue, New York, NY 10010. For examination copies only, call (800) 922-0579.

To order an examination copy online, go to *http://www.pearsonhighered.com* or send an e-mail to *exam.copies@pearsonhighered.com*.

THANKS

The collaboration necessary to create this new edition goes far beyond the partnership of its two editors. *Literature: An Introduction to Fiction, Poetry, Drama, and Writing* has once again been revised, corrected, and shaped by wisdom and advice from instructors who actually put it to the test—and also from a number who, in teaching literature, preferred other textbooks to it, but who generously criticized this book anyway and made suggestions for it. (Some responded to the book in part, focusing their comments on the previous editions of *An Introduction to Poetry* and *An Introduction to Fiction*.) Deep thanks to the following individuals:

Alvaro Aleman, University of Florida
Jonathan Alexander, University of Southern Colorado
Ann P. Allen, Salisbury State University
Karla Alwes, SUNY Cortland
Brian Anderson, Central Piedmont Community College
Kimberly Green Angel, Georgia State University
Carmela A. Arnoldt, Glendale Community College
Herman Asarnow, University of Portland
Beverly Bailey, Seminole Community College
Carolyn Baker, San Antonio College
Rosemary Baker, SUNY Morrisville
Lee Barnes, Community College of Southern Nevada, Las Vegas
Sandra Barnhill, South Plains College
Bob Baron, Mesa Community College
Melinda Barth, El Camino Community College
Robin Barrow, University of Iowa
Joseph Bathanti, Mitchell Community College
Judith Baumel, Adelphi University
Anis Bawarski, University of Kansas
Bruce Beckum, Colorado Mountain College
Elaine Bender, El Camino Community College
Pamela Benson, Tarrant County Junior College
Jennifer Black, McLennan Community College
Brian Blackley, North Carolina State University
Debbie Borchers, Pueblo Community College
Alan Braden, Tacoma Community College
Glenda Bryant, South Plains College
Paul Buchanan, Biola University
Andrew Burke, University of Georgia
Jolayne Call, Utah Valley State College
Stasia Callan, Monroe Community College
Uzzie T. Cannon, University of North Carolina at Greensboro
Al Capovilla, Folsom Lake Community College
Eleanor Carducci, Sussex County Community College
Thomas Carper, University of Southern Maine
Jean W. Cash, James Madison University
Michael Cass, Mercer University
Patricia Cearley, South Plains College
Fred Chancey, Chemeketa Community College
Kitty Chen, Nassau Community College
Edward M. Cifelli, County College of Morris
Marc Cirigliano, Empire State College
Bruce Clary, McPherson College
Maria Clayton, Middle Tennessee State University
Cheryl Clements, Blinn College
Jerry Coats, Tarrant County Community College
Peggy Cole, Arapahoe Community College
Doris Colter, Henry Ford Community College
Dean Cooledge, University of Maryland Eastern Shore
Patricia Connors, University of Memphis
Steve Cooper, California State University, Long Beach
Cynthia Cornell, DePauw University
Ruth Corson, Norwalk Community Technical College, Norwalk
James Finn Cotter, Mount St. Mary College
Dessa Crawford, Delaware Community College
Janis Adams Crowe, Furman University
Allison M. Cummings, University of Wisconsin, Madison
Elizabeth Curtin, Salisbury State University
Robert Darling, Keuka College
Denise David, Niagara County Community College
Alan Davis, Moorhead State University
Michael Degen, Jesuit College Preparatory School, Dallas
Kathleen De Grave, Pittsburgh State University
Apryl Denny, Viterbo University
Fred Dings, University of South Carolina
Leo Doobad, Stetson University
Stephanie Dowdle, Salt Lake Community College
Dennis Driewald, Laredo Community College
David Driscoll, Benedictine College
John Drury, University of Cincinnati
Tony D'Souza, Shasta College
Victoria Duckworth, Santa Rosa Junior College
Ellen Dugan-Barrette, Brescia University
Dixie Durman, Chapman University
Bill Dynes, University of Indianapolis
Janet Eber, County College of Morris
Terry Ehret, Santa Rosa Junior College
George Ellenbogen, Bentley College
Peggy Ellsberg, Barnard College
Toni Empringham, El Camino Community College
Lin Enger, Moorhead State University
Alexina Fagan, Virginia Commonwealth University
Lynn Fauth, Oxnard College
Annie Finch, University of Southern Maine
Katie Fischer, Clarke College
Susan Fitzgerald, University of Memphis
Juliann Fleenor, Harper College
Richard Flynn, Georgia Southern University
Billy Fontenot, Louisiana State University at Eunice
Deborah Ford, University of Southern Mississippi
Doug Ford, Manatee Community College
James E. Ford, University of Nebraska, Lincoln

Peter Fortunato, Ithaca College
Ray Foster, Scottsdale Community College
Maryanne Garbowsky, County College of Morris
John Gery, University of New Orleans
Mary Frances Gibbons, Richland College
Maggie Gordon, University of Mississippi
Joseph Green, Lower Columbia College
William E. Gruber, Emory University
Huey Guagliardo, Louisiana State University
R. S. Gwynn, Lamar University
Steven K. Hale, DeKalb College
Renée Harlow, Southern Connecticut State University
David Harper, Chesapeake College
John Harper, Seminole Community College
Iris Rose Hart, Santa Fe Community College
Karen Hatch, California State University, Chico
Jim Hauser, William Patterson College
Kevin Hayes, Essex County College
Jennifer Heller, Johnson County Community College
Hal Hellwig, Idaho State University
Gillian Hettinger, William Paterson University
Mary Piering Hiltbrand, University of Southern Colorado
Martha Hixon, Middle Tennessee State University
Jan Hodge, Morningside College
David E. Hoffman, Averett University
Mary Huffer, Lake-Sumter Community College
Patricia Hymson, Delaware County Community College
Carol Ireland, Joliet Junior College
Alan Jacobs, Wheaton College
Ann Jagoe, North Central Texas College
Kimberlie Johnson, Seminole Community College
Peter Johnson, Providence College
Ted E. Johnston, El Paso Community College
Cris Karmas, Graceland University
Howard Kerner, Polk Community College
Lynn Kerr, Baltimore City Community College
D. S. Koelling, Northwest College
Dennis Kriewald, Laredo Community College
Paul Lake, Arkansas Technical University
Susan Lang, Southern Illinois University
Greg LaPointe, Elmira College
Tracy Lassiter, Eastern Arizona College
Sherry Little, San Diego State University
Alfred Guy Litton, Texas Woman's University
Heather Lobban-Viravong, Grinnell College
Karen Locke, Lane Community College
Eric Loring, Scottsdale Community College
Deborah Louvar, Seminole State College
Gerald Luboff, County College of Morris
Susan Popkin Mach, UCLA
Samuel Maio, California State University, San Jose
Jim Martin, Mount Ida College
Paul Marx, University of New Haven
David Mason, Colorado College
Mike Matthews, Tarrant County Junior College
Beth Maxfield, Henderson State University
Janet McCann, Texas A&M University
Susan McClure, Indiana University of Pennsylvania
Kim McCollum-Clark, Millersville University
David McCracken, Texas A&M University
Nellie McCrory, Gaston College
William McGee, Jr., Joliet Junior College
Kerri McKeand, Joliet Junior College
Robert McPhillips, Iona College
Jim McWilliams, Dickinson State University
Elizabeth Meador, Wayne Community College
Bruce Meyer, Laurentian University
Tom Miller, University of Arizona
Joseph Mills, University of California at Davis
Cindy Milwe, Santa Monica High School
Dorothy Minor, Tulsa Community College
Mary Alice Morgan, Mercer University
Samantha Morgan, University of Tennessee
Bernard Morris, Modesto Junior College
Brian T. Murphy, Burlington Community College
William Myers, University of Colorado at Colorado Springs
Madeleine Mysko, Johns Hopkins University
Kevin Nebergall, Kirkwood Community College
Eric Nelson, Georgia Southern University
Jeff Newberry, University of West Florida
Marsha Nourse, Dean College
Hillary Nunn, University of Akron
James Obertino, Central Missouri State University
Julia O'Brien, Meredith College
Sally O'Friel, John Carroll University
Elizabeth Oness, Viterbo College
Regina B. Oost, Wesleyan College
Mike Osborne, Central Piedmont Community College
Jim Owen, Columbus State University
Jeannette Palmer, Motlow State Community College
Mark Palmer, Tacoma Community College
Dianne Peich, Delaware County Community College
Betty Jo Peters, Morehead State University
Timothy Peters, Boston University
Norm Peterson, County College of Morris
Susan Petit, College of San Mateo

Louis Phillips, School of Visual Arts
Robert Phillips, University of Houston
Jason Pickavance, Salt Lake Community College
Teresa Point, Emory University
Deborah Prickett, Jacksonville State University
William Provost, University of Georgia
Wyatt Prunty, University of the South, Sewanee
Allen Ramsey, Central Missouri State University
Ron Rash, Tri-County Technical College
Michael W. Raymond, Stetson University
Mary Anne Reiss, Elizabethtown Community College
Barbara Rhodes, Central Missouri State University
Diane Richard-Alludya, Lynn University
Gary Richardson, Mercer University
Fred Robbins, Southern Illinois University
Doulgas Robillard Jr., University of Arkansas at Pine Bluff
Daniel Robinson, Colorado State University
Dawn Rodrigues, University of Texas, Brownsville
Linda C. Rollins, Motlow State Community College
Mark Rollins, Ohio University
Laura Ross, Seminole Community College
Jude Roy, Madisonville Community College
M. Runyon, Saddleback College
Mark Sanders, College of the Mainland
Kay Satre, Carroll College
Ben Sattersfield, Mercer University
SueAnn Schatz, University of New Mexico
Roy Scheele, Doane College
Bill Schmidt, Seminole Community College
Beverly Schneller, Millersville University
Meg Schoerke, San Francisco State University
Janet Schwarzkopf, Western Kentucky University
William Scurrah, Pima Community College
Susan Semrow, Northeastern State University
Tom Sexton, University of Alaska, Anchorage
Chenliang Sheng, Northern Kentucky University
Roger Silver, University of Maryland–Asian Division
Phillip Skaar, Texas A&M University
Michael Slaughter, Illinois Central College
Martha K. Smith, University of Southern Indiana
Richard Spiese, California State, Long Beach
Lisa S. Starks, Texas A&M University
John R. Stephenson, Lake Superior State University
Jack Stewart, East Georgia College
Dabney Stuart, Washington and Lee University
David Sudol, Arizona State University
Stan Sulkes, Raymond Walters College
Gerald Sullivan, Savio Preparatory School
Henry Taylor, American University
Jean Tobin, University of Wisconsin Center, Sheboygan County
Linda Travers, University of Massachusetts, Amherst
Tom Treffinger, Greenville Technical College
Peter Ulisse, Housatonia Community College
Lee Upton, Lafayette College
Rex Veeder, St. Cloud University
Deborah Viles, University of Colorado, Boulder
Joyce Walker, Southern Illinois University–Carbondale
Sue Walker, University of South Alabama
Irene Ward, Kansas State University
Penelope Warren, Laredo Community College
Barbara Wenner, University of Cincinnati
Terry Witek, Stetson University
Sallie Wolf, Arapahoe Community College
Beth Rapp Young, University of Alabama
William Zander, Fairleigh Dickinson University
Tom Zaniello, Northern Kentucky University
Guanping Zeng, Pensacola Junior College
John Zheng, Mississippi Valley State University

Ongoing thanks go to our friends and colleagues who helped with earlier editions: Michael Palma, who scrupulously examined and updated every chapter of the previous edition; Diane Thiel of the University of New Mexico, who originally helped develop the Latin American poetry chapter; Susan Balée of Temple University, who contributed to the chapter on writing a research paper; April Lindner of Saint Joseph's University in Philadelphia, Pennsylvania, who served as associate editor for the writing sections; Mark Bernier of Blinn College in Brenham, Texas, who helped improve the writing material; Joseph Aimone of Santa Clara University, who helped integrate web-based materials and research techniques; and John Swensson of De Anza College, who provided excellent practical suggestions from the classroom.

On the publisher's staff, Joseph Terry, Katharine Glynn, and Joyce Nilsen made many contributions to the development and revision of the new edition. Savoula

Amanatidis and Lois Lombardo directed the complex job of managing the production of the book in all of its many versions from the manuscript to the final printed form. Beth Keister handled the difficult job of permissions. Rona Tuccillo and Jennifer Nonenmacher supervised the expansion of photographs in the new edition.

Mary Gioia was involved in every stage of planning, editing, and execution. Not only could the book not have been done without her capable hand and careful eye, but her expert guidance made every chapter better.

Past debts that will never be repaid are outstanding to hundreds of instructors named in prefaces past and to Dorothy M. Kennedy.

X. J. K. AND D. G.

ABOUT THE AUTHORS

X. J. KENNEDY, after graduation from Seton Hall and Columbia, became a journalist second class in the Navy ("Actually, I was pretty eighth class"). His poems, some published in the *New Yorker,* were first collected in *Nude Descending a Staircase* (1961). Since then he has published seven more collections, including a volume of new and selected poems in 2007, several widely adopted literature and writing textbooks, and seventeen books for children, including two novels. He has taught at Michigan, North Carolina (Greensboro), California (Irvine), Wellesley, Tufts, and Leeds. Cited in *Bartlett's Familiar Quotations* and reprinted in some 200 anthologies, his verse has brought him a Guggenheim fellowship, a Lamont Award, a Los Angeles Times Book Prize, an award from the American Academy and Institute of Arts and Letters, an Aiken-Taylor prize, and the Award for Poetry for Children from the National Council of Teachers of English. He now lives in Lexington, Massachusetts, where he and his wife Dorothy have collaborated on five books and five children.

DANA GIOIA is a poet, critic, and teacher. Born in Los Angeles of Italian and Mexican ancestry, he attended Stanford and Harvard before taking a detour into business. ("Not many poets have a Stanford M.B.A., thank goodness!") After years of writing and reading late in the evenings after work, he quit a vice presidency to write and teach. He has published four collections of poetry, *Daily Horoscope* (1986), *The Gods of Winter* (1991), *Interrogations at Noon* (2001), which won the American Book Award, and *Pity the Beautiful* (2012); and three critical volumes, including *Can Poetry Matter?* (1992), an influential study of poetry's place in contemporary America. Gioia has taught at Johns Hopkins, Sarah Lawrence, Wesleyan (Connecticut), Mercer, and Colorado College. From 2003 to 2009 he served as the Chairman of the National Endowment for the Arts. At the NEA he created the largest literary programs in federal history, including Shakespeare in American Communities and Poetry Out Loud, the national high school poetry recitation contest. He also led the campaign to restore active literary reading by creating The Big Read, which helped reverse a quarter century of decline in U.S. reading. He is currently the Judge Widney Professor of Poetry and Public Culture at the University of Southern California.

(The surname Gioia is pronounced JOY-A. As some of you may have already guessed, Gioia is the Italian word for joy.)

Susan Glaspell at work, around 1913.

WRITING

41 WRITING ABOUT LITERATURE

If one waits for the right time to come before writing,
the right time never comes.

—JAMES RUSSELL LOWELL

Assigned to write an essay on *Hamlet*, a student might well wonder, "What can I say that hasn't been said a thousand times before?" Often the most difficult aspect of writing about a story, poem, or play is the feeling that we have nothing of interest to contribute to the ongoing conversation about some celebrated literary work. There's always room, though, for a reader's fresh take on an old standby.

Remember that in the study of literature common sense is never out of place. For most of a class hour, a professor once rhapsodized about the arrangement of the contents of W. H. Auden's *Collected Poems*. Auden, he claimed, was a master of thematic continuity, who had brilliantly placed the poems in the order that they ingeniously complemented each other. Near the end of the hour, his theories were punctured—with a great inaudible pop—when a student, timidly raising a hand, pointed out that Auden had arranged the poems in the book not by theme but in alphabetical order according to the first word of each poem. The professor's jaw dropped: "Why didn't you say that sooner?" The student was apologetic: "I—I was afraid I'd sound too *ordinary*."

Don't be afraid to state a conviction, though it seems obvious. Does it matter that you may be repeating something that, once upon a time or even just the other day, has been said before? What matters more is that you are actively engaged in thinking about literature. There are excellent old ideas as well as new ones. You have something to say.

READ ACTIVELY

Most people read in a relaxed, almost passive way. They let the story or poem carry them along without asking too many questions. To write about literature well, however, you need to *read actively*, paying special attention to various aspects of the text. This special sort of attention will not only deepen your enjoyment of the story, poem, or play but will also help generate the information and ideas that will become your final paper. How do you become an active reader? Here are some steps to get you started:

- **Preview the text.** To get acquainted with a work of literature before you settle in for a closer reading, skim it for an overview of its content and organization. Take a quick look at all parts of the work. Even a book's cover, preface, introduction, footnotes, and biographical notes about the author can provide you with some context for reading the work itself.
- **Take notes. Annotate the text.** Read with a highlighter and pencil at hand, making appropriate annotations to the text. Later, you'll easily be able to review these highlights, and, when you write your paper, quickly refer to supporting evidence.
    - Underline words, phrases, or sentences that seem interesting or important, or that raise questions.
    - Jot down brief notes in the margin (*"key symbol—this foreshadows the ending,"* for example, or *"dramatic irony"*).
    - Use lines or arrows to indicate passages that seem to speak to each other—for instance, all the places in which you find the same theme or related symbols.

Robert Frost

Nothing Gold Can Stay

Nature's first green is gold,
Her hardest hue to hold.
Her early leaf's a flower;
But only so an hour.
Then leaf subsides to leaf.
So Eden sank to grief,
So dawn goes down to day.
Nothing gold can stay.

- Similar lines
- How can green=gold?
- Rhyme + end-stopped lines
- Spring leaves
- Spring blossoms (golden?)
- Exaggeration
- Everybody loses innocence
- To sink to a lower level (everything becomes less beautiful)
- Nothing good can last
- Youth, beauty, innocence
- rhyme pattern aabbccdd
- Adam+Eve: Getting kicked out of Eden was natural as seasons changing?

- **Read closely.** Once you have begun reading in earnest, don't skim or skip over words you don't recognize; sometimes, looking up those very words will unlock a piece's meaning.
- **Reread as needed.** If a piece is short, read it several times. Often, knowing the ending of a poem or short story will allow you to extract new meaning from its beginning and middle. If the piece is longer, reread the passages you thought important enough to highlight.

PLAN YOUR ESSAY

If you have actively reread the work you plan to write about and have made notes or annotations, you are already well on your way to writing your paper. Your mind has already begun to work through some initial impressions and ideas. Now you need to arrange those early notions into an organized and logical essay. Here is some advice on how to manage the writing process:

- **Leave yourself time.** Good writing involves thought and revision. Anyone who has ever been a student knows what it's like to pull an all-nighter, churning out a term paper hours before it is due. Still, the best writing evolves over time. Your ideas need to marinate. Sometimes, you'll make false starts, and you'll need to salvage what you can and do the rest from scratch. For the sake of your writing—not to mention your health and sanity—it's far better to get the job started well before your deadline.
- **Choose a subject you care about.** If you have been given a choice of literary works to write about, always choose the play, story, or poem that evokes the strongest emotional response. Your writing will be liveliest if you feel engaged by your subject.
- **Know your purpose.** As you write, keep the assignment in mind. You may have been asked to write a response, in which you describe your reactions to a literary work. Perhaps your purpose is to interpret a work, analyzing how one or more of its elements contribute to its meaning. You may have been instructed to write an evaluation, in which you judge a work's merits. Whatever the assignment, how you approach your essay will depend in large part on your purpose.
- **Think about your audience.** When you write journal entries or rough drafts, you may be composing for your own eyes only. More often, though, you are likely to be writing for an audience, even if it is an audience of one: your professor. Whenever you write for others, you need to be conscious of your readers. Your task is to convince them that your take on a work of literature is a plausible one. To do so, you need to keep your audience's needs and expectations in mind.
- **Define your topic narrowly.** Worried about having enough to say, students sometimes frame their topic so broadly that they can't do justice to it in the allotted number of pages. Your paper will be stronger if you go more deeply into your subject than if you choose a gigantic subject and touch on most aspects of it only superficially. A thorough explication of a short story is hardly possible in a 250-word paper, but an explication of a paragraph or two could work in that space. A profound topic ("The Character of Hamlet") might overflow a book, but a more focused one ("Hamlet's View of Acting" or "Hamlet's Puns") could result in a manageable paper. A paper entitled "Female Characters in *Hamlet*" couldn't help being too general and vague, but one on "Ophelia's Relationship to Laertes" could make for a good marriage of length and subject.

PREWRITING: DISCOVER YOUR IDEAS

Topic in hand, you can begin to get your ideas on the page. To generate new ideas and clarify the thoughts you already have, try one or more of the following useful prewriting techniques:

- **Brainstorm.** Writing quickly, list everything that comes into your mind about your subject. Set a time limit—ten or fifteen minutes—and force yourself to keep adding items to the list, even when you think you have run out of things to say. Sometimes, if you press onward past the point where you feel you are finished, you will surprise yourself with new and fresh ideas.

  gold = early leaves/blossoms
  Or gold = something precious (both?)
  early leaf = flower (yellow blossoms)
  spring (lasts an hour)
  Leaves subside (sink to lower level)
  Eden = paradise = perfection = beauty
  Loss of innocence?
  What about original sin?
  Dawn becomes day (dawn is more precious?)
  Adam and Eve had to fall? Part of natural order.
  seasons/days/people's lives
  Title = last line: perfection can't last
  spring/summer/autumn
  dawn/day
  Innocence can't last

- **Cluster.** This prewriting technique works especially well for visual thinkers. In clustering, you build a diagram to help you explore the relationships among your ideas. To get started, write your subject at the center of a sheet of paper. Circle it. Then jot down ideas, linking each to the central circle with lines. As you write down each new idea, draw lines to link it to related old ideas. The result will look something like the following web.

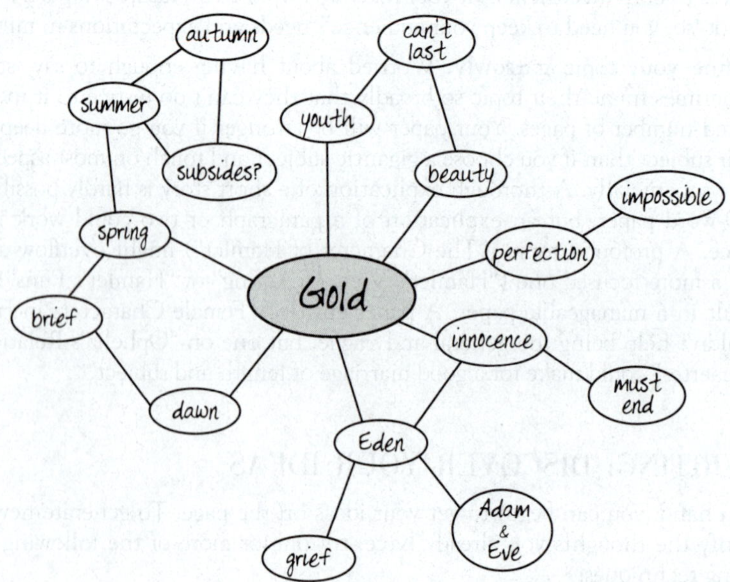

- **List.** Look over the notes and annotations that you made in your active reading of the work. You have probably already underlined or noted more information than you can possibly use. One way to sort through your material to find the most useful information is to make a list of the important items. It helps to make several short lists under different headings. Here are some lists you might make after rereading Frost's "Nothing Gold Can Stay." Don't be afraid to add more comments or questions on the lists to help your thought process.

Images	Colors
leaf ("early leaf")	green
flower	gold ("hardest hue to hold")
dawn	
day	
Eden	
gold	

Key Actions
gold is hard to hold
early leaf lasts only an hour
leaf subsides to leaf (what does this mean???)
Eden sinks to grief (paradise is lost)
dawn goes down to day
gold can't stay (perfection is impossible?)

- **Freewrite.** Most writers have snarky little voices in their heads, telling them that the words they're committing to paper aren't interesting or deep or elegant enough. To drown out those little voices, try freewriting. Give yourself a set amount of time (say, ten minutes) and write, nonstop, on your topic. Force your pen to keep moving or your fingers to keep typing, even if you have run out of things to say. If all you can think of to write is "I'm stuck" or "This is dumb," so be it. Keep writing and something else will most likely occur to you. Don't worry, yet, about grammar or spelling. When your time is up, read what you have written, highlighting the best ideas for later use.

> How can green be gold? By nature's first green, I guess he means the first leaves in spring. Are those leaves gold? They're more delicate and yellow than summer leaves . . . so maybe in a sense they look gold. Or maybe he means spring blossoms. Sometimes they're yellow. Also the first line seems to connect with the third one, where he comes right out and says that flowers are like early leaves. Still, I think he also means that the first leaves are the most precious ones, like gold. I don't think the poem wants me to take all of these statements literally. Flowers on trees last more than an hour, but that really beautiful moment in spring when blossoms are everywhere always ends too quickly, so maybe that's what he means by "only so an hour." I had to look up "subsides." It means to sink to a lower level . . . as if the later leaves will be less perfect than the first ones. I don't know if I agree. Aren't fall leaves precious? Then he says, "So Eden sank to grief" which seems to be saying that Adam and Eve's fall would

> have happened no matter what they did, because everything that seems perfect falls apart . . . nothing gold can stay. Is he saying Adam and Eve didn't really have a choice? No matter what, everything gets older, less beautiful, less innocent . . . even people.

- **Journal.** Your instructor might ask you to keep a journal in which you jot down your ideas, feelings, and impressions before they are fully formulated. Sometimes a journal is meant for your eyes only; in other instances your instructor might read it. Either way, it is meant to be informal and immediate, and to provide raw material that you may later choose to refine into a formal essay. Here are some tips for keeping a useful journal:

  - Get your ideas down as soon as they occur to you.
  - Write quickly.
  - Jot down your feelings about and first impressions of the story, poem, or play you are reading.
  - Don't worry about grammar, spelling, or punctuation.
  - Don't worry about sounding academic.
  - Don't worry about whether your ideas are good or bad ones; you can sort that out later.
  - Try out invention strategies such as freewriting, clustering, and outlining.
  - Keep writing, even after you think you have run out of things to say. You might surprise yourself.
  - Write about what interests you most.
  - Write in your journal on a regular basis.

  For a more detailed explanation of how to approach journal writing, read the chapter "Writing as Discovery: Keeping a Journal."

- **Outline.** Some topics by their very nature suggest obvious ways to organize a paper. "An Explication of a Sonnet by Wordsworth" might mean simply working through the poem line by line. If this isn't the case, some kind of outline will probably prove helpful. Your outline needn't be elaborate to be useful. While a long research paper on several literary works might call for a detailed outline, a 500-word analysis of a short story's figures of speech might call for just a simple list of points in the order that makes the most logical sense—not necessarily the order in which those thoughts first came to mind.

  1. Passage of time = fall from innocence
     - blossoms
     - gold
     - dawn
     - grief
  2. Innocence = perfection
     - Adam and Eve
     - loss of innocence = inevitable
     - real original sin = passing of time
     - paradise sinks to grief

2. Grief = knowledge
   experience of sin & suffering
   unavoidable as grow older

DEVELOP A LITERARY ARGUMENT

Once you have finished a rough outline of your ideas, you need to refine it into a clear and logical shape. You need to state your thesis (or basic idea) clearly and then support it with logical and accurate evidence. Here is a practical approach to this crucial stage of the writing process:

- **Consider your purpose.** As you develop your argument, be sure to refer back to the specific assignment; let it guide you. Your instructor might request one of the following kinds of papers:
  - *Response*, in which you explore your reaction to a work of literature.
  - *Evaluation*, in which you assess the literary merits of a work.
  - *Interpretation*, in which you discuss a work's meaning. If your instructor has assigned an interpretation, he or she may have more specifically asked for an *analysis*, *explication*, or *comparison/contrast* essay, among other possibilities.
- **Remember your audience.** Practically speaking, your professor (and sometimes your classmates) will be your paper's primary audience. Some assignments may specify a particular audience beyond your professor and classmates. Keep your readers in mind. Be sure to adapt your writing to meet their needs and interests. If, for example, the audience has presumably already read a story under discussion, you won't need to relate the plot in its entirety. Instead, you will be free to bring up only those plot points that serve as evidence for your thesis.
- **Narrow your topic to fit the assignment.** Though you may be tempted to choose a broad topic so that you will have no shortage of things to say, remember that a good paper needs focus. Your choice should be narrow enough for you to do it justice in the space and time allotted.
- **Decide on a thesis.** Just as you need to know your destination before you set out on a trip, you need to decide what point you're traveling toward before you begin your first draft. Start by writing a provisional thesis sentence: a summing up of the main idea or argument your paper will explore. While your thesis doesn't need to be outrageous or deliberately provocative, it does need to take a stand. A clear, decisive statement gives you something to prove and lends vigor to your essay.

WORKING THESIS

The poem argues that like Adam and Eve we all lose our innocence and the passage of time is inevitable.

This first stab at a thesis sentence gave its author a sense of purpose and direction that allowed him to finish his first draft. Later, as he revised his essay, he found he needed to refine his thesis to make more specific and focused assertions.

- **Build your argument**. Once you've formulated your thesis, your task will be clear: you need to convince your audience that your thesis is sound. To write persuasively, it helps to have an understanding of some key elements of argument:
  - ***Claims.*** Anytime you make a statement you hope will be taken as true, you have made a claim. Some claims are unlikely to be contradicted ("the sky is blue" or "today is Tuesday"), but others are debatable ("every college sophomore dreams of running off to see the world"). Your essay's main claim—your thesis—should not be something entirely obvious. Having to support your point of view will cause you to clarify your ideas about a work of literature.
  - ***Persuasion.*** If the word *argument* makes you think of raised voices and short tempers, it may help to think of your task as the gentler art of persuasion. To convince your audience of your thesis, you will need to present a cogent argument supported by evidence gathered from the text. If the assignment is a research paper, you will also need to cite what others have written on your topic.
  - ***Evidence.*** When you write about a work of literature, the most convincing evidence will generally come from the text itself. Direct quotations from the poem, play, or story under discussion can provide particularly convincing support for your claims. Be sure to introduce any quotation by putting it in the context of the larger work. It is even more important to follow up each quotation with your own analysis of what it shows about the work.
  - ***Warrants.*** Whenever you use a piece of evidence to support a claim, an underlying assumption connects one to the other. For instance, if you were to make the claim that today's weather is absolutely perfect and offer as your evidence the blue sky, your logic would include an unspoken warrant: sunny weather is perfect weather. Not everyone will agree with your warrant, though. Some folks (perhaps farmers) might prefer rain. In making any argument, including one about literature, you may find that you sometimes need to spell out your warrants to demonstrate that they are sound. This is especially true when the evidence you provide can lead to conclusions other than the one you are hoping to prove.
  - ***Credibility.*** When weighing the merits of a claim, you will probably take into account the credibility of the person making the case. Often this happens almost automatically. You are more likely to listen to the opinion that you should take vitamins if it is expressed by your doctor than if it is put forth by a stranger you meet on the street. An expert on any given topic has a certain brand of authority not available to most of us. Fortunately, there are other ways to establish your own credibility:

    Keep your tone thoughtful. Your reader will develop a sense of who you are through your words. If you come across as belligerent or disrespectful to those inclined to disagree with your views, you may lose your reader's goodwill. Therefore, express your ideas calmly and thoughtfully. A level tone demonstrates that you are interested in thinking through an issue or idea, not in bullying your reader into submission.

    Take opposing arguments into account. To make an argument more convincing, demonstrate familiarity with other possible points of view.

Doing so indicates that you have taken other claims into account before arriving at your thesis; it reveals your fairness as well as your understanding of your subject matter. In laying out other points of view, though, be sure to represent them fairly but also to respectfully make clear why your thesis is the soundest claim; you don't want your reader to doubt where you stand.

Demonstrate your knowledge. To gain your reader's trust, it helps to demonstrate a solid understanding of your subject matter. Always check your facts; factual errors can call your knowledge into doubt. It also helps to have a command of the conventions of writing. Errors in punctuation and spelling can undermine a writer's credibility.

- **Organize your argument.** Unless you are writing an explication that works its way line by line through a work of literature, you will need to make crucial decisions about how to shape your essay. Its order should be driven by the logic of your argument, not by the structure of the story, play, or poem you're discussing. In other words, you need not work your way from start to finish through your source material, touching on each major point. Instead, choose only the points needed to prove your thesis, and present them in whatever order best makes your point. A rough outline can help you to determine that order.

- **Make sure your thesis is supported by the evidence.** If you find you can't support certain aspects of your thesis, then refine it so that you can. Remember: until you turn it in, your essay is a work in progress. Anything can and should be changed if it doesn't further the development of the paper's main idea.

CHECKLIST: DEVELOPING AN ARGUMENT

- ☐ What is your essay's purpose?
- ☐ Who is your audience?
- ☐ Is your topic narrow enough?
- ☐ Is your thesis interesting and thought-provoking?
- ☐ Does everything in your essay support your thesis?
- ☐ Have you considered and refuted alternative views?
- ☐ Is your tone thoughtful?
- ☐ Is your argument sensibly organized? Are similar ideas grouped together? Does one point lead logically to the next?

WRITE A ROUGH DRAFT

Seated at last, you prepare to write, only to find yourself besieged with petty distractions. All of a sudden you remember a friend you had promised to call, some double-A batteries you were supposed to pick up, a neglected Coke (in another room) growing warmer and flatter by the minute. If your paper is to be written, you have only one course of action: collar these thoughts and for the moment banish them. Here are a few tips for writing your rough draft:

- **Review your argument.** The shape of your argument, its support, and the evidence you have collected will form the basis of your rough draft.
- **Get your thoughts down.** The best way to draft a paper is to get your ideas down quickly. At this stage, don't fuss over details. The critical, analytical side of your mind can worry about spelling, grammar, and punctuation later. For now, let your creative mind take charge. This part of yourself has the good ideas, insight, and confidence. Forge ahead. Believe in yourself and in your ideas.
- **Write the part you feel most comfortable with first.** There's no need to start at the paper's beginning and work your way methodically through to the end. Instead, plunge right into the parts of the paper you feel most prepared to write. You can always go back later and fill in the blanks.
- **Leave yourself plenty of space.** As you compose, leave plenty of space between lines and set wide margins. When you print out your draft, you will easily be able to go back and squeeze other thoughts in.
- **Focus on the argument.** As you jot down your first draft, you might not want to look at the notes you have compiled. When you come to a place where a note will fit, just insert a reminder to yourself such as "See card 19" or "See Aristotle on comedy." Also, whenever you bring up a new point, it's good to tie it back to your thesis. If you can't find a way to connect a point to your thesis, it's probably better to leave it out of your paper and come up with a point that advances your central claim.
- **Does your thesis hold up?** If, as you write, you find that most of the evidence you uncover is not helping you prove your paper's thesis, it may be that the thesis needs honing. Adjust it as needed.
- **Be open to new ideas.** Writing rarely proceeds in a straight line. Even after you outline your paper and begin to write and revise, expect to discover new thoughts—perhaps the best thoughts of all. If you do, be sure to invite them in.

Here is a student's rough draft for an analytical essay on "Nothing Gold Can Stay."

On Robert Frost's "Nothing Gold Can Stay"

Most of the lines in the poem "Nothing Gold Can Stay" by Robert Frost focus on the changing of the seasons. The poem's first line says that the first leaves of spring are actually blossoms, and the actual leaves that follow are less precious. Those first blossoms only last a little while. The reader realizes that nature is a metaphor for a person's state of mind. People start off perfectly innocent, but as time passes, they can't help but lose that innocence. The poem argues that like Adam and Eve we all lose our innocence and the passage of time is inevitable.

The poem's first image is of the color found in nature. The early gold of spring blossoms is nature's "hardest hue to hold." The color gold is associated with the mineral gold, a precious commodity. There's a hint that early spring is nature in its perfect state, and perfection is impossible to hold on to. To the poem's speaker, the colors of early spring seem to last only an hour. If you blink, they are gone. Like early spring, innocence can't last.

The line "leaf subsides to leaf" brings us from early spring through summer and fall. The golden blossoms and delicate leaves of spring subside, or sink to a lower level, meaning they become less special and beautiful. There's nothing more special and beautiful than a baby, so people are the same way. In literature, summer often means the prime of your life, and autumn often means the declining years. These times are less beautiful ones. "So dawn goes down to day" is a similar kind of image. Dawns are unbelievably colorful and beautiful but they don't last very long. Day is nice, but not as special as dawn.

The most surprising line in the poem is the one that isn't about nature. Instead it's about human beings. Eden may have been a garden (a part of nature), but it also represents a state of mind. The traditional religious view is that Adam and Eve chose to disobey God and eat from the tree of knowledge. They could have stayed in paradise forever if they had followed God's orders. So it's surprising that Frost writes "So Eden sank to grief" in a poem that is all about how inevitable change is. It seems like he's saying that no matter what Adam and Eve had done, the Garden of Eden wouldn't stay the paradise it started out being. When Adam and Eve ate the apple, they lost their innocence. The apple is supposed to represent knowledge, so they became wiser but less perfect. But the poem implies that no matter what Adam and Eve had done, they would have grown sadder and wiser. That's true for all people. We can't stay young and innocent.

It's almost as if Frost is defying the Bible, suggesting that there is no such thing as sin. We can't help getting older and wiser. It's a natural process. Suffering happens not because we choose to do bad things but because passing time takes our innocence. The real original sin is that time has to pass and we all have to grow wiser and less innocent.

The poem "Nothing Gold Can Stay" makes the point that people can't stay innocent forever. Suffering is the inevitable result of the aging process. Like the first leaves of spring, we are at the best at the very beginning, and it's all downhill from there.

REVISE YOUR DRAFT

A writer rarely—if ever—achieves perfection on the first try. For most of us, good writing is largely a matter of revision. Once your first draft is done, you can—and should—turn on your analytical mind. Painstaking revision is more than just tidying up grammar and spelling. It might mean expanding your ideas or sharpening the focus by cutting out any unnecessary thoughts. To achieve effective writing, you must have the courage to be merciless. Tear your rough drafts apart and reassemble their pieces into a stronger order. As you revise, consider the following:

- **Be sure your thesis is clear, decisive, and thought-provoking.** The most basic ingredient in a good essay is a strong thesis—the sentence in which you summarize the claim you are making. Your thesis should say something more than just the obvious; it should be clear and decisive and make a point that requires evidence to persuade your reader to agree. A sharp, bold thesis lends energy to your argument. A revision of the working thesis used in the rough draft above provides a good example.

  WORKING THESIS

  The poem argues that like Adam and Eve we all lose our innocence and the passage of time is inevitable.

  This thesis may not be bold or specific enough to make for an interesting argument. A careful reader would be hard pressed to disagree with the observation that Frost's poem depicts the passage of time or the loss of innocence. In a revision of his thesis, however, the essay's author pushes the claim further, going beyond the obvious to its implications.

  REVISED THESIS

  In "Nothing Gold Can Stay," Frost makes a bold claim: sin, suffering, and loss are inevitable because the passage of time causes everyone to fall from grace.

  Instead of simply asserting that the poem looks with sorrow on the passage of time, the revised thesis raises the issue of why this is so. It makes a more thought-provoking claim about the poem. An arguable thesis can result in a more energetic, purposeful essay. A thesis that is obvious to everyone, on the other hand, leads to a static, dull paper.

- **Ascertain whether the evidence you provide supports your theory.** Does everything within your paper work to support its thesis sentence? While a solid paper might be written about the poetic form of "Nothing Gold Can Stay," the student paper above would not be well served by bringing the subject up unless the author could show how the poem's form contributes to its message that time causes everyone to lose his or her innocence. If you find yourself including information that doesn't serve your argument, consider going back into the poem, story, or play for more useful evidence. On the other hand, if you're beginning to have a sneaking feeling that your thesis itself is shaky, consider reworking *it* so that it more accurately reflects the evidence in the text.

- **Check whether your argument is logical.** Does one point lead naturally to the next? Reread the paper, looking for logical fallacies, moments in which the claims you make are not sufficiently supported by evidence, or the connection between one thought and the next seems less than rational. Classic logical fallacies include making hasty generalizations, confusing cause and effect, or using a non sequitur, a statement that doesn't follow from the statement that precedes it. An example of two seemingly unconnected thoughts may be found in the second paragraph of the draft above:

> To the poem's speaker, the colors of early spring seem to last only an hour. If you blink, they are gone. Like early spring, innocence can't last.

Though there may well be a logical connection between the first two sentences and the third one, the paper doesn't spell that connection out. Asked to clarify the warrant, or assumption, that makes possible the leap from the subject of spring to the subject of innocence, the author revised the passage this way:

> To the poem's speaker, the colors of early spring seem to last only an hour. When poets write of seasons, they often also are commenting on the life cycle. To make a statement that spring can't last more than an hour implies that a person's youth (often symbolically associated with spring) is all too short. Therefore, the poem implies that innocent youth, like spring, lasts for only the briefest time.

The revised version spells out the author's thought process, helping the reader to follow the argument.

- **Supply transitional words and phrases.** To ensure that your reader's journey from one idea to the next is a smooth one, insert transitional words and phrases at the start of new paragraphs or sentences. Phrases such as "in contrast" and "however" signal a U-turn in logic, while those such as "in addition" and "similarly" alert the reader that you are continuing in the same direction you have been traveling. Seemingly inconsequential words and phrases such as "also" and "as well" or "as mentioned above" can smooth the reader's path from one thought to the next, as in the example below.

DRAFT

> Though Frost is writing about nature, his real subject is humanity. In literature, spring often represents youth. Summer symbolizes young adulthood, autumn stands for middle age, and winter represents old age. The adult stages of life are, for Frost, less precious than childhood, which passes very quickly. The innocence of childhood is, like those spring leaves, precious as gold.

ADDING TRANSITIONAL WORDS AND PHRASES

> Though Frost is writing about nature, his real subject is humanity. As mentioned above, in literature, spring often represents youth. Similarly, summer symbolizes young adulthood, autumn stands for middle age, and winter represents old age. The adult stages of life are, for Frost, less precious than childhood, which passes very quickly. Also, the innocence of childhood is, like those spring leaves, precious as gold.

- **Make sure each paragraph contains a topic sentence.** Each paragraph in your essay should develop a single idea; this idea should be conveyed in a topic sentence. As astute readers often expect to get a sense of a paragraph's purpose from its first few sentences, a topic sentence is often well placed at or near a paragraph's start.
- **Make a good first impression.** Your introductory paragraph may have seemed just fine as you began the writing process. Be sure to reconsider it in light of the entire paper. Does the introduction draw readers in and prepare them for what follows? If not, be sure to rework it, as the author of the rough draft above did. Look at his first paragraph again:

DRAFT OF OPENING PARAGRAPH

Most of the lines in the poem "Nothing Gold Can Stay" by Robert Frost focus on the changing of the seasons. The poem's first line says that the first leaves of spring are actually blossoms, and the actual leaves that follow are less precious. Those first blossoms only last a little while. The reader realizes that nature is a metaphor for a person's state of mind. People start off perfectly innocent, but as time passes, they can't help but lose that happy innocence. The poem argues that like Adam and Eve we all lose our innocence and the passage of time is inevitable.

While serviceable, this paragraph could be more compelling. Its author improved it by adding specifics to bring his ideas to more vivid life. For example, the rather pedestrian sentence "People start off perfectly innocent, but as time passes, they can't help but lose that innocence" became this livelier one: "As babies we are all perfectly innocent, but as time passes, we can't help but lose that innocence." By adding a specific image—the baby—the author gave the reader a visual picture to illustrate the abstract idea of innocence. He also sharpened his thesis sentence, making it less general and more thought-provoking. By varying the length of his sentences, he made the paragraph less monotonous.

REVISED OPENING PARAGRAPH

Most of the lines in Robert Frost's brief poem "Nothing Gold Can Stay" focus on nature: the changing of the seasons and the fading of dawn into day. The poem's opening line asserts that the first blossoms of spring are more precious than the leaves that follow. Likewise, dawn is more special than day. Though Frost's subject seems to be nature, the reader soon realizes that his real subject is human nature. As babies we are all perfectly innocent, but as time passes, we can't help but lose that happy innocence. In "Nothing Gold Can Stay," Frost makes a bold claim: sin, suffering, and loss are inevitable because the passage of time causes everyone to fall from grace.

- **Remember that last impressions count too.** Your paper's conclusion should give the reader some closure, tying up the paper's loose ends without simply (and boringly) restating all that has come before. The author of the rough draft above initially ended his paper with a paragraph that repeated the paper's main ideas without pushing those ideas any further:

DRAFT OF CONCLUSION

The poem "Nothing Gold Can Stay" makes the point that people can't stay innocent forever. Grief is the inevitable result of the aging process. Like the first leaves of spring, we are at the best at the very beginning, and it's all downhill from there.

While revising his paper, the author realized that the ideas in his next-to-last paragraph would serve to sum up the paper. The new final paragraph doesn't simply restate the thesis; it pushes the idea further, in its last two sentences, by exploring the poem's implications.

REVISED CONCLUSION

Some people might view Frost's poem as sacrilegious because it seems to say that Adam and Eve had no choice; everything in life is doomed to fall. Growing less innocent and more knowing seems less a choice in Frost's view than a natural process like the changing of golden blossoms to green leaves. "Eden sank to grief" not because we choose to do evil things but because time takes away our innocence as we encounter the suffering and loss of human existence. Frost suggests that the real original sin is that time has to pass and we all must grow wiser and less innocent.

- **Give your paper a compelling title.** Like the introduction, a title should be inviting to readers, giving them a sense of what's coming. Avoid a nontitle such as "A Rose for Emily," which serves as a poor advertisement for your paper. Instead, provide enough specifics to pique your reader's interest. "On Robert Frost's 'Nothing Gold Can Stay'" is a duller, less informative title than "Lost Innocence in Robert Frost's 'Nothing Gold Can Stay,'" which may spark the reader's interest and prepare him or her for what is to come.

CHECKLIST: Revising Your Draft

- ☐ Is your thesis clear? Can it be sharpened?
- ☐ Does all your evidence serve to advance the argument put forth in your thesis?
- ☐ Is your argument logical?
- ☐ Do transitional words and phrases signal movement from one idea to the next?
- ☐ Does each paragraph contain a topic sentence?
- ☐ Does your introduction draw the reader in? Does it prepare the reader for what follows?
- ☐ Does your conclusion tie up the paper's loose ends? Does it avoid merely restating what has come before?
- ☐ Is your title compelling?

FINAL ADVICE ON REWRITING

- **Whenever possible, get feedback from a trusted reader.** In every project there comes a time when the writer has gotten so close to the work that he or she can't see it clearly. A talented roommate or a tutor in the campus writing center can tell you what isn't yet clear on the page, what questions still need answering, or what line of argument isn't yet as persuasive as it could be.
- **Be willing to refine your thesis.** Once you have fleshed out your whole paper, you may find that your original thesis is not borne out by the rest of your argument. If so, you will need to rewrite your thesis so that it more precisely fits the evidence at hand.
- **Be prepared to question your whole approach to a work of literature.** On occasion, you may even need to entertain the notion of throwing everything you have written into the wastebasket and starting over again. Occasionally having to start from scratch is the lot of any writer.
- **Rework troublesome passages.** Look for skimpy paragraphs of one or two sentences—evidence that your ideas might need more fleshing out. Can you supply more evidence, more explanation, more examples or illustrations?
- **Cut out any unnecessary information.** Everything in your paper should serve to further its thesis. Delete any sentences or paragraphs that detract from your focus.
- **Aim for intelligent clarity when you use literary terminology.** Critical terms can help sharpen your thoughts and make them easier to handle. Nothing is less sophisticated or more opaque, however, than too many technical terms thrown together for grandiose effect: "The mythic *symbolism* of this *archetype* is the *antithesis* of the *dramatic situation*." Choose plain words you're already at ease with. When you use specialized terms, do so to smooth the way for your reader—to make your meaning more precise. It is less cumbersome, for example, to refer to the *tone* of a story than to say, "the way the author makes you feel that she feels about what she is talking about."
- **Set your paper aside for a while.** Even an hour or two away from your essay can help you see it with fresh eyes. Remember that the literal meaning of "revision" is "seeing again."
- **Finally, carefully read your paper one last time to edit it.** Now it's time to sweat the small stuff. Check any uncertain spellings, scan for run-on sentences and fragments, pull out a weak word and send in a stronger one. Like soup stains on a job interviewee's tie, finicky errors distract from the overall impression and prejudice your reader against your essay.

Here is the revised version of the student paper we have been examining.

Gabriel 1

Noah Gabriel

Professor James

English 2171

7 December 2011

Lost Innocence in
Robert Frost's "Nothing Gold Can Stay"

Most of the lines in Robert Frost's brief poem "Nothing Gold Can Stay" focus on nature: the changing of the seasons and the fading of dawn into day. The poem's opening line asserts that the first blossoms of spring are more precious than the leaves that follow. Likewise, dawn is more special than day. Though Frost's subject seems to be nature, the reader soon realizes that his real subject is human nature. As babies we are all perfectly innocent, but as time passes, we can't help but lose that happy innocence. In "Nothing Gold Can Stay," Frost makes a bold claim: sin, suffering, and loss are inevitable because the passage of time causes everyone to fall from grace.

Thesis sentence is specific and decisive

The poem begins with a deceptively simple sentence: "Nature's first green is gold." The subject seems to be the first, delicate leaves of spring which are less green and more golden than summer leaves. However, the poem goes on to say, "Her early leaf's a flower" (3), indicating that Frost is describing the first blossoms of spring. In fact, he's describing both the new leaves and blossoms. Both are as rare and precious as the mineral gold. They are precious because they don't last long; the early gold of spring blossoms is nature's "hardest hue to hold" (2). Early spring is an example of nature in its perfect state, and perfection is impossible to hold on to. To the poem's speaker, in fact, the colors of early spring seem to last only an hour. When poets write of seasons, they often also are commenting on the life cycle. To make a statement that spring can't last more than an hour implies that a person's youth (often symbolically associated with spring) is all too short. Therefore, the poem implies that innocent youth, like spring, lasts for only the briefest time.

Textual evidence to back up thesis

Warrant is spelled out

Claim

While Frost takes four lines to describe the decline of the spring blossoms, he picks up the pace when he describes what happens next. The line "Then leaf subsides to leaf" (5) brings us from early spring through summer and fall, compressing three seasons into a single line. Just as time seems to pass slowly

Gabriel 2

Significant word is looked at closely

when we are children, and then much more quickly when we grow up, the poem moves quickly once the first golden moment is past. The word "subsides" feels important. The golden blossoms and delicate leaves of spring subside, or sink to a lower level, meaning they become less special and beautiful.

Claim

Warrant spelled out

Though Frost is writing about nature, his real subject is humanity. As mentioned above, in literature, spring often represents youth. Similarly, summer symbolizes young adulthood, autumn stands for middle age, and winter represents old age. The adult stages of life are, for Frost, less precious than childhood, which passes very quickly, as we later realize. Also, the innocence of childhood is, like those spring leaves, precious as gold.

Key phrase is analyzed closely

Frost shifts his view from the cycle of the seasons to the cycle of a single day to make a similar point. Just as spring turns to summer, "So dawn goes down to day" (7). Like spring, dawn is unbelievably colorful and beautiful but doesn't last very long. Like "subsides," the phrase "goes down" implies that full daylight is actually a falling off from dawn. As beautiful as daylight is, it's ordinary, while dawn is special because it is more fleeting.

Claim

Among these natural images, one line stands out: "So Eden sank to grief" (6). This line is the only one in the poem that deals directly with human beings. Eden may have been a garden (a part of nature) but it represents a state of mind—perfect innocence. In the traditional religious view, Adam and Eve chose to disobey God by eating an apple from the tree of knowledge. They were presented with a choice: to be obedient and remain in paradise forever, or to disobey God's order. People often speak of that first choice as "original sin." In this religious view, "Eden sank to grief" because the first humans chose to sin.

Claim

Frost, however, takes a different view. He compares the Fall of Man to the changing of spring to summer, as though it was as inevitable as the passage of time. The poem implies that no matter what Adam and Eve did, they couldn't remain in paradise. Original sin in Frost's view seems less a voluntary moral action than a natural, if unhappy sort of maturation. The innocent perfection of the garden of Eden couldn't possibly last. The apple represents knowledge, so in a symbolic sense God wanted Adam and Eve to stay unknowing, or innocent. But the poem implies that it was inevitable that Adam and Eve would gain knowledge and lose their innocence, becoming wiser but less perfect. They lost Eden and encountered "grief," the knowledge of suffering and loss associated with the human condition. This is certainly true for the rest of us human beings. As much as we might like to, we can't stay young or innocent forever.

Gabriel 3

Some people might view Frost's poem as sacrilegious because it seems to say that Adam and Eve had no choice; everything in life is doomed to fall. Growing less innocent and more knowing seems less a choice in Frost's view than a natural process like the changing of golden blossoms to green leaves. "Eden sank to grief" not because we choose to do evil things but because time takes away our innocence as we encounter the suffering and loss of human existence. Frost suggests that the real original sin is that time has to pass and we all must grow wiser and less innocent.

Restatement of thesis

Gabriel 4

Work Cited

Frost, Robert. "Nothing Gold Can Stay." *Literature: An Introduction to Fiction, Poetry, Drama, and Writing*. Ed. X. J. Kennedy and Dana Gioia. 12th ed. New York: Pearson, 2013. 909. Print.

DOCUMENT SOURCES TO AVOID PLAGIARISM

Certain literary works, because they offer intriguing difficulties, have attracted professional critics by the score. On library shelves, great phalanxes of critical books now stand at the side of James Joyce's *Ulysses* and T. S. Eliot's allusive poem *The Waste Land*. The student who undertakes to study such works seriously is well advised to profit from the critics' labors. Chances are, too, that even in discussing a relatively uncomplicated work, you will want to seek the aid of some critics.

If you do so, you may find yourself wanting to borrow quotations for your own papers. This is a fine thing to do—provided you give credit for those words to their rightful author. To do otherwise is plagiarism—a serious offense—and most English instructors are likely to recognize it when they see it. In any but the most superlative student paper, a brilliant (or even not so brilliant) phrase from a renowned critic is likely to stand out like a golf ball in a garter snake's midriff.

To avoid plagiarism, you must reproduce the text you are using with quotation marks around it, and give credit where it is due. Even if you summarize a critic's idea in your own words, rather than quoting his or her exact words, you have to give credit to your source. A later chapter, "Writing a Research Paper," will discuss the topic of properly citing your sources in greater depth. For now, students should simply remember that claiming another's work as one's own is the worst offense of the learning community. It negates the very purpose of education, which is to learn to think for oneself.

THE FORM OF YOUR FINISHED PAPER

If your instructor has not specified the form of your finished paper, follow the guidelines in the current edition of the *MLA Handbook for Writers of Research Papers*, which you will find more fully described in the chapter "Writing a Research Paper." In brief:

- Choose standard letter-size ($8\frac{1}{2} \times 11$) white paper.
- Use standard, easy-to-read type fonts, such as Times New Roman. Be sure the italic type style contrasts with the regular style.
- Give your name, your instructor's name, the course number, and the date at the top left-hand corner of your first page, starting one inch from the top.
- On all pages, give your last name and the page number in the upper right-hand corner, one-half inch from the top.
- Remember to give your paper a title that reflects your thesis.
- Leave one inch of margin on all four sides of each page and a few inches of space or an additional sheet of paper after your conclusion, so that your instructor can offer comments.
- If you include a works-cited section, begin it on a new page.
- Double-space all your text, including quotations, notes, and the works-cited page.
- Italicize the titles of longer works—books, plays, periodicals, and book-length poems such as *The Odyssey*. The titles of shorter works—poems, articles, or short stories—should appear in quotation marks.

SPELL-CHECK AND GRAMMAR-CHECK PROGRAMS

Most computer software includes a program to automatically check spelling. While such programs make proofreading easier, there are certain kinds of errors they won't catch. Words that are perfectly acceptable in other contexts but not the ones you intended ("is" where you meant "in," or "he" where you meant "the") will slip by undetected, making it clear to your instructor that your computer—and not you—did the proofreading. This is why it's still crucial that you proofread and correct your papers the old-fashioned way—read them yourself.

Another common problem is that the names of most authors, places, and special literary terms won't be in many standard spell-check memories. Unfamiliar words will be identified during the spell-check process, but you still must check all proper nouns carefully, so that Robert Forst, Gwendolyn Broks, or Emily Dickensen doesn't make an unauthorized appearance midway in your otherwise exemplary paper. As the well-known authors Dina Gioia, Dan Goia, Dana Glola, Dona Diora, and Dana Gioia advise, always check the spelling of all names.

As an example of the kinds of mistakes your spell-checker won't catch, here are some cautionary verses that have circulated on the Internet. (Based on a charming piece of light verse by Jerrold H. Zar, "Candidate for a Pullet Surprise," this version reflects additions and revisions by numerous anonymous Internet collaborators.)

A Little Poem Regarding Computer Spell-Checkers 2000?

Eye halve a spelling checker
  It came with my pea sea
It plainly marques four my revue
  Miss steaks eye kin knot sea.

Eye strike a key and type a word
  And weight four it two say
Weather eye am wrong oar write
  It shows me strait a weigh.

As soon as a mist ache is made
  It nose bee fore two long
And eye can put the error rite
  Its rare lea ever wrong.

Eye have run this poem threw it
  I am shore your pleased two no
Its letter perfect awl the weigh
  My checker tolled me sew.

Another mixed blessing is the grammar-check program that highlights sentences containing obvious grammatical mistakes. Unfortunately, if you don't know what is wrong with your sentence in the first place, the grammar program won't always tell you. You can try reworking the sentence until the highlighting disappears (indicating that it's now grammatically correct). Better still, you can take steps to ensure that you have a good grasp of grammar already. Most colleges offer brief refresher courses in grammar, and, of course, writers' handbooks with grammar rules are readily available. Still, the best way to improve your grammar, your spelling, and your general command of language is to read widely and well.

To that end, we urge you to read the works of literature collected in this book beyond those texts assigned to you by your teacher. A well-furnished mind is a great place to live, an address you'll want to have forever.

42 WRITING ABOUT A STORY

Don't write merely to be understood.
Write so that you cannot possibly be misunderstood.

—ROBERT LOUIS STEVENSON

Writing about fiction presents its own set of challenges and rewards. Because a well-wrought work of fiction can catch us up in the twists and turns of its plot, we may be tempted to read it in a trance, passively letting its plot wash over us, as we might watch an entertaining film. Or, because stories, even short ones, unfold over time, there is often so much to say about them that narrowing down and organizing your thoughts can seem daunting.

To write compellingly about fiction, you need to read actively, identify a meaningful topic, and focus on making a point about which you feel strongly. (For pointers on finding a topic, organizing, writing, and revising your paper, see the previous chapter, "Writing About Literature." Some methods especially useful for writing about stories are described in the present chapter.)

In this chapter much of the discussions and many of the examples refer to Edgar Allan Poe's short story "The Tell-Tale Heart" (page 387). If you haven't already read it, you can do so in only a few minutes, so that the rest of this chapter will make more sense to you.

READ ACTIVELY

Unlike a brief poem or a painting that you can take in with one long glance, a work of fiction—even a short story—may be too complicated to hold all at once in the mind's eye. Before you can write about it, you may need to give it two or more careful readings, and even then, as you begin to think further about it, you will probably have to thumb through it to reread passages. The first time through, it is best just to read attentively, open to whatever pleasure and wisdom the story may afford. The second time, you will find it useful to read with pencil in hand, either to mark your text or to take notes to jog your memory. To work out the design and meaning of a story need not be a boring chore, any more than it is to land a fighting fish and to study it with admiration.

- **Read the story at least twice.** The first time through, allow yourself just to enjoy the story—to experience surprise and emotion. Once you know how the tale ends, you'll find it easier to reread with some detachment, noticing details you may have glossed over the first time.
- **Annotate the text.** Reread the story, taking notes in the margins or highlighting key passages as you go. When you sit down to write, you probably will have to skim the story to refresh your memory, and those notes and highlighted passages should prove useful. Here is a sample of an annotated passage, from paragraph 3 of Edgar Allan Poe's "The Tell-Tale Heart."

Who is his listener?

Is this true?

Now this is the point. You fancy me mad. Madmen know nothing. But you should have seen *me*. You should have seen how wisely I proceeded—with what caution—with what foresight—with what dissimulation I went to work! I was never kinder to the old man than during the whole week before I killed him. And every night, about midnight, I turned the latch of his door and opened it—oh, so gently! And then, when I had made an opening sufficient for my head, I put in a dark lantern, all closed, closed, so that no light shone out, and then I thrust in my head. Oh, you would have laughed to see how cunningly I thrust it in! I moved it slowly—very, very slowly, so that I might not disturb the old man's sleep. It took me an hour to place my whole head within the opening so far that I could see him as he lay upon his bed. Ha!—would a madman have been so wise as this? And then, when my head was well in the room, I undid the lantern cautiously—oh, so cautiously—cautiously (for the hinges creaked)—I undid it just so much that a single thin ray fell upon the vulture eye. And this I did for seven long nights—every night just at midnight—but I found the eye always closed; and so it was impossible to do the work; for it was not the old man who vexed me, but his Evil Eye.

He's not so mad he doesn't know what he's doing

He's strangely happy/excited

Careful planning

Creepy image. Who is the vulture here?

What did he expect?!

Peculiar obsession

THINK ABOUT THE STORY

Once you have reread the story, you can begin to process your ideas about it. To get started, try the following steps:

- **Identify the protagonist and the conflict.** Whose story is being told? What does that character desire more than anything else? What stands in the way of that character's achievement of his or her goal? The answers to these questions can give you a better handle on the story's plot.
- **Consider the story's point of view.** What does it contribute to the story? How might the tale change if told from another point of view?
- **Think about the setting.** Does it play a significant role in the plot? How does setting affect the story's tone?
- **Notice key symbols.** If any symbols catch your attention as you go, be sure to highlight each place in which they appear in the text. What do these symbols contribute to the story's meaning? (Remember, not every image is a symbol—only those important recurrent persons, places, or things that seem to suggest more than their literal meaning.)
- **Look for the theme.** Is the story's central meaning stated directly? If not, how does it reveal itself?
- **Think about tone and style.** How would you characterize the style in which the story is written? Consider elements such as diction, sentence structure, tone, and organization. How does the story's style contribute to its tone?

PREWRITING: DISCOVER YOUR IDEAS

Once you have given the story some preliminary thought, it is time to write as a means of discovering what it is you have to say. Brainstorming, clustering, listing, freewriting, keeping a journal, and outlining all can help you clarify your thoughts about the story and, in doing so, generate ideas for your paper. While you don't need to use *all* these techniques, try them to find the one or two that work best for you.

- **Brainstorm.** If you aren't sure what, exactly, to say about a story, try jotting down everything you can think of about it. Work quickly, without pausing to judge what you have written. Set yourself a time limit of ten or fifteen minutes and keep writing even if you think you have said it all. A list that results from brainstorming on "The Tell-Tale Heart" might look something like this:

  madness? seems crazy
  unreliable narrator
  Could story be a dream?
  Could heartbeat be supernatural?
  heartbeat = speaker's paranoia
  tone: dramatic, intense, quick mood changes
  glee/terror
  lots of exclamation points

telling his story to listener
old man = father? boss? friend?
old man's gold/treasures
old man's eye = motive
vulture eye = symbolic
Calls plotting murder "work"
careful/patient
Chops up body
perfect crime
Policemen don't hear heartbeat
Guilt makes him confess

- **Cluster.** Clustering involves generating ideas by diagramming the relationship among your many ideas. First, write your subject at the center of a sheet of paper and circle it. Then, jot down ideas as they occur to you, drawing lines to link each idea to related ones. Here is an example of how you might cluster your ideas about "The Tell-Tale Heart."

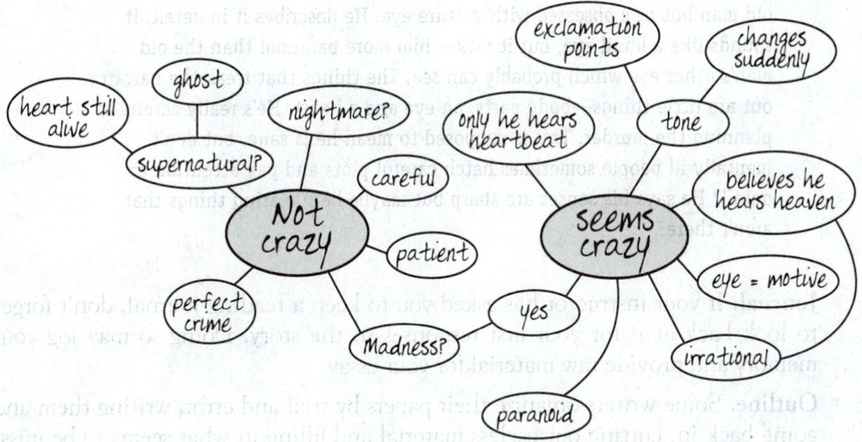

- **List.** Using your notes and annotations as a guide, list information that seems useful, adding any notes that help you to keep track of your thought process. Use different headings to organize related concepts. Your lists might look something like this:

<u>Unreliable Narrator</u>	<u>Other Possibilities</u>
mood swings	nightmare
insists too much on being sane	supernatural
confusion	heart still alive?
disease	ghost's heartbeat?
sharpened senses	
loved old man	
murder	
patience	
guilt	
hearing things	

- **Freewrite.** Before you try to write a coherent first draft of your essay, take time to write freely, exploring your ideas as they occur to you. Writing quickly, without thinking too hard about grammar or spelling, can call forth surprising new ideas that wouldn't arrive if you were composing in a more reflective, cautious manner. To freewrite, give yourself a set amount of time—fifteen or twenty minutes. Put your pen to paper (or your fingers to the keyboard) and write without pausing to think. Keep going even if you run out of things to say. A freewrite on "The Tell-Tale Heart" might look like this:

  The guy seems crazy. He keeps insisting he's sane, so maybe others have accused him of being insane. He's speaking to someone—a judge? a fellow inmate? The story feels spoken out loud, like a dramatic monologue. His mood changes really quickly. One minute he's gleeful, and then impatient, then terrified. The story is full of dashes and exclamation points. He says he can hear everything in heaven and earth and even some things in hell. That seems crazy. His disease has sharpened his senses. Is he the old man's son, or his employee? I don't think the story says. It does say he loves the old man but he's obsessed with vulture eye. He describes it in detail. It sounds like a blind eye, but it makes him more paranoid than the old man's other eye which probably can see. The things that freak the narrator out are little things—body parts, an eye and a heart. He's really careful in planning the murder. This is supposed to mean he is sane, but don't mentally ill people sometimes hatch careful plots and pay attention to detail? He says his senses are sharp but maybe he's hearing things that aren't there?

- **Journal.** If your instructor has asked you to keep a reading journal, don't forget to look back at it for your first responses to the story. Doing so may jog your memory and provide raw material for your essay.
- **Outline.** Some writers organize their papers by trial and error, writing them and going back in, cutting out useless material and filling in what seems to be missing. For a more efficient approach to organization, though, try making an outline—a simple list of points arranged in an order that makes logical sense. Such an outline might look like this:

  1. Point of view is ironic (speaker is mad/unreliable)
     hears things in heaven/hell
     excited tone
     focus on strange detail
  2. Can we trust story really happened?
     nightmare?
     more interesting if actual
  3. Supernatural elements?
     ghost heartbeat?
     heart still alive?
  4. More interesting/believable if speaker is mad

WRITE A ROUGH DRAFT

Once your prewriting exercises have sparked an idea or two, you will be ready to begin shaping your thoughts into a rough draft. Reread the section "Develop a Literary Argument" in the previous chapter for help getting started. You can still keep your approach loose and informal; don't worry yet about phrasing things perfectly or pinning down the ideal word. For now, your goal is to begin finding a shape for your argument.

- **Remember your purpose.** Before you begin work on your first draft, be sure to check the assignment you have been given. There is no sense in writing even the most elegant *analysis* (in which you focus on one particular element of a story) if you have been told to write an *explication* (a detailed, line-by-line interpretation of a passage).
- **Consider your audience.** Though your professor and classmates will likely be your paper's actual audience, the assignment might specify hypothetical readers. Whoever your audience may be, keep their needs in mind as you write.
- **Formulate your thesis.** Before you get going on your rough draft, you will need a thesis sentence summing up your paper's main idea. Begin with a provisional thesis to give your argument direction. As you write, be sure to keep your provisional thesis in mind; doing so will help you stay on track. Here is a working thesis for a paper on "The Tell-Tale Heart":

  WORKING THESIS

  The story contains many hints that the narrator of "The Tell-Tale Heart" is crazy.

  While this thesis gives its author something to work toward, it isn't yet as sharp as it could be. Most readers would agree that the story's narrator shows obvious signs of insanity. A more compelling thesis would go into the specifics of what, exactly, gives away the narrator's madness, or it might spell out the implications of this madness for the story. The following reworked version of this thesis sentence does both:

  REVISED THESIS

  The narrator's tenuous hold on reality and his wild shifts in mood indicate that he is insane and, therefore, that his point of view is untrustworthy.

  Like this statement, your thesis should be decisive and specific. As you write a rough draft, your task is to persuade readers of the wisdom of your thesis.

- **Back up your thesis with evidence.** The bulk of your essay should be spent providing evidence that proves your thesis. Because the most persuasive evidence tends to be that which comes from the story itself, be sure to quote as needed. As you flesh out your argument, check back frequently to make sure your thesis continues to hold up to the evidence. If you find that the facts of the story don't bear out your thesis, the problem may be with the evidence or with the thesis itself. Could your point be better proved by presenting different evidence? If so, exchange what you have for more convincing information. If not, go back in and refine your thesis sentence. Then make sure that the rest of the evidence bears out your new and improved thesis.

- **Organize your argument.** Choose the points you need to prove your thesis and present them, along with supporting evidence, in whatever order best makes your case. A rough outline is often a useful tool.

CHECKLIST: Writing a Rough Draft

- ☐ What is your essay's purpose?
- ☐ Who is your audience? What do they need to know?
- ☐ What is your thesis? Is it debatable?
- ☐ Does everything in your essay support your thesis?
- ☐ Is your argument sensibly organized?

REVISE YOUR DRAFT

Once your first draft has been committed to paper, you will need to begin revising—going back in and reworking it to make the argument as persuasive and the prose as seamless as can be. First, though, it is an excellent idea to get feedback on your draft from a trusted reader—a classmate, a roommate, a tutor in your school's writing center, or even your instructor—who can tell you which ideas are, and are not, coming across clearly, or where your argument is persuasive and where it could be more convincing. For writers at all levels of expertise, there simply is no substitute for constructive criticism from a thoughtful reader. If, however, you find readers are in short supply, put your rough draft away for at least an hour or two, and reread it with fresh eyes before you begin revising.

The following is an example of how one student used his instructor's comments to improve his paper's opening paragraph. (The final paper appears later in the chapter on page 1920.)

DRAFT OF OPENING PARAGRAPH

The narrator of Edgar Allan Poe's "The Tell-Tale Heart" is a very mysterious and murderous character. The reader doesn't know much about him, except for how he speaks and what he has to say for himself. There is one important fact revealed by evidence in the story. The story contains many hints that the narrator of "The Tell-Tale Heart" is crazy.

Provide specifics.

Tell me more!

Why is this important?

What are some of these?

REVISED OPENING PARAGRAPH

Although there are many things we do not know about the narrator of Edgar Allan Poe's story "The Tell-Tale Heart"—is he a son? a servant? a companion?—there is one thing we are sure of from the start. He is mad. In the opening paragraph, Poe makes the narrator's condition unmistakable, not only from his excited and worked-up speech (full of dashes and exclamation points), but also from his wild claims. He says it is merely some disease which has sharpened his senses that has made people call him crazy. Who but a madman, however, would say, "I heard all things in the heaven and in the earth," and brag how his ear is a kind of radio, listening in on hell? The narrator's tenuous hold on reality and his wild shifts in mood indicate that he is mad and, therefore, that his point of view is untrustworthy.

Remember that revision means more than just cleaning up typos and doing away with stray semicolons. Revision might mean fleshing out your ideas with new paragraphs, rearranging material, or paring away passages that detract from your focus. As you rewrite, make sure every paragraph has a topic sentence that announces its main idea. Feel free to link your ideas with transitional words and phrases such as "moreover," "in addition," or "in contrast" to help your reader understand how each new idea relates to the one that precedes it.

CHECKLIST: Revising Your Draft

- ☐ Is your thesis clear? Does it say something significant but not entirely obvious about the story?
- ☐ Does all your evidence serve to advance the argument put forth in your thesis?
- ☐ Is your argument clear and logical?
- ☐ Do transitional words and phrases help signal movement from one idea to the next?
- ☐ Does your introduction draw the reader in? Does it prepare the reader for what follows?
- ☐ Does your conclusion tie up the paper's loose ends? Does it avoid merely restating what has come before?
- ☐ Does each paragraph contain a topic sentence?
- ☐ Does the paper have an interesting and compelling title?

WHAT'S YOUR PURPOSE? COMMON APPROACHES TO WRITING ABOUT FICTION

It is crucial to keep your paper's purpose in mind. When you write an academic paper, you are likely to have been given a specific set of marching orders. Maybe you have been asked to write for a particular audience besides the obvious one (your professor, that is). Perhaps you have been asked to describe your personal reaction to a literary work. Maybe your purpose is to interpret a work, analyzing how one or more of its elements contribute to its meaning. You may have been instructed to write an evaluation in which you judge a work's merits. Let the assignment dictate your paper's tone and content. Below are several commonly used approaches to writing about fiction.

Explication

Explication is the patient unfolding of meanings in a work of literature. An explication proceeds carefully through a story, usually interpreting it line by line—perhaps even word by word—dwelling on details a casual reader might miss and illustrating how a story's smaller parts contribute to the whole. Alert and willing to take pains, the writer of such an essay notices anything meaningful that isn't obvious, whether it is a colossal theme suggested by a symbol or a little hint contained in a single word.

To write an honest explication of an entire story takes time and space, and it is a better assignment for a term paper, an honors thesis, or a dissertation than a short essay. A thorough explication of Nathaniel Hawthorne's "Young Goodman Brown," for example, would likely run much longer than the rich and intriguing short story itself. Ordinarily, explication is best suited to a short passage or section of a story: a key scene, a critical conversation, a statement of theme, or an opening or closing paragraph. In a long critical essay that doesn't adhere to one method all the way through, the method of explication may appear from time to time, as when the critic, in discussing a story, stops to unravel a particularly knotty passage. Here are tips for writing a successful explication of your own:

- **Focus on the details that strike you as most meaningful.** Do not try to cover everything.
- **Try working through the original passage sentence by sentence.** If you choose this method, be sure to vary your transitions from one point to the next, to avoid the danger of falling into a boring singsong: "In the first sentence I noticed . . . ," "In the next sentence . . . ," "Now in the third sentence . . . ," and "Finally, in the last sentence. . . ."
- **Consider working from a simple outline.** In writing the explication that follows of a passage from "The Tell-Tale Heart," the student began with a list of points she wanted to express:

1. Speaker's extreme care and exactness—typical of some mental illnesses.
2. Speaker doesn't act by usual logic but by a crazy logic.
3. Dreamlike connection between latch and lantern and old man's eye.

Storytellers who are especially fond of language invite closer attention to their words than others might. Edgar Allan Poe, for one, was a poet sensitive to the rhythms of his sentences and a symbolist whose stories abound in potent suggestions. Here is a student's explication of a short but essential passage in "The Tell-Tale Heart." The passage occurs in the third paragraph of the story, and to help us follow the explication, the student quotes the passage in full at the paper's beginning.

Kim 1

Susan Kim

Professor A. M. Lundy

English 100

20 March 2012

By Lantern Light: An Explication

of a Passage in Poe's "The Tell-Tale Heart"

> And every night, about midnight, I turned the latch of his door and opened it—oh, so gently! And then, when I had made an opening sufficient for my head, I put in a dark lantern, all closed, closed, so that no light shone out, and then I thrust in my head. Oh, you would have laughed to see how cunningly I thrust it in! I moved it slowly—very, very slowly, so that I might not disturb the old man's sleep. It took me an hour to place my whole head within the opening so far that I could see him as he lay upon his bed. Ha!—would a madman have been so wise as this? And then, when my head was well in the room, I undid the lantern cautiously—oh, so cautiously—cautiously (for the hinges creaked)—I undid it just so much that a single thin ray fell upon the vulture eye. And this I did for seven long nights—every night just at midnight—but I found the eye always closed; and so it was impossible to do the work; for it was not the old man who vexed me, but his Evil Eye. (par. 3)

Quotes passage to be explicated

Although Edgar Allan Poe has suggested in the first lines of his story "The Tell-Tale Heart" that the person who addresses us is insane, it is only when we come to the speaker's account of his preparations for murdering the old man that we find his madness fully revealed. Even more convincingly than his earlier words (for we might possibly think that someone who claims to hear things in heaven and hell is a religious mystic), these preparations reveal him to be mad. What strikes us is that they are so elaborate and meticulous. A significant detail is the exactness of his schedule for spying: "every night just at midnight." The words with which he describes his motions also convey the most extreme care (and I will indicate them by italics): "how wisely I proceeded—with *what caution*," "I turned the latch of his door and opened it—oh, so *gently*!" "how *cunningly* I thrust it [my head] in! I moved it slowly—*very, very slowly*," "I undid the lantern *cautiously*—oh, *so cautiously*—*cautiously*." Taking a whole hour to intrude his head into the room, he asks, "Ha!—would a madman have been so wise as this?" But of course the word

Thesis sentence

Textual evidence supports thesis

Kim 2

wise is unconsciously ironic, for clearly it is not wisdom the speaker displays, but an absurd degree of care, an almost fiendish ingenuity. Such behavior, I understand, is typical of certain mental illnesses. All his careful preparations that he thinks prove him sane only convince us instead that he is mad.

Topic sentence on narrator's mad logic

Obviously his behavior is self-defeating. He wants to catch the "vulture eye" open, and yet he takes all these pains not to disturb the old man's sleep. If he behaved logically, he might go barging into the bedroom with his lantern ablaze, shouting at the top of his voice. And yet, if we can see things his way, there *is* a strange logic to his reasoning. He regards the eye as a creature in itself, quite apart from its possessor. "It was not," he says, "the old man who vexed me, but his Evil Eye." Apparently, to be inspired to do his deed, the madman needs to behold the eye—at least, this is my understanding of his remark, "I found the eye always closed; and so it was impossible to do the work." Poe's choice of the word *work*, by the way, is also revealing. Murder is made to seem a duty or a job; and anyone who so regards murder is either extremely cold-blooded, like a hired killer for a gangland assassination, or else deranged. Besides, the word suggests again the curious sense of detachment that the speaker feels toward the owner of the eye.

Conclusion pushes thesis further, making it more specific.

In still another of his assumptions, the speaker shows that he is madly logical, or operating on the logic of a dream. There seems a dreamlike relationship between his dark lantern "all closed, closed, so that no light shone out," and the sleeping victim. When the madman opens his lantern so that it emits a single ray, he is hoping that the eye in the old man's head will be open too, letting out its corresponding gleam. The latch that he turns so gently, too, seems like the eye, whose lid needs to be opened in order for the murderer to go ahead. It is as though the speaker is *trying* to get the eyelid to lift. By taking such great pains and by going through all this nightly ritual, he is practicing some kind of magic, whose rules are laid down not by our logic, but by the logic of dreams.

Kim 3

Work Cited

Poe, Edgar Allan. "The Tell-Tale Heart." *Literature: An Introduction to Fiction, Poetry, Drama, and Writing.* Ed. X. J. Kennedy and Dana Gioia. 12th ed. New York: Pearson, 2013. 387–91. Print.

An unusually well written essay, "By Lantern Light" cost its author two or three careful revisions. Rather than attempting to say something about *everything* in the passage from Poe, she selects only the details that strike her as most meaningful. In her very first sentence, she briefly shows us how the passage functions in the context of Poe's story: how it clinches our suspicions that the narrator is mad. Notice too that the student who wrote the essay doesn't inch through the passage sentence by sentence, but freely takes up its details in an order that seems appropriate to her argument.

Analysis

Examining a single component of a story can afford us a better understanding of the entire work. This is perhaps why in most literature classes students are asked to write at least one **analysis** (from the Greek: "breaking up"), an essay that breaks a story or novel into its elements and, usually, studies one part closely. One likely topic for an analysis might be "The Character of James Baldwin's Sonny," in which the writer would concentrate on showing us Sonny's highly individual features and traits of personality. Other topics for an analysis might be "Irony in Anne Tyler's 'Teenage Wasteland,'" or "Setting in Kate Chopin's 'The Storm,'" or "The Unidentified Narrator in 'A Rose for Emily.'"

To be sure, no element of a story dwells in isolation from the story's other elements. In "The Tell-Tale Heart," the madness of the leading character apparently makes it necessary to tell the story from a special point of view and probably helps determine the author's choice of theme, setting, symbolism, tone, style, and ironies. But it would be mind-boggling to try to study all those elements simultaneously. For this reason, when we write an analysis, we generally study just one element, though we may suggest—probably at the start of the essay—its relation to the whole story. Here are two points to keep in mind when writing an analysis:

- **Decide upon a thesis, and include only relevant insights.** As tempting as it might be to include your every idea, stick to those that will help to prove your point.
- **Support your contentions with specific references to the story you are analyzing.** Quotations can be particularly convincing.

The following paper is an example of a solid, brief analysis. Written by a student, it focuses on just one element of "The Tell-Tale Heart"—the story's point of view.

Frederick 1

Mike Frederick

Professor Stone

English 110

18 January 2012

The Hearer of the Tell-Tale Heart

States author and work

Although there are many things we do not know about the narrator of Edgar Allan Poe's story "The Tell-Tale Heart"—is he a son? a servant? a companion?—there is one thing we are sure of from the start. He is mad. In the opening paragraph, Poe makes the narrator's condition unmistakable, not only from his excited and worked-up speech (full of dashes and exclamation points), but also from his wild claims. He says it is merely some disease which has sharpened his senses that has made people call him crazy. Who but a madman, however, would say, "I heard all things in the heaven and in the earth," and brag how his ear is a kind of radio, listening in on hell? The narrator's tenuous hold on reality and his wild shifts in mood indicate that he is insane and, therefore, that his point of view is untrustworthy.

Thesis statement

Topic sentence—how point of view determines emphasis

Because the participant narrator is telling his story in the first person, some details in the story stand out more than others. When the narrator goes on to tell how he watches the old man sleeping, he rivets his attention on the old man's "vulture eye." When a ray from his lantern finds the Evil Eye open, he says, "I could see nothing else of the old man's face or person" (par. 9). Actually, the reader can see almost nothing else about the old man anywhere in the rest of the story. All we are told is that the old man treated the younger man well, and we gather that the old man was rich, because his house is full of treasures. We do not have a clear idea of what the old man looks like, though, nor do we know how he talks, for we are not given any of his words. Our knowledge of him is mainly confined to his eye and its effect on the narrator. This confinement gives that symbolic eye a lot of importance in the story. The narrator tells us all we know and directs our attention to parts of it.

Raises question, then explores answer

This point of view raises an interesting question. Since we are dependent on the narrator for all our information, how do we know the whole story isn't just a nightmare in his demented mind? We have really no way to be sure it isn't, as far as I can see. I assume, however, that there really is a dark shuttered house and an old man and real policemen who start snooping around when

Frederick 2

screams are heard in the neighborhood because it is a more memorable story if it is a crazy man's view of reality than if it is all just a terrible dream. But we can't rely on the madman's interpretation of what happens. Poe keeps putting distances between what the narrator says and what we are apparently supposed to think. For instance: the narrator has boasted that he is calm and clear in the head, but as soon as he starts trying to explain why he killed the old man, we gather that he is confused, to say the least. "I think it was his eye!" the narrator exclaims, as if not quite sure (par. 2). As he goes on to explain how he conducted the murder, we realize that he is a man with a fixed idea working with a patience that is certainly mad, almost diabolical.

Topic sentence on how narrator's madness is revealed

Some readers might wonder if "The Tell-Tale Heart" is a story of the supernatural. Is the heartbeat that the narrator hears a ghost come back to haunt him? Here, I think, the point of view is our best guide to what to believe. The simple explanation for the heartbeat is this: it is all in the madman's mind. Perhaps he feels such guilt that he starts hearing things. Another explanation is possible, one suggested by Daniel Hoffman, a critic who has discussed the story: the killer hears the sound of his *own* heart (227). Hoffman's explanation (which I don't like as well as mine) also is a natural one, and it fits the story as a whole. Back when the narrator first entered the old man's bedroom to kill him, the heartbeat sounded so loud to him that he was afraid the neighbors would hear it too. Evidently they didn't, and so Hoffman may be right in thinking that the sound was only that of his own heart pounding in his ears. Whichever explanation you take, it is a more down-to-earth and reasonable explanation than (as the narrator believes) that the heart is still alive, even though its owner has been cut to pieces. Then, too, the police keep chatting. If they heard the heartbeat, wouldn't they leap to their feet, draw their guns, and look all around the room? As the author keeps showing us in the rest of the story, the narrator's view of things is untrustworthy. You don't kill someone just because you dislike the look in his eye. You don't think that such a murder is funny. For all its Gothic atmosphere of the old dark house with a secret hidden inside, "The Tell-Tale Heart" is not a ghost story. We have only to see its point of view to know it is a study in abnormal psychology.

Raises question, then explores answer

Secondary source paraphrase

Restatement of thesis

Frederick 3

Works Cited

Hoffman, Daniel. *Poe Poe Poe Poe Poe Poe Poe.* New York: Anchor, 1973. Print.

Poe, Edgar Allan. "The Tell-Tale Heart." *Literature: An Introduction to Fiction, Poetry, Drama, and Writing.* Ed. X. J. Kennedy and Dana Gioia. 12th ed. New York: Pearson, 2013. 387–91. Print.

The temptation in writing an analysis is to include all sorts of insights that the writer proudly wishes to display, even though they aren't related to the main idea. In the preceding essay, the student resists this temptation admirably. In fairly plump and ample paragraphs, he works out his ideas and supports his contentions with specific references to Poe's story. Although his paper is not brilliantly written and contains no insight so fresh as the suggestion (by the writer of the first paper) that the madman's lantern is like the old man's head, still, it is a good brief analysis. By sticking faithfully to his purpose and by confronting the problems he raises ("How do we know the whole story isn't just a nightmare?"), the writer persuades us that he understands not only the story's point of view but also the story in its entirety.

The Card Report

Another form of analysis, a **card report** breaks down a story into its various elements. Though card reports tend to include only as much information as can fit on both sides of a single 5- by 8-inch index card, they are at least as challenging to write as full-fledged essays. The author of a successful card report can dissect a story into its elements and describe them succinctly and accurately. A typical card report on "The Tell-Tale Heart" follows. In this assignment, the student was asked to include:

1. The story's title and the date of its original publication.
2. The author's name and dates of birth and death.
3. The name (if any) of the main character, along with a description of that character's dominant traits or features.
4. Similar information for other characters.
5. A short description of the setting.
6. The point of view from which the story is told.
7. A terse summary of the story's main events in chronological order.
8. A description of the general tone, or, in other words, the author's feelings toward the central character or the main event.
9. Some comments on the style in which the story is written. Brief illustrative quotations are helpful if space allows.
10. Whatever kinds of irony the story contains and what they contribute to the story.
11. The story's main theme, in a sentence.

12. Key symbols (if the story has any), with an educated guess at what each symbol suggests.
13. Finally, an evaluation of the story as a whole, concisely setting forth the student's opinion of it. (Some instructors consider this the most important part of the report, and most students find that, by the time they have so painstakingly separated the ingredients of the story, they have arrived at a definite opinion of its merits.)

Front of Card

Carly Grace English 101

Story: "The Tell-Tale Heart," 1850

Author: Edgar Allan Poe (1809-1849)

Central character: An unnamed younger man whom people call mad, who claims that a nervous disease has greatly sharpened his sense perceptions. He is proud of his own cleverness.

Other characters: The old man, whose leading feature is one pale blue, filmed eye; said to be rich, kind, and lovable. Also three policemen, not individually described.

Setting: A shuttered house full of wind, mice, and treasures; pitch dark even in the afternoon.

Narrator: The madman himself.

Events in summary: (1) Dreading one vulture-like eye of the old man he shares a house with, a madman determines to kill its owner. (2) Each night he spies on the sleeping old man, but finding the eye shut, he stays his hand. (3) On the eighth night, finding the eye open, he suffocates its owner beneath the mattress and conceals the dismembered body under the floor of the bedchamber. (4) Entertaining some inquiring police officers in the very room where the body lies hidden, the killer again hears (or thinks he hears) the beat of the victim's heart. (5) Terrified, convinced that the police also hear the heartbeat growing louder, the killer confesses.

Tone: Horror at the events described, skepticism toward the narrator's claims to be sane, detachment from his gaiety and laughter.

Back of Card

<u>Style</u>: Written as if told aloud by a deranged man eager to be believed, the story is punctuated by laughter, interjections ("Hearken!"), nervous halts, and fresh beginnings—indicated by dashes that grow more frequent as the story goes on and the narrator becomes more excited. Poe often relies on general adjectives ("mournful," "hideous," "hellish,") to convey atmosphere; also on exact details (the lantern that emits "a single dim ray, like the thread of a spider").

<u>Irony</u>: The whole story is ironic in its point of view. Presumably the author is not mad, nor does he share the madman's self-admiration. Many of the narrator's statements therefore seem verbal ironies: his account of taking an hour to move his head through the bedroom door.

<u>Theme</u>: Possibly "Murder will out," but I really don't find any theme either stated or clearly implied.

<u>Symbols</u>: The vulture eye, called an Evil Eye (in superstition, one that can implant a curse), perhaps suggesting too the all-seeing eye of God the Father, from whom no guilt can be concealed. The ghostly heartbeat, sound of the victim's coming back to be avenged (or the God who cannot be slain?). Death watches: beetles said to be death omens, whose ticking sound foreshadows the sound of the tell-tale heart *"as a watch makes when enveloped in cotton."*

<u>Evaluation</u>: Despite the overwrought style (to me slightly comic-bookish), a powerful story, admirable for its conclusion and for its memorable portrait of a deranged killer. Poe knows how it is to be mad.

As you might expect, fitting so much information on one card is like trying to engrave the Declaration of Independence on the head of a pin. The student who wrote this report had to spoil a few trial cards before she was able to complete the assignment. The card report is an extreme exercise in making every word count, a worthwhile discipline in almost any kind of writing. Some students enjoy the challenge, and most are surprised at how thoroughly they come to understand the story. A longer story, even a novel, may be analyzed in the same way, but insist on taking a second card if you are asked to analyze an especially hefty and complicated novel.

Comparison and Contrast

If you were to write on "The Humor of Alice Walker's 'Everyday Use' and John Updike's 'A & P,'" you would probably employ one or two methods. You might use **comparison,** placing the two stories side by side and pointing out their similarities, or **contrast,** pointing out their differences. Most of the time, in dealing with a pair of stories, you will find them similar in some ways and different in others, and you'll use both methods. Keep the following points in mind when writing a comparison-contrast paper:

- **Choose stories with something significant in common.** This will simplify your task and help ensure that your paper hangs together. Before you start writing, ask yourself if the two stories you've selected throw some light on each other. If the answer is no, rethink your story selection.
- **Choose a focus.** Simply ticking off every similarity and difference between two stories would make for a slack and rambling essay. More compelling writing would result from better-focused topics such as "The Experience of Coming of Age in James Joyce's 'Araby' and William Faulkner's 'Barn Burning'" or "Mother-Daughter Relationships in Alice Walker's 'Everyday Use' and Jamaica Kincaid's 'Girl.'"
- **Don't feel you need to spend equal amounts of time on comparing and contrasting.** If your chosen stories are more similar than different, you naturally will spend more space on comparison, and vice versa.
- **Don't devote the first half of your paper to one story and the second half to the other.** Such a paper wouldn't be a comparison or contrast so much as a pair of analyses yoked together. To reap the full benefits of the assignment, let the two stories mingle.
- **Before you start writing, draw up a brief list of points you would like to touch on.** Then address each point, first in one story and then in the other. A sample outline follows for a paper on William Faulkner's "A Rose for Emily" and Katherine Mansfield's "Miss Brill." The essay's topic is "Adapting to Change: The Characters of Emily Grierson and Miss Brill."

  1. Adapting to change (both women)
     Miss Brill more successful
  2. Portrait of women
     Miss Emily—unflattering
     Miss Brill—empathetic
  3. Imagery
     Miss Emily—morbid
     Miss Brill—cheerful
  4. Plot
     Miss Emily
     - loses sanity
     - refuses to adapt
     Miss Brill
     - finds place in society
     - adapts
  5. Summary: Miss Brill is more successful

- **Emphasize the points that interest you the most.** This strategy will help keep you from following your outline in a plodding fashion ("Well, now it's time to whip over to Miss Brill again . . . ").

- **If the assignment allows, consider applying comparison and contrast in an essay on a single story.** You might, for example, analyze the attitudes of the younger and older waiters in Hemingway's "A Clean, Well-Lighted Place." Or you might contrast Mrs. Turpin's smug view of herself with the young Mary Grace's merciless view of her in Flannery O'Connor's "Revelation."

The following student-written paper compares and contrasts the main characters in "A Rose for Emily" and "Miss Brill." Notice how the author focuses the discussion on a single aspect of each woman's personality—the ability to adapt to change and the passage of time. By looking through the lens of three different elements of the short story—diction, imagery, and plot—this clear and systematic essay convincingly argues its thesis.

Ortiz 1

Michelle Ortiz

Professor Gregg

English 200

25 February 2012

Successful Adaptation in

"A Rose for Emily" and "Miss Brill"

Clear statement of thesis

In William Faulkner's "A Rose for Emily" and Katherine Mansfield's "Miss Brill," the reader is given a glimpse into the lives of two old women living in different worlds but sharing many similar characteristics. Both Miss Emily and Miss Brill attempt to adapt to a changing environment as they grow older. Through the authors' use of language, imagery, and plot, it becomes clear to the reader that Miss Brill is more successful at adapting to the world around her and finding happiness.

Textual evidence on language supports thesis.

In "A Rose for Emily," Faulkner's use of language paints an unflattering picture of Miss Emily. His tone evokes pity and disgust rather than sympathy. The reader identifies with the narrator of the story and shares the townspeople's opinion that Miss Emily is somehow "perverse" (par. 51). In "Miss Brill," however, the reader can identify with the title character and feel sympathy for her because of the lonely life she leads. Mansfield's attitude toward the young couple at the end makes the reader hate them for ruining the happiness that Miss Brill has found, however small it may be.

Imagery in Faulkner's story supports argument.

The imagery in "A Rose for Emily" keeps the reader from further identifying with Miss Emily by creating several morbid images of her. For example, there are several images of decay throughout the story. The house she lived in is falling apart and described as "filled with dust and shadows" (par. 52), "an

Ortiz 2

eyesore among eyesores" (par. 2). Emily herself is described as looking "bloated, like a body long submerged in motionless water" (par. 6). Faulkner also uses words like "skeleton," "dank," "decay," and "cold" to reinforce these morbid, deathly images (par. 6, 5, 2, 8).

In "Miss Brill," however, Mansfield uses more cheerful imagery. The music and the lively action in the park make Miss Brill feel alive inside. She notices the other old people in the park are "still as statues," "odd," and "silent" (par. 5). She says they "looked as though they'd just come from dark little rooms or even—even cupboards!" (par. 5). In the final paragraph, her own room is described as "like a cupboard," but during the action of the story she does not include herself among those other old people. She still feels alive.

Contrasting imagery in Mansfield's story supports argument.

Through the plots of both stories the reader can also see that Miss Brill is more successful in adapting to her environment. Miss Emily loses her sanity and ends up committing a crime in order to control her environment. Throughout the story, she refuses to adapt to any of the changes going on in the town, such as the taxes or the mailboxes. Miss Brill is able to find her own special place in society where she can be happy and remain sane.

Characters contrasted with examples drawn from plots.

In "A Rose for Emily" and "Miss Brill" the authors' use of language and the plots of the stories illustrate that Miss Brill is more successful in her story. Instead of hiding herself away she emerges from the "cupboard" to participate in life. She adapts to the world that is changing as she grows older, without losing her sanity or committing crimes, as Miss Emily does. The language of "Miss Brill" allows the reader to sympathize with the main character. The imagery in the story is lighter and less morbid than in "A Rose for Emily." The resulting portrait is of an aging woman who has found creative ways to adjust to her lonely life.

The final conclusion is stated and the thesis is restated.

Ortiz 3

Works Cited

Faulkner, William. "A Rose for Emily." *Literature: An Introduction to Fiction, Poetry, Drama, and Writing*. Ed. X. J. Kennedy and Dana Gioia. 12th ed. New York: Pearson, 2013. 31–37. Print.

Mansfield, Katherine. "Miss Brill." *Literature: An Introduction to Fiction, Poetry, Drama, and Writing*. Ed. X. J. Kennedy and Dana Gioia. 12th ed. New York: Pearson, 2013. 102–5. Print.

Response Paper

One popular form of writing assignment is the **response paper,** a short essay that expresses your personal reaction to a work of literature. Both instructors and students often find the response paper an ideal introductory writing assignment. It provides you with an opportunity to craft a focused essay about a literary work, but it does not usually require any outside research. What it does require is careful reading, clear thinking, and honest writing.

The purpose of a response paper is to convey your thoughts and feelings about an aspect of a particular literary work. It isn't a book report (summarizing the work's content) or a book review (evaluating the quality of a work). A response paper expresses what you experienced in reading and thinking about the assigned text. Your reaction should reflect your background, values, and attitudes in response to the work, not what the instructor thinks about it. You might even consider your response paper a conversation with the work you have just read. What questions does it seem to ask you? What reactions does it elicit? You might also regard your paper as a personal message to your instructor telling him or her what you really think about one of the reading assignments.

Of course, you can't say everything you thought and felt about your reading in a short paper. Focus on an important aspect (such as a main character, setting, or theme) and discuss your reaction to it. Don't gush or meander. Personal writing doesn't mean disorganized writing. Identify your main ideas and present your point of view in a clear and organized way. Once you get started you might surprise yourself by discovering that it's fun to explore your own responses. Stranger things have happened.

Here are tips for writing a successful response paper of your own:

- **Make quick notes as you read or reread the work.** Don't worry about writing anything organized at this point. Just write a word or two in the margin noting your reactions as you read (e.g., "very interesting" or "reminds me of my sister"). These little notes will jog your memory when you go back to write your paper.
- **Consider which aspect of the work affected you the most.** That aspect will probably be a good starting point for your response.
- **Be candid in your writing.** Remember that the literary work is only half of the subject matter of your paper. The other half is your reaction.
- **Try to understand and explain why you have reacted the way you did.** It's not enough just to state your responses. You also want to justify or explain them.
- **Refer to the text in your paper.** Demonstrate to the reader that your response is based on the text. Provide specific textual details and quotations wherever relevant.

The following paper is one student's response to Tim O'Brien's story "The Things They Carried" (page 637).

Martin 1

Ethan Martin
English 99
Professor Merrill
31 March 2012

"Perfect Balance and Perfect Posture":
Reflecting on "The Things They Carried"

Reading Tim O'Brien's short story "The Things They Carried" became a very personal experience. It reminded me of my father, who is a Vietnam veteran, and the stories he used to tell me. Growing up, I regularly asked my dad to share stories from his past, especially about his service in the United States Marine Corps. He would rarely talk about his tour during the Vietnam War for more than a few minutes, and what he shared was usually the same: the monsoon rain could chill to the bone, the mosquitoes would never stop biting, and the M-16 rifles often jammed in a moment of crisis. He dug a new foxhole where he slept every night, he traded the cigarettes from his C-rations for food, and—since he was the radio man of his platoon—the combination of his backpack and radio was very heavy during the long, daily walks through rice paddies and jungles. For these reasons, "The Things They Carried" powerfully affected me.

While reading the story, I felt as if I was "humping" (par. 4) through Vietnam with Lieutenant Jimmy Cross, Rat Kiley, Ted Lavender, and especially Mitchell Sanders—who carries the 26-pound radio and battery. Every day, we carry our backpacks to school. Inside are some objects that we need to use in class: books, paper, and pens. But most of us probably include "unnecessary" items that reveal something about who we are or what we value—photographs, perfume, or good-luck charms. O'Brien uses this device to tell his story. At times he lists the things that the soldiers literally carried, such as weapons, medicine, and flak jackets. These military items weigh between 30 and 70 pounds, depending on one's rank or function in the platoon. The narrator says, "They carried all they could bear, and then some, including a silent awe for the terrible power of the things they carried" (par. 12).

Some of this "terrible power" comes from the sentimental objects the men keep. Although these are relatively light, they weigh down the hearts of the soldiers. Lt. Jimmy Cross carries 10-ounce letters and a pebble from Martha, a girl in his hometown who doesn't love him back. Rat Kiley carries comic books, and Norman Bowker carries a diary. I now own the small, water-logged Bible

Martin 2

that my father carried through his tour in Vietnam, which was a gift from his mother. When I open its pages, I can almost hear his voice praying to survive the war.

The price of such survival is costly. O'Brien's platoon carries ghosts, memories, and "the land itself" (par. 39). Their intangible burdens are heavier than what they carry in their backpacks. My father has always said that, while he was in Vietnam, an inexpressible feeling of death hung heavy in the air, which he could not escape. O'Brien notes that an emotional weight of fear and cowardice "could never be put down, it required perfect balance and perfect posture" (par. 77), and I wonder if this may be part of what my father meant.

Both Tim O'Brien and my father were wounded by shrapnel, and now they both carry a Purple Heart. They carry the weight of survival. They carry memories that I will never know. "The Things They Carried" is not a war story about glory and honor. It is a portrait of the psychological damage that war can bring. It is a story about storytelling and how hard it can be to find the truth. And it is a beautiful account of what the human heart can endure.

Martin 3

Work Cited

O'Brien, Tim. "The Things They Carried." *Literature: An Introduction to Fiction, Poetry, Drama, and Writing.* Ed. X. J. Kennedy and Dana Gioia. 12th ed. New York: Pearson, 2013. 637–49. Print.

TOPICS FOR WRITING

What kinds of topics are likely to result in papers that will reveal something about works of fiction? Here is a list of typical topics, suitable for papers of various lengths, offered in the hope of stimulating your own ideas. For additional ideas, see "More Topics for Writing" at the end of most chapters in this book.

TOPICS FOR WRITING BRIEF PAPERS (250–500 WORDS)

1. Explicate the opening paragraph or first few lines of a story. Show how the opening prepares the reader for what will follow. In an essay of this length, you will need to limit your discussion to the most important elements of the passage you explicate; there won't be room to deal with everything. Or, as thoroughly as the word count allows, explicate the final paragraph of a story. What does the ending imply about the fates of the story's characters, and about the story's take on its central theme?
2. Select a story that features a first-person narrator. Write a concise yet thorough analysis of how that character's point of view colors the story.
3. Following the directions in this chapter, write a card report on any short story in this book.
4. Consider a short story in which the central character has to make a decision or must take some decisive step that will alter the rest of his or her life. Faulkner's "Barn Burning" is one such story; another is Updike's "A & P." As concisely and as thoroughly as you can, explain the nature of the character's decision, the reasons for it, and its probable consequences (as suggested by what the author tells us).
5. Choose two stories that might be interesting to compare and contrast. Write a brief defense of your choice. How might these two stories illuminate each other?
6. Choose a key passage from a story you admire. As closely as the word count allows, explicate that passage and explain why it strikes you as an important moment in the story. Concentrate on the aspects of the passage that seem most essential.
7. Write a new ending to a story of your choice. Try to imitate the author's writing style. Add a paragraph explaining how this exercise illuminates the author's choices in the original.
8. Drawing on your own experience, make the case that a character in any short story behaves (or doesn't behave) as people do in real life. Your audience for this assignment is your classmates; tailor your tone and argument accordingly.

TOPICS FOR WRITING MORE EXTENDED PAPERS (600–1,000 WORDS)

1. Write an analysis of a short story, focusing on a single element, such as point of view, theme, symbolism, character, or the author's voice (tone, style, irony). For a sample paper in response to this assignment, see "The Hearer of the Tell-Tale Heart" (page 1920).
2. Compare and contrast two stories with protagonists who share an important personality trait. Make character the focus of your essay.
3. Write a thorough explication of a short passage (preferably not more than four sentences) in a story you admire. Pick a crucial moment in the plot, or a passage

that reveals the story's theme. You might look to the paper "By Lantern Light" (page 1917) as a model.

4. Write an analysis of a story in which the protagonist experiences an epiphany or revelation of some sort. Describe the nature of this change of heart. How is the reader prepared for it? What are its repercussions in the character's life? Some possible story choices are Alice Walker's "Everyday Use," William Faulkner's "Barn Burning," Raymond Carver's "Cathedral," James Baldwin's "Sonny's Blues," and, not surprisingly, Flannery O'Connor's "Revelation."
5. Imagine you are given the task of teaching a story to your class. Write an explanation of how you would address this challenge.
6. Imagine a reluctant reader, one who would rather play video games than crack a book. Which story in this book would you recommend to him or her? Write an essay to that imagined reader, describing the story's merits.

TOPICS FOR WRITING LONG PAPERS (1,500 WORDS OR MORE)

1. Write an analysis of a longer work of fiction. Concentrate on a single element of the story, quoting as necessary to make your point.
2. Read three or four short stories by an author whose work you admire. Concentrating on a single element treated similarly in all of the stories, write an analysis of the author's work as exemplified by your chosen stories.
3. Adapt a short story in this book into a one-act play. This may prove harder than it sounds; be sure to choose a story in which most of the action takes place in the physical world and not in the protagonist's mind. Don't forget to include stage directions.
4. Describe the process of reading a story for the first time and gradually learning to understand and appreciate it. First, choose a story you haven't yet read. As you read it for the first time, take notes on aspects of the story you find difficult or puzzling. Read the story a second time. Now write about the experience. What uncertainties were resolved when you read the story the second time? What, if any, uncertainties remain? What has this experience taught you about reading fiction?
5. Choose two stories that treat a similar theme. Compare and contrast the stance each story takes toward that theme, marshalling quotations and specifics as necessary to back up your argument.
6. Browse through newspapers and magazines for a story with the elements of good fiction. Now rewrite the story *as* fiction. Then write a one-page accompanying essay explaining the challenges of the task. What did it teach you about the relative natures of journalism and fiction?

43 WRITING ABOUT A POEM

I love being a writer.
What I can't stand is the paperwork.
—PETER DE VRIES

Many readers—even some enthusiastic ones—are wary of poems. "I don't know anything about poetry," some people say, if the subject arises. While poems aren't booby traps designed to trip up careless readers, it is true that poetry demands a special level of concentration. Poetry is language at its most intense and condensed, and in a good poem, every word counts. With practice, though, anyone can become a more confident reader—and critic—of poetry. Remember that the purpose of poetry isn't intimidation but wisdom and pleasure. Even writing a paper on poetry can occasion a certain enjoyment. Here are some tips.

- **Choose a poem that speaks to you.** Let pleasure be your guide in choosing the poem you write about. The act of writing is easier if your feelings are engaged. Write about something you dislike and don't understand, and your essay will be as dismal to read as it was for you to write. But write about something that interests you, and your essay will communicate that interest and enthusiasm.
- **Allow yourself time to get comfortable with your subject.** As most professors will tell you, when students try to fudge their way through a paper on a topic they don't fully understand, the lack of comfort shows, making for muddled, directionless prose. The more familiar you become with a poem, however, the easier and more pleasurable it will be to write about it. Expect to read the poem several times over before its meaning becomes clear. Better still, reread it over the course of several days.

READ ACTIVELY

A poem differs from most prose in that it should be read slowly, carefully, and attentively. Good poems yield more if read twice, and the best poems—after ten, twenty, or even thirty readings—keep on yielding. Here are some suggestions to enhance your reading of a poem you plan to write about.

- **Read the poem aloud.** There is no better way to understand a poem than to effectively read it aloud. Read slowly, paying attention to punctuation cues. Listen for the auditory effects.
- **Read closely and painstakingly, annotating as you go.** Keep your mind (and your pencil) sharp and ready. The subtleties of language are essential to a poem. Pay attention to the connotations or suggestions of words, and to the rhythm of phrases and lines. Underline words and images that jump out at you. Use arrows to link phrases that seem connected. Highlight key passages or take notes in the margins as ideas or questions occur to you.

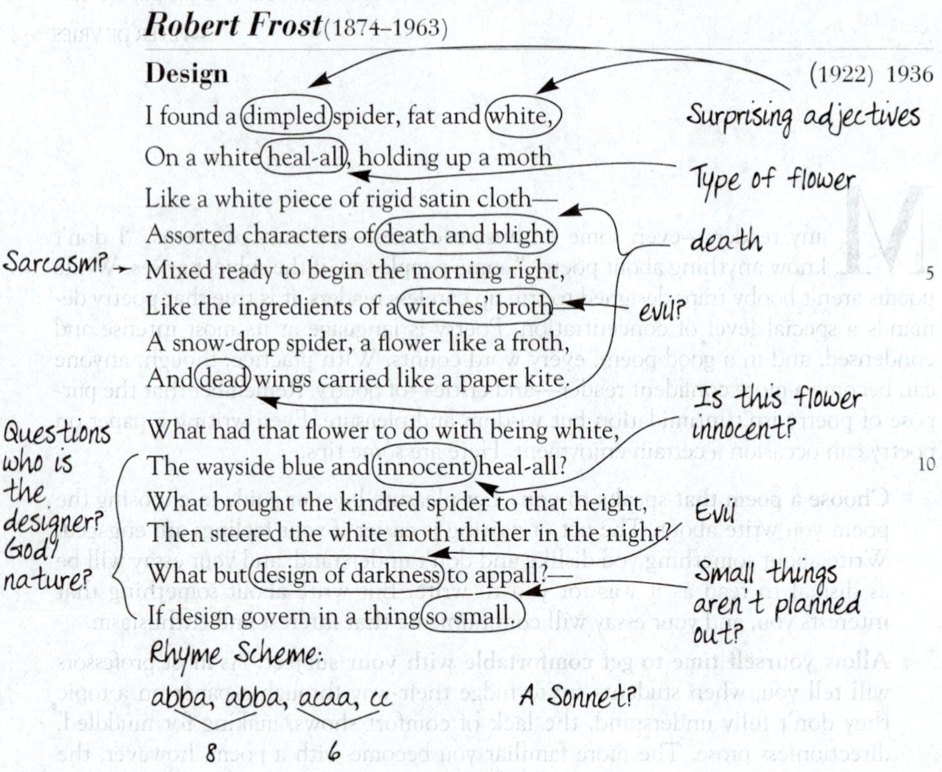

Robert Frost (1874–1963)

Design (1922) 1936

I found a dimpled spider, fat and white,
On a white heal-all, holding up a moth
Like a white piece of rigid satin cloth—
Assorted characters of death and blight
Mixed ready to begin the morning right,
Like the ingredients of a witches' broth—
A snow-drop spider, a flower like a froth,
And dead wings carried like a paper kite.

What had that flower to do with being white,
The wayside blue and innocent heal-all?
What brought the kindred spider to that height,
Then steered the white moth thither in the night?
What but design of darkness to appall?—
If design govern in a thing so small.

- **Look up any unfamiliar words, allusions, or references.** Often the very words you may be tempted to skim over will provide the key to a poem's meaning. Thomas Hardy's "The Ruined Maid" will remain elusive to a reader unfamiliar with the archaic meaning of the word "ruin"—a woman's loss of virginity to a man other than her husband. Similarly, be sure to acquaint yourself with any references or allusions that appear in a poem. H.D.'s poem "Helen" will make sense only to readers who are familiar with the story of Helen of Troy.

THINK ABOUT THE POEM

Before you begin writing, take some time to collect your thoughts. The following steps can be useful in thinking about a poem.

- **Let your emotions guide you into the poem.** Do any images or phrases call up a strong emotional response? If so, try to puzzle out why those passages seem so emotionally loaded. In a word or two, describe the poem's tone.
- **Determine what's literally happening in the poem.** Separating literal language from figurative or symbolic language can be one of the trickiest—and most essential—tasks in poetic interpretation. Begin by working out the literal. Who is speaking the poem? To whom? Under what circumstances? What happens in the poem?
- **Ask what it all adds up to.** Once you've pinned down the literal action of the poem, it's time to take a leap into the figurative. What is the significance of the poem? Address symbolism, any figures of speech, and any language that means one thing literally but suggests something else. In "My Papa's Waltz," for example, Theodore Roethke tells a simple story of a father dancing his small son around a kitchen. The language of the poem suggests much more, however, implying that while the father is rough to the point of violence, the young boy hungers for his attention.
- **Consider the poem's shape on the page, and the way it sounds.** What patterns of sound do you notice? Are the lines long, short, or a mixture of both? How do these elements contribute to the poem's effect?
- **Pay attention to form.** If a poem makes use of rime or regular meter, ask yourself how those elements contribute to its meaning. If it is in a fixed form, such as a sonnet or villanelle, how do the demands of that form serve to set its tone? If the form calls for repetition—of sounds, words, or entire lines—how does that repetition underscore the poem's message? If, on the other hand, the poem is in free verse—without a consistent pattern of rime or regular meter—how does this choice affect the poem's feel?
- **Take note of line breaks.** If the poem is written in free verse, pay special attention to its line breaks. Poets break their lines with care, conscious that readers pause momentarily over the last word in any line, giving that word special emphasis. Notice whether the lines tend to be broken at the ends of whole phrases and sentences or in the middle of phrases. Then ask yourself what effect is created by the poet's choice of line breaks. How does that effect contribute to the poem's meaning?

PREWRITING: DISCOVER YOUR IDEAS

Now that you have thought the poem through, it's time to let your ideas crystallize on the page (or screen). Try one or more of the following prewriting techniques.

- **Brainstorm.** With the poem in front of you, jot down every single thing you can think of about it. Write quickly, without worrying about the value of your thoughts; you can sort that out later. Brainstorming works best if you set a time limit of ten or fifteen minutes and force yourself to keep working until the time is up. A list that results from brainstorming on "Design" might look something like this:

white spider	white = strangeness
heal-all/flower	heal-all usually blue
dead moth like a kite	flower doesn't heal all
white = innocence?	design = God or nature
death/blight	design of darkness = the devil?
begin the morning right=oddly cheerful	maybe no design (no God?)
irony	God doesn't govern small things
witches' broth/scary	

▪ **Cluster.** If you are a visual thinker, you might find yourself drawn to clustering as a way to explore the relationships among your ideas. Begin by writing your subject at the center of a sheet of paper. Circle it. Then write ideas as they occur to you, drawing lines linking each new idea to ones that seem related. Here is an example of clustering on "Design."

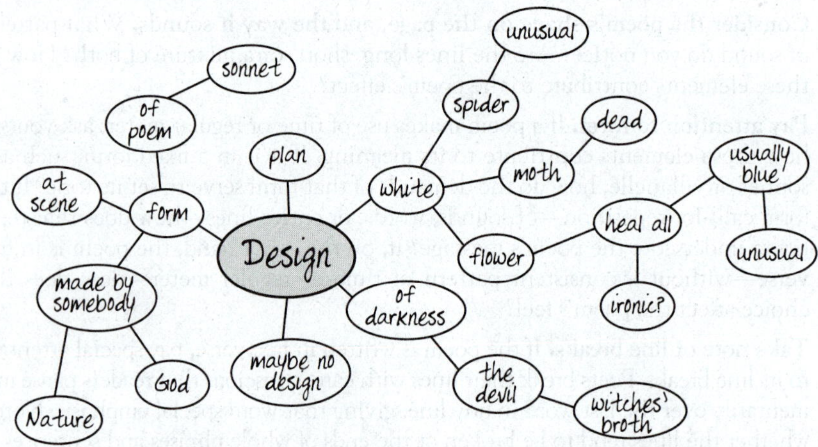

▪ **List.** Make a list of information that seems useful. Feel free to add notes that will help you to remember what you meant by each item. Headings can help you to organize related concepts. A list might look like this:

Odd Coincidence	Questions
white spider	Accidental or by design?
white flower (not blue, innocent)	Whose design?
white moth (stiff, dead)	Nature or God?
characters of death/blight	Does God care?
morning (hopeful) = ironic	**Form of Poem**
witches' broth	sonnet (strict, orderly)
	form of universe =
	not so orderly?

- **Freewrite.** Another approach to generating ideas is to let your thoughts pour out onto the page. To freewrite, give yourself a time limit: fifteen or twenty minutes will work well. Then write, without stopping to think, for that whole time. Keep writing. Don't worry about grammar or spelling or even logic; your task is to come up with fresh ideas that might evade you if you were writing more cautiously. Keep writing even (or especially) if you run out of ideas. New and surprising thoughts sometimes arrive when we least expect them. Here is a sample of freewriting on "Design."

> The scene seems strange. Spiders aren't usually white, and heal-alls are supposed to be blue. Moths are white, but this one is described as being like a rigid satin cloth or a paper kite. It's dead, which is why it is rigid, but the images seem to focus on its stiffness—its deadness—in a creepy way. The poet seems surprised at all this whiteness. Whiteness usually represents innocence, but here he says the flower would ordinarily be blue and innocent, so maybe it's not innocent now? I think he's saying this is a kind of deathly pageant; he calls the three things assorted characters though a flower can't be a character. The second part of the poem is all questions, no answers. What does he mean by "design of darkness"?
>
> Design seems to mean plan. It sounds like he's saying something sinister is going on. Like someone (God?) put the scene there for a purpose, maybe for him to notice. But then he seems to say no, God doesn't care about small things which maybe means he doesn't care about us either. I just noticed that this poem is (I think) a sonnet. It has rime and fourteen lines. It seems funny that a poem about there being no order to the universe is written in such a strict form.

- **Journal.** A journal of your reactions to the works you read can be an excellent place to look for raw material for more formal writing. If your instructor has assigned such a journal, page through to remind yourself of your first reactions to a poem you plan to write about.

- **Outline.** To think through your argument before you begin to flesh it out, make an outline (a list of points arranged in a logical order). Not all writers work from outlines, but some find them indispensable. Here is a sample outline.

1. Italian sonnet (define)
   - two parts
   - octave draws picture
   - sestet asks questions
2. Rime
   - "ite" sound stresses whiteness
3. Sonnet form = order
   - poem's subject = order
   - irony/no order in universe

4. Design of poem is unpredictable

   looks orderly but isn't

5. Design of universe is unpredictable

WRITE A ROUGH DRAFT

When your prewriting work has given you a sense of direction, you will be ready to begin forming your thoughts and writing a first draft of your essay. Reread the section "Develop a Literary Argument" in the chapter "Writing About Literature" for help getting started.

- **Review your purpose and audience.** Begin by referring back to the exact assignment you have been given. No matter how crystal clear your prose or intriguing your ideas, an essay that fails to respond to the assignment is likely to fall flat. As you begin your first draft, consider how best to focus your essay to fulfill the instructor's requirements. Whatever the assignment, you need to keep your purpose in mind as you write. You also need to consider your audience's needs, whether that audience is your professor, your fellow students, or some hypothetical set of readers.
- **Define your thesis.** To keep you focused on the task at hand, and to signal your intentions to your reader, you will need, first of all, to come up with a thesis. Like the rest of your first draft, that thesis sentence can be rough around the edges; you can refine it later in the process. For now, though, the thesis gives you something to work toward. You need to make a decisive statement that offers an insight that isn't entirely obvious about the work under discussion. In the final paper your task will be to convince readers that your thesis is sound. Here is a working thesis sentence for an analytical essay on Frost's poem "Design."

  WORKING THESIS

  The poem "Design" both is and isn't formal.

  This rough thesis defines the essay's focus—the poem's form. But the statement is still very vague. A later, sharper version will clarify the idea and show what the author means by the claim that the poem both is and isn't formal. The revision also will push this idea further by connecting the poem's form to its meaning.

  REVISED THESIS

  Although Frost's sonnet "Design" is a well-designed formal poem, the conclusions it presents are not predictable but both surprising and disturbing.

  In its revised form, this thesis makes a stronger and more specific claim. Because the revision says something specific about how the poem works, it is more compelling than the vaguer original.

- **Supply evidence to prove your point.** Once you've settled on a working thesis, your next task is to decide what evidence will best prove your point. Be sure to quote from the poem to back up each point you make; there is no evidence more convincing than the words of the poem itself.
- **Organize your argument.** You will need to make clear what each bit of evidence illustrates. Connect your argument back to the thesis as often as it takes to clarify your line of reasoning for the reader.

- **Concentrate on getting your ideas onto the page.** Later you will go back and revise, making your prose clearer and more elegant. At that point, you can add information that seems to be missing and discard passages that seem beside the point. For now, though, the goal is to spell out your argument while it is clear in your mind.

CHECKLIST: Writing a Rough Draft

- ☐ What is your assignment? Does the essay fulfill it?
- ☐ Who is your audience?
- ☐ What is your thesis?
- ☐ Is your thesis thought-provoking rather than a statement of the obvious?
- ☐ Have you provided evidence to support your thesis?
- ☐ Does anything in your essay undercut your thesis?
- ☐ Have you quoted from the poem? Would more quotations strengthen your argument?
- ☐ Is your argument organized in a logical way?

REVISE YOUR DRAFT

- **Have a reader review your paper.** Once you have completed your rough draft, consider enlisting the aid of a reader, professional (a writing center tutor) or otherwise (a trusted friend). The author of the paragraph below used her instructor's comments to improve her paper's introduction.

DRAFT OF OPENING PARAGRAPH

Robert Frost's poem "Design" is an Italian sonnet, a form that divides its argument into two parts, an octave and a sestet. The octave, or first part of the poem, concentrates on telling the reader about a peculiar scene the poet has noticed: a white spider holding a dead moth on a white flower. The sestet, or second part of the poem, asks what the scene means. It doesn't really provide any answers.

Good start. I'm glad you're thinking about the poem's form. How does the form suit the content?

Add a little more. Is the scene significant? How so?

Does it hint at answers? Be more specific.

REVISED OPENING PARAGRAPH

For Robert Frost's poem "Design," the sonnet form has at least two advantages. As in most Italian sonnets, the poem's argument falls into two parts. In the octave Frost's persona draws a still life of a spider, a flower, and a moth; then in the sestet he contemplates the meaning of his still life. The sestet focuses on a universal: the possible existence of a vindictive deity who causes the spider to catch the moth and, no doubt, also causes—when viewed anthropomorphically—other suffering.

To see this essay in its entirety, turn to page 1946. (It's worth noting that while the thesis sentence often appears in an essay's first paragraph, this paper takes a different tack. The first paragraph introduces the essay's focus—the benefits of the sonnet form for this particular poem—then builds carefully toward its thesis, which appears in the last paragraph.)

- **Make your argument more specific.** Use specifics instead of generalities in describing the poem. Writing imprecisely or vaguely, favoring the abstract over the concrete, is a common problem for student writers. When discussing ideas or principles, you can communicate more fully to your reader by supplying specific examples of those ideas or principles in action, as this student did when she reworked the ending of the paragraph above.

- **Make your language fresh and accurate.** It is easy to depend on habitual expressions and to overuse a few convenient words. Mechanical language may tempt you to think of the poem in mechanical terms. Here, for instance is a plodding discussion of Frost's "Design":

  DRAFT

  The symbols Frost uses in "Design" are very successful. Frost makes the spider <u>stand</u> <u>for</u> Nature. He <u>wants</u> us to see nature as blind and cruel. He also <u>employs</u> good sounds. He <u>uses</u> a lot of *i*'s because he is <u>trying</u> to make you think of falling rain.

  What's wrong with this "analysis"? The underscored words are worth questioning here. While understandable, the words *employs* and *uses* seem to lead the writer to see Frost only as a conscious tool-manipulator. To be sure, Frost in a sense "uses" symbols, but did he grab hold of them and lay them into his poem? For all we know, perhaps the symbols arrived quite unbidden and used the poet. To write a good poem, Frost maintained, the poet himself has to be surprised. (How, by the way, can we hope to know what a poet wants to do? And there isn't much point in saying that the poet is *trying* to do something. He has already done it, if he has written a good poem.) At least it is likely that Frost didn't plan to fulfill a certain quota of *i*-sounds. Writing his poem, not by following a blueprint but probably by bringing it slowly to the surface of his mind, Frost no doubt had enough to do without trying to engineer the reactions of his possible audience. Like all true symbols, Frost's spider doesn't *stand for* anything. The writer would be closer to the truth in saying that the spider *suggests* or *reminds us* of nature or of certain forces in the natural world. (Symbols just hint; they don't indicate.)

  After the student discussed the paper in a conference with her instructor, she rewrote her sentences:

  REVISION

  The symbols in Frost's "Design" are highly effective. The spider, for instance, suggests the blindness and cruelty of Nature. Frost's word-sounds, too, are part of the meaning of his poem, for the *i*'s remind the reader of falling rain.

  Not every reader of "Design" will hear rain falling, but the student's revision probably comes closer to describing the experience of the poem most of us have.

- **Be clear and precise.** Another very real pitfall of writing literary criticism is the temptation to write in official-sounding Critic Speak. Writers who aren't quite sure about what to say may try to compensate for this uncertainty with unnecessarily ornate sentences that don't say much of anything. Other times, they will begin a sentence and find themselves completely entangled in its structure, unable to make a perfectly sound idea clear to the reader. Should you feel yourself being tugged out to sea by an undertow of fancy language, here is a trick for getting back ashore: speak your ideas aloud, in the simplest terms possible, to a friend, or a tape recorder, or your mirror. When you've formulated your idea simply and clearly, write down your exact words. Most likely, your instructor will be grateful for the resulting clarity of expression.

CHECKLIST: Revising Your Draft

- ☐ Is your thesis clear and decisive?
- ☐ Does all your evidence advance your argument?
- ☐ Is information presented in the most logical order?
- ☐ Could your prose be clearer? More precise? More specific?
- ☐ Do transitional words and phrases signal movement from one idea to the next?
- ☐ Does your introduction draw the reader in? Does it prepare him or her for what follows?
- ☐ Does your conclusion tie up the essay's loose ends?
- ☐ Does each paragraph include a topic sentence?
- ☐ Does your title give a sense of the essay's subject?

COMMON APPROACHES TO WRITING ABOUT POETRY

Explication

In an **explication** (literally, "an unfolding"), a writer explains an entire poem in detail, unraveling its complexities. An explication, however, should not be confused with a paraphrase, which puts the poem's literal meaning into plain prose. While an explication might include some paraphrasing, it does more than simply restate. It explains a poem, in great detail, showing how each part contributes to the whole. In writing an explication, keep the following tips in mind:

- **Start with the poem's first line, and keep working straight through to the end.** As needed, though, you can take up points out of order.
- **Read closely, addressing the poem's details.** You may choose to include allusions, the denotations or connotations of words, the possible meanings of symbols, the effects of certain sounds and rhythms and formal elements (rime schemes, for instance), the sense of any statements that contain irony, and other particulars.
- **Show how each part of the poem contributes to the meaning of the whole.** Your explication should go beyond dissecting the pieces of a poem; it should also bring them together in a way that casts light on the poem in its entirety.

Here is a successful student-authored explication of Frost's "Design." The assignment was to explain, in not more than 750 words, whatever in the poem seemed most essential.

Jasper 1

Ted Jasper

Professor Koss

English 130

21 November 2011

An Unfolding of Robert Frost's "Design"

Interesting opening. Quotes author

"I always wanted to be very observing," Robert Frost once told an audience, after reading aloud his poem "Design." Then he added, "But I have always been afraid of my own observations" (qtd. in Cook 126–27). What could Frost have observed that could scare him? Let's examine the poem in question and see what we discover.

Central question raised

Defines key word. Sets up theme

Starting with the title, "Design," any reader of this poem will find it full of meaning. As the *Merriam-Webster Dictionary* defines *design*, the word can denote among other things a plan, purpose, or intention ("Design"). Some arguments for the existence of God (I remember from Sunday School) are based on the "argument from design": that because the world shows a systematic order, there must be a Designer who made it. But the word design can also mean "a deliberate undercover project or scheme" such as we attribute to a "designing person" ("Design"). As we shall see, Frost's poem incorporates all of these meanings. His poem raises the old philosophic question of whether there is a Designer, an evil Designer, or no Designer at all.

Topic sentence on significance of title

Begins line-by-line unfolding of meaning

Discusses images

Like many other sonnets, "Design" is divided into two parts. The first eight lines draw a picture centering on the spider, who at first seems almost jolly. It is *dimpled* and *fat* like a baby, or Santa Claus. The spider stands on a wildflower whose name, *heal-all*, seems ironic: a heal-all is supposed to cure any disease, but this flower has no power to restore life to the dead moth. (Later, in line ten, we learn that the heal-all used to be blue. Presumably, it has died and become bleached-looking.) In the second line we discover, too, that the spider has hold of another creature, a dead moth. We then see the moth described with an odd simile in line three: "Like a white piece of rigid satin cloth." Suddenly, the moth becomes not a creature but a piece of fabric—lifeless and dead—and yet *satin* has connotations of beauty. Satin is a luxurious material used in rich formal clothing, such as coronation gowns and brides' dresses. Additionally, there is great accuracy in the word: the smooth and slightly plush surface of satin is like the powder-smooth surface of moths' wings. But this "cloth," rigid and white, could be the lining to Dracula's coffin.

Explores language

Jasper 2

In the fifth line an invisible hand enters. The characters are "mixed" like ingredients in an evil potion. Some force doing the mixing is behind the scene. The characters in themselves are innocent enough, but when brought together, their whiteness and look of *rigor mortis* are overwhelming. There is something diabolical in the spider's feast. The "morning right" echoes the word *rite*, a ritual—in this case apparently a Black Mass or a Witches' Sabbath. The simile in line seven ("a flower like a froth") is more ambiguous and harder to describe. Froth is white, foamy, and delicate—something found on a brook in the woods or on a beach after a wave recedes. However, in the natural world, froth also can be ugly: the foam on a polluted stream or a rabid dog's mouth. The dualism in nature—its beauty and its horror—is there in that one simile.

Refers to sound

So far, the poem has portrayed a small, frozen scene, with the dimpled killer holding its victim as innocently as a boy holds a kite. Already, Frost has hinted that Nature may be, as Radcliffe Squires suggests, "Nothing but an ash-white plain without love or faith or hope, where ignorant appetites cross by chance" (87). Now, in the last six lines of the sonnet, Frost comes out and directly states his theme. What else could bring these deathly pale, stiff things together "but design of darkness to appall"? The question is clearly rhetorical; we are meant to answer, "Yes, there does seem to be an evil design at work here!" I take the next-to-last line to mean, "What except a design so dark and sinister that we're appalled by it?" "Appall," by the way, is the second pun in the poem: it sounds like a pall or shroud. (The derivation of *appall*, according to *Merriam-Webster*, is ultimately from a Latin word meaning "to be pale"—an interesting word choice for a poem full of pale white images ["Appall"].) *Steered* carries the suggestion of a steering-wheel or rudder that some pilot had to control. Like the word *brought*, it implies that some invisible force charted the paths of spider, heal-all, and moth, so that they arrived together.

Transition words

Quotes secondary source

Discusses theme

Defines key word

Having suggested that the universe is in the hands of that sinister force (an indifferent God? Fate? the Devil?), Frost adds a note of doubt. The Bible tells us that "His eye is on the sparrow," but at the moment the poet doesn't seem sure. Maybe, he hints, when things in the universe drop below a certain size, they pass completely out of the Designer's notice. When creatures are this little, maybe God doesn't bother to govern them but just lets them run wild. And possibly the same mindless chance is all that governs human lives. And because this is even more senseless than having an angry God intent on punishing us, it is, Frost suggests, the worst suspicion of all.

Answers question raised in introduction

Conclusion

Jasper 3

Works Cited

"Appall." *Merriam-Webster Online Dictionary.* Merriam-Webster, 2011. Web. 13 November 2011.

Cook, Reginald. *Robert Frost: A Living Voice.* Amherst: U of Massachusetts P, 1974. Print.

"Design." *Merriam-Webster Online Dictionary.* Merriam-Webster, 2011. Web. 11 November 2011.

Frost, Robert. "Design." *Collected Poems, Prose and Plays.* New York: Library of America, 1995. 275. Print.

Squires, Radcliffe. *The Major Themes of Robert Frost.* Ann Arbor: U of Michigan P, 1963. Print.

This excellent paper finds something worth unfolding in every line of Frost's poem, without seeming mechanical. Although the student proceeds sequentially through the poem from the title to the last line, he takes up some points out of order when it serves his purpose. In paragraph two, for example, he looks ahead to the poem's ending and briefly states its main theme in order to relate it to the poem's title. In the third paragraph, he explicates the poem's later image of the heal-all, relating it to the first image. He also comments on the poem's form ("Like many other sonnets"), on its similes and puns, and on its denotations and connotations.

This paper also demonstrates good use of manuscript form, following the *MLA Handbook*, 7th ed. Brief references (in parentheses) tell us where the writer found Frost's remarks and give the page number for his quotation from the book by Radcliffe Squires. At the end of the paper, a list of works cited uses abbreviations that the *MLA Handbook* recommends.

A Critic's Explication of Frost's "Design"

It might seem that to work through a poem line by line is a mechanical task, and yet there can be genuine excitement in doing so. Randall Jarrell once wrote an explication of "Design" in which he managed to convey just such excitement. See if you can sense Jarrell's joy in writing about the poem.

> Frost's details are so diabolically good that it seems criminal to leave some unremarked; but notice how *dimpled, fat,* and *white* (all but one; all but one) come from our regular description of any baby; notice how the *heal-all*, because of its name, is the one flower in all the world picked to be the altar for this Devil's Mass; notice how *holding up* the moth brings something ritual and hieratic, a ghostly, ghastly formality, to this priest and its sacrificial victim; notice how terrible to the fingers, how full of the stilling rigor of death, that *white piece of rigid satin cloth* is. And *assorted characters of death and blight* is, like so many things in this poem,

> sharply ambiguous: *a mixed bunch of actors* or *diverse representative signs*. The tone of the phrase *assorted characters of death and blight* is beautifully developed in the ironic Breakfast-Club-calisthenics, Radio-Kitchen heartiness of *mixed ready to begin the morning right* (which assures us, so unreassuringly, that this isn't any sort of Strindberg *Spook Sonata*, but hard fact), and concludes in the *ingredients* of the witches' broth, giving the soup a sort of cuddly shimmer that the cauldron in *Macbeth* never had; the *broth*, even, is brought to life—we realize that witches' broth *is* broth, to be supped with a long spoon.[1]

Evidently, Jarrell's cultural interests are broad: ranging from August Strindberg's ground-breaking modern play down to *The Breakfast Club* (a once-popular radio program that cheerfully exhorted its listeners to march around their tables). And yet breadth of knowledge, however much it deepens and enriches Jarrell's writing, isn't all that he brings to the reading of poetry. For him an explication isn't a dull plod, but a voyage of discovery. His prose—full of figures of speech (*diabolically good, cuddly shimmer*)—conveys the apparent delight he takes in showing off his findings. Such a joy, of course, can't be acquired deliberately. But it can grow, the more you read and study poetry.

Analysis

Like a news commentator's analysis of a crisis in the Middle East or a chemist's analysis of an unknown fluid, an **analysis** separates a poem into elements as a means to understanding that subject. Usually, the writer of an analysis focuses on one particular element: "Imagery of Light and Darkness in Frost's 'Design'" or "The Character of Satan in Milton's *Paradise Lost*." In this book, you probably already have encountered a few brief analyses: the discussion of connotations in William Blake's "London" (pages 741–42), for instance, or the examination of symbols in T. S. Eliot's "The *Boston Evening Transcript*" (page 893). In fact, most of the discussions in this book are analyses. To write an analysis, remember two key points:

- **Focus on a single, manageable element of a poem.** Some possible choices are tone, irony, literal meaning, imagery, figures of speech, sound, rhythm, theme, and symbolism.
- **Show how this element of the poem contributes to the meaning of the whole.** While no element of a poem exists apart from all the others, by taking a closer look at one particular aspect of the poem, you can see the whole more clearly.

The paper that follows analyzes a particularly tricky subject—the formal and technical elements of Frost's "Design." Long analyses of metrical feet, rime schemes, and indentations can make for ponderous reading, but this paper shows how formal analysis can be interesting and can cast light on a poem.

[1]*Poetry and the Age* (New York: Knopf, 1953), 42–43.

Lopez 1

Guadalupe Lopez

Professor Faber

English 210

16 April 2012

The Design of Robert Frost's "Design"

Introduction gives overview of poem's form.

Thesis sentence

For Robert Frost's poem "Design," the sonnet form has at least two advantages. As in most Italian sonnets, the poem's argument falls into two parts. In the octave Frost's persona draws a still life of a spider, a flower, and a moth; then in the sestet he contemplates the meaning of his still life. Although the poem is perfectly formal in its shape, the ideas it presents are not predictable, but are instead both surprising and disturbing. The sestet focuses on a universal: the possible existence of a vindictive deity who causes the spider to catch the moth and, no doubt, also causes—when viewed anthropomorphically—other suffering.

Topic sentence on how poem subtly makes its point

Frost's persona weaves his own little web. The unwary audience is led through the poem's argument from its opening "story" to a point at which something must be made of the story's symbolic significance. Even the rhyme scheme contributes to the poem's successful leading of the audience toward the sestet's theological questioning. The word *white* ends the first line of the sestet, and the same vowel sound is echoed in the lines that follow. All in all, half of the sonnet's lines end in the "ite" sound, as if to render significant the wh*ite*ness—the symbolic innocence—of nature's representation of a greater truth.

Topic sentence on how form relates to theme

A sonnet has a familiar design, and the poem's classical form points to the thematic concern that there seems to be an order to the universe that might be perceived by looking at even seemingly insignificant natural events. The sonnet must follow certain conventions, and nature, though not as readily apprehensible as a poetic form, is apparently governed by a set of laws. There is a ready-made irony in Frost's choosing such an order-driven form to meditate on whether or not there is any order in the universe. However, whether or not his questioning sestet is actually approaching an answer or, indeed, the answer, Frost has approached an order that seems to echo a larger order in his using the sonnet form. An approach through poetic form and substance is itself significant in Frost's own estimation, for he argues that what a poet achieves in writing poetry is "a momentary stay against confusion" (777).

Lopez 2

Although design clearly governs in this poem—in this "thing so small"—the design is not entirely predictable. The poem does start out in the form of an Italian sonnet, relying on only two rhyming sounds. However, unlike an Italian sonnet, one of the octave's rhyming sounds—the "ite"—continues into the sestet. And additionally, "Design" ends in a couplet, much in the manner of the Shakespearean sonnet, which frequently offers, in the final couplet, a summing up of the sonnet's argument. Perhaps not only nature's "story" of the spider, the flower, and the moth but also Frost's poem itself echoes the larger universe. It looks perfectly orderly until the details are given their due.

Conclusion

Lopez 3

Work Cited

Frost, Robert. "The Figure a Poem Makes." *Collected Poems, Prose and Plays.* New York: Library of America, 1995. 776–78. Print.

Comparison and Contrast

The process of **comparison** and **contrast** places two poems side by side and studies their differences and similarities in order to shed light on both works. Writing an effective comparison-contrast paper involves the following steps:

- **Pair two poems with much in common.** Comparing two poems with surface similarities—for example, Dorothy Parker's caustic "Résumé" and Ben Jonson's profoundly elegiac "On My First Son"—can be a futile endeavor. Though both poems are about death, the two seem hopelessly removed from each other in diction, tone, complexity, and scope. Instead, choose two poems with enough in common that their differences take on interesting weight.
- **Point to further, unsuspected resemblances.** Steer clear of the obvious ("'Design' and 'Wing-Spread' are both about bugs"). The interesting resemblances take some thought to discover.
- **Show noteworthy differences.** Avoid those your reader will see without any help.
- **Carefully consider your essay's organization.** While you may be tempted to discuss first one poem and then the other, this simple structure may weaken your essay if it leads you to keep the two poems in total isolation from each other. After all, the

point is to see what can be learned by comparison. There is nothing wrong in discussing all of poem A first, then discussing poem B—if in discussing B you keep referring back to A. Another strategy is to do a point-by-point comparison of the two poems all the way through your paper, dealing first, perhaps, with their themes, then with their central metaphors, and finally with their respective merits.

A comparison-contrast essay is often a kind of analysis—a study of a theme common to two poems, perhaps, or of two poets' similar fondness for the myth of Eden. In some cases, though, a comparison can also involve evaluation—a judgment on the relative worth of two poems.

Here, for example, is a poem by Abbie Huston Evans, followed by a paper that considers the merits of that poem and Frost's "Design." Through comparison and contrast, this student makes a case for his view of which poet deserves the brighter laurels.

Abbie Huston Evans (1881–1983)

Wing-Spread

1938

The midge spins out to safety
Through the spider's rope;
But the moth, less lucky,
Has to grope.

Mired in glue-like cable
See him foundered swing
By the gap he opened
With his wing,

Dusty web enlacing
All that blue and beryl.
In a netted universe
Wing-spread is peril.

Munjee 1

Tom Munjee
Professor Mickey
English 110
21 February 2012

"Wing-Spread" Does a Dip

Thesis sentence

Abbie Huston Evans's "Wing-Spread" is an effective short poem, but it lacks the complexity and depth of Robert Frost's "Design." These two poems were published only two years apart, and both present a murderous spider and an unlucky moth, but Frost's treatment differs from Evans's approach in at least

Munjee 2

two important ways. First, Frost uses poetic language more evocatively than Evans. Second, "Design" digs more deeply into the situation to uncover a more memorable theme.

Argument summary

If we compare the language of the two poems, we find "Design" is full of words and phrases rich with suggestions. The language of "Wing-Spread," by comparison, seems thinner. Frost's "dimpled spider, fat and white," for example, is certainly a more suggestive description. Actually, Evans does not describe her spider; she just says, "the spider's rope." (Evans does vividly show the spider and moth in action. In Frost's poem, they are already dead and petrified.) In "Design," the spider's dimples show that it is like a chubby little baby. This seems an odd way to look at a spider, but it is more original than Evans's conventional view (although I like her word *cable*, suggesting that the spider's web is a kind of high-tech food trap). Frost's word choice—his repetition of *white*—paints a more striking scene than Evans's slightly vague "All that blue and beryl." Except for her brief personification of the moth in the second stanza, Evans hardly uses any figures of speech, and even this one is not a clear personification—she simply gives the moth a sex by referring to it as "him." Frost's striking metaphors, similes, and even puns (*right*, *appall*) show him, as usual, to be a master of figures of speech. He calls the moth's wings "satin cloth" and "a paper kite"; Evans just refers in line 8 to a moth's wing. As far as the language of the two poems goes, we might as well compare a vase brimming with flowers and a single flower stuck in a vase. In fairness to Evans, I would say that her poem, while lacking complexity, still makes its point effectively. Her poem has powerful sounds: short lines with the riming words coming at us again and again.

Textual evidence—contrasts diction of two poems

In theme, however, "Wing-Spread" seems much more narrow than "Design." The first time I read Evans's poem, all I felt was: Ho hum, the moth's wings were too wide and got stuck. The second time I read it, I realized that she was saying something with a universal application. This message comes out in line 11, in "a netted universe." That metaphorical phrase is the most interesting part of her poem. *Netted* makes me imagine the universe as being full of nets rigged by someone who is fishing for us. Maybe, like Frost, Evans sees an evil plan operating. She does not, though, investigate it. She says that the midge escapes because it is tiny. On the other hand, things with wide wing-spreads get stuck. Her theme as I read it is, "Be small and inconspicuous if you want to survive," or maybe, "Isn't it too bad that in this world the big beautiful types

Contrasts thematic approach

Munjee 3

crack up and die, while the little puny punks keep sailing?" Now, this is a valuable idea. I have often thought that very same thing myself. But Frost's closing note ("If design govern in a thing so small") is really devastating because it raises a huge uncertainty. "Wing-Spread" leaves us with not much besides a moth stuck in a web and a moral. In both language and theme, "Design" climbs to a higher altitude.

Conclusion restates thesis

Munjee 4

Works Cited

Evans, Abbie Huston. "Wing-Spread." *Literature: An Introduction to Fiction, Poetry, Drama, and Writing*. Ed. X. J. Kennedy and Dana Gioia. 12th ed. New York: Pearson, 2013. 1948. Print.

Frost, Robert. "Design." *Collected Poems, Prose and Plays*. New York: Library of America, 1995. 275. Print.

HOW TO QUOTE A POEM

Quoted to illustrate some point, memorable lines can enliven your paper. Carefully chosen quotations can serve to back up your thesis, or to alert your readers to a phrase or passage they may have neglected. Quoting poetry accurately, however, raises certain difficulties you don't face in quoting prose. Poets choose their line breaks with deliberation, and part of a critic's job is to take those breaks into account. Here are guidelines for respecting a poet's line breaks and for making your essay more polished in the bargain.

- **Quoting a few lines.** If you are quoting fewer than four lines of poetry, transform the passage into prose form, separating each line by a space, diagonal (/), and another space. The diagonal (/) indicates where the poet's lines begin and end. Two diagonals (//) signal a new stanza. Do not change the poet's capitalization or punctuation. Be sure to identify the line numbers you are quoting, as follows:

  The color white preoccupies Frost. The spider is "fat and white, / On a white heal-all" (1–2), and even the victim moth is pale, too.

- **Quoting four or more lines.** If you are quoting four or more lines of verse, set them off from your text, and arrange them just as they occur on the page, white space and all. Be sure to identify the lines you are quoting. In general, follow these rules:
  - Indent the quotation one inch from the left-hand margin.
  - Double-space between the quoted lines.
  - Type the poem exactly as it appears in the original. You do not need to use quotation marks.
  - If you begin the quotation in the middle of a line of verse, position the starting word about where it occurs in the poem—not at the left-hand margin.
  - If a line you are quoting runs too long to fit on one line, indent the return one-quarter inch.
  - Cite the line numbers you are quoting in parentheses.

At the end of the poem, the poet asks what deity or fate cursed this particular mutant flower

with being white,
The wayside blue and innocent heal-all?
What brought the kindred spider to that height,
Then steered the white moth thither in the
night? (9–12)

- **Omitting words.** If you omit words from the lines you quote, indicate the omission with an ellipsis (. . .), as in the following example:

The color white preoccupies Frost in his description of the spider "fat and white, / On a white heal-all . . . / Like a white piece of rigid satin cloth" (1–3).

- **Quoting only a brief phrase.** There's no need for an ellipsis if it is obvious that only a phrase is being quoted.

The speaker says that he "found a dimpled spider," and he goes on to portray it as a kite-flying boy.

- **Omitting full lines of verse.** If you leave out lines of verse, indicate the omission by spaced periods about the length of a line of the poem you are quoting.

Maybe, she hints, when things in the universe drop below a certain size, they pass completely out of the Designer's notice:

The midge spins out to safety
Through the spider's rope;
. . . .
In a netted universe
Wing-spread is peril. (1–2, 11–12)

One last note: often a paper on a short poem will include the whole text of the poem at its beginning, with the lines numbered so that your reader can refer to it with ease. Ask your instructor whether he or she prefers the full text to be quoted this way.

TOPICS FOR WRITING BRIEF PAPERS (250–500 WORDS)

1. Write a concise *explication* of a short poem of your choice. Concentrate on those facets of the poem that you think most need explaining.
2. Write an *analysis* of a short poem, focusing on how a single key element shapes its meaning. Some possible topics are:
    - Tone in Edna St. Vincent Millay's "Recuerdo"
    - Rime and meter in Edgar Allan Poe's "A Dream Within a Dream"
    - Imagery in Wallace Stevens's "The Emperor of Ice-Cream"
    - Kinds of irony in Thomas Hardy's "The Workbox"
    - Theme in W. H. Auden's "Musée des Beaux Arts"
    - Extended metaphor in Langston Hughes's "The Negro Speaks of Rivers" (Explain the one main comparison that the poem makes and show how the whole poem makes it. Other poems that would lend themselves to a paper on extended metaphor include: Emily Dickinson's "Because I could not stop for Death," Robert Frost's "The Silken Tent," Robert Lowell's "Skunk Hour," Adrienne Rich's "Aunt Jennifer's Tigers.")

    (To locate any of these poems, see the Index of Authors and Titles.)

3. Select a poem in which the main speaker is a character who for any reason interests you. You might consider, for instance, Robert Browning's "Soliloquy of the Spanish Cloister," T. S. Eliot's "The Love Song of J. Alfred Prufrock," or Rhina Espaillat's "Bilingual/*Bilingüe*." Then write a brief profile of this character, drawing only on what the poem tells you (or reveals). What is the character's age? Situation in life? Attitude toward self? Attitude toward others? General personality? Do you find this character admirable?
4. Choose a brief poem that you find difficult. Write an essay in which you begin by listing the points in the poem that strike you as most impenetrable. Next, reread the poem at least twice. In the essay's second half, describe how further readings changed your experience of the poem.
5. Although each of these poems tells a story, what happens in the poem isn't necessarily obvious: E. E. Cummings's "anyone lived in a pretty how town," T. S. Eliot's "The Love Song of J. Alfred Prufrock," Edwin Arlington Robinson's "Luke Havergal." Choose one of these poems, and in a paragraph sum up what you think happens in it. Then in a second paragraph, ask yourself: what, *besides* the element of story, did you consider in order to understand the poem?
6. Imagine a reader who categorically dislikes poetry. Choose a poem for that person to read, and, addressing your skeptical reader, explain the ways in which this particular poem rewards a careful reader.

TOPICS FOR WRITING MORE EXTENDED PAPERS (600–1,000 WORDS)

1. Perform a line-by-line explication of a brief poem of your choice. Imagine that your audience is unfamiliar with the poem and needs your assistance in interpreting it.
2. Explicate a passage from a longer poem. Choose a passage that is, in your opinion, central to the poem's meaning.
3. Compare and contrast any two poems that treat a similar theme. Let your comparison bring you to an evaluation of the poems. Which is the stronger, more satisfying one?
4. Write a comparison-contrast essay on any two or more poems by a single poet. Look for two poems that share a characteristic thematic concern. (This book contains multiple selections by Auden, Blake, Cummings, Dickinson, Donne, Eliot, Frost, Hardy, Hopkins, Hughes, Keats, Shakespeare, Stevens, Tennyson, Whitman, Williams, Wordsworth, Yeats, and many others.) Here are some possible topics:
   - Mortality in the work of John Keats
   - Nature in the poems of William Wordsworth
   - How Emily Dickinson's lyric poems resemble hymns
   - E. E. Cummings's approach to the free-verse line
   - Gerard Manley Hopkins's sonic effects
5. Evaluate by the method of comparison two versions of a poem, one an early draft and one a late draft, or perhaps two translations of the same poem from another language.
6. If the previous topic appeals to you, consider this. In 1912, ten years before he published "Design," Robert Frost sent a correspondent this early version:

In White

A dented spider like a snow drop white
On a white Heal-all, holding up a moth
Like a white piece of lifeless satin cloth—
Saw ever curious eye so strange a sight?
Portent in little, assorted death and blight
Like the ingredients of a witches' broth?
The beady spider, the flower like a froth,

And the moth carried like a paper kite.
What had that flower to do with being white,
The blue Brunella every child's delight.
What brought the kindred spider to that height?
(Make we no thesis of the miller's plight.)
What but design of darkness and of night?
Design, design! Do I use the word aright?

Compare "In White" with "Design." In what respects is the finished poem superior?

TOPICS FOR WRITING LONG PAPERS (1,500 WORDS OR MORE)

1. Review an entire poetry collection by a poet featured in this book. You will need to communicate to your reader a sense of the work's style and thematic preoccupations. Finally, make a value judgment about the work's quality.
2. Read five or six poems by a single author. Start with a poet featured in this book, and then find additional poems at the library or on the Internet. Write an analysis of a single element of that poet's work—for example, theme, imagery, diction, or form.
3. Write a line-by-line explication of a poem rich in matters to explain or of a longer poem that offers ample difficulty. While relatively short, John Donne's "A Valediction: Forbidding Mourning" and Gerard Manley Hopkins's "The Windhover" are poems that will take a good bit of time to explicate. Even a short, apparently simple poem such as Robert Frost's "Stopping by Woods on a Snowy Evening" can provide more than enough material to explicate thoughtfully in a longer paper.
4. Write an analysis of a certain theme (or other element) that you find in the work of two or more poets. It is probable that in your conclusion you will want to set the poets' works side by side, comparing or contrasting them, and perhaps making some evaluation. Here are some sample topics to consider:
   - Langston Hughes, Gwendolyn Brooks, and Dudley Randall as Prophets of Social Change
   - What It Is to Be a Woman: The Special Knowledge of Sylvia Plath, Anne Sexton, and Adrienne Rich
   - The Complex Relations Between Fathers and Children in the Poetry of Robert Hayden, Rhina Espaillat, Theodore Roethke, and A. E. Stallings
   - Making Up New Words for New Meanings: Neologisms in Lewis Carroll and Kay Ryan
5. Apply the ideas in one of the critical excerpts in the "Writing Effectively" section found at the end of each chapter to a poem by the same author. Formulate a thesis about whether or not the prose excerpt sheds any light on the poetry. How do T. S. Eliot's thoughts on the music of poetry, or William Butler Yeats's observations on poetic symbolism, help you to better understand their poems? Quote as needed to back up your argument.

44 WRITING ABOUT A PLAY

The play was a great success,
but the audience was a total failure.

—OSCAR WILDE

Writing about a play you've read is similar, in many ways, to writing about poetry or fiction. If your subject is a play you have actually seen performed, however, some differences will quickly become apparent. Although, like a story or a poem, a play in print is usually the work of a single author, a play on stage may be the joint effort of seventy or eighty people—actors, director, costumers, set designers, and technicians. Though a play on the page stays fixed and changeless, a play in performance changes in many details from season to season—and even from night to night.

Later in this chapter you will find advice on reviewing a performance of a play, as you might do for a class assignment or for publication in a campus newspaper. In a literature course, though, you will probably write about the plays you quietly read and behold only in the theater of your mind.

READ CRITICALLY

- **Read the whole play—not just the dialogue, but also everything in italics, including stage directions and descriptions of settings.** The meaning of a scene, or even of an entire play, may depend on the tone of voice in which an actor is supposed to deliver a significant line. At the end of *A Doll's House*, for example, we need to pay attention to *how* Helmer's last line is spoken—"*A hope flashes across his mind*"—if we are to understand that Nora ignores his last desperate hope for reconciliation when she closes the door. The meaning of a line may depend upon the actions described in the stage directions. If Nora did not leave the house or close the door, but hesitated at Helmer's last line, the meaning of the play would be slightly different.
- **Highlight key passages and take notes as you read.** Later you will want to quote or refer to important moments in the play, and marking those moments will simplify your job. Following is an example of a student's notes on a key scene in Susan Glaspell's *Trifles*.

Mrs. Peters (*to the other woman*): Oh, her fruit; it did freeze. (*To the County Attorney*) She worried about that when it turned so cold. She said the fire'd go out and her jars would break.

Sheriff: Well, can you beat the women! Held for murder and worryin' about her preserves.

Both men are insulting toward Mrs. Wright.

County Attorney: I guess before we're through she may have something more serious than preserves to worry about.

He thinks he's being kind.

Hale: Well, women are used to worrying over trifles.

Is housework really insignificant?

(*The two women move a little closer together.*)

The women side with each other.

County Attorney (*with the gallantry of a young politician*): And yet, for all their worries, what would we do without the ladies? (*The women do not unbend. He goes to the sink, takes a dipperful of water from the pail and pouring it into a basin, washes his hands. Starts to wipe them on the roller towel, turns it for a cleaner place.*) Dirty towels! (*Kicks his foot against the pans under the sink.*) Not much of a housekeeper, would you say, ladies?

Courtesy toward women, but condescending

The two women aren't buying it.

Mrs. Hale (*stiffly*): There's a great deal of work to be done on a farm.

She holds back, but she's mad.

I don't like this guy!

Small, insignificant things or not?

Play's title. Significant word? The men miss the "clues"–too trifling.

- **If your subject is a play in verse—such as those by Sophocles and Shakespeare—keep track of act, scene, and line numbers as you take notes.** This will help you to easily relocate any text you want to refer to or quote.

> Iago's hypocrisy is apparent in his speech defending his good name (3.3.168–74).

COMMON APPROACHES TO WRITING ABOUT DRAMA

The methods commonly used to write about fiction and poetry—for example, explication, analysis, or comparison and contrast—are all well suited to writing about drama. These methods are discussed in depth in earlier chapters. Here are a few suggestions for using these methods to write about plays in particular.

Explication

A whole play is too much to cover in an ordinary **explication**, a line-by-line unfolding of meaning in a literary work. In drama, explication is best suited to brief passages—a key soliloquy, for example, or a moment of dialogue that lays bare the play's theme. Closely examining a critical moment in a play can shed light on the play in its entirety. To be successful, an explication needs to concentrate on a passage probably not much more than 20 lines long.

Analysis

A separation of a literary work into elements, **analysis** is a very useful method for writing about drama. To write an analysis, choose a single element in a play—for example, animal imagery in some speeches from *Othello*, or the theme of fragility in *The Glass Menagerie*. Plays certainly offer many choices of elements for analysis: characters, themes, tone, irony, imagery, figures of speech, and symbols, for example. Keep in mind, though, that not all plays contain the same elements you would find in poetry or fiction. Few plays have a narrator, and in most cases the point of view is that of the audience, which perceives the events not through a narrator's eyes but through its own. And while we might analyze a short story's all-pervading style, a play might contain as many styles as there are speaking characters. (Noteworthy exceptions do exist, though: you might argue that in Susan Glaspell's *Trifles*, both main characters speak the same language.) As for traditional poetic devices such as metaphor and metrical pattern, they may be found in plays such as *Othello*, but not in most contemporary plays, in which the dialogue tends to sound like ordinary conversation.

Comparison and Contrast

The method of **comparison** and **contrast** involves setting two plays side by side and pointing out their similarities and differences. Because plays are complicated entities, you need to choose a narrow focus, or you will find yourself overwhelmed. A profound topic—"The Self-Deception of Othello and Oedipus"—might do for a three-hundred-page dissertation, but an essay of a mere thousand words could never do it justice. A large but finite topic—say, attitudes toward marriage in *A Doll's House* and *Trifles*—would best suit a long term paper. To apply this method to a shorter term paper, you might compare and contrast a certain aspect of personality in two characters within the same play—for example, Willy's and Biff's illusions in *Death of a Salesman*.

Card Report

In place of an essay, some instructors like to assign a **card report**, a succinct but thorough method of analyzing the components of a play. For more information on this kind of assignment, see "The Card Report" on page 1922. Keep in mind, though, that when dealing with a play, you will find some elements that differ from those in a short story. Specifying the work's narrator may not be relevant to a play, for example. Also, for a full-length play, you may need to write on both sides of two 5- × 8-inch index cards instead of on one card, as you might for a short story. Still, in order to write a good card report, you have to be both brief and specific. Before you start, sort out your impressions of the play and try to decide which characters, scenes, and lines of dialogue are the most memorable and important. Reducing your scattered impressions to essentials, you will have to reexamine what you have read. When you finish, you will know the play much more thoroughly.

Here is an example: a card report on Susan Glaspell's one-act play *Trifles*. By including only the elements that seemed most important, the writer managed to analyze the brief play on the front and back of one card. Still, he managed to work in a few pertinent quotations to give a sense of the play's remarkable language. Although the report does not say everything about Glaspell's little masterpiece, an adequate criticism of the play could hardly be much briefer. For this report, the writer was assigned to include the following:

1. The playwright's name, nationality, and dates.
2. The title of the play and the date of its first performance.
3. The central character or characters, with a brief description that includes leading traits.
4. Other characters, also described.
5. The scene or scenes and, if the play does not take place in the present, the time of its action.
6. The dramatic question. This question is whatever the play leads us to ask ourselves: some conflict whose outcome we wonder about, some uncertainty whose resolution we look forward to.
7. A brief summary of the play's principal events, in the order in which the playwright presents them. If you are reporting on a play longer than *Trifles*, you may find it simplest to sum up what happens in each act, perhaps in each scene.
8. The tone of the play, as best you can detect it. Try to describe the playwright's apparent feelings toward the characters or what happens to them.
9. The language spoken in the play. Try to describe it. Does any character speak with a choice of words or with figures of speech that strike you as unusual, distinctive, poetic—or maybe dull and drab? Does language indicate a character's background or place of birth? Brief quotations, in what space you have, will be valuable.
10. A one-sentence summary of the play's central theme. If you find none, say so. Plays often contain more than one theme. Which of them seems most clearly borne out by the main events?
11. Any symbols you notice and believe to be important. Try to state in a few words what each suggests.
12. A concise evaluation of the play. What did you think of it? (For more suggestions on being a drama critic, see Chapter 39, "Evaluating a Play.")

A card report on *Trifles* begins on the following page.

Front of Card

Ben Nelson English 101

Susan Glaspell, American, 1876–1948 *Trifles,* 1916

<u>Central characters</u>: Mrs. Peters, the sheriff's nervous wife, dutiful but independent, not "married to the law"—whose sorrows make her able to sympathize with a woman accused of murder. Mrs. Hale, who knows the accused; more decisive.

<u>Other characters</u>: The County Attorney, self-important but short-sighted. The Sheriff, a man of only middling intelligence, another sexist. Hale, a farmer, a cautious man. Not seen on stage, two others are central: Minnie (Foster) Wright, the accused, a music lover reduced to near despair by years of grim marriage and isolation; and John Wright, the victim, known for his cruelty.

<u>Scene</u>: The kitchen of a gloomy farmhouse after the arrest of a wife on suspicion of murder; little things left in disarray.

<u>Major dramatic question</u>: Why did Minnie Wright kill her husband? When this question is answered, a new major dramatic question is raised: Will Mrs. Peters and Mrs. Hale cover up incriminating evidence?

<u>Events</u>: In the exposition, Sheriff and C.A., investigating the death of Wright, hear Hale tell how he found the body and a distracted Mrs. Wright. Then (1) C.A. starts looking for a motive. (2) His jeering at Mrs. Wright (and all women) for their concern with "trifles" causes Mrs. Peters and Mrs. Hale to rally to the woman's defense. (3) When the two women find evidence that Mrs. Wright had panicked (a patch of wild sewing in a quilt), Mrs. Hale destroys it.

[continued on back of card]

Back of Card

[Events, continued]

(4) Mrs. Peters finds more evidence: a wrecked birdcage. (5) The women find a canary with its neck wrung and realize that Minnie killed her husband in a similar way. (6) The women align themselves with Minnie when Mrs. Peters recalls her own sorrows, and Mrs. Hale decides her own failure to visit Minnie was "a crime." (7) The C.A. unwittingly provides Mrs. Peters with a means to smuggle out the canary. (8) The two women unite to seize the evidence.

Tone: Made clear in the women's dialogue: mingled horror and sadness at what has happened, compassion for a fellow woman, smoldering resentment toward men who crush women.

Language: The plain speech of farm people, with a dash of rural Midwestern slang (*red-up* for tidy; Hale's remark that the accused was "kind of done up"). Unschooled speech: Mrs. Hale says *ain't*—and yet her speech rises at moments to simple poetry: "She used to sing. He killed that too." Glaspell hints at the self-importance of the County Attorney by his heavy reliance on the first person.

Central theme: Women, in their supposed concern for trifles, see more deeply than men do.

Symbols: The broken birdcage and the dead canary, both suggesting the music and the joy that John Wright stifled in Minnie.

Evaluation: A powerful, successful, realistic play that conveys its theme with great economy—in its views, more than fifty years ahead of its time.

A Drama Review

Writing a **play review**, a brief critical account of an actual performance, involves going out on a limb and making an evaluation. It also can mean assessing various aspects of the production, including the acting, direction, sets, costumes, lighting, and possibly even the play itself. While reviews can be challenging to write, many students find them more stimulating—even more fun—than most writing assignments. There is no better way to understand—and appreciate—drama than by seeing live theater. Here are some tips for writing a review.

- **Clarify what you are evaluating.** Is it the play's script, or the performance? If the latter, are you concentrating on the performance in its entirety, or on certain elements, such as the acting or the direction? If the play is a classic one, the more urgent task for the reviewer will be not to evaluate the playwright's work but to comment on the success of the actors', director's, and production crew's particular interpretation of it. If the play is newer and less well established, you may profitably evaluate the script itself.
- **If the play itself is your subject, be aware of the conventions within which the playwright is working.** For a list of considerations see "Judging a Play" in Chapter 39.
- **Don't simply sneer or gush; give reasons for your opinions.** Ground your praise or criticism of a production in specifics. Incidentally, harsh evaluations can tempt a reviewer to flashes of wit. One celebrated flash was writer Eugene Field's observation of an actor in a production of *King Lear*, that "he played the king as though he were in constant fear that someone else was about to play the ace." The comment isn't merely nasty; it implies that Field had closely watched the actor's performance and had discerned what was wrong with it.
- **Early in the review, provide the basic facts.** Give the play's title and author, the theatrical company producing it, and the theater in which it is performed.
- **Give the names of actors in lead roles, and evaluate their performances.** How well cast do the leads seem? If an actor stands out—for good or ill—in a supporting role, he or she may deserve a mention as well.
- **Provide a brief plot summary.** Your reader may be unacquainted with the play, and will certainly want a general sense of what it is about. Out of consideration to the reader, however, it is best not to reveal any plot surprises, unless the play is a classic one with an ending likely to be common knowledge.
- **If the play is unfamiliar, summarize its theme.** This exercise will not only help your reader understand your review but probably sharpen your analysis.
- **For a well-known play, evaluate the director's approach to familiar material.** Is the production exactly what you'd expect, or are there any fresh and apparently original innovations? If a production is unusual, does it achieve newness by violating the play? The director of one college production of *Othello* emphasized the play's being partly set in Venice by staging it in the campus swimming pool, with actors floating on barges and a homemade gondola—a fresh, but not entirely successful, innovation.
- **Comment on the director's work.** Can you discern the director's approach to the play? Do the actors hurry their lines or speak too slowly? Do they speak and gesture naturally, or in an awkward, stylized manner? Are these touches effective or distracting?
- **Pay attention to costumes, sets, and lighting.** Though such matters may seem small, they have an effect on the play's overall tone.
- **Finally, to prepare yourself, read a few professional play reviews.** Reviews appear regularly in magazines such as the *New Yorker*, *Time*, the *New Criterion*, and *American Theatre*, and also on the entertainment pages of most metropolitan newspapers. Newspaper reviews can often be accessed online; for example, *New York Times* reviews may be found at <http://theater.nytimes.com>.

Here is a good, concise review of an amateur production of *Trifles*, as it might be written for a college newspaper or as a course assignment.

Trifles Scores Mixed Success in

Monday Players' Production

Opening paragraph gives information on play and production

Women have come a long way since 1916. At least, that impression was conveyed yesterday when the Monday Players presented Susan Glaspell's classic one-act play *Trifles* in Alpaugh Theater.

At first, in Glaspell's taut story of two subjugated farm women who figure out why a fellow farm woman strangled her husband, actors Lloyd Fox and Cal Federicci get to strut around. As a small-town sheriff and a county attorney, they lord it over the womenfolk, making sexist remarks about women in general. Fox and Federicci obviously enjoy themselves as the pompous types that Glaspell means them to be.

Evaluates performances

But of course it is the women with their keen eyes for small details who prove the superior detectives. In the demanding roles of the two Nebraska Miss Marples, Kathy Betts and Ruth Fine cope as best they can with what is asked of them. Fine is especially convincing. As Mrs. Hale, a friend of the wife accused of the murder, she projects a growing sense of independence. Visibly smarting under the verbal lashes of the menfolk, she seems to straighten her spine inch by inch as the play goes on.

Analyzes direction

Unluckily for Betts, director Alvin Klein seems determined to view Mrs. Peters as a comedian. Though Glaspell's stage directions call the woman "nervous," I doubt she is supposed to be quite so fidgety as Betts makes her. Betts vibrates like a tuning fork every time a new clue turns up, and when she is obliged to smell a dead canary bird (another clue), you would think she was whiffing a dead hippopotamus. Mrs. Peters, whose sad past includes a lost baby and a kitten some maniac chopped up with a hatchet, is no figure of fun to my mind. Played for laughs, her character fails to grow visibly on stage, as Fine makes Mrs. Hale grow.

Further elaborates on stage direction

Klein, be it said in his favor, makes the quiet action proceed at a brisk pace. Feminists in the audience must have been a little embarrassed, though, by his having Betts and Fine deliver every speech defending women in an extra-loud voice. After all, Glaspell makes her points clearly enough just by showing us what she shows. Not everything is overstated, however. As a farmer who found the murder victim, Ron Valdez acts his part with quiet authority.

Overall evaluation

Despite flaws in its direction, this powerful play still spellbinds an audience. Anna Winterbright's set, seen last week as a background for *Dracula* and just slightly touched up, provides appropriate gloom.

HOW TO QUOTE A PLAY

The guidelines for quoting prose or poetry generally apply to quoting from a play. Plays present certain challenges of their own, however. When you quote an extended section of a play or dialogue that involves more than one character, use the following MLA format to set the passage off from the body of your paper:

- Indent one inch.
- Type the character's name in all capitals, followed by a period.
- If a speech runs for more than a single line, indent any additional lines one-quarter inch.
- Provide a citation reference:

  If the play is written in prose, provide a page number.

  If the play is written in verse, provide the act, scene, and line numbers.

Here is an example of that format:

> The men never find a motive for the murder because, ironically, they consider all the real clues "trifles" that don't warrant their attention:
>
> SHERIFF. Well, can you beat the women! Held for murder and worryin' about her preserves.
>
> COUNTY ATTORNEY. I guess before we're through she may have something more serious than preserves to worry about.
>
> HALE. Well, women are used to worrying over trifles. (1155-56)

When you are quoting a verse play, be careful to respect the line breaks. For citation references, you should provide the act, scene, and line numbers, so that your reader will be able to find the quotation in any edition of the play. A quotation from a verse play should look like this:

> Even before her death, Othello will not confront Desdemona with his specific suspicions:
>
> OTHELLO. Think on thy sins.
> DESDEMONA. They are loves I bear to you.
> OTHELLO. Ay, and for that thou diest.
> DESDEMONA. That death's unnatural that kills for loving.
> Alas, why gnaw you so your nether lip?
> Some bloody passion shakes your very frame.
> These are portents; but yet I hope, I hope,
> They do not point on me. (5.2.42–48)

TOPICS FOR WRITING BRIEF PAPERS (250–500 WORDS)

1. Analyze a key character from any play in this book. Some choices might be Tom Wingfield in *The Glass Menagerie*, Torvald Helmer in *A Doll's House*, or Biff Loman in *Death of a Salesman.* What motivates that character? Point to specific moments in the play to make your case.
2. When the curtain comes down on the conclusion of some plays, the audience is left to decide exactly what finally happened. In a short informal essay, state your interpretation of the conclusion of one of these plays: *The Sound of a Voice, El Santo Americano, The Glass Menagerie.* Don't just give a plot summary; tell what you think the conclusion means.
3. Sum up the main suggestions you find in one of these meaningful objects (or actions): the handkerchief in *Othello;* the Christmas tree in *A Doll's House* (or Nora's doing a wild tarantella); Willy Loman's planting a garden in *Death of a Salesman;* Laura's collection of figurines in *The Glass Menagerie*.
4. Here is an exercise in being terse. Write a card report on a short, one-scene play (other than *Trifles*), and confine your remarks to both sides of one 5- × 8-inch card. (For further instructions see page 1958.) Possible subjects include *The Sound of a Voice*, *Beauty*, *Sure Thing.*
5. Attend a play and write a review. In an assignment this brief, you will need to concentrate your remarks on either the performance or the script itself. Be sure to back up your opinions with specific observations.

TOPICS FOR WRITING MORE EXTENDED PAPERS (600–1,000 WORDS)

1. From a play you have enjoyed, choose a passage that strikes you as difficult, worth reading closely. Try to pick a passage not longer than about 20 lines. Explicate it—give it a close, sentence-by-sentence reading—and explain how this small part of the play relates to the whole. For instance, any of the following passages might be considered memorable (and essential to their plays):

   - Othello's soliloquy beginning "It is the cause, it is the cause, my soul" (*Othello*, 5.2.1–22).
   - Oedipus to Teiresias, speech beginning "Wealth, power, craft of statemanship!" (*Oedipus the King*, 1.163–86).
   - Nora to Mrs. Linde, speech beginning "Yes, someday, maybe, in many years when I am not as pretty as I am now . . ." (*A Doll's House*, page 1608).

2. Analyze the complexities and contradictions to be found in a well-rounded character from a play of your choice. Some good subjects might be Hamlet, Othello, Nora Helmer (in *A Doll's House*), Willy Loman (in *Death of a Salesman*), or Tom Wingfield (in *The Glass Menagerie*).
3. Take just a single line or sentence from a play, one that stands out for some reason as greatly important. Perhaps it states a theme, reveals a character, or serves as a crisis (or turning point). Write an essay demonstrating its importance—how it functions, why it is necessary. Some possible lines include:

   - Iago to Roderigo: "I am not what I am" (*Othello*, 1.1.67).
   - Amanda to Tom: "You live in a dream; you manufacture illusions!" (*The Glass Menagerie*, Scene vii).

- Charley to Biff: "A salesman is got to dream, boy. It comes with the territory" (*Death of a Salesman*, the closing Requiem).

4. Write an analysis essay in which you single out an element of a play for examination—character, plot, setting, theme, dramatic irony, tone, language, symbolism, conventions, or any other element. Try to relate this element to the play as a whole. Sample topics: "The Function of Teiresias in *Oedipus the King*," "Imagery of Poison in *Othello*," "Irony in *Antigonê*," "Williams's Use of Magic-Lantern Slides in *The Glass Menagerie*," "The Theme of Success in *Death of a Salesman*."
5. How would you stage an updated production of a play by Shakespeare, Sophocles, or Ibsen, transplanting it to our time? Choose a play, and describe the challenges and difficulties of this endeavor. How would you overcome them—or, if they cannot be overcome, why not?
6. Louis Phillips, of the School of Visual Arts in New York City, developed the following assignment. Read this statement from Woody Allen:

   > Sports to me is like music. It's completely satisfying. There were times I would sit at a game with the old Knicks and think to myself in the fourth quarter, this is everything the theatre should be and isn't. There's an outcome that's unpredictable. The audience is not ahead of the dramatists. The drama is ahead of the audience.

   What does Allen mean by the notion of the audience being ahead of (or behind) the dramatist? Apply that to a play you have read. If Woody Allen feels that sports are more satisfying than drama, why does he continue to make movies?

TOPICS FOR WRITING LONG PAPERS (1,500 WORDS OR MORE)

1. Choose a play you admire from this book, and read a second play by the same author. Compare and contrast the two plays with attention to a single element—a theme they have in common, or a particular kind of imagery, for example.
2. Compare and contrast the ways in which *The Glass Menagerie* and *Death of a Salesman* approach the theme of fantasy and wishful thinking.
3. Read *Othello* and view a movie version of the play. You might choose Oliver Parker's 1995 take on the play with Laurence Fishburne and Kenneth Branagh, or even O (2001), an updated version that has a prep school as its setting and a basketball star as its protagonist. Review the movie. What does it manage to convey of the original? What gets lost in the translation?
4. Choosing any of the works in "Plays for Further Reading" or taking some other play your instructor suggests, report any difficulties you encountered in reading and responding to it. Explicate any troublesome passages for the benefit of other readers.
5. Attend a play and write an in-depth review, taking into account many elements of the drama: acting, direction, staging, costumes, lighting, and—if the work is relatively new and not a classic—the play itself.
6. Have you ever taken part in a dramatic production, either as an actor or a member of the crew? What did the experience teach you about the nature of drama and about what makes a play effective?
7. Write a one-act play of your own, featuring a minor character from one of the plays you have read for class. Think about what motivates that character, and let the play's central conflict grow from his or her preoccupations.

45 WRITING A RESEARCH PAPER

A writer is a person for whom writing is more difficult than it is for other people.

—THOMAS MANN

Oh no! You have been assigned a research paper, and every time you even think about starting it, your spirits sink and your blood pressure rises. You really liked the story by Ernest Hemingway, but when you entered his name in a search of the college library catalogue it listed 135 books about him. Time to switch authors, you decide. How about Emily Dickinson? She was fun to talk about in class, but when you Google her name, the computer states that there are over 8.4 million entries. What should you do? The paper is due in two weeks, not twenty years. Why would an otherwise very nice instructor put you through this mental trauma?

Why is it worthwhile to write a research paper? (Apart from the fact that you want a passing grade in the class, that is.) While you can learn much by exploring your own responses to a literary work, there is no substitute for entering into a conversation with others who have studied and thought about your topic. Literary criticism is that conversation. Your reading will expose you to the ideas of others who can shed light on a story, poem, or play. It will introduce you to the wide range of informed opinions that exist about literature, as about almost any subject. Sometimes, too, your research will uncover information about an author's life that leads you to new insights into a literary work. Undertaking a research paper gives you a chance to test your ideas against those of others, and in doing so to clarify your own opinions.

BROWSE THE RESEARCH

The most daunting aspect of the research paper may well be the mountains of information available on almost any literary subject. It can be hard to know where to begin. Sifting through books and articles is part of the research process. Unfortunately, the first material you uncover in the library or on the Internet is rarely the evidence you need to develop or support your thesis. Keep looking until you uncover helpful sources.

Another common pitfall in the process is the creeping feeling that your idea has already been examined a dozen times over. But take heart: like Odysseus, tie yourself to the mast so that when you hear the siren voices of published professors, you can listen without abandoning your own point of view. Your idea may have been treated, but not yet by you. Your particular take on a topic is bound to be different from someone else's. After all, thousands of books have been written on Shakespeare's plays, but people still find new things to say about them.

CHOOSE A TOPIC

- **Find a topic that interests you.** A crucial first step in writing a research paper is coming up with a topic that interests you. Start with a topic that bores you, and the process will be a chore and yield dull results. But if you come up with an intriguing research question, seeking the answer will be a more engaging process. The paper that results will inevitably be stronger and more interesting.
- **Find a way to get started.** Browsing through books of literary criticism in the library, or glancing at online journal articles, can help to spark an idea or two. Prewriting techniques such as brainstorming, freewriting, listing, and clustering can also help you to generate ideas on a specific work of literature. If you take notes and jot down ideas as they occur to you, when you start the formal writing process you will discover you have already begun.
- **Keep your purpose and audience in mind.** Refer often to the assignment, and approach your essay accordingly. Think of your audience as well. Is it your professor, your classmates, or some hypothetical reader? As you plan your essay, keep your audience's expectations and needs in mind.
- **Develop a general thesis that you hope to support with research, and look for material that will help you demonstrate its plausibility.** Remember: the ideal research paper is based on your own observations and interpretations of a literary text.

BEGIN YOUR RESEARCH

Print Resources

Writing a research paper on literature calls for two kinds of sources: primary sources, or the literary works that are your subject, and secondary sources, or the books, articles, and web resources that discuss your primary sources. When you are hunting down secondary sources, the best place to begin is your campus library. Plan to spend some time thumbing through scholarly books and journals, looking for passages that you find particularly interesting or that pertain to your topic. Begin your search with the online catalog to get a sense of where you might find the books and journals you need.

To choose from the many books available on your library's shelves and through interlibrary loan, you might turn to book reviews for a sense of which volumes would best suit your purpose. *Book Review Digest* contains the full texts of many book reviews and excerpts of others. The *Digest* may be found in printed form in the reference section of your campus library, which may also provide access to the online version. Whether you are using the online or print version, you will need the author's name, title, and date of first publication of any book for which you hope to find a review.

Scholarly journals are an excellent resource for articles on your topic. Indexes to magazines and journals may be found in your library's reference section. You may also find an index to print periodicals on your library's website.

Online Databases

Most college libraries subscribe to specialized online or CD-ROM database services covering all academic subjects—treasure troves of reliable sources. If you find yourself unsure how to use your library's database system, ask the reference librarian to help you get started. The following databases are particularly useful for literary research:

- The *MLA International Bibliography*, the Modern Language Association's database, is an excellent way to search for books and full-text articles on literary topics.
- *JSTOR*, a not-for-profit organization, indexes articles or abstracts from an archive of journals in over fifty disciplines.
- *Literature Resource Center* (Thomson Gale) provides biographies, bibliographies, and critical analyses of more than 120,000 authors and their work. This information is culled from journal articles and reference works.
- *Literature Online (LION)* provides a vast searchable database of critical articles and reference works as well as full texts of more than 300,000 works of prose, poetry, and drama.
- *Project Muse*, a collaboration between publishers and libraries, offers access to more than 400 journals in the humanities, arts, and social sciences.
- *EBSCO*, a multisubject resource, covers literature and the humanities, as well as the social sciences, medical sciences, linguistics, and other fields.

Your library may provide access to some or all of these databases, or it may offer other useful ones. Many college library home pages provide students with access to subscription databases, which means that if you really can't bear to leave your comfy desk at home, you can still pay a virtual visit.

Reliable Web Sources

While online databases are the most reliable source for high-quality information, you may find yourself looking to supplement journal articles with information and quotations from the Internet. If so, proceed with care. While the journal articles in online databases have been reviewed for quality by specialists and librarians, websites may be written and published by anybody for any purpose, with no oversight. Even the online reference site *Wikipedia*, for example, is an amalgamation of voluntary contributors, and is rife with small factual errors and contributor biases. Carefully analyze any material you gather online, or you may find yourself tangled in the spidery threads of a dubious website. To garner the best sources possible, take these steps:

- **Learn to use Internet search engines effectively.** If you enter general terms such as the author's name and story title into an Internet search engine, you may well find yourself bombarded with thousands of hits. For a more efficient approach to navigating the Internet, try using an "advanced" search option, entering keywords to get results that contain those words (LITERARY CRITICISM A DOLL'S HOUSE or SYMBOLISM THE LOTTERY).
- **Begin your search at a reliable website.** Helpful as an advanced search may be, it won't separate valuable sources from useless ones. To weed out sloppy and inaccurate sites, begin your search with one of the following excellent guides through cyberspace:

- *Library of Congress*. Fortunately, you don't have to trek to Washington to visit this venerable institution's annotated collection of websites in the Humanities and Social Sciences Division. For your purpose—writing a literary research paper—access the Subject Index <http://www.loc.gov/rr/main/alcove9>, click on "Literatures in English" and then on "Literary Criticism." This will take you to a list of metapages and websites with collections of reliable critical and biographical materials on authors and their works. (A metapage provides links to other websites.)
- *Internet Public Library*. Created and maintained by the University of Michigan School of Information and Library Studies, this site <http://www.ipl.org> lets you search for literary criticism by author, work, country of origin, or literary period.
- *Library Spot*. Visit <http://www.libraryspot.com> for a portal to over 5,000 libraries around the world, and to periodicals, online texts, reference works, and links to metapages and websites on any topic including literary criticism. This carefully maintained site is published by StartSpot Mediaworks, Inc., in the Northwestern University/Evanston Research Park in Evanston, Illinois.
- *Voice of the Shuttle*. Research links in over 25 categories in the humanities and social sciences, including online texts, libraries, academic websites, and metapages may be found at this site. Located at <http://vos.ucsb.edu> it was developed and is maintained by Dr. Alan Liu in the English Department of the University of California, Santa Barbara.

CHECKLIST: Finding Reliable Sources

- ☐ Begin at your campus library. Ask the reference librarian for advice.
- ☐ Check the library catalog for books and journals on your topic.
- ☐ Look into the online databases subscribed to by your library.
- ☐ Locate reputable websites by starting at a reputable website designed for that purpose.

Visual Images

The web is an excellent source of visual images. If a picture, chart, or graph will enhance your argument, you may find the perfect one via an image search on Google, PicSearch, or other search engines. The Library of Congress offers a wealth of images documenting American political, social, and cultural history—including portraits, letters, and original manuscripts—at <http://memory.loc.gov>. Remember, though, that not all images are available for use by the general public. Check for a copyright notice to see if its originator allows that image to be reproduced. If so, you may include the photograph, provided you credit your source as you would if you were quoting text.

One note on images: use them carefully. Choose visuals that provide supporting evidence for the point you are trying to make or that enhance your reader's understanding of the work. Label your images with captions. Your goal should be to make your argument more convincing. In the example below, a reproduction of Brueghel's painting helps to advance the author's argument and provide insight into Auden's poem.

Lombardo 4

Fig. 1. *Landscape with the Fall of Icarus* by Pieter Brueghel the Elder (c. 1558, Musées Royaux des Beaux-Arts de Belgique, Brussels)

W. H. Auden's poem "Musée des Beaux Arts" refers to a specific painting to prove its point that the most honest depictions of death take into account the way life simply goes on even after the most tragic of events. In line 14, Auden turns specifically to Pieter Brueghel the Elder's masterwork *The Fall of Icarus* (see Fig. 1), pointing to the painting's understated depiction of tragedy. In this painting, the death of Icarus does not take place on center stage. A plowman and his horse take up the painting's foreground, while the leg of Icarus falling into the sea takes up a tiny portion of the painting's lower-right corner. A viewer who fails to take the painting's title into account might not even notice Icarus at all.

CHECKLIST: Using Visual Images

- ☐ Use images as evidence to support your argument.
- ☐ Use images to enhance communication and understanding.
- ☐ Refer to the images in your text.
- ☐ Label image as "Fig. 1" and provide title or caption.
- ☐ Check copyrights.
- ☐ Include source in works-cited list.

EVALUATE YOUR SOURCES

Print Resources

It's an old saying, but a useful one: don't believe everything you read. The fact that a book or an article is printed and published doesn't necessarily mean it is accurate or unbiased. Be discriminating about printed resources.

Begin your search in a place that has taken some of the work out of quality control—your school library. Books and articles you find there are regarded by librarians as having some obvious merit. If your search takes you beyond the library, though, you will need to be discerning when choosing print resources. As you weigh the value of printed matter, take the following into account:

- **Look closely at information provided about the author.** Is he or she known for expertise in the field? What are the author's academic or association credentials? Is there any reason to believe that the author is biased in any way? For example, a biography of an author written by that author's son or daughter might not be as unbiased as one written by a scholar with no personal connections.
- **Determine the publisher's reliability.** Books or articles published by an advocacy group might be expected to take a particular—possibly biased—slant on an issue. Be aware also that some books are published by vanity presses, companies that are paid by an author to publish his or her books. As a result, vanity press-published books generally aren't subject to the same rigorous quality control as those put out by more reputable publishing houses.
- **Always check for a publication date.** If a document lists an edition number, check to see whether you are using the latest edition of the material.
- **For periodicals, decide whether a publication is an academic journal or a popular magazine.** What type of reputation does it have? Obviously, you do not want to use a magazine that periodically reports on Elvis sightings and alien births. And even articles on writers in magazines such as *Time* and *People* are likely to be too brief and superficial for purposes of serious research. Instead, choose scholarly journals designed to enhance the study of literature.

Web Resources

As handy and informative as the Internet is, it sometimes serves up some pretty iffy information. A website, after all, can be created by anyone with a computer and access to the Internet—no matter how poorly qualified that person might be. Be discerning when it comes to the Internet. Here are tips on choosing your sources wisely:

- **Check a site's author or sponsorship.** Is the site's creator or sponsor known to you or reputable by association? Look closely at information provided about the author. Is he or she known for expertise in the field? What are the author's academic or association credentials? Is the web entry unsigned and anonymous? If the website is sponsored by an organization, is it a reputable one? While government or university-sponsored sites may be considered reliable, think carefully about possible biases in sites sponsored by advocacy or special interest groups.

  A word of warning: individual student pages posted on university sites have not necessarily been reviewed by that university and are not reliable sources of information. Also, postings on the popular encyclopedia website *Wikipedia* are not subject to a scholarly review process and have been found to contain inaccuracies. It's safer to use a published encyclopedia.

- **Look at the site's date of publication.** When was it last updated? In some cases you may want to base your essay on the most current information or theories, so you will want to steer toward the most recently published material.
- **Is this an online version of a print publication?** If so, what type of reputation does it have?
- **Make your own assessment of the site.** Does the content seem consistent with demonstrated scholarship? Does it appear balanced in its point of view?
- **Consult experts.** Cornell University has two good documents with guidance for analyzing sources, posted at <http://www.olinuris.librarycornell.edu/content/skill-guides>. The titles are "Critically Analyzing Information Sources" and "Distinguishing Scholarly from Non-Scholarly Periodicals." Your school's research librarian or library website may have similar resources.

CHECKLIST: Evaluating Your Sources

Print

- ☐ Who wrote it? What are the author's credentials?
- ☐ Is he or she an expert in the field?
- ☐ Does he or she appear to be unbiased toward the subject matter?
- ☐ Is the publisher reputable? Is it an advocacy group or a vanity press?
- ☐ When was it published? Do later editions exist? If so, would a later edition be more useful?

Web

- ☐ Who wrote it? What are the author's credentials?
- ☐ Is he or she an expert in the field?
- ☐ Who sponsors the website? Is the sponsor reputable?
- ☐ When was the website published? When was it last updated?
- ☐ Is the website an online journal or magazine? Is it scholarly or popular?
- ☐ Does content seem consistent with demonstrated scholarship?
- ☐ Can you detect obvious bias?

ORGANIZE YOUR RESEARCH

- **Get your thoughts down on notecards or the equivalent on your laptop.** Once you have amassed your secondary sources, it will be time to begin reading in earnest. As you do so, be sure to take notes on any passage that pertains to your topic. A convenient way to organize your many thoughts is to write them down on index cards, which are easy to shuffle and rearrange. You'll need 3- × 5-inch cards for brief notes and titles and 5- × 8-inch cards for more in-depth notes. Confine your jottings to one side of the card; notes on the back can easily be overlooked. Write a single fact or opinion on each card. This will make it easier for you to shuffle the deck and re-envision the order in which you deliver information to your reader.

- **Keep careful track of the sources of quotations and paraphrases.** As you take notes, make it unmistakably clear which thoughts and phrases are yours and which derive from others. (Remember, *quotation* means using the exact words of your source and placing the entire passage in quotation marks and citing the author. *Paraphrase* means expressing the ideas of your source in your own words, again citing the author.) Bear in mind the cautionary tale of a well-known historian, Doris Kearns Goodwin. She was charged with plagiarizing sections of two of her famous books when her words were found to be jarringly similar to those published in other books. Because she had not clearly indicated on her notecards which ideas and passages were hers and which came from other sources, Goodwin was forced to admit to plagiarism. Her enormous reputation suffered from these charges, but you can learn from her mistakes and save your own reputation—and your grades.
- **Keep track of the sources of ideas and concepts.** When an idea is inspired by or directly taken from someone else's writing, be sure to jot down the source on that same card or in your computer file. Your deck of cards or computer list will function as a working bibliography, which later will help you put together a works-cited list. To save yourself work, keep a separate list of the sources you're using. Then, as you make the note, you need write only the material's author or title and page reference on the card in order to identify your source. It's also useful to classify the note in a way that will help you to organize your material, making it easy, for example, to separate cards that deal with a story's theme from cards that deal with point of view or symbolism.
- **Make notes of your own thoughts and reactions to your research.** When a critical article sparks your own original idea, be sure to capture that thought in your notes and mark it as your own. As you plan your paper, these notes may form the outline for your arguments.

Some useful note cards taken on a critical essay on page 2022 about Joyce Carol Oates's short story "Where Are You Going, Where Have You Been?" might look something like this:

Direct Quotation from Critic

THEME

Schulz and Rockwood, p. 2022

"There is a terrible irony here, for although the story is full of fairy tales, Connie, its protagonist, is not. Connie represents an entire generation of young people who have grown up—or tried to—without the help of those bedtime stories which not only entertain the child, but also enable him vicariously to experience and work through problems which he will encounter in adolescence."

Paraphrase of Critic

THEME

Schulz and Rockwood, p. 2022

Ironic that while story steeped in fairy tales, Connie is not. Connie stands for her whole generation that grew up without fairy tales.

Missed benefits of fairy tales for child: working through life's problems.

Critic's Idea

THEME

Schulz and Rockwood, p. 2022

Many fairy tales underlie "Where Are You Going ?" e.g.

Snow White
Cinderella
Sleeping Beauty
Little Red Riding Hood

Your Own Idea

THEME or CHARACTER?

My Idea

Is Arnold the big bad wolf?

Can I find clues in story?

■ **Make photocopies or printouts to simplify the process and ensure accuracy.** Scholars once had to spend long hours copying out prose passages by hand. Luckily, for a small investment you can simply photocopy your sources to ensure accuracy in quoting and citing your sources. In fact, some instructors will require you to hand in photocopies of your original sources with the final paper, along with printouts of articles downloaded from an Internet database. Even if this is not the case, photocopying your sources and holding onto your printouts can help you to reproduce quotations accurately in your essay—and accuracy is crucial.

REFINE YOUR THESIS

As you read secondary sources and take notes, you should begin to refine your essay's thesis. This, in turn, will help you to winnow your stacks of source material down to the secondary sources that will best help you to make your point. Even your revised thesis doesn't have to be etched in stone. It should simply give you a sense of direction as you start to plan your essay.

- **Be willing to fine-tune your thesis or even rework it completely.** Your research may reveal that you have misinterpreted an idea, or that there is not much evidence to support your thesis. Of course, it is annoying to find that you may be wrong about something, but don't let these discoveries put you off. Use your research to refine your thoughts.
- **Let your initial idea be the jumping-off point to other, better ideas.** Say, for example, that you plan to write about the peculiar physical description of Arnold Friend in Joyce Carol Oates's story "Where Are You Going, Where Have You Been?" You may have noticed he has trouble standing in his shoes, and you want to explore that odd detail. If you research this character, you may find Arnold Friend likened to the devil (whose cloven hooves might give him similar problems with standard-issue cowboy boots), or to the wolf in "Little Red Riding Hood" (also a character who would have a hard time managing human clothes). Use your research to sharpen your focus. Can you think of other stories that deal with potentially supernatural, possibly even evil, characters? What about Nathaniel Hawthorne's "Young Goodman Brown"? Or Flannery O'Connor's "A Good Man Is Hard to Find"? How might you compare Arnold Friend with Hawthorne's devil or O'Connor's Misfit?

ORGANIZE YOUR PAPER

With your thesis in mind and your notes spread before you, draw up an outline—a rough map of how best to argue your thesis and present your material. Determine what main points you need to make, and look for quotations that support those points. Even if you generally prefer to navigate the paper-writing process without a map, you will find that an outline makes the research-paper writing process considerably smoother. When organizing information from many different sources, it pays to plan ahead.

WRITE AND REVISE

As with any other kind of essay, a research paper rarely, if ever, reaches its full potential in a single draft. Leave yourself time to rewrite. The knowledge that your first draft won't be your final one can free you up to take chances and to jot down your ideas as quickly as they occur to you. If your phrasing is less than elegant, it hardly matters in a first draft; the object is to work out your ideas on paper. Rough out the paper, working as quickly as you can. Later you can rearrange paragraphs and smooth out any rough patches.

Once you've got the first draft down, it's an excellent idea to run it by a friend, a writing center tutor, or even your instructor. A writer can't know how clear or persuasive his or her argument is without a trusted reader to give feedback.

When you do revise, be open to making both large and small changes. Sometimes revising means adding needed paragraphs, or even refining the thesis a bit further. Be willing to start from scratch if you need to, but even as you take the whole picture into account, remember that details are important too. Before you hand in that final draft, be sure to proofread for small errors that could detract from the finished product.

MAINTAIN ACADEMIC INTEGRITY

Papers for Sale Are Papers that "F"ail

Do not be seduced by the apparent ease of cheating by computer. Your Internet searches may turn up several sites that offer term papers to download (just as you can find pornography, political propaganda, and questionable get-rich-quick schemes!). Most of these sites charge money for what they offer, but a few do not, happy to strike a blow against the "oppressive" insistence of English teachers that students learn to think and write.

Plagiarized term papers are an old game: the fraternity file and the "research assistance" service have been around far longer than the computer. It may seem easy enough to download a paper, put your name at the head of it, and turn it in for an easy grade. As any writing instructor can tell you, though, such papers usually stick out like a sore thumb. The style will be wrong, the work will not be consistent with other work by the same student in any number of ways, and the teacher will sometimes even have seen the same phony paper before. The ease with which electronic texts are reproduced makes this last possibility increasingly likely.

The odds of being caught and facing the unpleasant consequences are reasonably high. It is far better to take the grade you have earned for your own effort, no matter how mediocre, than to try to pass off someone else's work as your own. Even if, somehow, your instructor does not recognize your submission as a plagiarized paper, you have diminished your character through dishonesty and lost an opportunity to learn something on your own.

A Warning Against Internet Plagiarism

Plagiarism detection services are a professor's newest ally in the battle against academic dishonesty. Questionable research papers can be sent to these services (such as Turnitin.com and EVE2), which perform complex searches of the Internet and of a growing database of purchased term papers. The research paper will be returned to the professor with plagiarized sections annotated and the sources documented. The end result will certainly be a failing grade on the essay, possibly a failing grade for the course, and, depending on the policies of your university, the very real possibility of expulsion.

ACKNOWLEDGE ALL SOURCES

The brand of straight-out dishonesty described above is one type of plagiarism. There is, however, another, subtler kind: when students incorporate somebody else's words *or* ideas into their papers without giving proper credit. To avoid this second—sometimes quite accidental—variety of plagiarism, familiarize yourself with the conventions for acknowledging sources. First and foremost, remember to give credit to any writer who supplies you with ideas, information, or specific words and phrases.

Using Quotations

- **Acknowledge your source when you quote a writer's words or phrases.** When you use someone else's words or phrases, you should reproduce his or her exact words in quotation marks, and be sure to properly credit the source.

> Already, Frost has hinted that Nature may be, as Radcliffe Squires suggests, "Nothing but an ash-white plain without love or faith or hope, where ignorant appetites cross by chance" (87).

- **If you quote more than four lines, set your quotation off from the body of the paper.** Start a new line; indent one inch and type the quotation, double-spaced. (You do not need to use quotation marks, as the format tells the reader the passage is a quotation.)

> Samuel Maio made an astute observation about the nature of Weldon Kees's distinctive tone:
>
> > Kees has therefore combined a personal subject matter with an impersonal voice—that is, one that is consistent in its tone evenly recording the speaker's thoughts without showing any emotional intensity which might lie behind those thoughts. (136)

Citing Ideas

- **Acknowledge your source when you mention a critic's ideas.** Even if you are not quoting exact words or phrases, be sure to acknowledge the source of any original ideas or concepts you have used.

> Another explanation is suggested by Daniel Hoffman, a critic who has discussed the story: the killer hears the sound of his *own* heart (227).

- **Acknowledge your source when you paraphrase a writer's words.** To paraphrase a critic, you should do more than just rearrange his or her words: you should translate them into your own original sentences—again, always being sure to credit the original source. As an example, suppose you wish to refer to an insight of Randall Jarrell, who commented as follows on the images of spider, flower, and moth in Robert Frost's poem "Design":

RANDALL JARRELL'S ORIGINAL TEXT

> Notice how the *heal-all*, because of its name, is the one flower in all the world picked to be the altar for this Devil's Mass; notice how *holding up* the moth brings something ritual and hieratic, a ghostly, ghastly formality, to this priest and its sacrificial victim.[1]

[1]*Poetry and the Age* (New York: Knopf, 1953) 42.

It would be too close to the original to write, without quotation marks, these sentences:

PLAGIARIZED REWORDING

> Frost picks the *heal-all* as the one flower in all the world to be the altar for this Devil's Mass. There is a ghostly, ghastly formality to the spider *holding up* the moth, like a priest holding a sacrificial victim.

This rewording, although not exactly in Jarrell's language, manages to steal his memorable phrases without giving him credit. Nor is it sufficient just to include Jarrell's essay in the works-cited list at the end of your paper. If you do, you are still a crook; you merely point to the scene of the crime. Instead, think through Jarrell's words to the point he is making, so that it can be restated in your own original way. If you want to keep any of his striking phrases (and why not?), put them exactly as he wrote them in quotation marks:

APPROPRIATE PARAPHRASE, ACKNOWLEDGES SOURCE

> As Randall Jarrell points out, Frost portrays the spider as a kind of priest in a Mass, or Black Mass, elevating the moth like an object for sacrifice, with "a ghostly, ghastly formality" (42).

Note also that this improved passage gives Jarrell the credit not just for his words but for his insight into the poem. Both the idea and the words in which it was originally expressed are the properties of their originator. Finally, notice the page reference that follows the quotation (this system of documenting your sources is detailed in the next section).

DOCUMENT SOURCES USING MLA STYLE

You must document everything you take from a source. When you quote from other writers, when you borrow their information, when you summarize or paraphrase their ideas, make sure you give them proper credit. Identify the writer by name and cite the book, magazine, newspaper, pamphlet, website, or other source you have used.

The conventions that govern the proper way to document sources are available in the *MLA Handbook for Writers of Research Papers*, 7th ed. (New York: MLA, 2009). The following brief list of pointers is not meant to take the place of the *MLA Handbook* itself, but to give you a basic sense of the rules for documentation.

List of Sources

Keep a working list of your research sources—all the references from which you might quote, summarize, paraphrase, or take information. When your paper is in finished form, it will end with a neat copy of the works you actually used (once called a "Bibliography," now titled "Works Cited").

Parenthetical References

In the body of your paper, every time you refer to a source, you need to provide information to help a reader locate it in your works-cited list. You can usually give just the author's name and a page citation in parentheses. For example, if you are writing a paper on Weldon Kees's sonnet "For My Daughter" and want to include an observation you found on page 136 of Samuel Maio's book *Creating Another Self*, write:

> One critic has observed that the distinctive tone of "For My Daughter" depends on Kees's combination of "personal subject matter with an impersonal voice" (Maio 136).

If you mention the author's name in your sentence, you need give only the page number in your reference:

> As Samuel Maio has observed, Kees creates a distinctive tone in this sonnet by combining a "personal subject with an impersonal voice" (136).

If you have two books or magazine articles by Samuel Maio in your works-cited list, how will the reader tell them apart? In your text, refer to the title of each book or article by condensing it into a word or two. Condensed book titles are italicized, and condensed article titles are still placed within quotation marks.

> One critic has observed that the distinctive tone of "For My Daughter" depends on Kees's combination of "personal subject matter with an impersonal voice" (Maio, *Creating* 136).

Works-Cited List

Provide a full citation for each source on your works-cited page. At the end of your paper, in your list of works cited, your reader will find a full description of your source—for the above examples, a critical book:

> Maio, Samuel. *Creating Another Self: Voices in Modern American Personal Poetry*. 2nd ed. Kirksville: Thomas Jefferson UP, 2005. Print.

Put your works-cited list in proper form. The *MLA Handbook* provides detailed instructions for citing a myriad of different types of sources, from books to online databases. Here is a partial list of the *Handbook*'s recommendations for presenting your works-cited list.

1. Start a new page for the works-cited list, and continue the page numbering from the body of your paper.
2. Center the title, "Works Cited," one inch from the top of the page.
3. Double-space between all lines (including after title and between entries).
4. Type each entry beginning at the left-hand margin. If an entry runs longer than a single line, indent the following lines one-half inch from the left-hand margin.
5. Alphabetize each entry according to the author's last name.
6. Include three sections in each entry: author, title, publication or access information. (You will, however, give slightly different information for a book, journal article, online source, or other reference.)

Citing Print Sources in MLA Style

For a Book Citation

a. **Author's full name** as it appears on the title page, last name first, followed by a period.
b. **Book's full title** (and subtitle, if it has one, separated by a colon) followed by a period. Remember to italicize the title. Also provide edition and volume information, if applicable, followed by a period.
c. **Publication information:** city of publication followed by a colon; name of publisher followed by a comma; year of publication followed by a period; and publication medium—*Print*—followed by a period.
   (1) **Make your citation of the city of publication brief, but clear.** If the title page lists more than one city, cite only the first. You need not provide the state, province, or country.
   (2) **Shorten the publisher's name.** Eliminate articles (*A*, *An*, *The*), business abbreviations (*Co.*, *Corp.*, *Inc.*, *Ltd.*), and descriptive words (*Books*, *House*, *Press*, *Publishers*). The exception is a university press, for which you should use the letters *U* (for University) and *P* (for Press). Use only the first listed *surname* of the publisher.

Publisher's Name	**Proper Citation**
Harvard University Press	Harvard UP
University of Chicago Press	U of Chicago P
Farrar, Straus and Giroux, Inc.	Farrar
Alfred A. Knopf, Inc.	Knopf

d. **Optional additional information:** Any additional information that may be helpful for your reader can be provided at the end of a citation. For example, if the book is part of an established series or part of a multivolume set, put the name of the series or the complete work here.

The citation for a book should read:

> Author's Last name, First name. *Book Title*. Ed. or vol. Publication city:
>
> Publisher, Year. Print.

For a Journal or Periodical Article Citation

a. **Author's name,** last name first, followed by a period.
b. **Title of article** followed by a period, all within quotation marks.
c. **Journal publication information:** journal title (italicized); volume number followed by period, issue number; year of publication in parentheses followed by a colon; inclusive page numbers of the entire article followed by a period; and publication medium—*Print*—followed by a period.

or

Periodical publication information: periodical title (italicized); day month year followed by a colon; page numbers of article (for continuous articles use inclusive pages, such as 31–33; for newspapers use starting page, such as C1+) followed by a period; and publication medium—*Print*—followed by a period.

The citation for a journal article should read:

> Author's Last name, First name. "Article Title." *Journal* Volume.Issue (Year): Pages. Print.

The citation for a periodical article should read:

> Author's Last name, First name. "Article Title." *Periodical* Day Month Year: Pages. Print.

Citing Web Sources in MLA Style

Like print sources, Internet sources should be documented with care. Before you begin your Internet search, be aware of the types of information you will want for your works-cited list. You can then record the information as you go. Keep track of the following information:

- Author's name
- Title of document
- Full information about publication in print form, when available
- Title of scholarly project, database, periodical, or professional or personal site
- Name of editor of project or database
- Date of electronic publication or last update
- Institution or organization sponsoring the website
- Date *you* accessed the source
- Website address or URL

Although many websites provide much of this information at the beginning or ending of an article or at the bottom of the home page, you will find that it is not always available. Also note that as web pages and even sites may sometimes disappear or change, you are well advised to print out important pages for future reference.

For a Web Resource Citation

a. **Author or editor's name,** last name first, followed by a period.
b. **Title of work,** within quotation marks or italicized as appropriate, followed by a period.
c. **Title of website,** in italics, followed by a period.
d. **Sponsor or publisher of website** followed by a comma. If not available, use *N.p.*
e. **Publication date** followed by a period. If data is not available, use *n.d.*
f. **Publication medium—*Web*—**followed by a period.
g. **Date *you* accessed information:** day month year that you viewed the document online.
h. **Optional URL:** if there is some reason your reader may not be able to access your web page with the information provided, you may include the full URL, enclosed in angle brackets < >.

The citation for a web source should read:

Author's Last name, First name. "Document Title." *Website.* Website Sponsor, Publication date. Web. Access Day Month Year.

For a Print Journal Accessed on the Web

a. **Provide information for standard print citation**
   (1) **Author's name,** last name first, followed by a period.
   (2) **Title of work,** within quotation marks or italicized as appropriate, followed by a period.
   (3) **Print publication information:** journal title in italics; volume and issue number; year; page references, as available. If no pages are available, use *n. pag.*

b. **Provide web access information**
   (1) **Title of website or database,** italicized.
   (2) **Publication medium—*Web*—**followed by period.
   (3) **Date *you* accessed information:** day month year that you viewed document online.

The citation for a scholarly journal article obtained on the web should read:

Author's Last name, First name. "Article Title." *Journal* Volume.Issue (Year): Pages. Website or Online Database. Web. Access Day Month Year.

Sample List of Works Cited

For a paper on Weldon Kees's "For My Daughter," a student's works-cited list might look as follows:

Works Cited

Grosholz, Emily. "The Poetry of Memory." *Weldon Kees: A Critical Introduction*. Ed. Jim Elledge. Metuchen: Scarecrow, 1985. 46–47. Print.

Kees, Weldon. *The Collected Poems of Weldon Kees*. Ed. Donald Justice. Lincoln: U of Nebraska P, 1975. Print.

Lane, Anthony. "The Disappearing Poet: What Ever Happened to Weldon Kees?" *New Yorker*. Condé Nast Digital, 4 July 2005. Web. 22 Aug. 2011.

Maio, Samuel. *Creating Another Self: Voice in Modern American Personal Poetry*. 2nd ed. Kirksville: Thomas Jefferson UP, 2005. Print.

Nelson, Raymond. "The Fitful Life of Weldon Kees." *American Literary History* 1.3 (1989): 816–52. Print.

Reidel, James. *Vanished Act: The Life and Art of Weldon Kees.* Lincoln: U of Nebraska P, 2003. Print.

---, ed. "Weldon Kees." *Nebraska Center for Writers,* Creighton University n.d. Web. 26 Aug. 2011.

Ross, William T. *Weldon Kees.* Boston: Twayne, 1985. Print. Twayne's US Authors Ser. 484.

"Weldon Kees." *Poetry Out Loud.* National Endowment for the Arts and the Poetry Foundation, n.d. Web. 20 Sept. 2011.

See the Reference Guide for Citations at the end of this chapter for additional examples of the types of citations that you are likely to need for your papers, or check the seventh edition of the *MLA Handbook*.

As you put together your works-cited list, keep in mind that the little things—page numbers, quotation marks—count. Documentation may seem tedious, but it has an important purpose: it's for the reader of your paper who wants to pursue a topic you have researched. Luckily, you don't have to know the rules by heart. You can refer as necessary to the *MLA Handbook* or to the examples in this book.

ENDNOTES AND FOOTNOTES

Citations and quotations in the text of your essay should be brief and snappy, lest they bog down your prose. You may, however, wish to provide your reader with passages of less important (yet possibly valuable) information, or make qualifying statements ("On the other hand, not every expert agrees. John Binks finds poets are often a little magazine's only cash customers, while Molly MacGuire maintains that . . ."). To insert such information without awkwardly interrupting your paper, put it into an **endnote** (placed at the end of a paper) or a **footnote** (placed at the bottom of the page). Footnotes and endnotes are now used mainly for such asides, but they are also a time-honored way to document sources.

Adding Footnotes

When an aside seems appropriate, insert a number in the text of your essay to send your reader to the corresponding note. Use the "Insert Footnote" option in your word processing program, or create a superscript number from the font menu. This will lift the number slightly above the level of your prose, so that it stands out.

as many observers have claimed.[2]

Once you insert the number of your footnote into the text, your word processing program will cleverly take care of the formatting and placement of the footnote, automatically sending it to the bottom of the page.

2. On the other hand, not every expert agrees. John Binks, to name only one such observer, finds that poets are often a little magazine's only cash customers . . .

SAMPLE STUDENT RESEARCH PAPER—PAGE 350

Professor Michael Cass of Mercer University asked his class to select the fiction writer on their reading list whose work had seemed most impressive and write a research paper defending that author's claim to literary greatness. See page 350 to read the research essay Stephanie Crowe wrote to fulfill the assignment.

CONCLUDING THOUGHTS

A well-crafted research essay is a wondrous thing—as delightful, in its own way, as a well-crafted poem or short story or play. Good essays prompt thought and add to knowledge. Writing a research paper sharpens your own mind and exposes you to the honed insights of other thinkers. Think of anything you write as a piece that could be published for the benefit of other people interested in your topic. After all, such a goal is not as far-fetched as it seems: this textbook, for example, features a number of papers written by students. Why shouldn't yours number among them? Aim high.

REFERENCE GUIDE FOR MLA CITATIONS

Here are examples of the types of citations you are likely to need for most student papers. The formats follow current MLA style for works-cited lists.

PRINT PUBLICATIONS

Books

No Author Listed

The Chicago Manual of Style. 16th ed. Chicago: U of Chicago P, 2010. Print.

One Author

Middlebrook, Diane Wood. *Anne Sexton: A Biography.* Boston: Houghton, 1991. Print.

Two or Three Authors

Jarman, Mark, and Robert McDowell. *The Reaper: Essays.* Brownsville: Story Line, 1996. Print.

Four or More Authors

Phillips, Rodney, et al. *The Hand of the Poet.* New York: Rizzoli, 1997. Print.

or

Phillips, Rodney, Susan Benesch, Kenneth Benson, and Barbara Bergeron. *The Hand of the Poet.* New York: Rizzoli, 1997. Print.

Two Books by the Same Author

Bawer, Bruce. *The Aspect of Eternity.* St. Paul: Graywolf, 1993. Print.

---. *Diminishing Fictions: Essays on the Modern American Novel and Its Critics.* St. Paul: Graywolf, 1988. Print.

Corporate Author

Poets and Writers. *A Writer's Guide to Copyright.* New York: Poets and Writers, 1979. Print.

Author and Editor

Shakespeare, William. *The Sonnets.* Ed. G. Blakemore Evans. Cambridge: Cambridge UP, 1996. Print.

One Editor

Monteiro, George, ed. *Conversations with Elizabeth Bishop*. Jackson: UP of Mississippi, 1996. Print.

Two Editors

Craig, David, and Janet McCann, eds. *Odd Angles of Heaven: Contemporary Poetry by People of Faith*. Wheaton: Shaw, 1994. Print.

Translation

Dante Alighieri. *Inferno: A New Verse Translation.* Trans. Michael Palma. New York: Norton, 2002. Print.

Introduction, Preface, Foreword, or Afterword

Lapham, Lewis. Introduction. *Understanding Media: The Extensions of Man*. By Marshall McLuhan. Cambridge: MIT P, 1994. vi–x. Print.

Thwaite, Anthony. Preface. *Contemporary Poets*. Ed. Thomas Riggs. 6th ed. New York: St. James, 1996. vii–viii. Print.

Work in an Anthology

Rodriguez, Richard. "Aria: A Memoir of a Bilingual Childhood." *The Best American Essays of the Century*. Ed. Robert Atwan and Joyce Carol Oates. Boston: Houghton, 2001. 447–66. Print. Best American Ser.

Translation in an Anthology

Neruda, Pablo. "We Are Many." Trans. Alastair Reid. *Literature: An Introduction to Fiction, Poetry, Drama, and Writing*. Ed. X. J. Kennedy and Dana Gioia. 12th ed. New York: Pearson, 2013. 966. Print.

Multivolume Work

Wellek, René. *A History of Modern Criticism, 1750–1950.* 8 vols. New Haven: Yale UP, 1955–92. Print.

One Volume of a Multivolume Work

Wellek, René. *A History of Modern Criticism, 1750–1950.* Vol. 7. New Haven: Yale UP, 1991. Print.

Book in a Series

Ross, William T. *Weldon Kees.* Boston: Twayne, 1985. Print. Twayne's US Authors Ser. 484.

Republished Book

Ellison, Ralph. *Invisible Man.* 1952. New York: Vintage, 1995. Print.

Revised or Subsequent Edition

Janouch, Gustav. *Conversations with Kafka.* Trans. Goronwy Rees. Rev. ed. New York: New Directions, 1971. Print.

Reference Books

Signed Article in a Reference Book

Cavoto, Janice E. "Harper Lee's *To Kill a Mockingbird.*" *The Oxford Encyclopedia of American Literature.* Ed. Jay Parini. Vol. 2. New York: Oxford UP, 2004. 418–21. Print.

Unsigned Encyclopedia Article—Standard Reference Book

"James Dickey." *The New Encyclopaedia Britannica: Micropaedia.* 15th ed. 1987. Print.

Dictionary Entry

"Design." *Merriam-Webster's Collegiate Dictionary.* 11th ed. 2003. Print.

Periodicals

Journal

Salter, Mary Jo. "The Heart Is Slow to Learn." *New Criterion* 10.8 (1992): 23–29. Print.

Signed Magazine Article

Gioia, Dana. "Studying with Miss Bishop." *New Yorker* 5 Sept. 1986: 90–101. Print.

Unsigned Magazine Article

"The Real Test." *New Republic* 5 Feb. 2001: 7. Print.

Newspaper Article

Lyall, Sarah. "In Poetry, Ted Hughes Breaks His Silence on Sylvia Plath." *New York Times* 19 Jan. 1998, natl. ed.: A1+. Print.

Signed Book Review

Fugard, Lisa. "Divided We Love." Rev. of *Unaccustomed Earth*, by Jhumpa Lahiri. *Los Angeles Times* 30 Mar. 2008: R1. Print.

Unsigned, Untitled Book Review

Rev. of *Otherwise: New and Selected Poems*, by Jane Kenyon. *Virginia Quarterly Review* 72 (1996): 136. Print.

WEB PUBLICATIONS

Website

Liu, Alan, dir. Home Page. *Voice of the Shuttle*. Dept. of English, U of California, Santa Barbara, n.d. Web. 17 Oct. 2011.

Document on a Website

"A Hughes Timeline." *PBS Online*. Public Broadcasting Service, 2001. Web. 20 Sept. 2011.

"Wallace Stevens." *Poets.org*. Academy of American Poets, n.d. Web. 20 Sept. 2011.

Online Reference Database

"Brooks, Gwendolyn." *Encyclopaedia Britannica Online*. Encyclopaedia Britannica, 2011. Web. 15 Feb. 2011.

Entire Online Book, Previously Appeared in Print

Jewett, Sarah Orne. *The Country of the Pointed Firs*. 1896. *Project Gutenberg*, 8 July 2008. Web. 10 Oct. 2011.

Article in an Online Newspaper

Atwood, Margaret. "The Writer: A New Canadian Life-Form." *New York Times*. New York Times, 18 May 1997. Web. 20 Aug. 2008.

Article in an Online Magazine

Garner, Dwight. "Jamaica Kincaid: The *Salon* Interview." *Salon*. Salon Media Group, 13 Jan. 1996. Web. 15 Feb. 2011.

Article in an Online Scholarly Journal

Carter, Sarah. "From the Ridiculous to the Sublime: Ovidian and Neoplatonic Registers in *A Midsummer Night's Dream." Early Modern Literary Studies* 12.1 (2006): 1–31. Web. 18 Jan. 2011.

Article from a Scholarly Journal, Part of an Archival Online Database

Finch, Annie. "My Father Dickinson: On Poetic Influence." *Emily Dickinson Journal* 17.2 (2008): 24–38. *Project Muse*. Web. 18 Jan. 2011.

Article Accessed via a Library Subscription Service

Seitler, Dana. "Unnatural Selection: Mothers, Eugenic Feminism, and Charlotte Perkins Gilman's Regeneration Narratives." *American Quarterly* 55.1 (2003): 61–87. *ProQuest*. Web. 7 July 2011.

Online Blog

Gioia, Ted. *"The Road* by Cormac McCarthy." *The New Canon: The Best in Fiction Since 1985*. N.p., n.d. Web. 11 May 2011.

Vellala, Rob. "Gilman: No Trouble to Anyone." *The American Literary Blog*. N.p., 10 Sept. 2010. Web. 23 Feb. 2011.

Photograph or Painting Accessed Online

Alice Walker, Miami Book Fair International, 1989. Wikimedia Commons. Wikimedia Foundation, 22 Jan. 2009. Web. 11 May 2011.

Bruegel, Pieter, *Landscape with the Fall of Icarus*. 1558. Musées Royaux des Beaux-Arts de Belgique, Brussels. *ibiblio.org*. Center for the Public Domain and UNC-CH. Web. 21 Nov. 2011.

Video Accessed Online

Ozymandias: Percy Bysshe Shelley. YouTube. E-Verse Radio, 13 Mar. 2007. Web. 21 January 2011. <http://www.youtube.com/watch?v=6xGa-fNSHaM>.

CD-ROM REFERENCE WORKS

CD-ROM Publication

"Appall." *The Oxford English Dictionary*. 2nd ed. Oxford: Oxford UP, 1992. CD-ROM.

Periodically Published Information, Collected on CD-ROM

Kakutani, Michiko. "Slogging Surreally in the Vietnamese Jungle." Rev. of *The Things They Carried*, by Tim O'Brien. *New York Times* 6 Mar. 1990: C6. CD-ROM. *New York Times Ondisc*. UMI-ProQuest. Oct. 1993.

MISCELLANEOUS SOURCES

Compact Disc (CD)

Shakespeare, William. *The Complete Arkangel Shakespeare: 38 Fully-Dramatized Plays*. Narr. Eileen Atkins and John Gielgud. Read by Imogen Stubbs, Joseph Fiennes, et al. Audio Partners, 2003. CD.

Audiocassette

Roethke, Theodore. *Theodore Roethke Reads His Poetry*. Caedmon, 1972. Audiocassette.

Videocassette

Henry V. By William Shakespeare. Dir. Laurence Olivier. Perf. Laurence Olivier. Two Cities Films. 1944. Paramount, 1988. Videocassette.

DVD

Hamlet. By William Shakespeare. Perf. Laurence Olivier, Eileen Herlie, and Basil Sydney. Two Cities Films. 1948. Criterion, 2000. DVD.

Film

Hamlet. By William Shakespeare. Dir. Franco Zeffirelli. Perf. Mel Gibson, Glenn Close, Helena Bonham Carter, Alan Bates, and Paul Scofield. Warner, 1991. Film.

Television or Radio Program

Moby Dick. By Herman Melville. Dir. Franc Roddam. Perf. Patrick Stewart and Gregory Peck. 2 episodes. USA Network. 16–17 Mar. 1998. Television.

46 WRITING AS DISCOVERY: KEEPING A JOURNAL

I have all my life regretted
that I did not keep a regular journal.

—SIR WALTER SCOTT

The novelist E. M. Forster once remarked, "How do I know what I think until I see what I say?" Few writers know precisely what they are going to say before they begin. Writing isn't simply a way to communicate ideas; it is also a way to formulate them, to try out new thoughts and hash them through. It is also a wonderful way to explore ideas that may eventually grow into longer pieces of formal writing.

THE REWARDS OF KEEPING A JOURNAL

Many instructors ask students to respond to reading in a journal—a day-to-day account of what they read and how they react to it. One great advantage of a journal is that it allows you to express your thoughts and feelings immediately, in your own words, before they grow cold. You can set down all your miscellaneous reactions to the reading, whether or not they fit into a paper topic. (If you have to write a paper later on, your journal just might suggest topics galore.) Journals are a useful place for collecting impressions, working through your ideas, and trying out false starts until you find the one that leads to someplace interesting for both you and your reader.

Journals can be useful study tools, too. If your course includes a midterm or final examination, you may well find that rereading your journal will help you to remember details of the works you read earlier in the term.

While some instructors give directives for journal entries, assigning essay questions or particular topics to address, others will give a more open-ended assignment, asking only that students respond in a way that shows they are interacting with the material. Either way, to get the most out of the experience, you might consider a few tips:

- **Capture your first reaction.** Read with pen in hand, jotting down anything you wish to remember. Write about anything that catches your attention or defies your interpretation. Does a line of dialogue surprise you? Make a note of it. Does a particular sentence seem significant? Comment on it. Does something in the story not make sense? Record your bewilderment. Better still, try to push past it into understanding. If you're at first puzzled by a character's motivation or by a line of poetry that resists interpretation, try to work through your puzzlement. A snippet from a journal entry on Denise Levertov's poem "Ancient Stairway" (see page 870) might be as unprocessed as this:

> What does this poem mean? I'm on the first line, and I'm already confused. What does she mean by the line "Footsteps like water hollow?" How can water be hollow? Oh, wait . . . maybe hollow really goes with the line after it . . . so the footsteps hollow the "broad curves of stone" which I guess means the steps. But why didn't she break the lines to make the poem easier to read, I wonder. Why not break the line after water instead of hollow? But I like how the next line is just two words "ascending, descending." I guess this means the stairs go both ways like all stairs.

Writing as you read can help you to begin to get a handle on difficult passages. It can also focus your mind. If your thoughts tend to meander away from the pages before you, or if you find yourself tempted to skim instead of paying close attention, writing in your journal can keep you involved and alert.

- **Just get it down.** In keeping a journal, you are writing primarily for yourself. You aren't obliged to polish your prose. It isn't necessary to develop your ideas. Just jot them down. Your aim is to store information without delay, to record your observations and impressions. Although your instructor may read your journal, he or she is unlikely to be looking there for fully processed ideas; those will come in more formal pieces of writing. Your teacher will most likely be reading your journal to ascertain that you are thinking your way through the work and the issues it raises. To be safe, though, ask your professor how formal or informal the journal needs to be.
- **Get personal.** Your journal is a place in which to sound off and express gut reactions. Don't just copy your class notes into it. Don't simply record plot details: first X happened, then Y happened, then Z. Instead, note your own emotional responses to a piece of literature, and consider what about the work is causing you to react. Your first reactions can provide a jumping-off point for further exploration.
- **Keep writing after you've said it all.** You may think you've said everything you have to say after you've written for five minutes or covered half a page. Keep writing, working quickly, without agonizing over where your words are taking you. Sometimes when we write beyond the point where we'd rather stop, we surprise ourselves with new ideas and insights. This is why many instructors will assign a certain length to journal entries or ask students to write for a particular amount of time.
- **Read closely.** It can be tempting to paint your journal entries with a broad brush, writing about a poem's central theme or a story's plot. Don't forget the value of reading closely. Examine a paragraph, or a sentence, or even a particularly significant word. Like our DNA, which encodes genetic information about our whole selves, sometimes a small part of a poem, story, or play can reveal much about the work as a whole.
- **Stick with the text.** A moment in a story might remind you of something in your own past. Connie's encounter with Arnold Friend in "Where Are You Going, Where Have You Been?," for example, may cause you to hearken back to your own brush with a creepy character. It might be tempting to leave the story behind and write about your own experience, but doing so won't teach you much about the story. You will learn more by giving the literary work itself your full attention.

- **Try out risky ideas.** A journal is no place to play it safe. Try for new insights—go out on a limb. You can try on new ideas and discard the ones that don't fit. By taking some risks, you may come up with a more provocative thesis than you otherwise would have, one that eventually will lead you to write a more dynamic term paper.
- **Follow your interests.** If you aren't given a specific topic to treat in your journal, attack the aspects of a literary work that most intrigue you. This will make your journaling more interesting—both for you and for your reader. If you should find yourself stumped, you can always turn to any of the "Topics for Writing" that appear at the end of the chapter in which your subject appears. These can provide a good starting point for a journal entry.
- **Write often.** Journals are useful only if you keep them up to date. Jot down your insights while you still have a story, poem, or play freshly in mind. Fall weeks behind, and you will have to grind out a journal from scratch, the night before it is due, and the whole project will decay into meaningless drudgery. Instead, if you faithfully do a little reading and writing every day or so, you will find yourself keeping track of the life of your mind. You will have a lively record not only of the literature you have read, but also of your personal involvement with it.

SAMPLE JOURNAL ENTRY

The following journal entry was written by Virginia Andros, a student at Saint Joseph's University in Philadelphia. Her subject was the opening of T. S. Eliot's "The Love Song of J. Alfred Prufrock," which can be found on page 1038. She wrote these entries in longhand, in a notebook. (Some instructors will accept journals composed on and printed out from a computer; if unsure, have your professor clarify his or her preference.)

"Prufrock" Reflections

This poem begins with six lines written in a language I don't speak, Spanish, maybe, or Italian. I'm going to ignore those lines for now—they don't seem to be part of the poem itself. For now I'll worry about the actual poem. I like the first line: "Let us go then, you and I" because it feels like an invitation—like the lines are being spoken directly to me. I can picture the speaker stretching out his hand for me. The next lines are strange, though: "When the evening is spread out against the sky / Like a patient etherized upon a table." The part about the sky is beautiful, but the image that follows it is creepy. Already I'm wondering what kind of trip this is going to be, and if I should trust my guide.

So where are we going? We're traveling "through certain half-deserted streets" to get to "one-night cheap hotels / And sawdust restaurants with oyster-shells." What's a sawdust restaurant? Maybe the food tastes like sawdust? Or maybe the place is messy, with sawdust on the floor. It's interesting that the poem mentions "oyster shells" and not the oysters themselves. It's like we're concentrating on the garbage left over after the meal is done. The phrase "muttering retreats" is odd too

. . . again, it sounds pretty negative. What's muttering? A crowd of people in the hotel lobby or the restaurant? They're not laughing or having pleasant conversation. The word "muttering" even sounds nasty . . . as though the people are complaining under their breath about the bad décor and lousy service.

Here's the next two lines. "Streets that follow like a tedious argument / Of insidious intent." How can streets be like a tedious argument? Confusion! But I picture cramped streets, in the center of a city. Maybe one leads to the next, which leads to the next, and the next . . . the way in a tedious argument one line of reasoning leads you to the next and pretty soon you've forgotten what you were arguing about in the first place, because you're bickering about something else entirely. I had to look up "insidious": it means slowly destructive. Is it the streets that have insidious intent, or the argument? I think maybe it's the argument . . . but maybe the streets do too in some way. The streets are slowly destructive? To whom? Okay, my head's starting to hurt. Maybe the streets are destructive to me, the person the speaker is speaking to.

Now the speaker talks to me (or at least to someone) directly again: "Oh, do not ask, 'What is it?' / Let us go and make our visit." I like these lines! I notice that they rhyme, so now I'm looking back to see if the other lines I've already read do too. Some do, but I hadn't noticed. Anyway, these lines make me wonder, who is the speaker? Is it J. Alfred Prufrock? And how is this a love poem? Maybe the "you" in the poem is a girlfriend? If so, this isn't much of a date.

New stanza: "In the room the women come and go / Talking of Michelangelo." Maybe we're in a museum?

Here comes more description of a sad, dirty city. The fog is "yellow" and there's chimney soot. If I'm right, and the speaker is taking his girlfriend around the city, he's sort of a loser. Why isn't he taking her someplace beautiful . . . to a nice restaurant, or out dancing? Why is he making her walk down a dirty street? Why is this poem so unromantic? If I were the girlfriend, there wouldn't be a second date.

This journal entry examines its subject closely, using key words and phrases to begin to get at the poem's meaning. Its author freely admits her confusion over certain challenging lines, but isn't content to rest on first impressions. By puzzling her way line by line through part of the poem, she begins to get at issues central to the entire poem: its speaker, its tone, its form, and its literal meaning. Doing your thinking on the page can be a crucial step in the writing—and reading—process. Even if keeping a journal isn't one of your course assignments, you might profitably apply these techniques to taking notes as you read through a poem, short story, or play. When it comes time to write a more formal paper, you're likely to be glad you've been actively thinking the material through all along.

47 WRITING AN ESSAY EXAM

The test of literature is, I suppose,
whether we ourselves live more intensely for the reading of it.

—ELIZABETH DREW

Why might an instructor choose to give an essay examination? It may sometimes seem like sheer sadism, but there are good reasons for using essays to test your knowledge of a subject. Longer, more involved answers can reveal not just how well you have memorized course material but also how thoroughly you have processed it. An essay exam allows you to demonstrate that you can think critically about the literature you have read and the issues your reading has raised. It lets you show how well you can marshal evidence to support your assertions. It also gives you a chance to draw connections between the literary works you have read and the main themes of the course.

Whether your exam is take-home or in-class, open-book or closed, the following strategies will help you to show off what you know:

- **Be prepared.** Before you take the exam, review the readings. If you have been highlighting and annotating all semester, you will find yourself well rewarded for that extra bit of effort. A glance at highlighted portions of text can help refresh your memory about passages in a text that struck you as particularly important; your marginalia can help you to recall why that was the case.
- **Review your notes.** It is also a good idea to review any notes you have taken for the course. If you kept a reading journal, go back and reread it. (You will be surprised how many specific memories rereading your journal will trigger.) Even if you are permitted to use your books during the exam, reacquainting yourself with the material beforehand can help you better recall what it is you are looking for in those open books.

  As you review, be sure to think about the big picture. How do the literary works you have read relate to each other? If you have been reading theory and criticism, how might it apply to the course's content? If you have been given historical background about the period in which a work was written, how does the work embody its author's time? Sometimes it might help just to write down a few of the central ideas the course has explored on a separate sheet of paper—to summarize a few of the major insights the course has offered.

- **Think it through.** Once you have been given the exam, be sure to read it all the way through before you begin writing. Figure out how much time you can afford to spend per section. Pay attention to how many points each question is worth; you may well want to budget your time accordingly. Leave yourself time to proofread your responses and add any missing information.

  When you are ready to start, you might find it helpful first to attack questions about which you feel more confident. Go ahead, but save enough time to tackle the tougher ones as well.

- **Read the questions carefully.** To ensure that you are answering the actual questions you have been asked, pay special attention to words in the directions that seem important. Verbs such as "analyze," "summarize," "explicate," "compare," "contrast," "evaluate," "interpret," and "explain" give clues to what your focus should be. Highlight or underline these action words so that you can more readily keep them in mind as you write. Understanding what you are being asked to do is crucial. Failing to follow directions might lose you precious points, no matter how brilliantly you write on your subject.

  Careful reading and highlighting can also help you remember to address all parts of any given question. Don't get so caught up in answering one part of a question that you neglect the other parts.

- **Understand your purpose.** Whenever you write, it pays to consider your audience and your purpose. Inevitably, the audience for an essay exam response will be your instructor. It's likely that he or she will be looking to see whether you have understood the material on which you are being tested. As you consider the questions you are about to answer, think back to concepts stressed by the instructor during in-class discussions. Try to touch on these concepts as you write, as long as you can do so without losing your focus. Also, since your instructor is familiar with the literary work under discussion, there's no need to relate the whole story in your exam response. Unless you are specifically asked to summarize, don't give any more plot details than are needed to accomplish the assigned task.

  For clues about what your purpose should be, pay attention to those action words you have highlighted in the directions. Here are some common ones:

Analyze	Consider how a single element of the text contributes to its full meaning or effect.
Compare	Explore how two or more things resemble each other.
Contrast	Explore how two or more things differ from each other.
Evaluate	Examine a work with the purpose of determining its quality or importance.
Explain	Clarify a concept.
Explicate	Explain a brief work or a passage from a longer work in detail to show how its parts contribute to the work as a whole.
Interpret	Express a literary work's meaning in your own words.
Paraphrase	Restate a passage in your own words.
Prove	Provide evidence of the truth of a claim, drawing on information from the literary work under study.
Relate	Show a connection between two or more items.
Summarize	Give a shortened version of a literary work, touching on key points.

- **Plan before you write. Start with a clear thesis that accurately addresses the exam question.** A critical step in writing a good essay exam is creating a thesis sentence that succinctly expresses your main point. Using the exam question to provide direction for your thesis, come up with a statement that is both decisive and specific.

  For example, if you have been asked to describe the grandmother's transformation in Flannery O'Connor's "A Good Man Is Hard to Find," your thesis should say something specific about *how* or *why* she gains insight in her last moments of life. The first thesis below does not address the assignment—it describes the grandmother, not the grandmother's transformation. It is accurate but incomplete since it does not lead anywhere useful.

  IRRELEVANT THESIS
  The grandmother in "A Good Man Is Hard to Find" is self-centered and silly.

  The rough thesis that follows sticks with the merely obvious.

  ROUGH THESIS
  The grandmother in "A Good Man Is Hard to Find" is a silly, self-centered woman who undergoes a transformation at the end of the story.

  The revised thesis makes a more decisive statement, providing specifics about what happens at the story's climax.

  REVISED THESIS
  In "A Good Man Is Hard to Find," the grandmother is transformed from a silly, self-centered woman into a wiser, more caring one.

  A final revision goes further, venturing to say not only what happens in the story but why it happens. It provides a good road map for writing an essay exam.

  FINAL THESIS
  In "A Good Man Is Hard to Find," the grandmother is transformed by her proximity to death from a silly, self-centered woman into a wiser, more caring one.

- **Create a rough outline.** Though an essay question might seem like an occasion for off-the-cuff writing, it's a good idea to sketch a rough outline before you plunge in. As you write, follow the outline point by point. An outline for an essay response based on the final thesis above might look something like this:

  1. Grandmother transformed by closeness to death
  2. Starts out silly
     Lives in the past
     Gets directions wrong
  3. Becomes wiser
     Sees her mistakes
     Sees her connection to the Misfit

4. Starts out self-centered
   Smuggles cat on trip
   Makes family drive out of way
5. Becomes caring
   Reaches out to Misfit
   Sees him as her own child
6. Nearness to death
   Hears her son get shot
   Misfit's quotation

- **Make it shapely.** Like a more formal piece of writing, your answer will need an introduction that establishes the point you will be making. It also should include a conclusion that summarizes your argument (preferably without too much bald-faced restatement) and reinforces your thesis. The paragraphs in between should be used to flesh out your argument.
- **Give evidence.** Back up your thesis, and any assertion you make along the way, with proof from the story, poem, or play you are discussing. Direct quotations generally make the most convincing evidence, but if you are working from memory, you can do the job with references to the text. To make your argument more convincing and establish how familiar you are with the material, be as specific as you can manage.
- **Keep your focus.** As you write, refer frequently to your outline. Be sure to keep your argument on track. Don't ramble or repeat yourself to fill up space; to do so will give the impression that you are uncertain about your response or the material.
- **Make smooth transitions.** Use transitional words and phrases to connect each new idea to the one that precedes it. These handy tools can signal your intentions. If your argument is changing directions, you might signal as much with words and phrases such as "in contrast," "on the other hand," "however," "yet," or "conversely." If you are continuing along the same track you've been traveling, try "in addition," "similarly," "furthermore," or "moreover." To indicate cause and effect, you might use "because," "therefore," "as a result," or "consequently." If you make it easy for your reader to follow your train of thought, the end result is likely to be a grateful reader.
- **Pay attention to detail.** Be sure to proofread your essay before handing it in. Nothing undermines a writer's authority faster than spelling mistakes and grammatical errors. Even illegible handwriting can try a reader's patience—never a good idea when a grade is involved.

CHECKLIST: Taking an Essay Exam

Exam Preparation

- ☐ Skim the literary works that will be on the exam.
- ☐ Reread all your notes and, if you have kept one, your reader's journal.
- ☐ Consider how the literary works on the exam relate to each other.
- ☐ Consider possible relationships between the literary works and any literary criticism, theory, or historical background you have been given in the course.

Taking the Exam

- ☐ When you are given the exam, quickly read it all the way through.
- ☐ Calculate how much time you can spend per question.
- ☐ Read each essay question carefully, underlining key words. Take note of multipart questions.
- ☐ Understand your purpose before you begin.
- ☐ Write a thesis sentence that accurately answers the exam question.
- ☐ Sketch an outline for the essay response.
- ☐ Include an introductory paragraph and a conclusion.
- ☐ Back up each point you make with evidence from the text.
- ☐ Don't give plot summaries unless asked to.
- ☐ Use transitional phrases to link paragraphs and ideas.
- ☐ Proofread your exam before handing it in.

PRACTICE ESSAY EXAM

The purpose of an essay exam is to test your ability to read and to effectively discuss a literary work in writing. A well-constructed exam response reveals both how well you read and interpret a work and how capably you organize and present your argument. An exam essay will not be as carefully prepared or polished as a paper you write and revise at home, but it still needs to be clear, intelligent, well-structured, and accurately based on the assigned text.

If you have never done an essay exam before, it will help to try your hand at a practice test. Following is a celebrated story by Toni Cade Bambara, along with a typical essay exam question. If you invest 45 minutes in writing a response to this sample question, you will find your actual essay exam far less intimidating.

Practice Essay Exam Question

Write a short essay on the main theme of Toni Cade Bambara's "The Lesson." In your interpretation, discuss the theme in relation to the story's narrator, main characters, setting, tone, style, and title. Demonstrate how each of these elements contributes to the effective communication of the theme. Provide specific examples to support your analysis.

Toni Cade Bambara

The Lesson

1972

Toni Cade Bambara (1939–1995), author, teacher, and civil rights activist, was born Miltona Cade in New York, and legally added her new last name in 1970. She grew up in Harlem and in the troubled Bedford-Stuyvesant section of Brooklyn. After taking her master's degree at City College, she worked for the New York State Welfare Department as a case investigator. Later she set out to learn dance and filmmaking; she studied commedia dell'arte in Florence and mime in Paris. After her fiction began to make her well known, she accepted invitations to teach at Duke, Stephens, Emory, Spelman College, and Rutgers University. Bambara's works of fiction are Gorilla, My Love *(1972), which contains the story "The Lesson,"* The Sea Birds Are Still Alive *(1977),* The Salt Eaters *(1980), and* Those Bones Are Not My Child *(edited by Toni Morrison and posthumously published in 1999). She conducted workshops on writing and community organization at museums, prisons, libraries, colleges, and community centers, as well as recreation programs for psychiatric patients at New York City's Metropolitan Hospital. As a storyteller, Bambara devoted herself to correcting stereotypes of African Americans. In her 1984 critical essay "Salvation Is the Issue," Bambara articulated her purpose in writing: "Stories are important. They keep us alive. . . . We, the hero of the tales. Our lives preserved. How it was; how it be. Passing it along in the relay. That is what I work to do: to produce stories that save our lives." Bambara never becomes ponderous or tedious in this quest, but relies on humor to convey her message: "What I enjoy most in my work is the laughter and the outrage and the attention to language." "I come from a family of very gifted laughers." She also wrote screenplays and edited two anthologies of African American literature,* The Black Woman *(1970) and* Tales and Stories for Black Folks *(1971). She died of cancer in 1995.*

Back in the days when everyone was old and stupid or young and foolish and me and Sugar were the only ones just right, this lady moved on our block with nappy hair and proper speech and no makeup. And quite naturally we laughed at her, laughed the way we did at the junk man who went about his business like he was some big-time president and his sorry-ass horse his secretary. And we kinda hated her too, hated the way we did the winos who cluttered up our parks and pissed on our handball walls and stank up our hallways and stairs so you couldn't halfway play hide-and-seek without a goddamn gas mask. Miss Moore was her name. The only woman on the block with no first name. And she was black as hell, cept for her feet, which were fish-white and spooky. And she was always planning these boring-ass things for us to do, us being my cousin, mostly, who lived on the block cause we all moved North the same time and to the same apartment then spread out gradual to breathe. And our parents would yank our heads into some kinda shape and crisp up our clothes so we'd be presentable for travel with Miss Moore, who always looked like she was going to church, though she never did. Which is just one of the things the grownups talked about when they talked behind her back like a dog. But when she came calling with some sachet she'd sewed up or some gingerbread she'd made or some book, why then they'd all be too embarrassed to turn her down and we'd get handed over all spruced up. She'd been to college and said it was only right that she should take responsibility for the young ones' education, and she not even related by marriage or blood. So they'd go for it. Specially Aunt Gretchen. She was the main gofer in the family. You got some ole dumb shit foolishness you want somebody to go for, you send for Aunt Gretchen. She been screwed into the go-along for so long, it's a blood-deep natural thing with her. Which is how she got saddled with me and Sugar and Junior in the first place while our mothers were in a la-de-da apartment up the block having a good ole time.

So this one day Miss Moore rounds us all up at the mailbox and it's puredee° hot and she's knockin herself out about arithmetic. And school suppose to let up in summer I heard, but she don't never let up. And the starch in my pinafore scratching the shit outta me and I'm really hating this nappy-head bitch and her goddamn college degree. I'd much rather go to the pool or to the show where it's cool. So me and Sugar leaning on the mailbox being surly, which is a Miss Moore word. And Flyboy checking out what everybody brought for lunch. And Fat Butt already wasting his peanut-butter-and-jelly sandwich like the pig he is. And Junebug punchin on Q.T.'s arm for potato chips. And Rosie Giraffe shifting from one hip to the other waiting for somebody to step on her foot or ask her if she from Georgia so she can kick ass, preferably Mercedes'. And Miss Moore asking us do we know what money is, like we a bunch of retards. I mean real money, she say, like it's only poker chips or Monopoly papers we lay on the grocer. So right away I'm tired of this and say so. And would much rather snatch Sugar and go to the Sunset and terrorize the West Indian kids and take their hair ribbons and their money too. And Miss Moore files that remark away for next week's lesson on brotherhood, I can tell. And finally I say we oughta get to the subway cause it's cooler and besides we might meet some cute boys. Sugar done swiped her mama's lipstick, so we ready.

So we heading down the street and she's boring us silly about what things cost and what our parents make and how much goes for rent and how money ain't divided up right in this country. And then she gets to the part about we all poor and live in the slums, which I don't feature. And I'm ready to speak on that, but she steps out in the street and hails two cabs just like that. Then she hustles half the crew in with her and hands me a five-dollar bill and tells me to calculate 10 percent tip for the driver. And we're off. Me and Sugar and Junebug and Flyboy hangin out the window and hollering to everybody, putting lipstick on each other cause Flyboy a faggot anyway, and making farts with our sweaty armpits. But I'm mostly trying to figure how to spend this money. But they all fascinated with the meter ticking and Junebug starts laying bets as to how much it'll read when Flyboy can't hold his breath no more. Then Sugar lays bets as to how much it'll be when we get there. So I'm stuck. Don't nobody want to go for my plan, which is to jump out at the next light and run off to the first bar-b-que we can find. Then the driver tells us to get the hell out cause we there already. And the meter reads eighty-five cents. And I'm stalling to figure out the tip and Sugar say give him a dime. And I decide he don't need it bad as I do, so later for him. But then he tries to take off with Junebug foot still in the door so we talk about his mama something ferocious. Then we check out that we on Fifth Avenue and everybody dressed up in stockings. One lady in a fur coat, hot as it is. White folks crazy.

"This is the place," Miss Moore say, presenting it to us in the voice she uses at the museum. "Let's look in the windows before we go in."

5 "Can we steal?" Sugar asks very serious like she's getting the ground rules squared away before she plays. "I beg your pardon," say Miss Moore, and we fall out. So she leads us around the windows of the toy store and me and Sugar screamin, "This is mine, that's mine, I gotta have that, that was made for me, I was born for that," till Big Butt drowns us out.

"Hey, I'm going to buy that there."

"That there? You don't even know what it is, stupid."

puredee: pretty.

"I do so," he say punchin on Rosie Giraffe. "It's a microscope."

"Whatcha gonna do with a microscope, fool?"

"Look at things." 10

"Like what, Ronald?" ask Miss Moore. And Big Butt ain't got the first notion. So here go Miss Moore gabbing about the thousands of bacteria in a drop of water and the somethinorother in a speck of blood and the million and one living things in the air around us is invisible to the naked eye. And what she say that for? Junebug go to town on that "naked" and we rolling. Then Miss Moore ask what it cost. So we all jam into the window smudgin it up and the price tag say $300. So then she ask how long'd take for Big Butt and Junebug to save up their allowances. "Too long," I say. "Yeh," adds Sugar, "outgrown it by that time." And Miss Moore say no, you never outgrow learning instruments. "Why, even medical students and interns and," blah, blah, blah. And we ready to choke Big Butt for bringing it up in the first damn place.

"This here costs four hundred eighty dollars," say Rosie Giraffe. So we pile up all over her to see what she pointin out. My eyes tell me it's a chunk of glass cracked with something heavy, and different-color inks dripped into the splits, then the whole thing put into a oven or something. But for $480 it don't make sense.

"That's a paperweight made of semi-precious stones fused together under tremendous pressure," she explains slowly, with her hands doing the mining and all the factory work.

"So what's a paperweight?" asks Rosie Giraffe.

"To weigh paper with, dumbbell," say Flyboy, the wise man from the East. 15

"Not exactly," say Miss Moore, which is what she say when you warm or way off too. "It's to weigh paper down so it won't scatter and make your desk untidy." So right away me and Sugar curtsy to each other and then to Mercedes who is more the tidy type.

"We don't keep paper on top of the desk in my class," say Junebug, figuring Miss Moore crazy or lyin one.

"At home, then," she say. "Don't you have a calendar and a pencil case and a blotter and a letter-opener on your desk at home where you do your homework?" And she know damn well what our homes look like cause she nosys around in them every chance she gets.

"I don't even have a desk," say Junebug. "Do we?"

"No. And I don't get no homework neither," say Big Butt. 20

"And I don't even have a home," say Flyboy like he do at school to keep the white folks off his back and sorry for him. Send this poor kid to camp posters, is his specialty.

"I do," says Mercedes. "I have a box of stationery on my desk and a picture of my cat. My godmother bought the stationery and the desk. There's a big rose on each sheet and the envelopes smell like roses."

"Who wants to know about your smelly-ass stationery," say Rosie Giraffe fore I can get my two cents in.

"It's important to have a work area all your own so that . . ."

"Will you look at this sailboat, please," say Flyboy, cuttin her off and pointin to the thing like it was his. So once again we tumble all over each other to gaze at this magnificent thing in the toy store which is just big enough to maybe sail two kittens across the pond if you strap them to the posts tight. We all start reciting the price tag like we in assembly. "Handcrafted sailboat of fiberglass at one thousand one hundred ninety-five dollars." 25

"Unbelievable," I hear myself say and am really stunned. I read it again for myself just in case the group recitation put me in a trance. Same thing. For some reason this pisses me off. We look at Miss Moore and she lookin at us, waiting for I dunno what.

"Who'd pay all that when you can buy a sailboat set for a quarter at Pop's, a tube of glue for a dime, and a ball of string for eight cents? It must have a motor and a whole lot else besides," I say. "My sailboat cost me about fifty cents."

"But will it take water?" say Mercedes with her smart ass.

"Took mine to Alley Pond Park once," say Flyboy. "String broke. Lost it. Pity."

"Sailed mine in Central Park and it keeled over and sank. Had to ask my father for another dollar."

"And you got the strap," laugh Big Butt. "The jerk didn't even have a string on it. My old man wailed on his behind."

Little Q.T. was staring hard at the sailboat and you could see he wanted it bad. But he too little and somebody'd just take it from him. So what the hell. "This boat for kids, Miss Moore?"

"Parents silly to buy something like that just to get all broke up," say Rosie Giraffe.

"That much money it should last forever," I figure.

"My father'd buy it for me if I wanted it."

"Your father, my ass," say Rosie Giraffe getting a chance to finally push Mercedes.

"Must be rich people shop here," say Q.T.

"You are a very bright boy," say Flyboy. "What was your first clue?" And he rap him on the head with the back of his knuckles, since Q.T. the only one he could get away with. Though Q.T. liable to come up behind you years later and get his licks in when you half expect it.

"What I want to know is," I says to Miss Moore though I never talk to her, I wouldn't give the bitch that satisfaction, "is how much a real boat costs? I figure a thousand'd get you a yacht any day."

"Why don't you check that out," she says, "and report back to the group?" Which really pains my ass. If you gonna mess up a perfectly good swim day least you could do is have some answers. "Let's go in," she say like she got something up her sleeve. Only she don't lead the way. So me and Sugar turn the corner to where the entrance is, but when we get there I kinda hang back. Not that I'm scared, what's there to be afraid of, just a toy store. But I feel funny, shame. But what I got to be shamed about? Got as much right to go in as anybody. But somehow I can't seem to get hold of the door, so I step away for Sugar to lead. But she hangs back too. And I look at her and she looks at me and this is ridiculous. I mean, damn, I have never ever been shy about doing nothing or going nowhere. But then Mercedes steps up and then Rosie Giraffe and Big Butt crowd in behind and shove, and next thing we all stuffed into the doorway with only Mercedes squeezing past us, smoothing out her jumper and walking right down the aisle. Then the rest of us tumble in like a glued-together jigsaw done all wrong. And people lookin at us. And it's like the time me and Sugar crashed into the Catholic church on a dare. But once we got in there and everything so hushed and holy and the candles and the bowin and the handkerchiefs on all the drooping heads, I just couldn't go through with the plan. Which was for me to run up to the altar and do a tap dance while Sugar played the nose flute and messed around in the holy water. And Sugar kept givin me the elbow. Then later teased me so bad I tied her up in the shower and turned it on and locked her in. And she'd be there till this day if Aunt Gretchen hadn't finally figured I was lyin about the boarder takin a shower.

Same thing in the store. We all walkin on tiptoe and hardly touchin the games and puzzles and things. And I watched Miss Moore who is steady watchin us like she waitin for a sign. Like Mama Drewery watches the sky and sniffs the air and takes note of just how much slant is in the bird formation. Then me and Sugar bump smack into each other, so busy gazing at the toys, 'specially the sailboat. But we don't laugh and go into our fat-lady bump-stomach routine. We just stare at that price tag. Then Sugar run a finger over the whole boat. And I'm jealous and want to hit her. Maybe not her, but I sure want to punch somebody in the mouth.

"Whatcha bring us here for, Miss Moore?"

"You sound angry, Sylvia. Are you mad about something?" Givin me one of them grins like she tellin a grown-up joke that never turns out to be funny. And she's lookin very closely at me like maybe she plannin to do my portrait from memory. I'm mad, but I won't give her that satisfaction. So I slouch around the store bein very bored and say, "Let's go."

Me and Sugar at the back of the train watchin the tracks whizzin by large then small then gettin gobbled up in the dark. I'm thinking about this tricky toy I saw in the store. A clown that somersaults on a bar then does chin-ups just cause you yank lightly at his leg. Cost $35. I could see me askin my mother for a $35 birthday clown. "You wanna who that costs what?" she'd say, cocking her head to the side to get a better view of the hole in my head. Thirty-five dollars could buy new bunk beds for Junior and Gretchen's boy. Thirty-five dollars and the whole household could go visit Granddaddy Nelson in the country. Thirty-five dollars would pay for the rent and the piano bill too. Who are these people that spend that much for performing clowns and $1000 for toy sailboats? What kinda work they do and how they live and how come we ain't in on it? Where we are is who we are, Miss Moore always pointin out. But it don't necessarily have to be that way, she always adds then waits for somebody to say that poor people have to wake up and demand their share of the pie and don't none of us know what kind of pie she talking about in the first damn place. But she ain't so smart cause I still got her four dollars from the taxi and she sure ain't gettin it. Messin up my day with this shit. Sugar nudges me in my pocket and winks.

Miss Moore lines us up in front of the mailbox where we started from, seem like 45 years ago, and I got a headache for thinkin so hard. And we lean all over each other so we can hold up under the draggy-ass lecture she always finishes us off with at the end before we thank her for borin us to tears. But she just looks at us like she readin tea leaves. Finally she say, "Well, what did you think of F.A.O. Schwarz?"

Rosie Giraffe mumbles, "White folks crazy."

"I'd like to go there again when I get my birthday money," says Mercedes, and we shove her out the pack so she has to lean on the mailbox by herself.

"I'd like a shower. Tiring day," say Flyboy.

Then Sugar surprises me by sayin, "You know, Miss Moore, I don't think all of us here put together eat in a year what that sailboat costs." And Miss Moore lights up like somebody goosed her. "And?" she say, urging Sugar on. Only I'm standin on her foot so she don't continue.

"Imagine for a minute what kind of society it is in which some people can spend 50 on a toy what it would cost to feed a family of six or seven. What do you think?"

"I think," say Sugar pushing me off her feet like she never done before, cause I whip her ass in a minute, "that this is not much of a democracy if you ask me. Equal chance to pursue happiness means an equal crack at the dough, don't it?" Miss Moore is besides herself and I am disgusted with Sugar's treachery. So I stand on her foot one more time to see if she'll shove me. She shuts up, and Miss Moore looks at me, sorrowfully I'm thinkin. And somethin weird is goin on, I can feel it in my chest.

"Anybody else learn anything today?" lookin dead at me. I walk away and Sugar has to run to catch up and don't even seem to notice when I shrug her arm off my shoulder.

"Well, we got four dollars anyway," she says.

"Uh hunh."

"We could go to Hascombs and get half a chocolate layer and then go to the Sunset and still have plenty money for potato chips and ice-cream sodas."

"Uh hunh."

"Race you to Hascombs," she say.

We start down the block and she gets ahead which is O.K. by me cause I'm going to the West End and then over to the Drive to think this day through. She can run if she want to and even run faster. But ain't nobody gonna beat me at nuthin.

48 CRITICAL APPROACHES TO LITERATURE

Literary criticism should arise out of a debt of love.

—GEORGE STEINER

Literary criticism is not an abstract, intellectual exercise; it is a natural human response to literature. If a friend informs you she is reading a book you have just finished, it would be odd indeed if you did not begin swapping opinions. Literary criticism is nothing more than discourse—spoken or written—about literature. A student who sits quietly in a morning English class, intimidated by the notion of literary criticism, will spend an hour that evening talking animatedly about the meaning of rock lyrics or comparing the relative merits of the *Star Wars* trilogies. It is inevitable that people will ponder, discuss, and analyze the works of art that interest them.

The informal criticism of friends talking about literature tends to be casual, unorganized, and subjective. Since Aristotle, however, philosophers, scholars, and writers have tried to create more precise and disciplined ways of discussing literature. Literary critics have borrowed concepts from other disciplines, such as philosophy, history, linguistics, psychology, and anthropology, to analyze imaginative literature more perceptively. Some critics have found it useful to work in the abstract area of **literary theory**, criticism that tries to formulate general principles rather than discuss specific texts. Mass media critics, such as newspaper reviewers, usually spend their time evaluating works—telling us which books are worth reading, which plays not to bother seeing. But most serious literary criticism is not primarily evaluative; it assumes we know that *Othello* or *The Metamorphosis* is worth reading. Instead, such criticism is analytic; it tries to help us better understand a literary work.

In the following pages you will find overviews of ten critical approaches to literature. While these ten methods do not exhaust the total possibilities of literary criticism, they represent the most widely used contemporary approaches. Although presented separately, the approaches are not necessarily mutually exclusive; many critics mix methods to suit their needs and interests. For example, a historical critic may use formalist techniques to analyze a poem; a biographical critic will frequently use psychological theories to analyze an author. The summaries try neither to provide a history of each approach nor to present the latest trends in each school. Their purpose is to give you a practical introduction to each critical method and then provide representative examples of it. If one of these critical methods interests you, why not try to write a class paper using the approach?

FORMALIST CRITICISM

Formalist criticism regards literature as a unique form of human knowledge that needs to be examined on its own terms. "The natural and sensible starting point for work in literary scholarship," René Wellek and Austin Warren wrote in their influential *Theory of Literature*, "is the interpretation and analysis of the works of literature themselves." To a formalist, a poem or story is not primarily a social, historical, or biographical document; it is a literary work that can be understood only by reference to its intrinsic literary features—that is, those elements found in the text itself. To analyze a poem or story, therefore, the formalist critic focuses on the words of the text rather than facts about the author's life or the historical milieu in which the text was written. The critic pays special attention to the formal features of the text—the style, structure, imagery, tone, and genre. These features, however, are usually not examined in isolation, because formalist critics believe that what gives a literary text its special status as art is how all its elements work together to create the reader's total experience. As Robert Penn Warren commented, "Poetry does not inhere in any particular element but depends upon the set of relationships, the structure, which we call the poem."

A key method that formalists use to explore the intense relationships within a poem is **close reading,** a careful step-by-step analysis and explication of a text. The purpose of close reading is to understand how various elements in a literary text work together to shape its effects on the reader. Since formalists believe that the various stylistic and thematic elements of a literary work influence each other, these critics insist that form and content cannot be meaningfully separated. The complete interdependence of form and content is what makes a text literary. When we extract a work's theme or paraphrase its meaning, we destroy the aesthetic experience of the work.

When Robert Langbaum examines Robert Browning's "My Last Duchess," he uses several techniques of formalist criticism. First, he places the poem in relation to its literary form, the dramatic monologue. Second, he discusses the dramatic structure of the poem—why the duke tells his story, whom he addresses, and the physical circumstances in which he speaks. Third, Langbaum analyzes how the duke tells his story—his tone, his manner, even the order in which he makes his disclosures. Langbaum neither introduces facts about Browning's life into his analysis, nor relates the poem to the historical period or social conditions that produced it. He focuses on the text itself to explain how it produces a complex effect on the reader.

Cleanth Brooks (1906–1994)

The Formalist Critic 1951

Here are some articles of faith I could subscribe to:

That literary criticism is a description and an evaluation of its object.

That the primary concern of criticism is with the problem of unity—the kind of whole which the literary work forms or fails to form, and the relation of the various parts to each other in building up this whole.

That the formal relations in a work of literature may include, but certainly exceed, those of logic.

That in a successful work, form and content cannot be separated.

That form is meaning.

That literature is ultimately metaphorical and symbolic.

That the general and the universal are not seized upon by abstraction, but got at through the concrete and the particular.

That literature is not a surrogate for religion.

That, as Allen Tate says, "specific moral problems" are the subject matter of literature, but that the purpose of literature is not to point a moral.

That the principles of criticism define the area relevant to literary criticism; they do not constitute a method for carrying out the criticism.

• • •

The formalist critic knows as well as anyone that poems and plays and novels are written by men—that they do not somehow happen—and that they are written as expressions of particular personalities and are written from all sorts of motives—for money, from a desire to express oneself, for the sake of a cause, etc. Moreover, the formalist critic knows as well as anyone that literary works are merely potential until they are read—that is, that they are recreated in the minds of actual readers, who vary enormously in their capabilities, their interests, their prejudices, their ideas. But the formalist critic is concerned primarily with the work itself. Speculation on the mental processes of the author takes the critic away from the work into biography and psychology. There is no reason, of course, why he should not turn away into biography and psychology. Such explorations are very much worth making. But they should not be confused with an account of the work. Such studies describe the process of composition, not the structure of the thing composed, and they may be performed quite as validly for the poor work as for the good one. They may be validly performed for any kind of expression—non-literary as well as literary.

From "The Formalist Critic"

Michael Clark (b. 1946)

Light and Darkness in "Sonny's Blues" 1985

"Sonny's Blues" by James Baldwin is a sensitive story about the reconciliation of two brothers, but it is much more than that. It is, in addition, an examination of the importance of the black heritage and of the central importance of music in that heritage. Finally, the story probes the central role that art must play in human existence. To examine all of these facets of human existence is a rather formidable undertaking in a short story, even in a longish short story such as this one. Baldwin not only undertakes this task, but he does it superbly. One of the central ways that Baldwin fuses all of these complex elements is by using a metaphor of childhood, which is supported by ancillary images of light and darkness. He does the job so well that the story is a *tour de force*, a penetrating study of American culture.

• • •

Sonny's quest is best described by himself when he writes to the narrator: "I feel like a man who's been trying to climb up out of some deep, real deep and funky hole and just saw the sun up there, outside. I got to get outside." Sonny is a person who finds his life a living hell, but he knows enough to strive for the "light." As it is chronicled in this story, his quest is for regaining something from the past—from his own childhood and from the pasts of all who have come before him. The means for doing this is his music, which is consistently portrayed in terms of light imagery. When Sonny has a discussion with the narrator about the future, the narrator describes Sonny's face as a mixture of concern and hope: "[T]he worry, the thoughtfulness, played on it still, the way shadows play on a face which is staring into the fire." This fire image is reinforced shortly afterward when the narrator describes Sonny's aspirations once more in terms of light: "[I]t was as though he were all wrapped up in some cloud, some fire, some vision all his own." To the narrator and to Isabel's family, the music that Sonny plays is simply "weird and disordered," but to Sonny, the music is seen in starkly positive terms: his failure to master the music will mean "death," while success will mean "life."

The light and dark imagery culminates in the final scene, where the narrator, apparently for the first time, listens to Sonny play the piano. The location is a Greenwich Village club. Appropriately enough, the narrator is seated "in a dark corner." In contrast, the stage is dominated by light, which Baldwin reiterates with a succession of images: "light . . . circle of light . . . light . . . flame . . . light." Although Sonny has a false start, he gradually settles into his playing and ends the first set with some intensity: "Everything had been burned out of [Sonny's face], and at the same time, things usually hidden were being burned in, by the fire and fury of the battle which was occurring in him up there."

The culmination of the set occurs when Creole, the leader of the players, begins to play "Am I Blue?" At this point, "something began to happen." Apparently, the narrator at this time realizes that this music *is* important. The music is central to the experience of the black experience, and it is described in terms of light imagery:

> Creole began to tell us what the blues were all about. They were not about anything very new. He and his boys up there were keeping it new, at the risk of ruin, destruction, madness, and death, in order to find new ways to make us listen. For, while the tale of how we suffer, and how we are delighted, and how we may triumph is never new, it always must be heard. There isn't any other tale to tell, it's the only light we've got in all this darkness.

From "James Baldwin's 'Sonny's Blues': Childhood, Light, and Art"

Robert Langbaum (b. 1924)

On Robert Browning's "My Last Duchess" 1957

When we have said all the objective things about Browning's "My Last Duchess," we will not have arrived at the meaning until we point out what can only be substantiated by an appeal to effect—that moral judgment does not figure importantly in our response to the duke, that we even identify ourselves with him. But how is such an effect produced in a poem about a cruel Italian duke of the Renaissance who out of unreasonable jealousy has had his last duchess put to death, and is now about to contract a second marriage for the sake of dowry? Certainly, no summary or paraphrase would indicate that condemnation is not our principal response. The difference must be laid to form, to that extra quantity which makes the difference in artistic discourse between content and meaning.

The objective fact that the poem is made up entirely of the duke's utterance has of course much to do with the final meaning, and it is important to say that the poem is in form a monologue. But much more remains to be said about the way in which the content is laid out, before we can come near accounting for the whole meaning. It is important that the duke tells the story of his kind and generous last duchess to, of all people, the envoy from his prospective duchess. It is important that he tells his story while showing off to the envoy the artistic merits of a portrait of the last duchess. It is above all important that the duke carries off his outrageous indiscretion, proceeding triumphantly in the end downstairs to conclude arrangements for the dowry. All this is important not only as content but also as form, because it establishes a relation between the duke on the one hand, and the portrait and the envoy on the other, which determines the reader's relation to the duke and therefore to the poem—which determines, in other words, the poem's meaning.

The utter outrageousness of the duke's behavior makes condemnation the least interesting response, certainly not the response that can account for the poem's success. What interests us more than the duke's wickedness is his immense attractiveness. His conviction of matchless superiority, his intelligence and bland amorality, his poise, his taste for art, his manners—high-handed aristocratic manners that break the ordinary rules and assert the duke's superiority when he is being most solicitous of the envoy, waiving their difference of rank ("Nay, we'll go / Together down, sir"); these qualities overwhelm the envoy, causing him apparently to suspend judgment of the duke, for he raises no demur. The reader is no less overwhelmed. We suspend moral judgment because we prefer to participate in the duke's power and freedom, in his hard core of character fiercely loyal to itself. Moral judgment is in fact important as the thing to be suspended, as a measure of the price we pay for the privilege of appreciating to the full this extraordinary man.

It is because the duke determines the arrangement and relative subordination of the parts that the poem means what it does. The duchess's goodness shines through the duke's utterance; he makes no attempt to conceal it, so preoccupied is he with his own standard of judgment and so oblivious of the world's. Thus the duchess's case is subordinated to the duke's, the novelty and complexity of which engages our attention. We are busy trying to understand the man who can combine the connoisseur's pride in the lady's beauty with a pride that caused him to murder the lady rather than tell her in what way she displeased him, for in that

> would be some stooping; and I choose
> Never to stoop.
>
> (lines 42–43)

The duke's paradoxical nature is fully revealed when, having boasted how at his command the duchess's life was extinguished, he turns back to the portrait to admire of all things its life-likeness:

> There she stands
> As if alive.
>
> (lines 46–47)

This occurs ten lines from the end, and we might suppose we have by now taken the duke's measure. But the next ten lines produce a series of shocks that outstrip each time our understanding of the duke, and keep us panting after revelation with no opportunity to consolidate our impression of him for moral judgment. For it is at this point that we learn to whom he has been talking; and he goes on to talk about dowry, even allowing himself to murmur the hypocritical assurance that the new bride's self and not the dowry is of course his object. It seems to me that one side of the duke's nature is here stretched as far as it will go; the dazzling figure threatens to decline into paltriness admitting moral judgment, when Browning retrieves it with two brilliant strokes. First, there is the lordly waiving of rank's privilege as the duke and the envoy are about to proceed downstairs, and then there is the perfect all-revealing gesture of the last two and a half lines when the duke stops to show off yet another object in his collection:

> Notice Neptune, though,
> Taming a sea-horse, thought a rarity,
> Which Claus of Innsbruck cast in bronze for me!
>
> (lines 54–56)

The lines bring all the parts of the poem into final combination, with just the relative values that constitute the poem's meaning. The nobleman does not hurry on his way to business, the connoisseur cannot resist showing off yet another precious object, the possessive egotist counts up his possessions even as he moves toward the acquirement of a new possession, a well-dowered bride; and most important, the last duchess is seen in final perspective. She takes her place as one of a line of objects in an art collection; her sad story becomes the *cicerone's* anecdote° lending piquancy to the portrait. The duke has taken from her what he wants, her beauty, and thrown the life away; and we watch with awe as he proceeds to take what he wants from the envoy and by implication from the new duchess. He carries all before him by sheer force of will so undeflected by ordinary compunctions as even, I think, to call into question—the question rushes into place behind the startling illumination of the last lines, and lingers as the poem's haunting afternote—the duke's sanity.

From *The Poetry of Experience*

BIOGRAPHICAL CRITICISM

Biographical criticism begins with the simple but central insight that literature is written by actual people and that understanding an author's life can help readers more thoroughly comprehend the work. Anyone who reads the biography of a writer quickly sees how much an author's experience shapes—both directly and indirectly—what he or she creates. Reading that biography will also change (and usually deepen) our response to the work. Sometimes even knowing a single important fact illuminates our reading of a poem or story. Learning, for example, that poet Josephine Miles was confined to a wheelchair or that Weldon Kees committed suicide at forty-one will certainly make us pay attention to certain aspects of their poems we might otherwise have missed or considered unimportant. A formalist critic might complain that we would also have noticed those things through careful textual analysis, but biographical information provides the practical assistance of underscoring subtle but important meanings in the poems. Though many literary theorists have assailed biographical criticism on philosophical grounds, the biographical approach to literature has never disappeared because of its obvious practical advantage in illuminating literary texts.

cicerone's anecdote: the Duke's tale. (In Italian, a *cicerone* is one who conducts guided tours for sightseers.)

It may be helpful here to make a distinction between biography and biographical criticism. **Biography** is, strictly speaking, a branch of history; it provides a written account of a person's life. To establish and interpret the facts of a poet's life, for instance, a biographer would use all the available information—not just personal documents such as letters and diaries but also the poems—for the possible light they might shed on the subject's life. A biographical *critic*, however, is not concerned with re-creating the record of an author's life. Biographical criticism focuses on explicating the literary work by using the insight provided by knowledge of the author's life. Quite often, biographical critics, such as Brett C. Millier in her discussion of Elizabeth Bishop's "One Art," will examine the drafts of a poem or story to see both how the work came into being and how it might have been changed from its autobiographical origins.

A reader, however, must use biographical interpretations cautiously. Writers are notorious for revising the facts of their own lives; they often delete embarrassments and invent accomplishments while changing the details of real episodes to improve their literary impact. John Cheever, for example, frequently told reporters about his sunny, privileged youth; after the author's death, his biographer Scott Donaldson discovered a childhood scarred by a distant mother; a failed, alcoholic father; and nagging economic uncertainty. Likewise, Cheever's outwardly successful adulthood was plagued by alcoholism, sexual promiscuity, and family tension. The unsettling facts of Cheever's life significantly changed the way critics read his stories. The danger in the case of a famous writer (Sylvia Plath and F. Scott Fitzgerald are two modern examples) is that the life story can overwhelm and eventually distort the work. A shrewd biographical critic always remembers to base an interpretation on what is in the text itself; biographical data should amplify the meaning of the text, not drown it out with irrelevant material.

Leslie Fiedler (1917-2003)

The Relationship of Poet and Poem — 1960

A central dogma of much recent criticism asserts that biographical information is irrelevant to the understanding and evaluation of poems, and that conversely, poems cannot legitimately be used as material for biography. This double contention is part of a larger position which holds that history is history and art is art, and that to talk about one in terms of the other is to court disaster. Insofar as this position rests upon the immortal platitude that it is good to know what one is talking about, it is unexceptionable; insofar as it is a reaction based upon the procedures of pre-Freudian critics, it is hopelessly outdated; and insofar as it depends upon the extreme nominalist definition of a work of art, held by many "formalists" quite unawares, it is metaphysically reprehensible. It has the further inconvenience of being quite unusable in the practical sphere (all of its proponents, in proportion as they are sensitive critics, immediately betray it when speaking of specific works, and particularly of large bodies of work); and, as if that were not enough, it is in blatant contradiction with the assumptions of most serious practicing writers.

That the anti-biographical position was once "useful," whatever its truth, cannot be denied; it was even once, what is considerably rarer in the field of criticism, amusing; but for a long time now it has been threatening to turn into one of those annoying clichés of the intellectually middle-aged, profferred with all the air of a stimulating heresy. The position was born in dual protest against an excess of Romantic criticism and one of "scientific scholarship." Romantic aesthetics appeared bent on dissolving the formally realized "objective" elements in works of art into "expression of personality"; while the "scholars," in revolt against Romantic subjectivity, seemed set on casting out all the more shifty questions of value and *gestalt* as "subjective," and concentrating on the kind of "facts" amenable to scientific verification. Needless to say, it was not the newer psychological sciences that the "scholars" had in mind, but such purer disciplines as physics and biology. It was at this point that it became fashionable to talk about literary study as "research," and graphs and tables began to appear in analyses of works of art.

• • •

The poet's life is the focusing glass through which pass the determinants of the shape of his work: the tradition available to him, his understanding of "kinds," the impact of special experiences (travel, love, etc.). But the poet's life is more than a burning glass; with his work, it makes up his total meaning. I do not intend to say, of course, that some meanings of works of art, satisfactory and as far as they go sufficient, are not available in the single work itself (only a really *bad* work depends for all substantial meaning on a knowledge of the life-style of its author); but a whole body of work will contain larger meanings, and, where it is available, a sense of the life of the writer will raise that meaning to a still higher power. The latter two kinds of meaning fade into each other; for as soon as two works by a single author are considered side by side, one has begun to deal with biography—that is, with an interconnectedness fully explicable only in terms of a personality, inferred or discovered.

One of the essential functions of the poet is the assertion and creation of a personality, in a profounder sense than any nonartist can attain. We ask of the poet a definition of man, at once particular and abstract, stated and acted out. It is impossible to draw a line between the work the poet writes and the work he lives, between the life he lives and the life he writes. And the agile critic, therefore, must be prepared to move constantly back and forth between life and poem, not in a pointless circle, but in a meaningful spiraling toward the absolute point.

No! in Thunder

Brett C. Millier (b. 1958)

On Elizabeth Bishop's "One Art" 1993

Elizabeth Bishop left seventeen drafts of the poem "One Art" among her papers. In the first draft, she lists all the things she's lost in her life—keys, pens, glasses, cities—and then she writes "One might think this would have prepared me / for losing one average-sized not exceptionally / beautiful or dazzlingly intelligent person . . . / But it doesn't seem to have at all. . . ." By the seventeenth draft, nearly every word has been transformed, but most importantly, Bishop discovered along the way that there might be a way to master this loss.

One way to read Bishop's modulation between the first and last drafts from "the loss of you is impossible to master" to something like "I am still the master of losing even though losing you looks like a disaster" is that in the writing of such a disciplined, demanding poem as this villanelle ("[*Write* it!]") lies the potential mastery of the loss. Working through each of her losses—from the bold, painful catalog of the first draft to the finely-honed and privately meaningful final version—is the way to overcome them or, if not to overcome them, then to see the way in which she might possibly master herself in the face of loss. It is all, perhaps "one art"—writing elegy, mastering loss, mastering grief, self-mastery. Bishop had a precocious familiarity with loss. Her father died before her first birthday, and four years later her mother disappeared into a sanitarium, never to be seen by her daughter again. The losses in the poem are real: time in the form of the "hour badly spent" and, more tellingly for the orphaned Bishop, "my mother's watch": the lost houses, in Key West, Petrópolis, and Ouro Prêto, Brazil. The city of Rio de Janeiro and the whole South American continent (where she had lived for nearly two decades) were lost to her with the suicide of her Brazilian companion. And currently, in the fall of 1975, she seemed to have lost her dearest friend and lover, who was trying to end their relationship. But each version of the poem distanced the pain a little more, depersonalized it, moved it away from the tawdry self-pity and "confession" that Bishop disliked in so many of her contemporaries.

Bishop's friends remained for a long time protective of her personal reputation, and unwilling to have her grouped among lesbian poets or even among the other great poets of her generation—Robert Lowell, John Berryman, Theodore Roethke—as they seemed to self-destruct before their readers' eyes. Bishop herself taught them this reticence by keeping her private life to herself, and by investing what "confession" there was in her poems deeply in objects and places, thus deflecting biographical inquiry. In the development of this poem, discretion is both a poetic method and a part of a process of self-understanding, the seeing of a pattern in her own life.

Adapted by the author from *Elizabeth Bishop: Life and the Memory of It*

Emily Toth (b. 1944)

The Source for Alcée Laballière in "The Storm" 1990

In January 1898, right after Kate Chopin had finished writing her controversial novel *The Awakening*, about one woman's quest for love (and sexual fulfillment) outside of marriage, a St. Louis newspaper asked her to answer the question, "Is Love Divine?"

Chopin's response was telling. She wrote, "I am inclined to think that love springs from animal instinct, and therefore is, in a measure, divine. One can never resolve to love this man, this woman or child, and then carry out the resolution unless one feels irresistibly drawn by an indefinable current of magnetism."

In that case, it was no doubt magnetism that led Kate Chopin to the handsome, wealthy Creole planter Albert Sampité (pronounced "Al-bear Sam-pi-TAY") after the death of her husband Oscar. This may also be why Kate Chopin's widowhood stories emphasize hope, not bereavement; spring, not winter; possibility, not loss. After Oscar died, Kate—who had grown up in a house full of widows who managed their own lives and their own money—decided to run Oscar's businesses herself.

She became an accomplished entrepreneur, a brisk businesswoman during the day who nevertheless kept the dark night as her own, with its prospects for silence and mystery and sin. Men flocked to aid the handsome widow in 1883, but when villagers gossiped generations later about who was "sweet on Kate," one name kept recurring. It was no secret to anyone—including his wife—that Albert Sampité was pursuing Kate Chopin. An examination of Chopin's stories show that the male characters who kindle desire and who devote themselves to sexual pleasure are named Alcée, an abbreviated form of Albert Sampité. Al. S——é and Alcée are both pronounced "Al-say."

It was not unseemly, or even odd, for Monsieur Sampite (his family dropped the accent mark, though they continued to use French pronunciation) to meet with Madame Chopin at the point where their lands intersected. When merchandise arrived for Kate's store, by boat from New Orleans, she had to go down to the landing to get her goods. It was not uncommon for a local planter like Albert Sampite to be at the landing at the same time. Somehow, too, Albert Sampite became involved in Kate Chopin's money matters. Papers that he saved show that Albert was apparently helping Kate to collect money owed her—and he also valued her financial records enough to keep them with his own personal papers.

There were still other ways in which a willing couple could make connections. And in a sudden storm, it was not impossible for two people to take refuge alone together in a house—a sensual scenario Kate Chopin sketched out, years later, in her most explicit short story, "The Storm."

Kate and Albert were discreet about their romance, by the standards of a century later. If anyone wrote down dates and places and eyewitness descriptions, none of those survive—although Cloutierville residents would certainly have been able to recognize him in her writings. But an affair in the 1880s was not simply a matter of physical consummation. Much less than that could be called "making love": flirting, significant glances, stolen kisses, secret silences.

Kate Chopin, in her diary eleven years after the first spring of her widowhood, suggested that more than flirting had gone on in her life: "I had loved—lovers who were not divine," she wrote, and "And then, there are so many ways of saying good night!" And even in her published writings, Kate left proof that her relationship with Albert Sampite was much more than a casual friendship. It shaped what she wrote about women and men, and love and lust and forbidden desires.

Adapted from *Kate Chopin*

HISTORICAL CRITICISM

Historical criticism seeks to understand a literary work by investigating the social, cultural, and intellectual context that produced it—a context that necessarily includes the artist's biography and milieu. Historical critics are less concerned with explaining a work's literary significance for today's readers than with helping us understand the work by recreating, as nearly as possible, the exact meaning and impact it had for its original audience. A historical reading of a literary work begins by exploring the possible ways in which the meaning of the text has changed over time. An analysis of William Blake's poem "London," for instance, carefully examines how certain words had different connotations for the poem's original readers than they do today. It also explores the probable associations an eighteenth-century English reader would have made with certain images and characters, like the poem's persona, the chimney sweep—a type of exploited child laborer who, fortunately, no longer exists in our society.

No one doubts the value of historical criticism in reading ancient literature. There have been so many social, cultural, and linguistic changes that some older texts are incomprehensible without scholarly assistance. But historical criticism can even help one better understand modern texts. To return to Weldon Kees's "For My Daughter," for example, one learns a great deal by considering two rudimentary historical facts—the year in which the poem was first published (1940) and the nationality of its author (American)—and then asking how this information has shaped the meaning of the poem. In 1940 war had already broken out in Europe, and most Americans realized that their country, still recovering from the Depression, would soon be drawn into it. For a young man like Kees, the future seemed bleak, uncertain, and personally dangerous. Even this simple historical analysis helps explain at least part of the bitter pessimism of Kees's poem, though a psychological critic would rightly insist that Kees's dark personality also played a crucial role. In writing a paper on a poem, you might explore how the time and place of its creation affect its meaning. For a splendid example of how to recreate the historical context of a poem's genesis, read the following account by Hugh Kenner of Ezra Pound's imagistic "In a Station of the Metro."

Hugh Kenner (1923–2003)

Imagism

1971

For it was English post-Symbolist verse that Pound's Imagism set out to reform, by deleting its self-indulgences, intensifying its virtues, and elevating the glimpse into the vision. The most famous of all Imagist poems commenced, like any poem by Arthur Symons,° with an accidental glimpse. Ezra Pound, on a visit to Paris in 1911, got out of the Metro at La Concorde, and "saw suddenly a beautiful face, and then another and another, and then a beautiful child's face, and then another beautiful woman, and I tried all that day to find words for what they had meant to me, and I could not find any words that seemed to me worthy, or as lovely as that sudden emotion."

The oft-told story is worth one more retelling. This was just such an experience as Arthur Symons cultivated, bright unexpected glimpses in a dark setting, instantly to melt into the crowd's kaleidoscope. And a poem would not have given Symons any trouble. But Pound by 1911 was already unwilling to write a Symons poem.

He tells us that he first satisfied his mind when he hit on a wholly abstract vision of colors, splotches on darkness like some canvas of Kandinsky's (whose work he had not then seen). This is a most important fact. Satisfaction lay not in preserving the vision, but in devising with mental effort an abstract equivalent for it, reduced, intensified. He next wrote a 30-line poem and destroyed it; after six months he wrote a shorter poem, also destroyed; and after another year, with, as he tells us, the Japanese *hokku* in mind, he arrived at a poem which needs every one of its 20 words, including the six words of its title:

In a Station of the Metro

The apparition of these faces in the crowd;
Petals on a wet, black bough.

We need the title so that we can savor that vegetal contrast with the world of machines: this is not any crowd, moreover, but a crowd seen underground, as Odysseus and Orpheus and Koré saw crowds in Hades. And carrying forward the

Arthur Symons: Symons (1865–1945) was a British poet who helped introduce French symbolist verse into English. His own verse was often florid and impressionistic.

suggestion of wraiths, the word "apparition" detaches these faces from all the crowded faces, and presides over the image that conveys the quality of their separation:

Petals on a wet, black bough.

Flowers, underground; flowers, out of the sun; flowers seen as if against a natural gleam, the bough's wetness gleaming on its darkness, in this place where wheels turn and nothing grows. The mind is touched, it may be, with a memory of Persephone, as we read of her in the 106th Canto,

Dis' bride, Queen over Phlegethon,
    girls faint as mist about her.

—the faces of those girls likewise "apparitions."

What is achieved, though it works by way of the visible, is no picture of the thing glimpsed, in the manner of

The light of our cigarettes
Went and came in the gloom.

It is a simile with "like" suppressed: Pound called it an equation, meaning not a redundancy, *a* equals *a*, but a generalization of unexpected exactness. The statements of analytic geometry, he said, "are 'lords' over fact. They are the thrones and dominations that rule over form and recurrence. And in like manner are great works of art lords over fact, over race-long recurrent moods, and over tomorrow." So this tiny poem, drawing on Gauguin and on Japan, on ghosts and on Persephone, on the Underworld and on the Underground, the Metro of Mallarmé's capital and a phrase that names a station of the Metro as it might a station of the Cross, concentrates far more than it need ever specify, and indicates the means of delivering post-Symbolist poetry from its pictorialist impasse. "An 'Image' is that which presents an intellectual and emotional complex in an instant of time": that is the elusive Doctrine of the Image. And, just 20 months later, "The image . . . is a radiant node or cluster; it is what I can, and must perforce, call a VORTEX, from which, and through which, and into which, ideas are constantly rushing." And: "An *image* . . . is real because we know it directly."

From *The Pound Era*

Seamus Deane (b. 1940)

Joyce's Vision of Dublin

1990

Although Joyce was opposed to the folkish, even folksy, elements of the Irish Revival, he is himself a dominant figure in that movement. Officially, he stands apart, as ever. Yeats, George Moore, Edward Martyn, Lady Gregory, Synge, Padraic Colum and their supporters seemed to him to be dangerously close to committing themselves to a version of the pseudo-Irishness which had once been the preserve of the stage-Irishman of nineteenth-century England and was, by the last decade of the century, becoming the property of the Celtic Irishman of the day. Yet, despite his difference, Joyce had much in common with these writers. In the work of all of them, Ireland, or an idea of Ireland, played a special role. For the revivalists, who were intent on turning nationalist political energies into cultural channels, the idea of Ireland was an invigorating and positive force. It embodied vitality and the possibility of a new kind of community, radically different from the aggregate crowds of the industrialized democracies. The distinction was enhanced by the predominantly rural character of Irish society, transformed by the writers into something very different from its harsh reality.

• • •

Joyce made it clear that, in his opinion, the Revival was conceding to public pressure by allowing the caricatured, but popular, version of Ireland to become the abiding image of the Abbey Theatre. This was wrong on a number of grounds. It deprived the artist of his independence; it nurtured provincialism; and it did this in the guise of a return to the "natural." Exile safe-guarded independence; cosmopolitanism helped to avoid provincialism; and the return to the natural was to be achieved, not by a romanticizing of rural and peasant life, or of the idea of the Celt and his lost language, but by an unflinching realism which, like that of Ibsen, stripped the mask from the pharisaic middle-class society of urban Europe and exposed its spiritual hypocrisy and impoverishment. In that respect, Ireland was indeed a special country. It lived under the political domination of England and the religious domination of Rome while it espoused a rhetoric of freedom, uniqueness, especial privilege. Ireland was, in fact, especially underprivileged and was, on that account, more susceptible to and more in need of an exemplary art than any other European country. It was in Joyce's art that the interior history of his country could be, for the first time, written.

• • •

Joyce's civilization was not, therefore, that of Myles Joyce, of Yeats and Lady Gregory and the Abbey Theatre, or of Mangan. Equally, it was not that of the comic dramatists, Sheridan, Goldsmith, Wilde, and Shaw, all of whom performed the role of "court jester to the English." It was the civilization of Catholic Dublin, related to but distinct from that of Catholic Ireland. Joyce tried to persuade the publisher, Grant Richards, that his collection of stories, *Dubliners*, was about a city that still had not been presented, or represented, to the world. He insists, on many occasions, on the emptiness that preceded his own writings about that city. It is an historical but not yet an imaginative reality. Although Dublin has been a capital for thousands of years and is said to be the second city of the British Empire, Joyce claims that no writer has yet "presented Dublin to the world." Furthermore, "the expression 'Dubliner' seems to me to have some meaning and I doubt that the same can be said for such words as 'Londoner' and 'Parisian.'" In the following year, 1906, the same publisher received from Joyce a sequence of famous letters, defending his text from charges of indecency and suggestions for changes, and declaring the importance of this "chapter of moral history" as "the first step towards the spiritual liberation of my country." Richards is asked to "Reflect for a moment on the history of the literature of Ireland as it stands at present written in the English language before you condemn this genial illusion of mine. . . ." "It is not my fault," he writes a month later, "that the odor of ashpits and old weeds and offal hangs round my stories. I seriously believe that you will retard the course of civilization in Ireland by preventing the Irish people from having one good look at themselves in my nicely polished looking-glass." The mirror held up to Culture was going to reflect a reality no one had presented before. Dublin would find it an unwelcome sight, but Dublin and Ireland would be liberated by it. Joyce is an author without native predecessors; he is an artist who intends to have the effect of a missionary.

By insisting that Dublin had not been represented before in literature, Joyce was intensifying the problem of representation for himself. He abjured the possibility of being influenced by any other Irish writer, because there was, in effect, none who belonged to his specific and peculiar version of his civilization. He was bound, therefore, to find a mode of representation that was, as far as Irish literature was concerned, unique. But the literature of Europe did offer possible models, and Joyce repeatedly spoke of Dublin—as in the letter to Grant Richards—as a European city. Indeed, he saw it as a city that inhabited three spheres of civilization. The first was that of the British Empire; the second that of Roman Catholicism; the third that of the ancient Europe to which Ireland had made such an important contribution. All three of these co-existed in Dublin, the only major European city which had not yet been commemorated in art.

From "Joyce the Irishman"

Kathryn Lee Seidel

The Economics of Zora Neale Hurston's "Sweat" 1991

"Sweat" functions at one level as a documentary of the economic situation of Eatonville in the early decades of the twentieth century. Hurston uses a naturalistic narrator to comment on the roles of Delia and Sykes Jones as workers as well as marriage partners, but ultimately the story veers away from naturalistic fiction and becomes a modernist rumination on Delia as an artist figure. The story's coherence of theme and structure makes it one of Hurston's most powerful pieces of fiction.

Preserved not only as a place but as an idea of a place, Eatonville, Florida, retains the atmosphere of which Hurston wrote. As putatively the oldest town in the United States incorporated by blacks, Eatonville possesses understandable pride in its unique history. When Hurston writes of Eatonville in "How It Feels To Be Colored Me," she implies that her childhood place was idyllic because "it is exclusively a colored town," one in which the young Zora was happily unaware of the restrictions that race conferred elsewhere. However, this gloss of nostalgia can be read simultaneously with "Sweat," published only two years earlier . . . [where] Hurston reveals the somber and multifaced variations of life in Eatonville in the first part of this century.

Economically Eatonville in "Sweat" exists as a twin, a double with its neighbor, the town of Winter Park. Far from being identical, the twin towns are configured like Siamese twins, joined as they are by economic necessity. Winter Park is an all-white, wealthy town that caters to rich northerners from New England who journey south each fall to "winter" in Florida—"snowbirds," as the natives call them. Winter Park then as now boasts brick streets, huge oaks, landscaped lakes, and large, spacious houses. To clean these houses, tend these gardens, cook the meals, and watch the children of Winter Park, residents of Eatonville made a daily exodus across the railroad tracks on which Amtrak now runs to work as domestics. . . . What is unique about Eatonville and Winter Park is that they are not one town divided in two but two towns. Eatonville's self-governance, its pride in its historic traditions, and its social mores were thus able to develop far more autonomously than those in the many towns . . . where the black community had to struggle to develop a sense of independent identity.

In "Sweat" we see the results of this economic situation. On Saturdays the men of the town congregate on the porch of the general store chewing sugarcane and discussing the lamentable marriage of Delia and Sykes Jones. Although these men may be employed during the week, Sykes is not. Some working people mentioned besides Joe Clarke, the store owner, are the woman who runs a rooming house where Bertha,

Sykes's mistress, stays, the minister of the church Delia attends, and the people who organize dances that Sykes frequents. Work as farm laborers on land owned by whites is probably available, but it pays very little and is seasonal. Jacqueline Jones points out that in 1900, not long before the time of the story, 50 to 70 percent of adult black women were employed full time as compared to only 20 percent of men.[1] A black man might be unemployed 50 percent of the time. One reason that unemployed men congregated at the local general store was not merely out of idleness, as whites alleged, nor out of a desire to create oral narratives, as we Hurston critics would like to imagine, but there they could be "visible to potential employers," as Jones asserts.

There is not enough work for the men as it is, but the townspeople discuss Sykes's particular aversion to what work is available. Old man Anderson reports that Sykes was always "ovahbearin' . . . but since dat white 'oman from up north done teached 'im how to run a automobile, he done got too biggety to live—an' we oughter kill 'im." The identity of this woman and her exact role in Sykes's life is not referred to again, but if she was a Winter Park woman, then perhaps Sykes worked for a time as a driver for residents there. All the more ironic, then, his comment to Delia in which he berates her for doing white people's laundry: "ah done tole you time and again to keep them white folks' clothes outa this house." The comment suggests that Sykes does not work out of protest against the economic system of Eatonville in which blacks are dependent on whites for their livelihood. Has he chosen to be unemployed to resist the system? Within the story, this reading is fragile at best. The townspeople point out that Sykes has used and abused Delia; he has "squeezed" her dry, like a piece of sugarcane. They report that she was in her youth a pert, lively, and pretty girl, but that marriage to a man like Sykes has worn her out.

In fact, Delia's work is their only source of income. In the early days of their marriage Sykes was employed, but he "took his wages to Orlando," the large city about ten miles from Eatonville, where he spent every penny. At some point Sykes stopped working and began to rely entirely on Delia for income. As she says, "Mah tub of suds is filled yo' belly with vittles more times than yo' hands is filled it. Mah sweat is done paid for this house." Delia's sense of ownership is that of the traditional work ethic; if one works hard, one can buy a house and support a family. That Delia is the breadwinner, however, is a role reversal but not ostensibly a liberation; her sweat has brought her some meager material rewards but has enraged her husband.

Although she may at one time have considered stopping work so that Sykes might be impelled to "feel like man again" and become a worker once more, at the time of the story that possibility is long past. Sykes wants her to stop working so she can be dainty, not sweaty, fat, not thin. Moreover, he wants to oust her from the house so that he and his girlfriend can live there. . . . Sykes's brutality is a chosen compensation because he does not participate in the work of the community. He chooses instead to become the town's womanizer and bully who spends his earnings when he has them; he lives for the moment and for himself.

. . . With her house she possesses not only a piece of property, but she also gains the right to declare herself as a person, not a piece of property. Because Sykes has not shared in the labor that results in the purchase of this property, he remains in a dependent state. He is rebellious against Delia who he feels controls him by denying

[1]Jacqueline Jones, *Labor of Love, Labor of Sorrow: Black Women, Work, and the Family from Slavery to the Present* (New York: Basic Books, 1985) 113.

him the house he feels ought to be his; his only reason for this assertion is that he is a man and Delia is his wife.

Thus, the economics of slavery in "Sweat" becomes a meditation on marriage as an institution that perpetuates the possession of women for profit. Indeed, Sykes is the slaveholder here; he does not work, he is sustained by the harsh physical labor of a black woman, he relies on the work of another person to obtain his own pleasure (in this case buying presents for his mistress Bertha). He regards Delia's property and her body as his possessions to be disposed of as he pleases. Sykes's brutal beatings of Delia and his insulting remarks about her appearance are the tools with which he perpetuates her subordination to him for the sixteen years of their marriage.

From "The Artist in the Kitchen: The Economics of Creativity in Hurston's 'Sweat'"

PSYCHOLOGICAL CRITICISM

Modern psychology has had an immense effect on both literature and literary criticism. The psychoanalytic theories of the Austrian neurologist Sigmund Freud changed our notions of human behavior by exploring new or controversial areas such as wish fulfillment, sexuality, the unconscious, and repression. Perhaps Freud's greatest contribution to literary study was his elaborate demonstration of how much human mental process was unconscious. He analyzed language, often in the form of jokes and conversational slips of the tongue (now often called "Freudian slips"), to show how it reflected the speaker's unconscious fears and desires. He also examined symbols, not only in art and literature but also in dreams, to study how the unconscious mind expressed itself in coded form to avoid the censorship of the conscious mind. His theory of human cognition asserted that much of what we apparently forget is actually stored deep in the unconscious mind, including painful traumatic memories from childhood that have been repressed.

Freud admitted that he himself had learned a great deal about psychology from studying literature. Sophocles, Shakespeare, Goethe, and Dostoyevsky were as important to the development of his ideas as were his clinical studies. Some of Freud's most influential writing was, in a broad sense, literary criticism, such as his psychoanalytic examination of Sophocles's Oedipus in *The Interpretation of Dreams* (1900). In analyzing Sophocles's tragedy *Oedipus the King,* Freud paid the classical Greek dramatist the considerable compliment that the playwright had such profound insight into human nature that his characters display the depth and complexity of real people. In focusing on literature, Freud and his disciples such as Carl Jung, Ernest Jones, Marie Bonaparte, and Bruno Bettelheim endorsed the belief that great literature truthfully reflects life.

Psychological criticism is a diverse category, but it often employs three approaches. First, it investigates the creative process of the arts: what is the nature of literary genius, and how does it relate to normal mental functions? Such analysis may also focus on literature's effects on the reader. How does a particular work register its impact on the reader's mental and sensory faculties? The second approach involves the psychological study of a particular artist. Most modern literary biographers employ psychology to understand their subject's motivations and behavior. One book, Diane Middlebrook's controversial *Anne Sexton: A Biography* (1991), actually used tapes of the poet's sessions with her psychiatrist as material for the study. The third common approach is the analysis of fictional characters. Freud's study of Oedipus is the prototype for this approach, which tries to bring modern insights about human behavior into the study of how fictional people act. While psychological criticism carefully examines the surface of the literary work, it customarily speculates on what lies underneath the text—the unspoken or perhaps even unspeakable memories, motives, and fears that covertly shape the work, especially in fictional characterizations.

Sigmund Freud (1856–1939)

The Nature of Dreams 1933

Let us go back once more to the latent dream-thoughts. Their dominating element is the repressed impulse, which has obtained some kind of expression, toned down and disguised though it may be, by associating itself with stimuli which happen to be there and by tacking itself on the residue of the day before. Just like any other impulse this one presses forward toward satisfaction in action, but the path to motor discharge is closed to it on account of the physiological characteristics of the state of sleep, and so it is forced to travel in the retrograde direction to perception, and content itself with an hallucinatory satisfaction. The latent dream-thoughts are therefore turned into a collection of sensory images and visual scenes. As they are travelling in this direction something happens to them which seems to us new and bewildering. All the verbal apparatus by means of which the more subtle thought-relations are expressed, the conjunctions and prepositions, the variations of declension and conjugation, are lacking, because the means of portraying them are absent: just as in primitive, grammarless speech, only the raw material of thought can be expressed, and the abstract is merged again in the concrete from which it sprang. What is left over may very well seem to lack coherence. It is as much the result of the archaic regression in the mental apparatus as of the demands of the censorship that so much use is made of the representation of certain objects and processes by means of symbols which have become strange to conscious thought. But of more far-reaching import are the other alterations to which the elements comprising the dream-thoughts are subjected. Such of them as have any point of contact are *condensed* into new unities. When the thoughts are translated into pictures those forms are indubitably preferred which allow of this kind of telescoping, or condensation; it is as though a force were at work which subjected the material to a process of pressure or squeezing together. As a result of condensation one element in a manifest dream may correspond to a number of elements of the dream-thoughts; but conversely one of the elements from among the dream-thoughts may be represented by a number of pictures in the dream.

From *New Introductory Lectures on Psychoanalysis*

Gretchen Schulz (b. 1943) *and R. J. R. Rockwood*

Fairy Tale Motifs in "Where Are You Going, Where Have You Been?" 1980

In her fiction both short and long Miss Oates makes frequent use of fairy tale material. Again and again she presents characters and situations which parallel corresponding motifs from the world of folk fantasy. And never is this more true than in the present story ["Where Are You Going, Where Have You Been?"]—never in all the novels and collections of short stories which she has written at last count. Woven into the complex texture of "Where Are You Going, Where Have You Been?" are motifs from such tales as "The Spirit in the Bottle," "Snow White," "Cinderella," "Sleeping Beauty," "Rapunzel," "Little Red Riding Hood," and "The Three Little Pigs." *The Pied Piper of Hamelin*, which ends tragically and so according to [Bruno] Bettelheim does not qualify as a proper fairy tale, serves as the "frame device" that contains all the other tales.

There is a terrible irony here, for although the story is full of fairy tales, Connie, its protagonist, is not. Connie represents an entire generation of young people who have grown up—or tried to—without the help of those bedtime stories which not only entertain the child, but also enable him vicariously to experience and work through problems which he will encounter in adolescence. The only "stories" Connie knows are those of the sexually provocative but superficial lyrics of the popular songs she loves or of the equally insubstantial movies she attends. Such songs and movies provide either no models of behavior for her to imitate, or dangerously inappropriate ones. Connie has thus been led to believe that life and, in particular, love will be "sweet, gentle, the way it was in the movies and promised in songs." She has no idea that life actually can be just as grim as in folk fairy tales. The society that is depicted in "Where Are You Going, Where Have You Been?" has failed to make available to children like Connie maps of the unconscious such as fairy tales provide, because it has failed to recognize that in the unconscious past and future coalesce, and that, psychologically, where the child is going is where he has already been. Since Connie has been left—in the words of yet another of the popular songs—to "wander through that wonderland alone"—it is small wonder, considering her lack of spiritual preparation, that Connie's journey there soon becomes a terrifying schizophrenic separation from reality, with prognosis for recovery extremely poor.

• • •

Bettelheim points out that a fairy tale like "Spirit in the Bottle" deals with two problems that confront the child as he struggles to establish a sense of identity: parental belittlement, and integration of a divided personality. In Connie's case, her mother's belittling remarks that "Connie couldn't do a thing, her mind was all filled with trashy daydreams," certainly have contributed to Connie's two-sidedness, with her one personality "for home" and another for "anywhere that was not home," a division also apparent in the relationship between Connie and the "girl friend" who accompanies her to the bottle-shaped restaurant—the two are so poorly differentiated as to suggest a mere *doubling* of Connie, rather than two separate individuals. While such personality division may at first glance seem pathological, it is not, according to Bettelheim, necessarily abnormal, since the "manner in which the child can bring some order into his world view is by dividing everything into opposites," and that "in the late-oedipal and post-oedipal ages, this splitting extends to the child himself."

• • •

To be assured of safe passage through what Bettelheim terms "that thorniest of thickets, the oedipal period," a child like Connie would need to have absorbed the wisdom of the other fairy tales to which Miss Oates alludes, tales such as "Snow White," "Cinderella," "Rapunzel," and "Little Red Riding Hood." By their applicability to Connie's situation, these tales reveal that at its deepest level Connie's most compelling psychological problem is *unresolved oedipal conflict, aggravated by sibling rivalry*.

Suggestive of "Snow White" is Connie's "habit of craning her neck to glance into mirrors, or checking other people's faces to make sure her own was all right" (as though other people's faces were mirrors, too); and we are told also that her mother, "who noticed everything and knew everything"—as though with the wicked queen's magic power—"hadn't much reason any longer to look at her own face," and so was jealous of her daughter's beauty and "always after Connie." Arnold Friend's sunglasses also mirror everything, which means that, in this instance, he personifies the Magic Mirror and, of course, he finds Connie the fairest one of all. In his words, "Seen you that night and thought, that's the one, yes sir, I never needed to look anymore." Though he thus serves as Prince, there is a hint of the dwarf motif in Arnold's short stature and obvious phallicism; and most particularly is this true of his friend, Ellie Oscar, a case of arrested development, whose face is that of a "forty-year-old baby." Connie's "Someday My Prince Will Come" daydreams, plus the many references to how dazed and sleepy she always is, especially the day Arnold comes for her, when she "lay languidly about the airless little room" and "breathed in and breathed out with each gentle rise and fall of her chest"—these too, suggest "Snow White" and, for that matter, "Sleeping Beauty," whose heroine in the Brothers Grimm is, like Connie, fifteen.

The oedipal implications of "Snow White" are evident in the fact that, as Bettelheim points out, the queen's Magic Mirror speaks not with the mother's but the daughter's voice, revealing the jealous child's own sense of inferiority and frustration projected onto her mother. The father's romantic feelings for the daughter are never at issue in such a fairy tale and he is generally depicted as weak, ineffectual, and oblivious to the struggle that issues between mother and daughter—exactly as in Miss Oates's story.

From "In Fairyland Without a Map: Connie's Exploration Inward in Joyce Carol Oates's 'Where Are You Going, Where Have You Been?'"

Harold Bloom (b. 1930)

Poetic Influence

1975

Let me reduce my argument to the hopelessly simplistic; poems, I am saying, are neither about "subjects" nor about "themselves." They are necessarily about *other poems;* a poem is a response to a poem, as a poet is a response to a poet, or a person to his parent. Trying to write a poem takes the poet back to the origins of what a poem *first was* for him, and so takes the poet back beyond the pleasure principle to the decisive initial encounter and response that began him. We do not think of W. C. Williams as a Keatsian poet, yet he *began and ended as one*, and his late celebration of his Greeny Flower is another response to Keats's odes. *Only a poet challenges a poet as poet*, and so only a poet makes a poet. To the poet-in-a-poet, a poem is always *the other man*, the precursor, and so a poem is always a person, always the father of one's Second Birth. To live, the poet must *misinterpret* the father, by the crucial act of misprision, which is the rewriting of the father.

But who, what is the poetic father? The voice of the other, of the *daimon*, is always speaking in one; the voice that cannot die because already it has survived death—*the dead poet lives in one*. In the last phase of strong poets, they attempt to join the undying *by living in the dead poets* who are already alive in them. This late Return of the Dead recalls us, as readers, to a recognition of the original motive for the catastrophe of poetic incarnation. Vico, who identified the origins of poetry with the impulse towards divination (to foretell, but also to become a god by foretelling), implicitly understood (as did Emerson, and Wordsworth) that a poem is written to escape dying. Literally, poems are refusals of mortality. Every poem therefore has two makers: the precursor, and the ephebe's rejected mortality.

A poet, I argue in consequence, is not so much a man speaking to men as a man rebelling against being spoken to by a dead man (the precursor) outrageously more alive than himself.

From A *Map of Misreading*

MYTHOLOGICAL CRITICISM

Mythological critics look for the recurrent universal patterns underlying most literary works. **Mythological criticism** is an interdisciplinary approach that combines the insights of anthropology, psychology, history, and comparative religion. If psychological criticism examines the artist as an individual, mythological criticism explores the artist's common humanity by tracing how the individual imagination uses symbols and situations—consciously or unconsciously—in ways that transcend its own historical milieu and resemble the mythology of other cultures or epochs.

A central concept in mythological criticism is the **archetype**, a symbol, character, situation, or image that evokes a deep universal response. The idea of the archetype came into literary criticism from the Swiss psychologist Carl Jung, a lifetime student of myth and religion. Jung believed that all individuals share a "collective unconscious," a set of primal memories common to the human race, existing below each person's conscious mind. Archetypal images (which often relate to experiencing primordial phenomena like the sun, moon, fire, night, and blood), Jung believed, trigger the collective unconscious. We do not need to accept the literal truth of the collective unconscious, however, to endorse the archetype as a helpful critical concept. Northrop Frye defined the archetype in considerably less occult terms as "a symbol, usually an image, which recurs often enough in literature to be recognizable as an element of one's literary experience as a whole."

Identifying archetypal symbols and situations in literary works, mythological critics almost inevitably link the individual text under discussion to a broader context of works that share an underlying pattern. In discussing Shakespeare's *Hamlet*, for instance, a mythological critic might relate Shakespeare's Danish prince to other mythic sons avenging the deaths of their fathers, like Orestes from Greek myth or Sigmund of Norse legend; or, in discussing *Othello*, relate the sinister figure of Iago to the devil in traditional Christian belief. Critic Joseph Campbell took such comparisons even further; his compendious study *The Hero with a Thousand Faces* demonstrates how similar mythic characters appear in virtually every culture on every continent.

Carl Jung (1875–1961)

The Collective Unconscious and Archetypes 1931

Translated by R. F. C. Hull

A more or less superficial layer of the unconscious is undoubtedly personal. I call it the *personal unconscious*. But this personal unconscious rests upon a deeper layer, which does not derive from personal experience and is not a personal acquisition but is inborn. This deeper layer I call the *collective unconscious*. I have chosen the term "collective" because this part of the unconscious is not individual but universal; in contrast to the personal psyche, it has contents and modes of behavior that are more or less the same everywhere and in all individuals. It is, in other words, identical in all men and thus constitutes a common psyche substrate of a suprapersonal nature which is present in every one of us.

Psychic existence can be recognized only by the presence of contents that are *capable of consciousness*. We can therefore speak of an unconscious only in so far as we are able to demonstrate its contents. The contents of the personal unconscious are chiefly the *feeling-toned complexes*, as they are called; they constitute the personal and private side of psychic life. The contents of the collective unconscious, on the other hand, are known as *archetypes*. . . .

For our purposes this term is apposite and helpful, because it tells us that so far as the collective unconscious contents are concerned we are dealing with archaic or—I would say—primordial types, that is, with universal images that have existed since the remotest times. The term "representations collectives," used by Lévy-Bruhl to denote the symbolic figures in the primitive view of the world, could easily be applied to unconscious contents as well, since it means practically the same thing. Primitive tribal lore is concerned with archetypes that have been modified in a special way. They are no longer contents of the unconscious, but have already been changed into conscious formulae taught according to tradition, generally in the form of esoteric teaching. This last is a typical means of expression for the transmission of collective contents originally derived from the unconscious.

Another well-known expression of the archetypes is myth and fairy tale. But here too we are dealing with forms that have received a specific stamp and have been handed down through long periods of time. The term "archetype" thus applies only indirectly to the "representations collectives," since it designates only those psychic contents which have not yet been submitted to conscious elaboration and are therefore an immediate datum of psychic experience. In this sense there is a considerable difference between the archetype and the historical formula that has evolved. Especially on the higher levels of esoteric teaching the archetypes appear in a form that reveals quite unmistakably the critical and evaluating influence of conscious elaboration. Their immediate manifestation, as we encounter it in dreams and visions, is much more individual, less understandable, and more naïve than in myths, for example. The archetype is essentially an unconscious content that is altered by becoming conscious and by being perceived, and it takes its color from the individual consciousness in which it happens to appear.

From *The Collected Works of* C. G. *Jung*, Volume 9

Northrop Frye (1912–1991)

Mythic Archetypes 1957

We begin our study of archetypes, then, with a world of myth, an abstract or purely literary world of fictional and thematic design, unaffected by canons of plausible adaptation to familiar experience. In terms of narrative, myth is the imitation of actions near or at the conceivable limits of desire. The gods enjoy beautiful women, fight one another with prodigious strength, comfort and assist man, or else watch his miseries from the height of their immortal freedom. The fact that myth operates at the top level of human desire does not mean that it necessarily presents its world as attained or attainable by human beings. . . .

Realism, or the art of verisimilitude, evokes the response "How like that is to what we know!" When what is written is *like* what is known, we have an art of extended or implied simile. And as realism is an art of implicit simile, myth is an art of implicit metaphorical identity. The word "sun-god," with a hyphen used instead of a predicate, is a pure ideogram, in Pound's terminology, or literal metaphor, in ours. In myth we see the structural principles of literature isolated; in realism we see the *same* structural principles (not similar ones) fitting into a context of plausibility. (Similarly in music, a piece by Purcell and a piece by Benjamin Britten may not be in the least *like* each other, but if they are both in D major their tonality will be the same.) The presence of a mythical structure in realistic fiction, however, poses certain technical problems for making it plausible, and the devices used in solving these problems may be given the general name of *displacement*.

Myth, then, is one extreme of literary design; naturalism is the other, and in between lies the whole area of romance, using that term to mean, not the historical mode of the first essay, but the tendency, noted later in the same essay, to displace myth in a human direction and yet, in contrast to "realism," to conventionalize content in an idealized direction. The central principle of displacement is that what can be metaphorically identified in a myth can only be linked in romance by some form of simile: analogy, significant association, incidental accompanying imagery, and the like. In a myth we can have a sun-god or a tree-god; in a romance we may have a person who is significantly associated with the sun or trees.

From *Anatomy of Criticism*

Edmond Volpe (1922–2007)

Myth in Faulkner's "Barn Burning" 1964

"Barn Burning" however is not really concerned with class conflict. The story is centered upon Sarty's emotional dilemma. His conflict would not have been altered in any way if the person whose barn Ab burns had been a simple poor farmer, rather than an aristocratic plantation owner. The child's tension, in fact, begins to surface during the hearing in which a simple farmer accuses Ab of burning his barn. The moral antagonists mirrored in Sarty's conflict are not sharecropper and aristocrat. They are the father, Ab Snopes, versus the rest of mankind. Major De Spain is not developed as a character; his house is important to Sarty because it represents a totally new and totally different social and moral entity. Within the context of the society Faulkner is dealing with, the gap between the rich aristocrat and the poor sharecropper provides a viable metaphor for dramatizing the crisis Sarty is undergoing. Ab Snopes is by no means a social crusader. The De Spain manor is Sarty's first contact with a rich man's house, though he can recall, in the short span of his life, at least a dozen times the family had to move because Ab burned barns. Ab does not discriminate between rich and poor. For him there are only two categories: blood kin and "they," into which he lumps all the rest of mankind. Ab's division relates to Sarty's crisis and only by defining precisely the nature of the conflict the boy is undergoing can we determine the moral significance Faulkner sees in it. The clue to Sarty's conflict rests in its resolution.

• • •

The boy's anxiety is created by his awakening sense of his own individuality. Torn between strong emotional attachment to the parent and his growing need to assert his own identity, Sarty's crisis is psychological and his battle is being waged far below the level of his intellectual and moral awareness.

Faulkner makes this clear in the opening scene with imagery that might be described as synesthesia. The real smell of cheese is linked with the smell of the hermetic meat in the tin cans with the scarlet devils on the label that his "intestines believed he smelled coming in intermittent gusts momentary and brief between the other constant one, the smell and sense just a little of fear because mostly of despair and grief, the old fierce pull of blood." The smells below the level of the olfactory sense link the devil image and the blood image to identify the anxiety the father creates in the child's psyche. Tension is created by the blood demanding identification with his father against "*our enemy* he thought in that despair; *ourn! mine and hisn both! He's my father!*" Sarty's conflict is played out in terms of identification, not in moral terms. He does not think of his father as bad, his father's enemies as good.

Ab unjustly accuses Sarty of intending to betray him at the hearing, but he correctly recognizes that his son is moving out of childhood, developing a mind and will of his own and is no longer blindly loyal. In instructing the boy that everyone is the enemy and his loyalty belongs to his blood, Ab's phrasing is revealing: "'Don't you know all they wanted was a chance to get at me because they knew I had them beat?'" Ab does not use the plural "us." It is "I" and "they." Blood loyalty means total identification with Ab, and in the ensuing scenes, Snopes attempts to make his son an extension of himself by taking him to the De Spain house, having him rise up before dawn to be with Ab when he returns the rug, having him accompany Ab to the hearing against De Spain and finally making him an accomplice in the burning of De Spain's barn.

The moral import of Ab's insistence on blood loyalty is fully developed by the satanic imagery Faulkner introduces in the scene at the mansion. As they go up the drive, Sarty follows his father, seeing the stiff black form against the white plantation house. Traditionally the devil casts no shadow, and Ab's figure appears to the child as having "that impervious quality of something cut ruthlessly from tin, depthless, as though sidewise to the sun it would cast no shadow." The cloven hoof of the devil is suggested by Ab's limp upon which the boy's eyes are fixed as the foot unwaveringly comes down into the manure. Sarty's increasing tension resounds in the magnified echo of the limping foot on the porch boards, "a sound out of all proportion to the displacement of the body it bore, as though it had attained to a sort of vicious and ravening minimum not to be dwarfed by anything." At first Sarty thought the house was impervious to his father, but his burgeoning fear of the threat the father poses is reflected in his vision of Ab becoming magnified and monstrous as the black arm reaches up the white door and Sarty sees "the lifted hand like a curled claw."

The satanic images are projected out of the son's nightmarish vision of his father, but they are reinforced by the comments of the adult narrator. Sarty believes Snopes fought bravely in the Civil War, but Ab, we are told, wore no uniform, gave his fealty to no cause, admitted the authority of no man. He went to war for booty. Ab's ego is so great it creates a centripetal force into which everything must flow or be destroyed. The will-less, abject creature who is his wife symbolizes the power of his will. What Ab had done to his wife, he sets out to do to the emerging will of his son.

Ab cannot tolerate any entity that challenges the dominance of his will. By allowing his hog to forage in the farmer's corn and by dirtying and ruining De Spain's rug, he deliberately creates a conflict that requires the assertion of primacy. Fire, the element of the devil, is the weapon for the preservation of his dominance. Ab's rage is not fired by social injustice. It is fired by a pride, like Lucifer's, so absolute it can accept no order beyond its own. In the satanic myth, Lucifer asserts his will against the divine order and is cast out of heaven. The angels who fall with Lucifer become extensions of his will. In the same way, Ab is an outcast and pariah among men. He accepts no order that is not of his blood.

From "'Barn Burning': A Definition of Evil"

SOCIOLOGICAL CRITICISM

Sociological criticism examines literature in the cultural, economic, and political context in which it is written or received. "Art is not created in a vacuum," critic Wilbur Scott observed, "it is the work not simply of a person, but of an author fixed in time and space, answering a community of which he is an important, because articulate part." Sociological criticism explores the relationships between the artist and society. Sometimes it looks at the sociological status of the author to evaluate how the profession of the writer in a particular milieu affected what was written. Sociological criticism also analyzes the social content of literary works—what cultural, economic, or political values a particular text implicitly or explicitly promotes. Finally, sociological criticism examines the role the audience has in shaping literature. A sociological view of Shakespeare, for example, might look at the economic position of Elizabethan playwrights and actors; it might also study the political ideas expressed in the plays or discuss how the nature of an Elizabethan theatrical audience (which was usually all male unless the play was produced at court) helped determine the subject, tone, and language of the plays.

An influential type of sociological criticism has been Marxist criticism, which focuses on the economic and political elements of art. Marxist criticism, as in the work of the Hungarian philosopher Georg Lukacs, often explores the ideological content of literature. Whereas a formalist critic would maintain that form and content are inextricably blended, Lukacs believed that content determines form and that, therefore, all art is political. Even if a work of art ignores political issues, it makes a political statement, Marxist critics believe, because it endorses the economic and political status quo. Consequently, Marxist criticism is frequently evaluative and judges some literary work better than others on an ideological basis; this tendency can lead to reductive judgment, as when Soviet critics rated Jack London a novelist superior to William Faulkner, Ernest Hemingway, Edith Wharton, and Henry James, because he illustrated the principles of class struggle more clearly. London was America's first major working-class writer. To examine the political ideas and observations found in his fiction can be illuminating, but to fault other authors for lacking his instincts and ideas is not necessarily helpful in understanding their particular qualities. There is always a danger in sociological criticism—Marxist or otherwise—of imposing the critic's personal politics on the work in question and then evaluating it according to how closely it endorses that ideology. As an analytical tool, however, Marxist criticism and sociological methods can illuminate political and economic dimensions of literature that other approaches overlook.

Georg Lukacs (1885–1971)

Content Determines Form 1962

What determines the style of a given work of art? How does the intention determine the form? (We are concerned here, of course, with the intention realized in the work; it need not coincide with the writer's conscious intention.) The distinctions that concern us are not those between stylistic "techniques" in the formalistic sense. It is the view of the world, the ideology or *Weltanschauung*° underlying a writer's work, that counts. And it is the writer's attempt to reproduce this view of the world which constitutes his "intention" and is the formative principle underlying the style of a given piece of writing. Looked at in this way, style ceases to be a formalistic category. Rather, it is rooted in content; it is the specific form of a specific content.

Content determines form. But there is no content of which Man himself is not the focal point. However various the *données*° of literature (a particular experience, a didactic purpose), the basic question is, and will remain: what is Man?

Here is a point of division: if we put the question in abstract, philosophical terms, leaving aside all formal considerations, we arrive—for the realist school—at the traditional Aristotelian dictum (which was also reached by other than purely aesthetic considerations): Man is *zoon politikon*,° a social animal. The Aristotelian dictum is applicable to all great realistic literature. Achilles and Werther, Oedipus and Tom Jones, Antigone and Anna Karenina: their individual existence—their *Sein an sich*,° in the Hegelian terminology; their "ontological being," as a more fashionable terminology has it—cannot be distinguished from their social and historical environment. Their human significance, their specific individuality cannot be separated from the context in which they were created.

From *Realism in Our Time*

Daniel P. Watkins (b. 1952)

Money and Labor in "The Rocking-Horse Winner" 1987

It is a commonplace that D. H. Lawrence's "The Rocking-Horse Winner" is a story about the devastating effect that money can have on a family, and, further, that Lawrence's specific objections in the story are not to money abstractly conceived but to money as it is understood and valued by capitalist culture. This is one of Lawrence's most savage and compact critiques of what he elsewhere calls "the goddamn bourgeoisie" and of individuals who, despite their natural or potential goodness, "swallow the culture bait" and hence become victims to the world they (wrongly) believe holds the key to human happiness.

• • •

The class nature of labor under capital is presented symbolically in the story in terms of the adult and non-adult worlds. That is, social reality is controlled by parents whose primary concern is to bring in money sufficient to "the social position which they (have) to keep up." While they have a small income, and while "The

Weltanschauung: German for "world view," an outlook on life. *données* French for "given"; it means the materials a writer uses to create his or her work or the subject or purpose of a literary work. *zoon politikon*: Greek for "political animal." *Sein an sich*: the German philosopher G. W. F. Hegel's term for "pure existence."

father went in to town to some office," they never are really seen to work actively and productively. Rather, they set a tone of need in their world that generates intense and pervasive anxiety, which then is passed down to their children, who interiorize the values and attitudes of the adult world and set about (as best they can) to satisfy the demands of that world. Even when money is produced, however, the demands of the adult world are never fully met, but, quite the reverse, intensify further, so that more labor is necessary. In this context, work is not a means of meeting basic human needs, but rather only a way of producing greater sums of money, and thus it is clearly socially unproductive. Seen from this perspective, it is not important that the parents are not capitalists in the crudest sense (that is, they are not drawn as investors of money); what is important is that they both set the tone (economic scarcity) and determine the values (consumerism) of the world they inhabit, and in addition expropriate the wealth that others produce for their own private consumption.

Young Paul exemplifies vividly the sort of work that arises under capital. Simply put, he is a laborer for his mother, to whom he gives all of his money, only to find that the more he gives the more she needs. It is true, of course, that as a handicapper he invests money, betting on a profitable return on his investment, and that in this sense he is a sort of capitalist; indeed, it is his betting that is the literal sign of the economic relations controlling the world of the story. But at the same time his character is made to carry a much larger symbolic significance, for what he is investing, in real terms, is himself, selling his skills to generate wealth that he is not free to possess, but that is necessary to the maintenance of existing social relations. As his mother touches the money he earns, she uses it not to satisfy family needs—it has little or no *use* value—but to extend her social position and social power, and the process of extension of course is never-ending, requiring ever greater sums of money: "There were certain new furnishings, and Paul had a tutor. He was *really* going to Eton, his father's school, in the following autumn. There were flowers in the winter, and a blossoming of the luxury Paul's mother had been used to. And yet the voices in the house, behind the sprays of mimosa and almond-blossom, and from under the piles of iridescent cushions, simply trilled and screamed in a sort of ecstasy: 'There *must* be more money!'" This passage clearly focuses the priority of money over commodity and the relentlessness with which the power associated with money controls even the most personal dimension of life.

The work itself that Paul performs cannot, under such conditions, be personally satisfying, and this is shown powerfully by the sort of work he does. The rocking horse is a brilliant symbol of non-productive labor, for even while it moves it remains stationary: even while Paul is magically (humanly) creative, producing untold wealth for his mother, he does not advance in the least, and in fact becomes increasingly isolated and fearful that even the abilities he now possesses will be taken from him. The labor, which drives him to "a sort of madness," that consumes him to an ever greater degree, leaves him nothing for himself, driving him down a terrible path to emotional and then physical distress. He is never satisfied with what he produces because it in no way relieves the pressure that his world places on him, and thus his anxiety and alienation grow to the point of destroying any sense of real personal worth and removing him literally from all meaningful social exchange, as when he takes his rocking horse to his bedroom and rides alone late into the night trying to find the key to wealth.

From "Labor and Religion in D. H. Lawrence's 'The Rocking-Horse Winner'"

Alfred Kazin (1915–1998)

Walt Whitman and Abraham Lincoln 1984

In Lincoln's lifetime Whitman was the only major writer to describe him with love. Whitman identified Lincoln with himself in the worshipful fashion that became standard after Lincoln's death. That Lincoln was a class issue says a good deal about the prejudices of American society in the East. A leading New Yorker, George Templeton Strong, noted in his diary that while he never disavowed the "lank and hard featured man," Lincoln was "despised and rejected by a third of the community, and only tolerated by the other two-thirds." Whitman the professional man of the people had complicated reasons for loving Lincoln. The uneasiness about him among America's elite was based on the fear that this unknown, untried man, elected without administrative experience (and without a majority) might not be up to his "fearful task."

• • •

Whitman related himself to the popular passion released by war and gave himself to this passion as a political cause. He understood popular opinion in a way that Emerson, Thoreau, and Hawthorne did not attempt to understand it. Emerson said, like any conventional New England clergyman, that the war was holy. He could not speak for the masses who bore the brunt of the war. Whitman was able to get so much out of the war, to create a lasting image of it, because he knew what people were feeling. He was not above the battle like Thoreau and Hawthorne, not suspicious of the majority like his fellow New Yorker Herman Melville, who in "The House-top," the most personal poem in *Battle-Pieces*, denounced the "ship-rats" who had taken over the city in the anti-draft riots of 1863.

Despite Whitman's elusiveness—he made a career out of longings it would have ended that career to fulfill—he genuinely felt at home with soldiers and other "ordinary" people who were inarticulate by the standards of men "from the schools." He was always present, if far from available, presenting the picture of a nobly accessible and social creature. He certainly got on better with omnibus drivers, workingmen, and now "simple" soldiers (especially when they were wounded and open to his ministrations) than he did with "scribblers." By the time Whitman went down after Fredericksburg to look for brother George, the war was becoming a revolution of sorts and Whitman's old radical politics were becoming "the nation." This made him adore Lincoln as the symbol of the nation's unity. An essential quality of Whitman's Civil War "memoranda" is Whitman's libidinous urge to associate himself with the great, growing, ever more powerful federal cause. Whitman's characteristic lifelong urge to join, to combine, to see life as movement, unity, totality, became during the Civil War an actively loving association with the broad masses of the people and *their* war. In his cult of the Civil War, Whitman allies himself with a heroic and creative energy which sees itself spreading out from the people and their representative men, Lincoln and Whitman.

Hawthorne's and Thoreau's horror of America as the Big State did not reflect Whitman's image of the Union. His passion for the "cause" reflected his intense faith in democracy at a juncture when the United States at war represented the revolutionary principle to Marx, the young Ibsen, Mill, Browning, Tolstoy. Whitman's deepest feeling was that his own rise from the city streets, his future as a poet of democracy, was tied up with the Northern armies.

From *An American Procession*

GENDER CRITICISM

Gender criticism examines how sexual identity influences the creation and reception of literary works. Gender studies began with the feminist movement and was influenced by such works as Simone de Beauvoir's *The Second Sex* (1949) and Kate Millett's *Sexual Politics* (1970) as well as sociology, psychology, and anthropology. Feminist critics believe that culture has been so completely dominated by men that literature is full of unexamined "male-produced" assumptions. They see their criticism correcting this imbalance by analyzing and combating patriarchal attitudes. Feminist criticism has explored how an author's gender influences—consciously or unconsciously—his or her writing. While a formalist critic such as Allen Tate emphasized the universality of Emily Dickinson's poetry by demonstrating how powerfully the language, imagery, and mythmaking of her poems combine to affect a generalized reader, Sandra M. Gilbert, a leading feminist critic, has identified attitudes and assumptions in Dickinson's poetry that she believes are essentially female. Another important theme in feminist criticism is analyzing how sexual identity influences the reader of a text. If Tate's hypothetical reader was deliberately sexless, Gilbert's reader sees a text through the eyes of his or her sex. Finally, feminist critics carefully examine how the images of men and women in imaginative literature reflect or reject the social forces that have historically kept the sexes from achieving total equality.

Recently, gender criticism has expanded beyond its original feminist perspective. In the last twenty years or so, critics in the field of gay and lesbian studies—some of whom describe their discipline as "queer theory"—have explored the impact of different sexual orientations on literary creation and reception. Seeking to establish a canon of classic gay and lesbian authors, these critics argue that sexual orientation is so central a component of human personality (especially when it necessarily puts one at odds with established social and moral norms) that to ignore it in connection with such writers amounts to a fundamental misreading and misunderstanding of their work. A men's movement has also emerged in response to feminism, seeking not to reject feminism but to rediscover masculine identity in an authentic, contemporary way. Led by poet Robert Bly, the men's movement has paid special attention to interpreting poetry and fables as myths of psychic growth and sexual identity.

Elaine Showalter (b. 1941)

Toward a Feminist Poetics 1979

Feminist criticism can be divided into two distinct varieties. The first type is concerned with *woman as reader* —with woman as the consumer of male-produced literature, and with the way in which the hypothesis of a female reader changes our apprehension of a given text, awakening us to the significance of its sexual codes. I shall call this kind of analysis the *feminist critique*, and like other kinds of critique it is a historically grounded inquiry which probes the ideological assumptions of literary phenomena. Its subjects include the images and stereotypes of women in literature, the omissions of and misconceptions about women in criticism, and the fissures in male-constructed literary history. It is also concerned with the exploitation and manipulation of the female audience, especially in popular culture and film; and with the analysis of woman-as-sign in semiotic systems. The second type of feminist criticism is concerned with *woman as writer*—with woman as the producer of textual meaning, with the history, themes, genres, and structures of literature by women. Its subjects include the psychodynamics of female creativity; linguistics and the problem of a female language; the trajectory of the individual or collective female literary career; literary history; and, of course, studies of particular writers and works. No term exists in English for such a specialized discourse, and so I have adapted the French term *la gynocritique*: "gynocritics" (although the significance of the male pseudonym in the history of women's writing also suggested the term "georgics").

The feminist critique is essentially political and polemical, with theoretical affiliations to Marxist sociology and aesthetics; gynocritics is more self-contained and experimental, with connections to other modes of new feminist research. In a dialogue between these two positions, Carolyn Heilbrun, the writer, and Catharine Stimpson, editor of the journal *Signs: Women in Culture and Society*, compare the feminist critique to the Old Testament, "looking for the sins and errors of the past," and gynocritics to the New Testament, seeking "the grace of imagination." Both kinds are necessary, they explain, for only the Jeremiahs of the feminist critique can lead us out of the "Egypt of female servitude" to the promised land of the feminist vision. That the discussion makes use of these Biblical metaphors points to the connections between feminist consciousness and conversion narratives which often appear in women's literature; Carolyn Heilbrun comments on her own text, "When I talk about feminist criticism, I am amazed at how high a moral tone I take."

From "Toward a Feminist Poetics"

Nina Pelikan Straus

Transformations in *The Metamorphosis* 1989

Traditionally, critics of *Metamorphosis* have underplayed the fact that the story is about not only Gregor's but also his family's and, especially, Grete's metamorphosis. Yet it is mainly Grete, woman, daughter, sister, on whom the social and psychoanalytic resonances of the text depend. It is she who will ironically "blossom" as her brother deteriorates; it is she whose mirror reflects women's present situations as we attempt to critique patriarchal dominance in order to create new lives that avoid the replication of invalidation. . . .

If Grete is a symbol of anything, it is the irony of self-liberation in relation to the indeterminacy of gender roles. Grete's role as a woman unfolds as Gregor's life as a man collapses. It is no accident that this gender scrolling takes place in the literature of a writer who had curious experiences in his life with women—experiences of his own weakness and of women's strengths. Traditionally, the text has been read not as revealing brother-sister or gender-based relationships, however, but as revealing a father-son conflict or Oedipus complex.

• • •

The word "shame" is central to both Grete and Gregor's experiences. It is a shame that Gregor cannot get out of bed, that he cannot get up to go to work, that his voice fails him, that he cannot open the door of his room with his insect pincers, that he must be fed, that he stinks and must hide his body that is a shame to others. Shame comes from seeing oneself through another's eyes, from Gregor's seeing himself through Grete's eyes, and from the reader's seeing Grete through the narrator's eyes. The text graphically mirrors how we see each other in various shameful (and comic) conditions. Through Gregor's condition, ultimately shameful because he is reduced to the dependency of an ugly baby, Kafka imagines what it is like to be dependent on the care of women. And Kafka is impressed with women's efforts to keep their households and bodies clean and alive. This impression is enlarged with every detail that humiliates and weakens Gregor while simultaneously empowering Grete, who cares for Gregor, ironically, at his own—and perhaps at Kafka's—expense.

The change or metamorphosis is in this sense a literary experiment that plays with problems the story's title barely suggests. For Kafka there can be no change without an exchange, no flourishing of Grete without Gregor's withering; nor can the meaning of transformation entail a final closure that prevents further transformations. The metamorphosis occurs both in the first sentence of the text—"When Gregor Samsa awoke one morning from unsettling dreams, he found himself changed in his bed into a monstrous vermin"—and in the last paragraph of the story, which describes Grete's transformation into a woman "blossoming" and "stretching" toward the family's "new dreams" once Gregor has been transformed into garbage. Grete's final transformation, rendered in concrete bodily terms, is foreshadowed in Gregor's initial transformation from human into vermin. This deliberately reflective textual pattern implies that only when the distorting mirrors of the sexist fun house are dismantled can the sons of the patriarchs recognize themselves as dehumanized and dehumanizing. Only when Grete blooms into an eligible young woman, ripe for the job and marriage markets, can we recognize that her empowerment is also an ironic reification. She has been transformed at another's expense, and she will carry within her the marketplace value that has ultimately destroyed Gregor.

From "Transforming Franz Kafka's *Metamorphosis*"

Richard R. Bozorth (b. 1965)

"Tell Me the Truth About Love" 2001

The 1994 film *Four Weddings and a Funeral* has probably done more to popularize Auden than any other recent event. It is also an instructive moment in his reception, for where the academy has often praised his work for its universality, the film invokes him as a gay sage: before reciting "Funeral Blues" at his lover's funeral, the character Matthew prefaces it by calling Auden "another splendid bugger" like the late Gareth.

This scene makes visible a number of significant occlusions in Auden's love poetry, including those he himself instigated. This lyric first appeared in Auden and Isherwood's play *The Ascent of F6* (1936), recited to "A Blues" at the death of James Ransom, the protagonist's brother.[2] The version used in the film dates from 1938 and gained the title "Funeral Blues" in *Another Time* (1940). Included there as one of "Four Cabaret Songs for Miss Hedli Anderson," it is presented as an exercise in light verse. As Mendelson notes, its dedication to Benjamin Britten's favorite soprano was a form of disguise Auden used only for love poems with masculine pronouns.[3] By putting the text in the voice of a gay male character, *Four Weddings and a Funeral* outs the poem, much as Matthew uses it to affirm before the mourners the romantic nature of his relationship with Gareth. Auden's words become a poignant utterance about the public unspeakability of gay love:

[2]W. H. Auden and Christopher Isherwood, *Plays and Other Dramatic Writings by W. H. Auden, 1928–1938*, ed. Edward Mendelson (Princeton: Princeton UP, 1988) 350–51.
[3]Edward Mendelson, *Later Auden* (New York: Farrar, 1999) 32.

Let aeroplanes circle moaning overhead
Scribbling on the sky the message He Is Dead,
Put crêpe bows round the white necks of the public doves,
Let the traffic policemen wear black cotton gloves.[4]

In cinematic context, such extravagance is not just an effect of the conventions of light verse, or an expression of anguish that the world goes blithely on—a feeling hardly limited, of course, to gay mourners. For these campy pleas for public ritual point up a gap between gay romantic loss and official forms of lament.

To read "Funeral Blues" as expressing a universal sense of the unfairness of death is to be so taken by Auden's facility with romantic commonplace as to be deaf to its sexual-political implications. For its part, *Four Weddings and a Funeral* risks another illusion in recovering Auden as a master of gay pathos. Perhaps his most touching line came with the 1938 revision: "I thought that love would last forever; I was wrong." Auden was evidently responding not to death but to the end of the affair that had generated most of his love poetry since 1932.[5] But while it is almost irresistible to see the poem as voicing utter desolation at a breakup, impermanence had always haunted Auden's love poems. "Certainty" and "fidelity," in his famous words, are delusions of lovers "in their ordinary swoon."[6] From this angle, "Funeral Blues" might sound contrived or even cruel, since it mourned someone still living. But the poem might also be read as a confession that grief can be a self-indulgent performance, as manipulative of oneself as it is of others. Rather than obscuring the personal, Auden's title invites moral reflection: grieving can indeed be "Funeral Blues"—a way of acting out romantic pathos.

Both universalizing and "gay-positive" readings of "Funeral Blues" find it confirming what we—however "we" may be defined—already feel: we sentimentally construe the mourning voice as echoing our own desires. To read the poem instead as Auden's private response to the end of a homosexual love affair is to see its expression of grief as a means for reflection on love. We have seen how Auden used "parable" to articulate the social value of poetry as an antiuniversalizing form, and this chapter extends my concern with his poetic theory. My largest claim is that Auden came to treat poetry itself as a kind of lovers' discourse: a site of intimate relation between poet and reader in all their particularities. Poetry would be an erotic "game of knowledge," as Auden writes in the 1948 essay "Squares and Oblongs": "a bringing to consciousness . . . of emotions and their hidden relationships."[7]

From *Auden's Games of Knowledge: Poetry and the Meanings of Homosexuality*

READER-RESPONSE CRITICISM

Reader-response criticism attempts to describe what happens in the reader's mind while interpreting a text. If traditional criticism assumes that imaginative writing is a creative act, reader-response theory recognizes that reading is also a creative process. Reader-response critics believe that no text provides self-contained meaning; literary texts do not exist independently of readers' interpretations. A text, according to this

[4]W. H. Auden, *The English Auden: Poems, Prose and Dramatic Writings* (London: Faber, 1977) 163.
[5]Mendelson, *Later Auden* 32.
[6]Auden, *English Auden* 207.
[7]W. H. Auden, "Squares and Oblongs," *Poets at Work*, ed. Charles D. Abbot (New York: Harcourt, 1948) 173.

critical school, is not finished until it is read and interpreted. As Oscar Wilde remarked in the preface to his novel *The Picture of Dorian Gray* (1891), "It is the spectator, and not life, that art really mirrors." The practical problem then arises, however, that no two individuals necessarily read a text in exactly the same way. Rather than declare one interpretation correct and the other mistaken, reader-response criticism recognizes the inevitable plurality of readings. Instead of trying to ignore or reconcile the contradictions inherent in this situation, it explores them.

The easiest way to explain reader-response criticism is to relate it to the common experience of rereading a favorite book after many years. Rereading a novel as an adult, for example, that "changed your life" as an adolescent, is often a shocking experience. The book may seem substantially different. The character you remembered liking most now seems less admirable, and another character you disliked now seems more sympathetic. Has the book changed? Very unlikely, but *you* certainly have in the intervening years. Reader-response criticism explores how different individuals (or classes of individuals) see the same text differently. It emphasizes how religious, cultural, and social values affect readings; it also overlaps with gender criticism in exploring how men and women read the same text with different assumptions.

While reader-response criticism rejects the notion that there can be a single correct reading for a literary text, it doesn't consider all readings permissible. Each text creates limits to its possible interpretations. As Stanley Fish admits in the following critical selection, we cannot arbitrarily place an Eskimo in William Faulkner's story "A Rose for Emily" (though Professor Fish does ingeniously imagine a hypothetical situation where this bizarre interpretation might actually be possible).

Stanley Fish (b. 1938)

An Eskimo "A Rose for Emily" 1980

The fact that it remains easy to think of a reading that most of us would dismiss out of hand does not mean that the text excludes it but that there is as yet no elaborated interpretive procedure for producing that text. . . . Norman Holland's analysis of Faulkner's "A Rose for Emily" is a case in point. Holland is arguing for a kind of psychoanalytic pluralism. The text, he declares, is "at most a matrix of psychological possibilities for its readers," but, he insists, "only some possibilities . . . truly fit the matrix": "One would not say, for example, that a reader of . . . 'A Rose for Emily' who thought the 'tableau' [of Emily and her father in the doorway] described an Eskimo was really responding to the story at all—only pursuing some mysterious inner exploration."

Holland is making two arguments: first, that anyone who proposes an Eskimo reading of "A Rose for Emily" will not find a hearing in the literary community. And that, I think, is right. ("We are right to rule out at least some readings.") His second argument is that the unacceptability of the Eskimo reading is a function of the text, of what he calls its "sharable promptuary," the public "store of structured language" that sets limits to the interpretations the words can accommodate. And that, I think, is wrong. The Eskimo reading is unacceptable because there is at present no interpretive strategy for producing it, no way of "looking" or reading (and remember, all acts of looking or reading are "ways") that would result in the emergence of obviously Eskimo meanings. This does not mean, however, that no such strategy could ever come into play, and it is not difficult to imagine the circumstances under which it would establish itself. One such circumstance would be the discovery of a letter in which Faulkner confides that he has always believed himself to be an Eskimo changeling.

(The example is absurd only if one forgets Yeats's *Vision* or Blake's Swedenborgianism° or James Miller's recent elaboration of a homosexual reading of *The Waste Land*.) Immediately the workers in the Faulkner industry would begin to reinterpret the canon in the light of this newly revealed "belief" and the work of reinterpretation would involve the elaboration of a symbolic or allusive system (not unlike mythological or typological criticism) whose application would immediately transform the text into one informed everywhere by Eskimo meanings. It might seem that I am admitting that there is a text to be transformed, but the object of transformation would be the text (or texts) given by whatever interpretive strategies the Eskimo strategy was in the process of dislodging or expanding. The result would be that whereas we now have a Freudian "A Rose for Emily," a mythological "A Rose for Emily," a Christological "A Rose for Emily," a regional "A Rose for Emily," a sociological "A Rose for Emily," a linguistic "A Rose for Emily," we would in addition have an Eskimo "A Rose for Emily," existing in some relation of compatibility or incompatibility with the others.

Again the point is that while there are always mechanisms for ruling out readings, their source is not the text but the presently recognized interpretive strategies for producing the text. It follows, then, that no reading, however outlandish it might appear, is inherently an impossible one.

From *Is There a Text in This Class?*

Robert Scholes (b. 1929)

"How Do We Make a Poem?" 1982

Let us begin with one of the shortest poetic texts in the English language, "Elegy" by W. S. Merwin:

Who would I show it to

One line, one sentence, unpunctuated, but proclaimed an interrogative by its grammar and syntax—what makes it a poem? Certainly without its title it would not be a poem; but neither would the title alone constitute a poetic text. Nor do the two together simply make a poem by themselves. Given the title and the text, the *reader* is encouraged to make a poem. He is not forced to do so, but there is not much else he can do with this material, and certainly nothing else so rewarding. (I will use the masculine pronoun here to refer to the reader, not because all readers are male but because I am, and my hypothetical reader is not a pure construct but an idealized version of myself.)

How do we make a poem out of this text? There are only two things to work on, the title and the question posed by the single, colloquial line. The line is not simply colloquial, it is prosaic; with no words of more than one syllable, concluded by a preposition, it is within the utterance range of every speaker of English. It is, in a sense, completely intelligible. But in another sense it is opaque, mysterious. Its three pronouns—who, I, it—pose problems of reference. Its conditional verb phrase—would . . . show to—poses a problem of situation. The context that would supply the

Yeats's Vision or *Blake's Swedenborgianism:* Irish poet William Butler Yeats and Swedish mystical writer Emanuel Swedenborg both claimed to have received revelations from the spirit world; some of Swedenborg's ideas are embodied in the long poems of William Blake.

information required to make that simple sentence meaningful as well as intelligible is not there. It must be supplied by the reader.

To make a poem of this text the reader must not only know English, he must know a poetic code as well: the code of the funeral elegy, as practiced in English from the Renaissance to the present time. The "words on the page" do not constitute a poetic "work," complete and self-sufficient, but a "text," a sketch or outline that must be completed by the active participation of a reader equipped with the right sort of information. In this case part of that information consists of an acquaintance with the elegiac tradition: its procedures, assumptions, devices, and values. One needs to know works like Milton's "Lycidas," Shelley's "Adonais," Tennyson's *In Memoriam*, Whitman's "When Lilacs Last in the Dooryard Bloom'd," Thomas's "Refusal to Mourn the Death, by Fire, of a Child in London," and so on, in order to "read" this simple poem properly. In fact, it could be argued that the more elegies one can bring to bear on a reading of this one, the better, richer poem this one becomes. I would go even further, suggesting that a knowledge of the critical tradition—of Dr. Johnson's objections to "Lycidas," for instance, or Wordsworth's critique of poetic diction—will also enhance one's reading of this poem. For the poem is, of course, an anti-elegy, a refusal not simply to mourn, but to write a sonorous, eloquent, mournful, but finally acquiescent, accepting—in a word, "elegiac"—poem at all.

Reading the poem involves, then, a special knowledge of its tradition. It also involves a special interpretive skill. The forms of the short, written poem as they have developed in English over the past few centuries can be usefully seen as compressed, truncated, or fragmented imitations of other verbal forms, especially the play, story, public oration, and personal essay. The reasons for this are too complicated for consideration here, but the fact will be apparent to all who reflect upon the matter. Our short poems are almost always elliptical versions of what can easily be conceived of as dramatic, narrative, oratorical, or meditative texts. Often, they are combinations of these and other modes of address. To take an obvious example, the dramatic monologue in the hands of Robert Browning is like a speech from a play (though usually more elongated than most such speeches). But to "read" such a monologue we must imagine the setting, the situation, the context, and so on. The dramatic monologue is "like" a play but gives us less information of certain sorts than a play would, requiring us to provide that information by decoding the clues in the monologue itself in the light of our understanding of the generic model. Most short poems work this way. They require both special knowledge and special skills to be "read."

To understand "Elegy" we must construct a situation out of the clues provided. The "it" in "Who would I show it to" is of course the elegy itself. The "I" is the potential writer of the elegy. The "Who" is the audience for the poem. But the verb phrase "would . . . show to" indicates a condition contrary to fact. Who would I show it to *if* I were to write it? This implies in turn that for the potential elegiac poet there is one person whose appreciation means more than that of all the rest of the potential audience for the poem he might write, and it further implies that the death of this particular person is the one imagined in the poem. If this person were dead, the poet suggests, so would his inspiration be dead. With no one to write for, no poem would be forthcoming. This poem is not only a "refusal to mourn," like that of Dylan Thomas, it is a refusal to elegize. The whole elegiac tradition, like its cousin the funeral oration, turns finally away from mourning toward acceptance, revival, renewal, a return to the concerns of life, symbolized by the very writing of the poem. Life goes on; there *is* an audience; and the mourned person will live through accomplishments, influence, descendants, and also (not least) in the elegiac poem itself. Merwin rejects all that. *If* I wrote an elegy for X, the person for whom I have always written, X would not be alive to read it; therefore, there is no reason to write an elegy for the one person in my life who most deserves one; therefore, there is no reason to write any elegy, anymore, ever. Finally, and of course, this poem called "Elegy" is not an elegy.

From *Semiotics and Interpretation*

Michael J. Colacurcio (b. 1936)

The End of Young Goodman Brown 1995

Having begun by assuming that all visible sanctity was real sanctity and by presuming his own final perseverance in faith, having next despaired of *all* virtue, he [Goodman Brown] ends by doubting the existence of any unblighted goodness but his own. There is simply no other way to account for the way Goodman Brown spends the rest of his life. Evidently he clings to the precious knowledge that he, at least, resisted the wicked one's final invitation to diabolical communion; accordingly, the lurid satisfactions of Satan's anti-covenant are not available to him. But neither are the sweet delights of the Communion of the Saints. He knows he resisted the "last, last crime" of witchcraft, but his deepest suspicion seems to be that Faith did not resist. Or if that seems too strong a formulation for tender-minded readers, he cannot make his faith in Faith prevail. Without such a prevailing faith, he is left outside the bounds of all communion: his own unbartered soul is the only certain locus of goodness in a world otherwise altogether blasted.

It would be easy enough to praise Young Goodman Brown for his recovery from the blasphemous nihilism of his mid-forest rage against the universe; for his refusal to translate his cosmic paranoia into an Ahabian plan of counterattack. Or, from another point of view, it would even be possible to suggest that if the Devil's proffered community of evil is the only community possible, perhaps he should have accepted membership instead of protecting the insular sacredness of his own separate and too precious soul. Perhaps salvation is not worth having—perhaps it is meaningless—in a universe where depravity has undone so many. But both of these moral prescriptions miss Hawthorne's principal emphasis, which, as I read the tale, is on the problem of faith and evidence; on that peculiar kind of "doubt" (in epistemological essence, really a kind of negative faith) which follows from a discrediting of evidences formerly trusted. Brown is damned to stony moral isolation because his "evidential" Puritan biases have led him all unprepared into a terrifying betrayal of Faith. He believes the Devil's spectral suggestions not merely because he is naive, though he is that; and not merely because he is incapable of the sort of evidential subtlety by which John Cotton instructed the very first members of those newly purified New England churches in the art of separating sheep and goats, or by which the Mathers sermonized the court of Oyer and Terminer on the occult art of the distinguishing of spirits. Brown believes the Devil because, at one level, the projected guilt of a man in bad faith *is* specter evidence and because, even more fundamentally, absolute moral quality is related to outward appearance as a real person is to his specter.

In short, Hawthorne suggests, one had better not raise such ultimate questions at all: to do so is to risk the appearance-and-reality question in its most pernicious, even "paranoic" form. At best one would be accepting the deceptive appearances of sanctity, as Goodman Brown evidently continued to be accepted at the communion table of a community which never suspected his presumption, despair, blasphemy, and his near approach to witchcraft. . . . And at worst, if one is already in bad faith, his penetrating glimpses into the "reality" behind the appearances will be no more than spectral projections of his own guilty wishes. . . . The truly naive will simply accept the smiling light of daytime, church-day appearances; the already compromised will "see" in others (as irrevocable commitment) what already pre-exists in themselves (as fantasy, wish, desire, or momentary intention). The only alternative would seem to be the acceptance of some ultimate and fundamental equality in a common moral struggle; a healthy skepticism about all moral appearances, firmly wedded to the faith that, whatever men may fantasize, or however they may fall, they generally love the good and hate the evil.

From *The Province of Piety: Moral History in Hawthorne's Early Tales*

DECONSTRUCTIONIST CRITICISM

Deconstructionist criticism rejects the traditional assumption that language can accurately represent reality. Language, according to deconstructionists, is a fundamentally unstable medium; consequently, literary texts, which are made up of words, have no fixed, single meaning. Deconstructionists insist, according to critic Paul de Man, on "the impossibility of making the actual expression coincide with what has to be expressed, of making the actual signs coincide with what is signified." Since they believe that literature cannot definitively express its subject matter, deconstructionists tend to shift their attention away from *what* is being said to *how* language is being used in a text.

Paradoxically, deconstructionist criticism often resembles formalist criticism; both methods usually involve close reading. But while a formalist usually tries to demonstrate how the diverse elements of a text cohere into meaning, the deconstructionist approach attempts to show how the text "deconstructs," that is, how it can be broken down—by a skeptical critic—into mutually irreconcilable positions. A biographical or historical critic might seek to establish the author's intention as a means to interpreting a literary work, but deconstructionists reject the notion that the critic should endorse the myth of authorial control over language. Deconstructionist critics like Roland Barthes and Michel Foucault have therefore called for "the death of the author," that is, the rejection of the assumption that the author, no matter how ingenious, can fully control the meaning of a text. They have also announced the death of literature as a special category of writing. In their view, poems and novels are merely words on a page that deserve no privileged status as art; all texts are created equal—equally untrustworthy, that is.

Deconstructionists focus on how language is used to achieve power. Since they believe, in the words of critic David Lehman, that "there are no truths, only rival interpretations," deconstructionists try to understand how some "interpretations" come to be regarded as truth. A major goal of deconstruction is to demonstrate how those supposed truths are at best provisional and at worst contradictory.

Deconstruction, as you may have inferred, calls for intellectual subtlety and skill. If you pursue your literary studies beyond the introductory stage, you will want to become more familiar with its assumptions. Deconstruction may strike you as a negative, even destructive, critical approach, and yet its best practitioners are adept at exposing the inadequacy of much conventional criticism. By patient analysis, they can sometimes open up the most familiar text and find unexpected significance.

Roland Barthes (1915–1980)

The Death of the Author 1968

Translated by Stephen Heath

Succeeding the Author, the scriptor no longer bears within him passions, humours, feelings, impressions, but rather this immense dictionary from which he draws a writing that can know no halt: life never does more than imitate the book, and the book itself is only a tissue of signs, an imitation that is lost, infinitely deferred.

Once the Author is removed, the claim to decipher a text becomes quite futile. To give a text an Author is to impose a limit on that text, to furnish it with a final signified, to close the writing. Such a conception suits criticism very well, the latter then allotting itself the important task of discovering the Author (or its hypostases: society, history, psyché, liberty) beneath the work: when the Author has been found, the text is "explained"—victory to the critic. Hence there is no surprise in the fact that, historically, the reign of the Author has also been that of the Critic, nor again in the fact that criticism (be it new) is today undermined along with the Author. In the multiplicity of writing, everything is to be *disentangled*, nothing *deciphered;* the structure can be followed, "run" (like the thread of a stocking) at every point and at every level, but there is nothing beneath: the space of writing is to be ranged over, not pierced; writing ceaselessly posits meaning ceaselessly to evaporate it, carrying out a systematic exemption of meaning. In precisely this way literature (it would be better from now on to say *writing*), by refusing to assign a "secret," an ultimate meaning, to the text (and to the world as text), liberates what may be called an anti-theological activity, an activity that is truly revolutionary since to refuse to fix meaning is, in the end, to refuse God and his hypostases—reason, science, law.

From "The Death of the Author"

Barbara Johnson (b. 1947)

Rigorous Unreliability 1987

As a critique of a certain Western conception of the nature of signification, deconstruction focuses on the functioning of claim-making and claim-subverting structures within texts. A deconstructive reading is an attempt to show how the conspicuously foregrounded statements in a text are systematically related to discordant signifying elements that the text has thrown into its shadows or margins, an attempt both to recover what is lost and to analyze what happens when a text is read solely in function of intentionality, meaningfulness, and representativity. Deconstruction thus confers a new kind of readability on those elements in a text that readers have traditionally been trained to disregard, overcome, explain away, or edit out—contradictions, obscurities, ambiguities, incoherences, discontinuities, ellipses, interruptions, repetitions, and plays of the signifier. In this sense it involves a reversal of values, a revaluation of the signifying function of everything that, in a signified-based theory of meaning, would constitute "noise." Derrida° has chosen to speak of the values involved in this reversal in terms of "speech" and "writing," in which "speech" stands for the privilege accorded to meaning as immediacy, unity, identity, truth, and presence,

Derrida: Jacques Derrida (1930–2004), French philosopher active in the development of deconstructionism.

while "writing" stands for the devalued functions of distance, difference, dissimulation, and deferment.

This transvaluation has a number of consequences for the appreciation of literature. By shifting the attention from intentional meaning to writing as such, deconstruction has enabled readers to become sensitive to a number of recurrent literary topoi° in a new way.

• • •

In addition, by seeing interpretation itself as a fiction-making activity, deconstruction has both reversed and displaced the narrative categories of "showing" and "telling," mimesis and diegesis.° Instead of according moments of textual self-interpretation an authoritative metalinguistic status, deconstruction considers anything the text says about itself to be another fiction, an allegory of the reading process. Hence, the privilege traditionally granted to showing over telling is reversed: "telling" becomes a more sophisticated form of "showing," in which what is "shown" is the breakdown of the show/tell distinction. Far from doing the reader's work for her, the text's self-commentary only gives the reader more to do. Indeed, it is the way in which a text subverts the possibility of any authoritative reading by inscribing the reader's strategies into its own structures that often, for de Man, ends up being constitutive of literature as such.

Deconstructors, therefore, tend to privilege texts that are self-reflexive in interestingly and rigorously unreliable ways. Since self-reflexive texts often explicitly posit themselves as belated or revolutionary with respect to a tradition on which they comment, deconstruction can both reinstate the self-consciously outmoded or overwritten (such as Melville's *Pierre*°) and canonize the experimental or avant-garde. But because deconstruction has focused on the ways in which the Western white male philosophico-literary tradition subverts itself *from within*, it has often tended to remain within the confines of the established literary and philosophical canon. . . . If it has questioned the boundary lines of literature, it has done so not with respect to the non-canonical but with respect to the line between literature and philosophy or between literature and criticism. It is as a rethinking of those distinctions that deconstruction most radically displaces certain traditional evaluative assumptions.

From *A World of Difference*

Geoffrey Hartman (b. 1929)

On Wordsworth's "A Slumber Did My Spirit Seal" 1987

Take Wordsworth's well-known lyric of eight lines, one of the "Lucy" poems, which has been explicated so many times without its meaning being fully determined:

A slumber did my spirit seal;
    I had no human fears—
She seemed a thing that could not feel
    The touch of earthly years.

topoi: the plural of the Greek *topos*, for "place"; it means a commonly used literary device. *diegesis*: the main events of a story, the basic plot, as distinct from the narration. *Pierre*: *Pierre, or the Ambiguities* (1852), a complex novel by Herman Melville, was a failure during the author's lifetime; it was not widely read until the mid-twentieth century.

No motion has she now, no force;
She neither hears nor sees;
Rolled round in earth's diurnal course,
With rocks, and stones, and trees.

It does not matter whether you interpret the second stanza (especially its last line) as tending toward affirmation, or resignation, or a grief verging on bitterness. The tonal assignment of one rather than another possible meaning, to repeat Susanne Langer° on musical form, is curiously open or beside the point. Yet the lyric does not quite support Langer's general position, that "Articulation is its life, but not assertion," because the poem is composed of a series of short and definitive statements, very like assertions. You could still claim that the poem's life is not in the assertions but somewhere else: but where then? What would articulation mean in that case? Articulation is not anti-assertive here; indeed the sense of closure is so strong that it thematizes itself in the very first line.

Nevertheless, is not the harmony or aesthetic effect of the poem greater than this local conciseness; is not the sense of closure broader and deeper than our admiration for a perfect technical construct? The poem is surely something else than a fine box, a well-wrought coffin.

That it is a kind of epitaph is relevant, of course. We recognize, even if genre is not insisted on, that Wordsworth's style is laconic, even lapidary. There may be a mimetic or formal motive related to the ideal of epitaphic poetry. But the motive may also be, in a precise way, meta-epitaphic. The poem, first of all, marks the closure of a life that has never opened up: Lucy is likened in other poems to a hidden flower or the evening star. Setting overshadows rising, and her mode of existence is inherently inward, westering. I will suppose then, that Wordsworth was at some level giving expression to the traditional epitaphic wish: Let the earth rest lightly on the deceased. If so, his conversion of this epitaphic formula is so complete that to trace the process of conversion might seem gratuitous. The formula, a trite if deeply grounded figure of speech, has been catalyzed out of existence. Here it is formula itself, or better, the adjusted words of the mourner that lie lightly on the girl and everyone who is a mourner.

I come back, then, to the "aesthetic" sense of a burden lifted, rather than denied. A heavy element is made lighter. One may still feel that the term "elation" is inappropriate in this context; yet elation is, as a mood, the very subject of the first stanza. For the mood described is love or desire when it *eternizes* the loved person, when it makes her a star-like being that "could not feel / The touch of earthly years." This *naive* elation, this spontaneous movement of the spirit upward, is reversed in the downturn or catastrophe of the second stanza. Yet this stanza does not close out the illusion; it preserves it within the elegaic form. The illusion is elated, in our use of the word: *aufgehoben*° seems the proper term. For the girl is still, and all the more, what she seemed to be: beyond touch, like a star, if the earth in its daily motion is a planetary and erring rather than a fixed star, and if all on this star of earth must partake of its sublunar, mortal, temporal nature.

• • •

Susanne Langer: Langer (1895–1985) was an American philosopher who discussed the relationship between aesthetics and artistic form. *aufgehoben:* German for "taken up" or "lifted up," but this term can also mean "canceled" or "nullified." Hartman uses the term for its double meaning.

To sum up: In Wordsworth's lyric the specific gravity of words is weighed in the balance of each stanza; and this balance is as much a judgment on speech in the context of our mortality as it is a meaningful response to the individual death. At the limit of the medium of words, and close to silence, what has been purged is not concreteness, or the empirical sphere of the emotions—shock, disillusion, trauma, recognition, grief, atonement—what has been purged is a series of flashy schematisms and false or partial mediations: artificial plot, inflated consolatory rhetoric, the coercive absolutes of logic or faith.

From "Elation in Hegel and Wordsworth"

CULTURAL STUDIES

Unlike the other critical approaches discussed in this chapter, cultural criticism (or **cultural studies**) does not offer a single way of analyzing literature. No central methodology is associated with cultural studies. Nor is cultural criticism solely, or even mainly, concerned with literary texts in the conventional sense. Instead, the term *cultural studies* refers to a relatively recent interdisciplinary field of academic inquiry. This field borrows methodologies from other approaches to analyze a wide range of cultural products and practices.

To understand cultural studies, it helps to know a bit about its origins. In the English-speaking world, the field was first defined at the Centre for Contemporary Cultural Studies of Birmingham University in Britain. Founded in 1964, this graduate program tried to expand the range of literary study beyond traditional approaches to canonic literature in order to explore a broader spectrum of historical, cultural, and political issues. The most influential teacher at the Birmingham Centre was Raymond Williams (1921–1983), a Welsh socialist with wide intellectual interests. Williams argued that scholars should not study culture as a canon of great works by individual artists but rather examine it as an evolutionary process that involves the entire society. "We cannot separate literature and art," Williams said, "from other kinds of social practice." The cultural critic, therefore, does not study fixed aesthetic objects so much as dynamic social processes. The critic's challenge is to identify and understand the complex forms and effects of the process of culture.

A Marxist intellectual, Williams called his approach cultural materialism (a reference to the Marxist doctrine of dialectical materialism), but later scholars soon discarded that name for two broader and more neutral terms, cultural criticism and cultural studies. From the start, this interdisciplinary field relied heavily on literary theory, especially Marxist and feminist criticism. It also employed the documentary techniques of historical criticism combined with political analysis focused on issues of social class, race, and gender. (This approach flourished in the United States, where it is called New Historicism.) Cultural studies is also deeply antiformalist, since the field concerns itself with investigating the complex relationships among history, politics, and literature. Cultural studies rejects the notion that literature exists in an aesthetic realm separate from ethical and political categories.

A chief goal of cultural studies is to understand the nature of social power as reflected in "texts." For example, if the object of analysis were a sonnet by Shakespeare, the cultural studies adherent might investigate the moral, psychological, and political assumptions reflected in the poem and then deconstruct them to see what individuals, social classes, or gender might benefit from having those assumptions perceived as true. The relevant mission of cultural studies is to identify both the overt and covert values reflected in a cultural practice. The cultural studies critic also tries to trace out and understand the structures of meaning that hold those assumptions in place and give them the appearance of objective representation. Any analytical technique that helps illuminate these issues is employed.

In theory, a cultural studies critic might employ any methodology. In practice, however, he or she will most often borrow concepts from deconstruction, Marxist analysis, gender criticism, race theory, and psychology. Each of these earlier methodologies provides particular analytical tools that cultural critics find useful. What cultural studies borrows from deconstructionism is its emphasis on uncovering conflict, dissent, and contradiction in the works under analysis. Whereas traditional critical approaches often sought to demonstrate the unity of a literary work, cultural studies often seeks to portray social, political, and psychological conflicts that the work masks. What cultural studies borrows from Marxist analysis is an attention to the ongoing struggle between social classes, each seeking economic (and therefore political) advantage. Cultural studies often asks questions about what social class created a work of art and what class (or classes) served as its audience. Among the many things that cultural studies borrowed from gender criticism and race theory is a concern with social inequality between the sexes and races. It seeks to investigate how these inequities have been reflected in the texts of a historical period or a society. Cultural studies is, above all, a political enterprise that views literary analysis as a means of furthering social justice.

Since cultural studies does not adhere to any single methodology (or even a consistent set of methodologies), it is impossible to characterize the field briefly, because there are exceptions to every generalization offered. What one sees most clearly are characteristic tendencies, especially the commitment to examining issues of class, race, and gender. There is also the insistence on expanding the focus of critical inquiry beyond traditional high literary culture. British cultural studies guru Anthony Easthope can, for example, analyze with equal aplomb Gerard Manley Hopkins's "The Windhover," Edgar Rice Burroughs's *Tarzan of the Apes*, a Benson and Hedges cigarette advertisement, and Sean Connery's eyebrows. Cultural studies is infamous—even among its practitioners—for its habitual use of literary jargon. It is also notorious for its complex intellectual analysis of mundane materials, such as Easthope's analysis of a cigarette ad, which may be interesting in its own right but remote from most readers' literary experience. Some scholars, such as Camille Paglia, however, use the principles of cultural studies to provide new social, political, and historical insights into canonic texts such as William Blake's "The Chimney Sweeper." Omnivorous, iconoclastic, and relentlessly analytic, cultural criticism has become a major presence in contemporary literary studies.

Vincent B. Leitch (b. 1944)

Poststructuralist Cultural Critique 1992

Whereas a major goal of New Criticism and much other modern formalistic criticism is aesthetic evaluation of freestanding texts, a primary objective of cultural criticism is cultural critique, which entails investigation and assessment of ruling and oppositional beliefs, categories, practices, and representations, inquiring into the causes, constitutions, and consequences as well as the modes of circulation and consumption of linguistic, social, economic, political, historical, ethical, religious, legal, scientific, philosophical, educational, familial, and aesthetic discourses and institutions. In rendering a judgment on an aesthetic artifact, a New Critic privileges such key things as textual coherence and unity, intricacy and complexity, ambiguity and irony, tension and balance, economy and autonomy, literariness and spatial form. In mounting a critique of a cultural "text," an advocate of poststructuralist cultural criticism evaluates such things as degrees of exclusion and inclusion, of complicity and resistance, of domination and letting-be, of abstraction and situatedness, of violence and tolerance, of monologue and polylogue, of quietism and activism, of sameness and otherness, of oppression and emancipation, of centralization and decentralization. Just as the aforementioned system of evaluative criteria underlies the exegetical and judgmental labor of New Criticism, so too does the above named set of commitments undergird the work of poststructuralist cultural critique.

Given its commitments, poststructuralist cultural criticism is, as I have suggested, suspicious of literary formalism. Specifically, the trouble with New Criticism is its inclination to advocate a combination of quietism and asceticism, connoisseurship and exclusiveness, aestheticism and apoliticism. . . . The monotonous practical effect of New Critical reading is to illustrate the subservience of each textual element to a higher, overarching, economical poetic structure without remainders. What should be evident here is that the project of poststructuralist cultural criticism possesses a set of commitments and criteria that enable it to engage in the enterprise of cultural critique. It should also be evident that the cultural ethicopolitics of this enterprise is best characterized, using current terminology, as "liberal" or "leftist," meaning congruent with certain socialist, anarchist, and libertarian ideals, none of which, incidentally, are necessarily Marxian. Such congruence, derived from extrapolating a generalized stance for poststructuralism, constitutes neither a party platform nor an observable course of practical action; avowed tendencies often account for little in the unfolding of practical engagements.

From *Cultural Criticism, Literary Theory, Poststructuralism*

Mark Bauerlein (b. 1959)

What Is Cultural Studies?

1997

Traditionally, disciplines naturally fell into acknowledged subdivisions, for example, as literary criticism broke up into formalist literary criticism, philological criticism, narratological analysis, and other methodologically distinguished pursuits, all of which remained comfortably within the category "literary criticism." But cultural studies eschews such institutional disjunctions and will not let any straitening adjective precede the "cultural studies" heading. There is no distinct formalist cultural studies or historicist cultural studies, but only cultural studies. (Feminist cultural studies may be one exception.) Cultural studies is a field that will not be parceled out to the available disciplines. It spans culture at large, not this or that institutionally separated element of culture. To guarantee this transcendence of disciplinary institutions, cultural studies must select a name for itself that has no specificity, that has too great an extension to mark off any expedient boundaries for itself. "Cultural studies" serves well because, apart from distinguishing between "physical science" and "cultural analysis," the term provides no indication of where any other boundaries lie.

This is exactly the point. To blur disciplinary boundaries and frustrate the intellectual investments that go along with them is a fundamental motive for cultural studies practice, one that justifies the vagueness of the titular term. This explains why the related label "cultural criticism," so much in vogue in 1988, has declined. The term "criticism" has a narrower extension than does "studies," ruling out some empirical forms of inquiry (like field work) that "studies" admits. "Studies" preserves a methodological openness that "criticism" closes. Since such closures have suspect political intentions behind them, cultural studies maintains its institutional purity by disdaining disciplinary identity and methodological uniformity.

• • •

A single approach will miss too much, will overlook important aspects of culture not perceptible to that particular angle of vision. A multitude of approaches will pick up an insight here and a piece of knowledge there and more of culture will enter into the inquiry. A diversity of methods will match the diversity of culture, thereby sheltering the true nature of culture from the reductive appropriations of formal disciplines.

But how do cultural critics bring all these methods together into a coherent inquiry? Are there any established rules of incorporating "important insights and knowledge" coming out of different methods into a coherent scholarly project of cultural studies? How might a scholar use both phonemic analysis and deconstruction in a single inquiry when deconstructionist arguments call into question the basic premises of phonetics? What scholar has the competence to handle materials from so many disciplines in a rigorous and knowing manner? Does cultural criticism as a "studies" practice offer any transdisciplinary evaluative standards to apply to individual pieces of cultural criticism? If not, if there are no clear methodological procedures or evaluative principles in cultural studies, it is hard to see how one might popularize it, teach it, make it into a recognized scholarly activity. In practical terms, one does not know how to communicate it to others or show students how to do it when it assumes so many different methodological forms. How does one create an academic department out of an outspokenly antidisciplinary practice? What criteria can faculty members jointly invoke when they are trying to make curricular and personnel decisions?

Once again, this is precisely the point. One reason for the generality of the term is to render such institutional questions unanswerable. Cultural studies practice mingles methods from a variety of fields, jumps from one cultural subject matter to another, simultaneously proclaims superiority to other institutionalized inquiries (on a correspondence to culture basis) and renounces its own institutionalization—gestures that strategically forestall disciplinary standards being applied to it. By studying culture in heterogenous ways, by clumping texts, events, persons, objects, and ideologies into a cultural whole (which, cultural critics say, is reality) and bringing a melange of logical argument, speculative propositions, empirical data, and political outlooks to bear upon it, cultural critics invent a new kind of investigation immune to methodological attack.

From *Literary Criticism: An Autopsy*

Camille Paglia (b. 1947)

A Reading of William Blake's "The Chimney Sweeper" 2005

Romantic writers glorified childhood as a state of innocence. Blake's "The Chimney Sweeper," written in the same year as the French Revolution, combines the Romantic cult of the child with the new radical politics, which can both be traced to social thinker Jean-Jacques Rousseau. It is the boy sweep, rather than Blake, who speaks: he acts as the poet's dramatic persona or mask. There is no anger in his tale. On the contrary, the sweep's gentle acceptance of his miserable life makes his exploitation seem all the more atrocious. Blake shifts responsibility for protest onto us.

The poem begins as autobiography, a favorite Romantic genre. Having lost his mother, his natural protector, the small child was "sold" into slavery by his father (1–2). That is, he was apprenticed to a chimney-sweeping firm whose young teams would probably have worked simply for food, lodging, and clothing—basics that the boy's widowed working-class father might well have been unable to provide for his family. Children, soberly garbed in practical black, were used for chimney sweeping because they could wriggle into narrow, cramped spaces. The health risks of this filthy job were many—deformation of a boy's growing skeleton as well as long-term toxic effects from coal dust, now known to be carcinogenic. Chronic throat and lung problems as well as skin irritation must have been common. (Among the specimens floating in formaldehyde at Philadelphia's Mütter Museum, a nineteenth-century medical collection, is a chimney sweep's foot deformed by a bulbous tumor on the instep.)

Blake's sweep was so young when indentured into service that, he admits, he still lisped (2–3). The hawking of products and services by itinerant street vendors was once a lively, raucous feature of urban life. "Sweep, sweep, sweep!" cried the wandering crews seeking a day's employment. But this tiny boy couldn't even form the word: "Weep weep weep weep!" is how it came out—inadvertently sending a damning message to the oblivious world. It's really the thundering indictment of Blake as poet-prophet: Weep, you callous society that enslaves and murders its young; weep for yourself and your defenseless victims.

"So your chimneys I sweep and in soot I sleep": this singsong, matter-of-fact line implicates the reader in the poem's crimes—a confrontational device ordinarily associated with ironically self-conscious writers like Baudelaire (4). The boy may be peacefully resigned to the horror of his everyday reality, but we, locked in our own routines and distanced by genteel book reading, are forced to face our collective indifference. The boy represents the invisible army of manual laborers, charwomen, and janitors who do our dirty work. Scrubbing the infernal warren of brick and stone tunnels, he absorbs soot (symbolizing social sin) into his own skin and clothes, while we stay neat and clean.

The anonymous sweep—made faceless by his role—chatters cheerfully away about his friend "little Tom Dacre," whom he has taken under his wing (5). In this moral vacuum, where parents and caretakers are absent or negligent, the children must nurture each other. When the newcomer's curly hair was shaved off (to keep it from catching fire from live coals), he cried at his disfigurement, experienced as loss of self. Head shaving is a familiar initiatory practice in military and religious settings to reduce individuality and enforce group norms. To soothe little Tom, the solicitous sweep resorts to consolation of pitiful illogic: "when your head's bare / You know that the soot cannot spoil your white hair" (7–8). That's like saying, "Good thing you lost your leg—now you'll never stub your toe!" Tom's white (that is, blond) "lamb's back" hair represents the innocence of the Christlike sacrificial lamb: children, according to Blake, have become scapegoats for society's amorality and greed (6). Their white hair seems unnatural, as if the boys have been vaulted forward to old age without enjoying the freedoms and satisfactions of virile adulthood. For modern readers, the bald children's caged sameness is disturbingly reminiscent of that of emaciated survivors of Nazi concentration camps, where liberation was met with blank stoicism.

Amazingly, the sweep's desperate reassurance works: Tom goes "quiet," and for the next three stanzas, the whole center of the text, we enter his dreams (9–20). The poem seems to crack open in an ecstatic allegory of rebirth: the children of industrial London escape by the "thousands" from a living death, the locked "coffins of black" that are their soot-stained bodies as well as the chimneys where they spend their days (11–12). Alas, Tom's vision of paradise is nothing more than a simple, playful childhood—the birthright that was robbed from them. The poem overflows with the boys' repressed energy and vitality, as "leaping, laughing, they run" across the "green plain" of nature, then plunge into the purifying "river." Bathed "white," they "shine" with their own inner light, bright as the "sun" (15–18).

But something goes terribly wrong. The "Angel" with the "bright key" who was their liberator inexplicably turns oppressor (13, 19). As the sweeps "rise upon clouds" toward heaven and "sport in the wind" like prankish cherubs casting off their burdens (the "bags" of brushes and collected soot), an officiously moralistic voice cuts into the dream and terminates it: "And the Angel told Tom, if he'd be a good boy, / He'd have God for his father, and never want joy" (17–20). That Tom wakes right up suggests that the voice actually belongs to the boss or overseer, briskly rousing his charges before dawn. The angel's homily, heavy with conventional piety, stops the children's fun and free motion dead: If you'll be good boys—that is, do what we say—you'll win God's approval and find your reward in heaven. (In British English, to "never want joy" means never to *lack* it.) But God is another false father in this poem.

The trusting, optimistic children grab their bags and brushes and get right to work in the "cold" and "dark" (21–23). They want to do right, and their spirit is unquenched. But they've been brainwashed into pliability by manipulative maxims such as the one recited by our first sweep in the ominous last line: "So if all do their duty they need not fear harm" (24). This bromide is an outrageous lie. If the children were to rebel, to run away to the green paradise lying just outside the city, they would be safe. Their naive goodwill leads straight to their ruin—a short, limited life of sickliness and toil. The final stanza's off rhymes ("dark"/"work," "warm"/"harm") subtly unbalance us and make us sense the fractures in the sweep's world. The poem shows him betrayed by an ascending row of duplicitous male authority figures—his father, the profiteering boss, the turncoat angel, and God himself, who tacitly endorses or tolerates an unjust social system. As Tom's dream suggests, the only deliverance for the sweep and his friends will be death.

From *Break, Blow, Burn*

TERMS FOR *review*

Formalist criticism ▶ A school of criticism that focuses on the *form* of a literary work. A key method that formalists use is close reading, a step-by-step analysis of the elements in a text.

Biographical criticism ▶ The practice of analyzing a literary work by using knowledge of the author's life to gain insight. Although the work is understood as an independent creation, the *biography* of the author provides the practical assistance of underscoring subtle but important meanings.

Historical criticism ▶ The practice of analyzing a literary work by investigating the social, cultural, and intellectual context that produced it, including the author's biography and milieu.

Psychological criticism ▶ The application of the analytical tools of psychology and psychoanalysis to authors and/or fictional characters in order to understand the underlying motivations and meanings of a literary work.

Mythological criticism ▶ The practice of analyzing a literary work by looking for recurrent universal patterns. It explores the ways in which an individual imagination uses myths and symbols shared by different cultures and epochs.

Sociological criticism ▶ The practice of analyzing a literary work by examining the cultural, economic, and political context in which it was written or received. It primarily explores the relationship between the artist and society.

Gender criticism ▶ The examination of the ways in which sexual identity influences the creation, interpretation, and evaluation of literary works. Feminism, gay culture, and the men's movement all play key roles in gender criticism.

Reader-response criticism ▶ The practice of analyzing a literary work by describing what happens in the reader's mind while interpreting the text, on the assumption that no literary text exists independently of readers' interpretations and that there is no single fixed interpretation of any literary work.

Deconstructionist criticism ▶ A school of criticism that rejects the traditional assumption that language can accurately represent reality. Deconstructionists believe that literary texts can have no single meaning; therefore, they concentrate their attention on *how* language is being used in a text, rather than what is being said.

Cultural studies ▶ A contemporary interdisciplinary field of academic study that focuses on understanding the social power encoded in "texts"—which may include any analyzable phenomenon from a traditional poem to an advertising image or actor's face.

GLOSSARY OF LITERARY TERMS

Abstract diction *See* **Diction.**

Accent An emphasis or stress placed on a syllable in speech. Clear pronunciation of polysyllabic words almost always depends on correct placement of their accents (e.g., *de*-sert and de-*sert* are two different words and parts of speech, depending on their accent). Accent or speech stress is the basis of most meters in English. (*See also* **Accentual meter, Meter.**)

Accentual meter A meter that uses a consistent number of strong speech stresses per line. The number of unstressed syllables may vary, as long as the accented syllables do not. Much popular poetry, such as rap and nursery rhymes, is written in accentual meter.

Acrostic A poem in which the initial letters of each line, when read downward, spell out a hidden word or words (often the name of a beloved person). Acrostics date back as far as the Hebrew Bible and classical Greek poetry.

Allegory A narrative in verse or prose in which the literal events (persons, places, and things) consistently point to a parallel sequence of symbolic ideas. This narrative strategy is often used to dramatize abstract ideas, historical events, religious systems, or political issues. An allegory has two levels of meaning: a literal level that tells a surface story and a symbolic level in which the abstract ideas unfold. The names of allegorical characters often hint at their symbolic roles. For example, in Nathaniel Hawthorne's "Young Goodman Brown," Faith is not only the name of the protagonist's wife but also a symbol of the protagonist's religious faith.

Alliteration The repetition of two or more consonant sounds in successive words in a line of verse or prose. Alliteration can be used at the beginning of words ("cool cats"—**initial alliteration**) or internally on stressed syllables ("In *k*itchen cups concupiscent curds"—which combines initial and **internal alliteration**). Alliteration was a central feature of Anglo-Saxon poetry and is still used by contemporary writers.

All-knowing narrator *See* **Omniscient narrator.**

Allusion A brief (and sometimes indirect) reference in a text to a person, place, or thing—fictitious or actual. An allusion may appear in a literary work as an initial quotation, a passing mention of a name, or as a phrase borrowed from another writer—often carrying the meanings and implications of the original. Allusions imply a common set of knowledge between reader and writer and operate as a literary shorthand to enrich the meaning of a text.

Analysis The examination of a piece of literature as a means of understanding its subject or structure. An effective analysis often clarifies a work by focusing on a single element such as tone, irony, symbolism, imagery, or rhythm in a way that enhances the reader's understanding of the whole. *Analysis* comes from the Greek word meaning to "undo," to "loosen."

Anapest A metrical foot in verse in which two unstressed syllables are followed by a stressed syllable, as in "on a *boat*" or "in a *slump*" (⏑ ⏑ ʹ). (*See also* **Meter.**)

Antagonist The most significant character or force that opposes the protagonist in a narrative or drama. The antagonist may be another character, society itself, a force of nature, or even—in modern literature—conflicting impulses within the protagonist.

Anticlimax An unsatisfying and trivial turn of events in a literary work that occurs in place of a genuine climax. An anticlimax often involves a surprising shift in tone from the lofty or serious into the petty or ridiculous. The term is often used negatively to denote a feeble moment in a plot in which an author fails to create an intended effect. Anticlimax, however, can also be a strong dramatic device when a writer uses it for humorous or ironic effect.

Antihero A protagonist who is lacking in one or more of the conventional qualities attributed to a hero. Instead of being dignified, brave, idealistic, or purposeful, for instance, the antihero may be buffoonish, cowardly, self-interested, or weak. The antihero is often considered an essentially modern form of characterization, a satiric or frankly realistic commentary on traditional portrayals of idealized heroes or heroines. Modern examples range from Kafka's many protagonists to Beckett's tramps in *Waiting for Godot.*

Antithesis Words, phrases, clauses, or sentences set in deliberate contrast to one another. Antithesis balances opposing ideas, tones, or structures, usually to heighten the effect of a statement.

Apostrophe A direct address to someone or something. In poetry an apostrophe often addresses something not ordinarily spoken to (e.g., "O mountain!"). In an apostrophe, a speaker may address an inanimate object, a dead or absent person, an abstract thing, or a spirit. Apostrophe is often used to provide a speaker with means to articulate thoughts aloud.

Apprenticeship novel *See* ***Bildungsroman.***

Archetype A recurring symbol, character, landscape, or event found in myth and literature across different cultures and eras. The idea of the archetype came into literary criticism from the Swiss psychologist Carl Jung, who believed that all individuals share a "collective unconscious," a set of primal memories common to the human race that exists in our subconscious. An example of an archetypal character is the devil who may appear in pure mythic form (as in John Milton's *Paradise Lost*) but occurs more often in a disguised form like Fagin in Charles Dickens's *Oliver Twist* or Abner Snopes in William Faulkner's "Barn Burning."

Aside In drama a few words or short passage spoken in an undertone or to the audience. By convention, other characters onstage are deaf to the aside.

Assonance The repetition of two or more vowel sounds in successive words, which creates a kind of rhyme. Like alliteration, the assonance may occur initially ("*a*ll the *aw*ful *au*guries") or internally ("wh*i*te l*i*lacs"). Assonance may be used to focus attention on key words or concepts. Assonance also helps make a phrase or line more memorable.

Atmosphere The dominant mood or feeling that pervades all or part of a literary work. Atmosphere is the total effect conveyed by the author's use of language, images, and physical setting. Atmosphere is often used to foreshadow the ultimate climax in a narrative.

Auditory imagery A word or sequence of words that refers to the sense of hearing. (*See also* **Imagery.**)

Ballad Traditionally, a song that tells a story. The ballad was originally an oral verse form—sung or recited and transmitted from performer to performer without being written down. Ballads are characteristically compressed, dramatic, and objective in their narrative style. There are many variations to the ballad form, most consisting of quatrains (made up of lines of three or four metrical feet) in a simple rhyme scheme. (*See also* **Ballad stanza.**)

Ballad stanza The most common pattern of ballad makers consists of four lines rhymed *abcb*, in which the first and third lines have four metrical feet and the second and fourth lines have three feet (4, 3, 4, 3).

Bathos In poetry, an unintentional lapse from the sublime to the ridiculous or trivial. Bathos differs from anticlimax, in that the latter is a deliberate effect, often for the purpose of humor or contrast, whereas bathos occurs through failure.

Bildungsroman German for "novel of growth and development." Sometimes called an **apprenticeship novel,** this genre depicts a youth who struggles toward maturity, forming a worldview or philosophy of life. Dickens's *David Copperfield* and Joyce's *Portrait of the Artist as a Young Man* are classic examples of the genre.

Biographical criticism The practice of analyzing a literary work by using knowledge of the author's life to gain insight.

Biography A factual account of a person's life, examining all available information or texts relevant to the subject.

Blank verse The most common and well-known meter of unrhymed poetry in English. Blank verse contains five iambic feet per line and is never rhymed. (*Blank* means "unrhymed.") Many literary works have been written in blank verse, including Tennyson's "Ulysses" and Frost's "Mending Wall." Shakespeare's plays are written primarily in blank verse. (*See also* **Iambic pentameter.**)

Blues A type of folk music originally developed by African Americans in the South, often about some pain or loss. Blues lyrics traditionally consist of three-line stanzas in which the first two identical lines are followed by a third concluding, rhyming line. The influence of the blues is fundamental in virtually all styles of contemporary pop—jazz, rap, rock, gospel, country, and rhythm and blues.

Box set The illusion of scenic realism for interior rooms was achieved in the early nineteenth century with the development of the box set, consisting of three walls that joined in two corners and a ceiling that tilted as if seen in perspective. The "fourth wall," invisible, ran parallel to the proscenium arch. By the middle of the nineteenth century, the addition of realistic props and furnishings made it possible for actors to behave onstage as if they inhabited private space, oblivious to the presence of an audience, even turning their backs to the audience if the dramatic situation required it.

Broadside ballads Poems printed on a single sheet of paper, often set to traditional tunes. Most broadside ballads, which originated in the late sixteenth century, were an early form of verse journalism, cheap to print, and widely circulated. Often they were humorous or pathetic accounts of sensational news events.

Burlesque Incongruoutation of either the style or subject matter of a serious genre, humorous due to the disparity between the treatment and the subject. On the nineteenth-century English stage, the burlesque was a broad caricature, parody, travesty, or take-off of popular plays, opera, or current events. Gilbert and Sullivan's Victorian operettas, for example, burlesqued grand opera.

Cacophony A harsh, discordant sound often mirroring the meaning of the context in which it is used. For example, "Grate on the scrannel pipes of wretched straw" (Milton's "Lycidas"). The opposite of cacophony is **euphony.**

Caesura, cesura A pause within a line of verse. Traditionally, caesuras appear near the middle of a line, but their placement may be varied to create expressive rhythmic effects. A caesura will usually occur at a mark of punctuation, but there can be a caesura even if no punctuation is present.

Carpe diem Latin for "seize the day." Originally said in Horace's famous "Odes I (11)," this phrase has been applied to characterize much lyric poetry concerned with human mortality and the passing of time.

Central intelligence The character through whose sensibility and mind a story is told. Henry James developed this term to describe a narrator—not the author—whose perceptions shape the way a story is presented. (*See also* **Narrator.**)

Character An imagined figure inhabiting a narrative or drama. By convention, the reader or spectator endows the fictional character with moral, dispositional, and emotional qualities expressed in what the character says—the dialogue—and by what he or she does—the action. What a character says and does in any particular situation is motivated by his or her desires, temperament, and moral nature. (*See also* **Dynamic character** and **Flat character.**)

Character development The process in which a character is introduced, advanced, and possibly transformed in a story. This development can prove to be either static (the character's personality is unchanging throughout the narrative) or dynamic (the character's personality undergoes some meaningful change during the course of the narrative). (*See also* **Dynamic character.**)

Characterization The techniques a writer uses to create, reveal, or develop the characters in a narrative. (*See also* **Character.**)

Child ballads American scholar Francis J. Child compiled a collection of over three hundred authentic ballads in his book *The English and Scottish Popular Ballads* (1882–1898). He demonstrated that these ballads were the creations of oral folk culture. These works have come to be called Child ballads.

Clerihew A comic verse form named for its inventor, Edmund Clerihew Bentley. A clerihew begins with the name of a person and consists of two metrically awkward, rhymed couplets. Humorous and often insulting, clerihews serve as ridiculous biographies, usually of famous people.

Climax The moment of greatest intensity in a story, which almost inevitably occurs toward the end of the work. The climax often takes the form of a decisive confrontation between the protagonist and antagonist. In a conventional story, the climax is followed by the **resolution** or **dénouement** in which the effects and results of the climactic action are presented. (*See also* **Falling action, Rising action.**)

Closed couplet Two rhymed lines that contain an independent and complete thought or statement. The closed couplet usually pauses lightly at the end of the first line; the second is more heavily end-stopped, or "closed." When such couplets are written in rhymed iambic pentameter, they are called **heroic couplets**. (*See also* **Couplet.**)

Closed dénouement One of two types of conventional dénouement or resolution in a narrative. In closed dénouement, the author ties everything up at the end of the story so that little is left unresolved. (*See also* **Open dénouement.**)

Closed form A generic term that describes poetry written in some preexisting pattern of meter, rhyme, line, or stanza. A closed form produces a prescribed structure as in the triolet, with a set rhyme scheme and line length. Closed forms include the sonnet, sestina, villanelle, ballade, and rondeau.

Close reading A method of analysis involving careful step-by-step explication of a poem in order to understand how various elements work together. Close reading is a common practice of formalist critics in the study of a text.

Colloquial English The casual or informal but correct language of ordinary native speakers, which may include contractions, slang, and shifts in grammar, vocabulary, and diction. Wordsworth helped introduce colloquialism into English poetry, challenging the past constraints of highly formal language in verse and calling for the poet to become "a man speaking to men." Conversational in tone, *colloquial* is derived from the Latin *colloquium*, "speaking together." (*See also* **Diction, Levels of diction.**)

Comedy A literary work aimed at amusing an audience. Comedy is one of the basic modes of storytelling and can be adapted to most literary forms—from poetry to film. In traditional comic plotting, the action often involves the adventures of young lovers, who face obstacles and complications that threaten disaster but are overturned at the last moment to produce a happy ending. Comic situations or comic characters can provide humor in tragicomedy and even in tragedies (the gravediggers in *Hamlet*).

Comedy of manners A realistic form of comic drama that flourished with seventeenth-century playwrights such as Molière and English Restoration dramatists. It deals with the social relations and sexual intrigues of sophisticated, intelligent, upper-class men and women, whose verbal fencing and witty repartee produce the principal comic effects. Stereotyped characters from contemporary life, such as would-be wits, jealous husbands, conniving rivals, country bumpkins, and foppish dandies, reveal by their deviations from the norm the decorum and conventional behaviors expected in polite society. Modern examples include G. B. Shaw (*Arms and the Man*), Noel Coward (*Private Lives*), or Tom Stoppard (*Arcadia*).

Comic relief The appearance of a comic situation, character, or clownish humor in the midst of a serious action that introduces a sharp contrast in mood. The drunken porter in *Macbeth*, who imagines himself the doorkeeper of Hell, not only provides comic relief but intensifies the horror of Macbeth's murder of King Duncan.

Coming-of-age story *See* **Initiation story.**

Commedia dell'arte A form of comic drama developed by guilds of professional Italian actors in the mid-sixteenth century. Playing stock characters, masked *commedia* players improvised dialogue around a given scenario (a brief outline marking entrances of characters and the main course of action). In a typical play a pair of young lovers (played without masks), aided by a clever servant (Harlequin), outwit older masked characters.

Common meter A highly regular form of ballad meter with two sets of rhymes—*abab*. "Amazing Grace" and many other hymns are in common meter. (*See also* **Ballad stanza.**)

Comparison In the analysis or criticism of literature, one may place two works side-by-side to point out their similarities. The product of this, a comparison, may be more meaningful when paired with its counterpart, a **contrast.**

Complication The introduction of a significant development in the central conflict in a drama or narrative between characters (or between a character and his or her situation). Traditionally, a complication begins the rising action of a story's plot. Dramatic conflict (motivation versus obstacle) during the complication is the force that drives a literary work from action to action. Complications may be *external* or *internal* or a combination of the two. A fateful blow such as an illness or an accident that affects a character is a typical example of an *external* complication—a problem the characters cannot turn away from. An *internal* complication, in contrast, might not be immediately apparent, such as the result of some important aspect of a character's values or personality.

Conceit A poetic device using elaborate comparisons, such as equating a loved one with the graces and beauties of the world. Most notably used by the Italian poet Petrarch in praise of his beloved Laura, *conceit* comes from the Italian *concetto*, "concept" or "idea."

Conclusion In plotting, the logical end or outcome of a unified plot, shortly following the climax. Also called **resolution** or **dénouement** ("the untying of the knot"), as in resolving or untying the knots created by plot complications during the rising action. The action or intrigue ends in success or failure for the protagonist, the mystery is solved, or misunderstandings are dispelled. Sometimes a conclusion is ambiguous; at the climax of the story the characters are changed, but the conclusion suggests different possibilities for what that change is or means.

Concrete diction *See* **Diction.**

Concrete poetry A visual poetry composed exclusively for the page in which a picture or image is made of printed letters and words. Concrete poetry attempts to blur the line between language and visual art. Concrete poetry was especially popular as an experimental movement in the 1960s.

Confessional poetry A poetic genre emerging in the 1950s and 1960s primarily concerned with autobiography and the unexpurgated exposure of the poet's personal life. Notable practitioners included Robert Lowell, W. D. Snodgrass, and Anne Sexton.

Conflict In Greek, ***agon,*** or contest. The central struggle between two or more forces in a story. Conflict generally occurs when some person or thing prevents the protagonist from achieving his or her intended goal. Opposition can arise from another character, external events, preexisting situations, fate, or even some aspect of the main character's own personality. Conflict is the basic material out of which most plots are made. (*See also* **Antagonist, Character, Complication, Rising action.**)

Connotation An association or additional meaning that a word, image, or phrase may carry, apart from its literal denotation or dictionary definition. A word picks up connotations from all the uses to which it has been put in the past. For example, an owl in literature is not merely the literal bird. It also carries the many associations (connotations, that is) attached to it.

Consonance Also called **Slant rhyme**. A kind of rhyme in which the linked words share similar consonant sounds but different vowel sounds, as in *reason* and *raisin*, *mink* and *monk*. Sometimes only the final consonant sound is identical, as in *fame* and *room*, *crack* and *truck*. Used mostly by modern poets, consonance often registers more subtly than exact rhyme, lending itself to special poetic effects.

Contrast A contrast of two works of literature is developed by placing them side-by-side to point out their differences. This method of analysis works well with its opposite, a **comparison,** which focuses on likenesses.

Convention Any established feature or technique in literature that is commonly understood by both authors and readers. A convention is something generally agreed on to be appropriate for its customary uses, such as the sonnet form for a love poem or the opening "Once upon a time" for a fairy tale.

Conventional symbols Literary symbols that have a conventional or customary effect on most readers. We would respond similarly to a black cat crossing our path or a young bride in a white dress. These are conventional symbols because they carry recognizable connotations and suggestions.

Cosmic irony Also called **irony of fate,** it is the irony that exists between a character's aspiration and the treatment he or she receives at the hands of fate. Oedipus's ill-destined relationship with his parents is an example of cosmic irony.

Cothurni High thick-soled boots worn by Greek and Roman tragic actors in late classical times to make them appear taller than ordinary men. (Earlier, in the fifth-century classical Athenian theater, actors wore soft shoes or boots or went barefoot.)

Couplet A two-line stanza in poetry, usually rhymed, which tends to have lines of equal length. Shakespeare's sonnets were famous for ending with a summarizing, rhymed couplet: "Give my love fame faster than Time wastes life; / So thou prevent'st his scythe and crookèd knife." (*See also* **Closed couplet.**)

Cowboy poetry A contemporary genre of folk poetry written by people with firsthand experience in the life of horse, trail, and ranch. Plainspoken and often humorous, cowboy poetry is usually composed in rhymed ballad stanzas and meant to be recited aloud.

Crisis The point in a drama when the crucial action, decision, or realization must be made, marking the turning point or reversal of the protagonist's fortunes. From the Greek word *krisis*, meaning "decision." For example, Hamlet's decision to refrain from killing Claudius while the guilty king is praying is a crisis that leads directly to his accidental murder of Polonius, pointing forward to the catastrophe of Act V. Typically, the crisis inaugurates the falling action (after Hamlet's murder of Polonius, Claudius controls the events) until the catastrophe (or conclusion), which is decided by the death of the hero, King Claudius, Queen Gertrude, and Laertes. In *Oedipus*, the crisis occurs as the hero presses forward to the horrible truth, to realize he is an incestuous parricide and to take responsibility by blinding himself.

Cultural studies A contemporary interdisciplinary field of academic study that focuses on understanding the social power encoded in "texts." Cultural studies defines "texts" more broadly than literary works; they include any analyzable phenomenon from a traditional poem to an advertising image or an actor's face. Cultural studies has no central critical methodology but uses whatever intellectual tools are appropriate to the analysis at hand.

Dactyl A metrical foot of verse in which one stressed syllable is followed by two unstressed syllables (′ ˘ ˘ , as in *bat*-ter-y or *par*-a-mour). The dactylic meter is less common to English than it was to classical Greek and Latin verse. Longfellow's *Evangeline* is the most famous English-language long dactylic poem.

Deconstructionist criticism A school of criticism that rejects the traditional assumption that language can accurately represent reality. Deconstructionists believe that literary texts can have no single meaning; therefore, they concentrate their attentions on *how* language is being used in a text, rather than on *what* is being said.

Decorum Propriety or appropriateness. In poetry, decorum usually refers to a level of diction that is proper to use in a certain occasion. Decorum can also apply to characters, setting, and the harmony that exists between the elements in a poem. For example, aged nuns speaking inner-city jive might violate decorum.

Denotation The literal, dictionary meaning of a word. (*See also* **Connotation.**)

Dénouement The resolution or conclusion of a literary work as plot complications are unraveled after the climax. In French, *dénouement* means "unknotting" or "untying." (*See also* **Closed dénouement, Conclusion, Open dénouement.**)

Deus ex machina Latin for "a god from a machine." The phrase refers to the Greek playwrights' frequent use of a god, mechanically lowered to the stage from the *skene* roof, to resolve human conflict with judgments and commands. Conventionally, the phrase now refers to any forced or improbable device in plot resolution.

Dialect A particular variety of language spoken by an identifiable regional group or social class of persons. Dialects are often used in literature in an attempt to present a character more realistically and to express significant differences in class or background.

Dialogue The direct representation of the conversation between two or more characters. (*See also* **Monologue.**)

Diction Word choice or vocabulary. Diction refers to the class of words that an author decides is appropriate to use in a particular work. Literary history is the story of diction being challenged, upheld, and reinvented. **Concrete diction** involves a highly specific word choice in the naming of something or someone. **Abstract diction** contains words that express more general ideas or concepts. More concrete diction would offer *boxer puppy* rather than *young canine*, *Lake Ontario* rather than *body of fresh water*. Concrete words refer to what we can immediately perceive with our senses. (*See also* **Levels of diction.**)

Didactic fiction A narrative that intends to teach a specific moral lesson or provide a model for proper behavior. This term is now often used pejoratively to describe a story in which the events seem manipulated in order to convey an uplifting idea, but much classic fiction has been written in the didactic mode—Aesop's *Fables*, John Bunyan's *The Pilgrim's Progress*, and Harriet Beecher Stowe's *Uncle Tom's Cabin*.

Didactic poetry Kind of poetry intended to teach the reader a moral lesson or impart a body of knowledge. Poetry that aims for education over art.

Dimeter A verse meter consisting of two metrical feet, or two primary stresses, per line.

Doggerel Verse full of irregularities often due to the poet's incompetence. Doggerel is crude verse that brims with cliché, obvious rhyme, and inept rhythm.

Double plot Also called **subplot.** Familiar in Elizabethan drama, a second story or plotline that is complete and interesting in its own right, often doubling or inverting the main plot. By analogy or counterpoint, a skillful subplot broadens perspective on the main plot to enhance rather than dilute its effect. In Shakespeare's *Othello*, for instance, Iago's duping of Rodrigo reflects the main plot of Iago's treachery to Othello.

Drama Derived from the Greek *dran*, "to do," *drama* means "action" or "deed." Drama is the form of literary composition designed for performance in the theater, in which actors take the roles of the characters, perform the indicated action, and speak the written dialogue. In the *Poetics*, Aristotle described tragedy or dramatic enactment as the most fully evolved form of the impulse to imitate or make works of art.

Dramatic irony A special kind of suspenseful expectation, when the audience or reader understands the implication and meaning of a situation onstage and foresees the oncoming disaster (in tragedy) or triumph (in comedy) but the character does not. The irony forms between the contrasting levels of knowledge of the character and the audience. Dramatic irony is pervasive throughout Sophocles's *Oedipus*, for example, because we know from the beginning what Oedipus does not. We watch with dread and fascination the spectacle of a morally good man, committed to the salvation of his city, unwittingly preparing undeserved suffering for himself.

Dramatic monologue A poem written as a speech made by a character at some decisive moment. The speaker is usually addressing a silent listener as in T. S. Eliot's "The Love Song of J. Alfred Prufrock" or Robert Browning's "My Last Duchess."

Dramatic poetry Any verse written for the stage, as in the plays of classical Greece, the Renaissance (Shakespeare), and neoclassical periods (Molière, Racine). Also a kind of poetry that presents the voice of an imaginary character (or characters) speaking directly, without any additional narration by the author. In poetry, the term usually refers to the dramatic monologue, a lyric poem written as a speech made by a character at some decisive moment, such as Lord, Alfred Tennyson's "Ulysses." (*See also* **Dramatic monologue.**)

Dramatic point of view A point of view in which the narrator merely reports dialogue and action with minimal interpretation or access to the characters' minds. The dramatic point of view, as the name implies, uses prose fiction to approximate the method of plays (where readers are provided only with set descriptions, stage directions, and dialogue, and thus must supply motivations based solely on this external evidence).

Dramatic question The primary unresolved issue in a drama as it unfolds. The dramatic question is the result of artful plotting, raising suspense and expectation in a play's action as it moves toward its outcome. Will the Prince in *Hamlet*, for example, achieve what he has been instructed to do and what he intends to do?

Dramatic situation The basic conflict that initiates a work or establishes a scene. It usually describes both a protagonist's motivation and the forces that oppose its realization. (*See also* **Antagonist, Character, Complication, Plot, Rising action.**)

Dumb show In Renaissance theater, a mimed dramatic performance whose purpose is to prepare the audience for the main action of the play to follow. Jacobean playwrights like John Webster used it to show violent events that occur some distance from the play's locale. The most famous Renaissance example is the dumb show preceding the presentation of "The Murder of Gonzago" in *Hamlet*.

Dynamic character A character who, during the course of the narrative, grows or changes in some significant way. (*See also* **Character development.**)

Echo verse A poetic form in which the final syllables of the lines are repeated back as a reply or commentary, often using puns. Echo verse dates back to late classical Greek poetry.

Editorial omniscience When an omniscient narrator goes beyond reporting the thoughts of his or her characters to make a critical judgment or commentary, making explicit the narrator's own thoughts or philosophies.

Editorial point of view The effect that occurs when a third-person narrator adds his or her own comments (which presumably represent the ideas and opinions of the author) into the narrative.

Elegy A lament or a sadly meditative poem, often written on the occasion of a death or other solemn theme. An elegy is usually a sustained poem in a formal style.

Endnote An additional piece of information that the author includes in a note at the end of a paper or chapter. Endnotes usually contain information that the author feels is important to convey but not appropriate to fit into the main body of text. (*See also* **Footnote.**)

End rhyme Rhyme that occurs at the ends of lines, rather than within them (as internal rhyme does). End rhyme is the most common kind of rhyme in English-language poetry.

End-stopped line A line of verse that ends in a full pause, usually indicated by a mark of punctuation.

English sonnet Also called **Shakespearean sonnet.** The English sonnet has a rhyme scheme organized into three quatrains with a final couplet: *abab cdcd efef* gg. The poem may turn, that is, shift in mood or tone, between any of the quatrains (although it usually occurs on the ninth line). (*See also* **Sonnet.**)

Envoy A short, often summarizing stanza that appears at the end of certain poetic forms (most notably the sestina, chant royal, and the French ballade). The envoy contains the poet's parting words. The word comes from the French *envoi*, meaning "sending forth."

Epic A long narrative poem usually composed in an elevated style tracing the adventures of a legendary or mythic hero. Epics are usually written in a consistent form and meter throughout. Famous epics include Homer's *Iliad* and *Odyssey*, Virgil's *Aeneid*, and Milton's *Paradise Lost*.

Epigram A very short poem, often comic, usually ending with some sharp turn of wit or meaning.

Epigraph A brief quotation preceding a story or other literary work. An epigraph usually suggests the subject, theme, or atmosphere the story will explore.

Epiphany A moment of insight, discovery, or revelation by which a character's life is greatly altered. An epiphany generally occurs near the end of a story. The term, which means "showing forth" in Greek, was first used in Christian theology to signify the manifestation of God's presence in the world. This theological idea was first borrowed by James Joyce to refer to a heightened moment of secular revelation.

Episode An incident in a large narrative that has unity in itself. An episode may bear close relation to the central narrative, but it can also be a digression.

Episodic plot, episodic structure A form of plotting where the individual scenes and events are presented chronologically without any profound sense of cause-and-effect relationship. In an episodic narrative the placement of many scenes could be changed without greatly altering the overall effect of the work.

Epistolary novel Novel in which the story is told by way of letters written by one or more of the characters. This form often lends an authenticity to the story, a sense that the author may have discovered these letters; but in fact they are a product of the author's invention.

Euphony The harmonious effect when the sounds of the words connect with the meaning in a way pleasing to the ear and mind. An example is found in Tennyson's lines, "The moan of doves in immemorial elms, / And murmuring of innumerable bees." The opposite of euphony is **cacophony.**

Exact rhyme A full rhyme in which the sounds following the initial letters of the words are identical in sound, as in *follow* and *hollow*, *go* and *slow*, *disband* and *this hand*.

Explication Literally, an "unfolding." In an explication an entire poem is explained in detail, addressing every element and unraveling any complexities as a means of analysis.

Exposition The opening portion of a narrative or drama. In the exposition, the scene is set, the protagonist is introduced, and the author discloses any other background information necessary to allow the reader to understand and relate to the events that are to follow.

Expressionism A dramatic style developed between 1910 and 1924 in Germany in reaction against realism's focus on surface details and external reality. To draw an audience into a dreamlike subjective realm, expressionistic artistic styles used episodic plots, distorted lines, exaggerated shapes, abnormally intense coloring, mechanical physical movement, and telegraphic speech (the broken syntax of a disordered psyche). Staging the contents of the unconscious, expressionist plays ranged from utopian visions of a fallen, materialistic world redeemed by the spirituality of "new men" to pessimistic nightmare visions of universal catastrophe.

Eye rhyme Rhyme in which the spelling of the words appears alike, but the pronunciations differ, as in *laughter* and *daughter*, *idea* and *flea*.

Fable A brief, often humorous narrative told to illustrate a moral. The characters in fables are traditionally animals whose personality traits symbolize human traits. Particular animals have conventionally come to represent specific human qualities or values. For example, the ant represents industry, the fox craftiness, and the lion nobility. A fable often concludes by summarizing its moral message in abstract terms. For example, Aesop's fable "The North Wind and the Sun" concludes with the moral "Persuasion is better than force." (*See also* **Allegory.**)

Fairy tale A traditional form of short narrative folklore, originally transmitted orally, that features supernatural characters such as witches, giants, fairies, or animals with human personality traits. Fairy tales often feature a hero or heroine who seems destined to achieve some desirable fate—such as marrying a prince or princess, becoming wealthy, or destroying an enemy.

Falling action The events in a narrative that follow the climax and bring the story to its conclusion, or dénouement.

Falling meter Trochaic and dactylic meters are called falling meters because their first syllable is accented, followed by one or more unaccented syllables. A foot of falling meter falls in its level of stress, as in the words *co*-medy or *aw*-ful.

Fantasy A narrative that depicts events, characters, or places that could not exist in the real world. Fantasy has limited interest in portraying experience realistically. Instead, it freely pursues the possibilities of the imagination. Fantasy usually includes elements of magic or the supernatural. Sometimes it is used to illustrate a moral message as in fables. Fantasy is a type of romance that emphasizes wish fulfillment (or nightmare fulfillment) instead of verisimilitude.

Farce A type of comedy featuring exaggerated character types in ludicrous and improbable situations, provoking belly laughs with sexual mix-ups, crude verbal jokes, pratfalls, and knockabout horseplay (like the comic violence of the Punch and Judy show).

Feminine rhyme A rhyme of two or more syllables with a stress on a syllable other than the last, as in *tur*-tle and *fer*-tile. (*See also* **Masculine rhyme, Rhyme.**)

Feminist criticism *See* **Gender criticism.**

Fiction From the Latin *ficio*, "act of fashioning, a shaping, a making." Fiction refers to any literary work that—although it might contain factual information—is not bound by factual accuracy, but creates a narrative shaped or made up by the author's imagination. Drama and poetry (especially narrative poetry) can be considered works of fiction, but the term now usually refers more specifically to prose stories and novels. Historical and other factual writing also requires shaping and making, but it is distinct from fiction because it is not free to invent people, places, and events; forays from documented fact must identify themselves as conjecture or hypothesis. Nonfiction, as the name suggests, is a category conventionally separate from fiction. Certainly an essay or work of literary journalism is "a made thing," and writers of nonfiction routinely employ the techniques used by fiction writers (moving forward and backward in time, reporting the inner thoughts of characters, etc.), but works of nonfiction must be not only true but factual. The truth of a work of fiction depends not on facts, but on how convincingly the writer creates the world of the story.

Figure of speech An expression or comparison that relies not on its literal meaning, but rather on its connotations and suggestions. For example, "He's dumber than dirt" is not literally true; it is a figure of speech. Major figures of speech include **metaphor, metonymy, simile,** and **synecdoche.**

First-person narrator A story in which the narrator is a participant in the action. Such a narrator refers to himself or herself as "I" and may be a major or minor character in the story. His or her attitude and understanding of characters and events shapes the reader's perception of the story being told.

Fixed form A traditional verse form requiring certain predetermined elements of structure, for example, a stanza pattern, set meter, or predetermined line length. A fixed form like the sonnet, for instance, must have no more nor less than fourteen lines, rhymed according to certain conventional patterns. (*See also* **Closed form.**)

Flashback A scene relived in a character's memory. Flashbacks can be related by the narrator in a summary or they can be experienced by the characters themselves. Flashbacks allow the author to include events that occurred before the opening of the story, which may show the reader something significant that happened in the character's past or give an indication of what kind of person the character used to be.

Flat character A term coined by English novelist E. M. Forster to describe a character with only one outstanding trait. Flat characters are rarely the central characters in a narrative and are often based on **stock characters.** Flat characters stay the same throughout a story. (*See also* **Dynamic character.**)

Folk ballads Anonymous narrative songs, usually in ballad meter, that were originally transmitted orally. Although most well-known ballads have been transcribed and published in order to protect them from being lost, they were originally created for oral performance, often resulting in many versions of a single ballad.

Folk epic Also called **Traditional epic.** A long narrative poem that traces the adventures of a tribe or nation's popular heroes. Some examples of epics are the *Iliad* and the *Odyssey* (Greek), *The Song of Roland* (French), and *The Cid* (Spanish). A folk epic originates in an oral tradition as opposed to a literary epic, which is written by an individual author consciously emulating earlier epic poetry.

Folklore The body of traditional wisdom and customs—including songs, stories, myths, and proverbs—of a people as collected and continued through oral tradition.

Folktale A short narrative drawn from folklore that has been passed down through an oral tradition. (*See also* **Fairy tale, Legend.**)

Foot The unit of measurement in metrical poetry. Different meters are identified by the pattern and order of stressed and unstressed syllables in their foot, usually containing two or three syllables, with one syllable accented.

Footnote An additional piece of information that the author includes at the bottom of a page, usually noted by a small reference number in the main text. A footnote might supply the reader with brief facts about a related historical figure or event, the definition of a foreign word or phrase, or any other relevant information that may help in understanding the text. (*See also* **Endnote.**)

Foreshadowing In plot construction, the technique of arranging events and information in such a way that later events are prepared for, or shadowed, beforehand. The author may introduce specific words, images, or actions in order to suggest significant later events. The effective use of foreshadowing by an author may prevent a story's outcome from seeming haphazard or contrived.

Form The means by which a literary work conveys its meaning. Traditionally, form refers to the way in which an artist expresses meaning rather than the content of that meaning, but it is now commonplace to note that form and content are inextricably related. Form, therefore, is more than the external framework of a literary work. It includes the totality of ways in which it unfolds and coheres as a structure of meaning and expression.

Formal English The heightened, impersonal language of educated persons, usually only written, although possibly spoken on dignified occasions. (*See also* **Levels of diction.**)

Formalist criticism A school of criticism which argues that literature may only be discussed on its own terms; that is, without outside influences or information. A key method that formalists use is close reading, a step-by-step analysis of the elements in a text.

Found poetry Poetry constructed by arranging bits of "found" prose. A found poem is a literary work made up of nonliterary language arranged for expressive effect.

Free verse From the French ***vers libre.*** Free verse describes poetry that organizes its lines without meter. It may be rhymed (as in some poems by H.D.), but it usually is not. There is no one means of organizing free verse, and different authors have used irreconcilable systems. What unites the two approaches is a freedom from metrical regularity. (*See also* **Open form.**)

Gender criticism Gender criticism examines how sexual identity influences the creation, interpretation, and evaluation of literary works. This critical approach began with feminist criticism in the 1960s and 1970s which stated that literary study had been so dominated by men that it contained many unexamined "male-produced" assumptions. Feminist criticism sought to address this imbalance in two ways: first in insisting that sexless interpretation was impossible, and second by articulating responses to the texts that were explicitly male or female. More recently, gender criticism has focused on gay and lesbian literary identity as interpretive strategies.

General English The ordinary speech of educated native speakers. Most literate speech and writing is general English. Its diction is more educated than **colloquial English,** yet not as elevated as **formal English.** (*See also* **Levels of diction.**)

Genre A conventional combination of literary form and subject matter, usually aimed at creating certain effects. A genre implies a preexisting understanding between the artist and the reader about the purpose and rules of the work. A horror story, for example, combines the form of the short story with certain conventional subjects, style, and theme with the expectation of frightening the reader. Major short story genres include science fiction, gothic, horror, and detective tales.

Gothic fiction A genre that creates terror and suspense, usually set in an isolated castle, mansion, or monastery populated by mysterious or threatening individuals. The Gothic form, invented by Horace Walpole in *The Castle of Otranto* (1764), has flourished in one form or another ever since. The term *Gothic* is also applied to medieval architecture, and Gothic fiction almost inevitably exploits claustrophobic interior architecture in its plotting—often featuring dungeons, crypts, torture chambers, locked rooms, and secret passageways. In the nineteenth century, writers such as Nathaniel Hawthorne, Edgar Allan Poe, and Charlotte Perkins Gilman brought the genre into the mainstream of American fiction.

Haiku A Japanese verse form that has three unrhymed lines of five, seven, and five syllables. Traditional haiku is often serious and spiritual in tone, relying mostly on imagery, and usually set in one of the four seasons.

Hamartia Greek for "error." An offense committed in ignorance of some material fact (without deliberate criminal intent) and therefore free of blameworthiness. A big mistake unintentionally made as a result of an intellectual error (not vice or criminal wickedness) by a morally good person, usually involving the identity of a blood relation. The *hamartia* of Oedipus, quite simply, is based on his ignorance of his true parentage; inadvertently and unwittingly, then, he commits the *hamartia* of patricide and incest. (*See also* **Recognition.**)

Heptameter A verse meter consisting of seven metrical feet, or seven primary stresses, per line.

Hero The central character in a narrative. The term is derived from the Greek epic tradition, in which *heroes* were the leading warriors among the princes. By extension, *hero* and *heroine* have come to mean the principal male and female figures in a narrative or dramatic literary work, although many today call protagonists of either sex *heroes*. When a critic terms the protagonist a *hero*, the choice of words often implies a positive moral assessment of the character. (*See also* **Antihero.**)

Heroic couplet *See* **Closed couplet.**

Hexameter A verse meter consisting of six metrical feet, or six primary stresses, per line.

High comedy A comic genre evoking so-called intellectual or thoughtful laughter from an audience that remains emotionally detached from the play's depiction of the folly, pretense, and incongruity of human behavior. The French playwright Molière and the English dramatists of the Restoration period developed a special form of high comedy in the **comedy of manners,** focused on the social relations and amorous intrigues of sophisticated upper-class men and women, conducted through witty repartee and verbal combat.

Historical criticism The practice of analyzing a literary work by investigating the social, cultural, and intellectual context that produced it—a context that necessarily includes the artist's biography and milieu. Historical critics strive to recreate the exact meaning and impact a work had on its original audience.

Historical fiction A type of fiction in which the narrative is set in another time or place. In historical fiction, the author usually attempts to recreate a faithful picture of daily life during the period. For example, Robert Graves's *I, Claudius* depicts the lives of the ancient Roman ruling class in the early Imperial age. Historical fiction sometimes introduces well-known figures from the past. More often it places imaginary characters in a carefully reconstructed version of a particular historical era.

Hubris Overweening pride, outrageous behavior, or the insolence that leads to ruin, hubris was in the Greek moral vocabulary the antithesis of moderation or rectitude. Creon, in Sophocles's *Antigonê*, is a good example of a character brought down by his hubris.

Hyperbole *See* **Overstatement.**

Iamb A metrical foot in verse in which an unaccented syllable is followed by an accented one, as in "ca-*ress*" or "a *cat*" (⏑ ʹ). The iambic measure is the most common meter used in English poetry.

Iambic meter A verse meter consisting of a specific recurring number of iambic feet per line. (*See also* **Iamb, Iambic pentameter.**)

Iambic pentameter The most common meter in English verse—five iambic feet per line. Many fixed forms, such as the sonnet and heroic couplets, are written in iambic pentameter. Unrhymed iambic pentameter is called **blank verse.**

Image A word or series of words that refers to any sensory experience (usually sight, although also sound, smell, touch, or taste). An image is a direct or literal recreation of physical experience and adds immediacy to literary language.

Imagery The collective set of images in a poem or other literary work.

Impartial omniscience Refers to an omniscient narrator who, although he or she presents the thoughts and actions of the characters, does not judge them or comment on them. (Contrasts with **Editorial omniscience.**)

Implied metaphor A metaphor that uses neither connectives nor the verb *to be*. If we say, "John crowed over his victory," we imply metaphorically that John is a rooster but do not say so specifically. (*See also* **Metaphor.**)

In medias res A Latin phrase meaning "in the midst of things" that refers to a narrative device of beginning a story midway in the events it depicts (usually at an exciting or significant moment) before explaining the context or preceding actions. Epic poems such as Virgil's *Aeneid* or John Milton's *Paradise Lost* commonly begin *in medias res*, but the technique is also found in modern fiction.

Initial alliteration *See* **Alliteration.**

Initiation story Also called **Coming-of-age story.** A narrative in which the main character, usually a child or adolescent, undergoes an important experience or rite of passage—often a difficult or disillusioning one—that prepares him or her for adulthood. James Joyce's "Araby" is a classic example of an initiation story.

Innocent narrator Also called **naive narrator.** A character who fails to understand all the implications of the story he or she tells. Of course, virtually any narrator has some degree of innocence or naiveté, but the innocent narrator—often a child or childlike adult—is used by an author trying to generate irony, sympathy, or pity by creating a gap between what the narrator knows and what the reader knows. Mark Twain's Huckleberry Finn—despite his mischievous nature—is an example of an innocent narrator.

Interior monologue An extended presentation of a character's thoughts in a narrative. Usually written in the present tense and printed without quotation marks, an interior monologue reads as if the character were speaking aloud to himself or herself, for the reader to overhear. A famous example of interior monologue comes at the end of *Ulysses* when Joyce gives us the rambling memories and reflections of Molly Bloom.

Internal alliteration *See* **Alliteration.**

Internal refrain A refrain that appears within a stanza, generally in a position that stays fixed throughout a poem. (*See also* **Refrain.**)

Internal rhyme Rhyme that occurs within a line of poetry, as opposed to **end rhyme.** Read aloud, these Wallace Stevens lines are rich in internal rhyme: "Chieftain Iffucan of Azcan in caftan / Of tan with henna hackles, halt!" (from "Bantams in Pine-Woods").

Ironic point of view The perspective of a character or narrator whose voice or position is rich in ironic contradictions. (*See also* **Irony.**)

Irony A literary device in which a discrepancy of meaning is masked beneath the surface of the language. Irony is present when a writer says one thing but means something quite the opposite. There are many kinds of irony, but the two major varieties are **verbal irony** (in which the discrepancy is contained in words) and **situational irony** (in which the discrepancy exists when something is about to happen to a character or characters who expect the opposite outcome). (*See also* **Cosmic irony, Irony of fate, Sarcasm, Verbal irony.**)

Irony of fate A type of situational irony that can be used for either tragic or comic purposes. Irony of fate is the discrepancy between actions and their results, between what characters deserve and what they get, between appearance and reality. In Sophocles's tragedy, for instance, Oedipus unwittingly fulfills the prophecy even as he takes the actions a morally good man would take to avoid it. (*See also* **Cosmic irony.**)

Italian sonnet Also called **Petrarchan sonnet**, a sonnet with the following rhyme pattern for the first eight lines (the **octave**): *abba, abba*; the final six lines (the **sestet**) may follow any pattern of rhymes, as long as it does not end in a couplet. The poem traditionally turns, or shifts in mood or tone, after the octave. (*See also* **Sonnet.**)

Katharsis*, catharsis** Often translated as purgation or purification, the term is drawn from the last element of Aristotle's definition of tragedy, relating to the final cause or purpose of tragic art. Catharsis generally refers to the feeling of emotional release or calm the spectator feels at the end of tragedy. In Aristotle ***katharsis is the final effect of the playwright's skillful use of plotting, character, and poetry to elicit pity and fear from the audience. Through ***katharsis*,** drama taught the audience compassion for the vulnerabilities of others and schooled it in justice and other civic virtues.

Legend A traditional narrative handed down through popular oral tradition to illustrate and celebrate a remarkable character, an important event, or to explain the unexplainable. Legends, unlike other folktales, claim to be true and usually take place in real locations, often with genuine historical figures.

Levels of diction In English, there are conventionally four basic levels of formality in word choice, or four levels of diction. From the least formal to the most elevated they are **vulgate, colloquial English, general English,** and **formal English.** (*See also* **Diction.**)

Limerick A short and usually comic verse form of five anapestic lines usually rhyming *aabba*. The first, second, and fifth lines traditionally have three stressed syllables each; the third and fourth have two stresses each (3, 3, 2, 2, 3).

Limited omniscience Also called third-person limited point of view. A type of point of view in which the narrator sees into the minds of some but not all of the characters. Most typically, limited omniscience sees through the eyes of one major or minor character. In limited omniscience, the author can compromise between the immediacy of first-person narration and the mobility of third person.

Literary ballad Ballad not meant for singing, written for literate readers by sophisticated poets rather than arising from the anonymous oral tradition. (*See also* **Ballad.**)

Literary epic A crafted imitation of the oral folk epic written by an author living in a society where writing has been invented. Examples of the literary epic are *The Aeneid* by Virgil and *The Divine Comedy* by Dante Alighieri. (*See also* **Folk epic.**)

Literary genre *See* **Genre.**

Literary theory Literary criticism that tries to formulate general principles rather than discuss specific texts. Theory operates at a high level of abstraction and often focuses on understanding basic issues of language, communication, art, interpretation, culture, and ideological content.

Local color The use of specific regional material—unique customs, dress, habits, and speech patterns of ordinary people—to create atmosphere or realism in a literary work.

Locale The location where a story takes place.

Low comedy A comic style arousing laughter through jokes, slapstick humor, sight gags, and boisterous clowning. Unlike **high comedy,** it has little intellectual appeal. (*See also* **Comedy.**)

Lyric A short poem expressing the thoughts and feelings of a single speaker. Often written in the first person, lyric poetry traditionally has a songlike immediacy and emotional force.

Madrigal A short secular song for three or more voices arranged in counterpoint. The madrigal is often about love or pastoral themes. It originated in Italy in the fourteenth century and enjoyed great success during the Elizabethan Age.

Magic realism Also called **magical realism**. A type of contemporary narrative in which the magical and the mundane are mixed in an overall context of realistic storytelling. The term was coined by Cuban novelist Alejo Carpentier in 1949 to describe the matter-of-fact combination of the fantastic and everyday in Latin American fiction. Magic realism has become the standard name for an international trend in contemporary fiction such as Gabriel García Márquez's *One Hundred Years of Solitude*.

Masculine rhyme Either a rhyme of one syllable words (as in *fox* and *socks*) or—in polysyllabic words—a rhyme on the stressed final syllables: con-*trive* and sur-*vive*. (*See also* **Feminine rhyme.**)

Masks In Latin, *personae*. In classical Greek theater, full facial masks made of leather, linen, or light wood, with headdress, allowed male actors to embody the conventionalized characters (or *dramatis personae*) of the tragic and comic stage. Later, in the seventeenth and eighteenth centuries, stock characters of the ***commedia dell' arte*** wore characteristic half masks made of leather. (*See also* **Persona.**)

Melodrama Originally a stage play featuring background music and sometimes songs to underscore the emotional mood of each scene. Melodramas were notoriously weak in characterization and motivation but famously strong on action, suspense, and passion. Melodramatic characters were stereotyped villains, heroes, and young lovers. When the term *melodrama* is applied to fiction, it is almost inevitably a negative criticism implying that the author has sacrificed psychological depth and credibility for emotional excitement and adventurous plotting.

Metafiction Fiction that consciously explores its own nature as a literary creation. The Greek word *meta* means "upon"; metafiction consequently is a mode of narrative that does not try to create the illusion of verisimilitude but delights in its own fictional nature, often by speculating on the story it is telling. The term is usually associated with late-twentieth-century writers like John Barth, Italo Calvino, and Jorge Luis Borges.

Metaphor A statement that one thing *is* something else, which, in a literal sense, it is not. By asserting that a thing is something else, a metaphor creates a close association between the two entities and usually underscores some important similarity between them. An example of metaphor is "Richard is a pig."

Meter A recurrent, regular, rhythmic pattern in verse. When stresses recur at fixed intervals, the result is meter. Traditionally, meter has been the basic organizational device of world poetry. There are many existing meters, each identified by the different patterns of recurring sounds. In English most common meters involve the arrangement of stressed and unstressed syllables.

Metonymy Figure of speech in which the name of a thing is substituted for that of another closely associated with it. For instance, in saying "The White House decided," one could mean that the president decided.

Minimalist fiction Contemporary fiction written in a deliberately flat, unemotional tone and an appropriately unadorned style. Minimalist fiction often relies more on dramatic action, scene, and dialogue than complex narration or authorial summary. Examples of minimalist fiction can be found in the short stories of Raymond Carver and Bobbie Ann Mason.

Mixed metaphor A metaphor that trips over another metaphor—usually unconsciously—already in the statement. Mixed metaphors are the result of combining two or more incompatible metaphors resulting in ridiculousness or nonsense. For example, "Mary was such a tower of strength that she breezed her way through all the work" ("towers" do not "breeze").

Monologue An extended speech by a single character. The term originated in drama, where it describes a solo speech that has listeners (as opposed to a **soliloquy**, where the character speaks only to himself or herself). A short story or even a novel can be written in monologue form if it is an unbroken speech by one character to another silent character or characters.

Monometer A verse meter consisting of one metrical foot, or one primary stress, per line.

Monosyllabic foot A foot, or unit of meter, that contains only one syllable.

Moral A paraphrasable message or lesson implied or directly stated in a literary work. Commonly, a moral is stated at the end of a fable.

Motif An element that recurs significantly throughout a narrative. A motif can be an image, idea, theme, situation, or action (and was first commonly used as a musical term for a recurring melody or melodic fragment). A motif can also refer to an element that recurs across many literary works like a beautiful lady in medieval romances who turns out to be an evil fairy or three questions that are asked a protagonist to test his or her wisdom.

Motivation What a character in a story or drama wants. The reasons an author provides for a character's actions. Motivation can be either *explicit* (in which reasons are specifically stated in a story) or *implicit* (in which the reasons are only hinted at or partially revealed).

Myth A traditional narrative of anonymous authorship that arises out of a culture's oral tradition. The characters in traditional myths are usually gods or heroic figures. Myths characteristically explain the origins of things—gods, people, places, plants, animals, and natural events—usually from a cosmic view. A culture's values and belief systems are traditionally passed from generation to generation in myth. In literature, myth may also refer to boldly imagined narratives that embody primal truths about life. Myth is usually differentiated from legend, which has a specific historical base.

Mythological criticism The practice of analyzing a literary work by looking for recurrent universal patterns. Mythological criticism explores the artist's common humanity by tracing how the individual imagination uses myths and symbols that are shared by different cultures and epochs.

Naive narrator *See* **Innocent narrator.**

Narrative poem A poem that tells a story. Narrative is one of the four traditional modes of poetry, along with lyric, dramatic, and didactic. **Ballads** and **epics** are two common forms of narrative poetry.

Narrator A voice or character that provides the reader with information and insight about the characters and incidents in a narrative. A narrator's perspective and personality can greatly affect how a story is told. (*See also* **Omniscient narrator, Point of view.**)

Naturalism A type of fiction or drama in which the characters are presented as products or victims of environment and heredity. Naturalism, considered an extreme form of realism, customarily depicts the social, psychological, and economic milieu of the primary characters. Naturalism was first formally developed by French novelist Émile Zola in the 1870s. In promoting naturalism as a theory of animal behavior, Zola urged the modeling of naturalist literature and drama on the scientific case study. The writer, like the scientist, was to record objective reality with detachment;

events onstage should be reproduced with sufficient exactness to demonstrate the strict laws of material causality. Important American Naturalists include Jack London, Theodore Dreiser, and Stephen Crane. (*See also* **Realism.**)

New Formalism A term for a contemporary literary movement (begun around 1980) in which young poets began using rhyme, meter, and narrative again. New Formalists attempt to write poetry that appeals to an audience beyond academia. Timothy Steele, Vikram Seth, R. S. Gwynn, David Mason, A. E. Stallings, and Marilyn Nelson are poets commonly associated with the movement.

New naturalism A term describing some American plays of the 1970s and 1980s, frankly showing the internal and external forces that shape the lives of unhappy, alienated, dehumanized, and often impoverished characters. Examples include the plays of Sam Shepard, August Wilson, and David Mamet.

Nonfiction novel A genre in which actual events are presented as a novel-length story, using the techniques of fiction (flashback, interior monologues, etc.). Truman Capote's *In Cold Blood* (1966), which depicts a multiple murder and subsequent trial in Kansas, is a classic example of this modern genre.

Nonparticipant narrator A narrator who does not appear in the story as a character but is capable of revealing the thoughts and motives of one or more characters. A nonparticipant narrator is also capable of moving from place to place in order to describe action and report dialogue. (*See also* **Omniscient narrator.**)

Novel An extended work of fictional prose narrative. The term *novel* usually implies a book-length narrative (as compared to more compact forms of prose fiction such as the short story). Because of its extended length, a novel usually has more characters, more varied scenes, and a broader coverage of time than a short story.

Novella In modern terms, a prose narrative longer than a short story but shorter than a novel (approximately 30,000 to 50,000 words). Unlike a short story, a novella is long enough to be published independently as a brief book. Classic modern novellas include Franz Kafka's *The Metamorphosis*, Joseph Conrad's *Heart of Darkness*, and Thomas Mann's *Death in Venice*. During the Renaissance, however, the term *novella* originally referred to short prose narratives such as those found in Giovanni Boccaccio's *Decameron*.

Objective point of view *See* **Dramatic point of view.**

Observer A type of first-person narrator who is relatively detached from or plays only a minor role in the events described.

Octameter A verse meter consisting of eight metrical feet, or eight primary stresses, per line.

Octave A stanza of eight lines. *Octave* is a term usually used when speaking of sonnets to indicate the first eight-line section of the poem, as distinct from the *sestet* (the final six lines). Some poets also use octaves as separate stanzas as in W. B. Yeats's "Sailing to Byzantium," which employs the *ottava rima* ("eighth rhyme") stanza—*abababcc*.

Off rhyme *See* **Slant rhyme.**

Omniscient narrator Also called **all-knowing narrator.** A narrator who has the ability to move freely through the consciousness of any character. The omniscient narrator also has complete knowledge of all of the external events in a story. (*See also* **Nonparticipant narrator.**)

Onomatopoeia A literary device that attempts to represent a thing or action by the word that imitates the sound associated with it (e.g., *crash*, *bang*, *pitter-patter*).

Open dénouement One of the two conventional types of dénouement or resolution. In open dénouement, the author ends a narrative with a few loose ends, or unresolved matters, on which the reader is left to speculate. (*See also* **Closed dénouement.**)

Open form Verse that has no set formal scheme—no meter, rhyme, or even set stanzaic pattern. Open form is always in free verse. (*See also* **Free verse.**)

Oral tradition The tradition within a culture that transmits narratives by word of mouth from one generation to another. Fables, folktales, ballads, and songs are examples of some types of narratives found originally in an oral tradition.

Orchestra In classical Greek theater architecture, "the place for dancing," a circular, level performance space at the base of a horseshoe-shaped amphitheater, where twelve, then later (in Sophocles's plays) fifteen, young, masked, male chorus members sang and danced the odes interspersed between dramatic episodes making up the classical Greek play. Today the orchestra refers to the ground floor seats in a theater or concert hall.

Overstatement Also called **hyperbole.** Exaggeration used to emphasize a point.

Parable A brief, usually allegorical narrative that teaches a moral. The parables found in Christian literature, such as "The Parable of the Prodigal Son" (Luke 15:11–32), are classic examples of the form. In parables, unlike fables (where the moral is explicitly stated within the narrative), the moral themes are implicit and can often be interpreted in several ways. Modern parables can be found in the works of Franz Kafka and Jorge Luis Borges.

Paradox A statement that at first strikes one as self-contradictory, but that on reflection reveals some deeper sense. Paradox is often achieved by a play on words.

Parallelism An arrangement of words, phrases, clauses, or sentences side-by-side in a similar grammatical or structural way. Parallelism organizes ideas in a way that demonstrates their coordination to the reader.

Paraphrase The restatement in one's own words of what we understand a literary work to say. A paraphrase is similar to a summary, although not as brief or simple.

Parody A mocking imitation of a literary work or individual author's style, usually for comic effect. A parody typically exaggerates distinctive features of the original for humorous purposes.

Participant narrator A narrator that participates as a character within a story. (*See also* **First-person narrator.**)

Pentameter A verse meter consisting of five metrical feet, or five primary stresses, per line. In English, the most common form of pentameter is iambic.

Peripeteia Anglicized as *peripety*, Greek for "sudden change." Reversal of fortune. In a play's plotting, a sudden change of circumstance affecting the protagonist, often also including a reversal of intent on the protagonist's part. The play's peripety occurs usually when a certain result is expected and instead its opposite effect is produced. For example, at the beginning of *Oedipus*, the protagonist expects to discover the identity of the murderer of Laius. However, after the Corinthian messenger informs Oedipus that he was adopted, the hero's intent changes to encompass the search for his true parentage. A comedy's peripety restores a character to good fortune, when a moment in which the worst can happen is suddenly turned into happy circumstance.

Persona Latin for "mask." A fictitious character created by an author to be the speaker of a poem, story, or novel. A persona is always the narrator of the work and not merely a character in it.

Personification A figure of speech in which a thing, an animal, or an abstract term is endowed with human characteristics. Personification allows an author to dramatize the nonhuman world in tangibly human terms.

Petrarchan sonnet *See* **Italian sonnet.**

Picaresque A type of narrative, usually a novel, that presents the life of a likable scoundrel who is at odds with respectable society. The narrator of a picaresque was originally a *picaro* (Spanish for "rascal" or "rogue") who recounts his adventures tricking the rich and gullible. This type of narrative rarely has a tight plot, and the episodes or adventures follow in a loose chronological order.

Picture-frame stage Developed in sixteenth-century Italian playhouses, the picture-frame stage held the action within a proscenium arch, a gateway standing "in front of the scenery" (as the word *proscenium* indicates). The proscenium framed painted scene panels (receding into the middle distance) designed to give the illusion of three-dimensional perspective. Only one seat in the auditorium, reserved for the theater's royal patron or sponsor, enjoyed the complete perspectivist illusion. The raised and framed stage separated actors from the audience and the world of the play from the real world of the auditorium. Picture-frame stages became the norm throughout Europe and England up into the twentieth century.

Play review A critical account of a performance, providing the basic facts of the production, a brief plot summary, and an evaluation (with adequate rationale) of the chief elements of performance, including the acting, the direction, scene and light design, and the script, especially if the play is new or unfamiliar.

Plot The particular arrangement of actions, events, and situations that unfold in a narrative. A plot is not merely the general story of a narrative but the author's artistic pattern made from the parts of the narrative, including the exposition, complications, climax, and dénouement. How an author chooses to construct the plot determines the way the reader experiences the story. Manipulating a plot, therefore, can be the author's most important expressive device when writing a story. More than just a story made up of episodes or a bare synopsis of the temporal order of events, the plotting is the particular embodiment of an action that allows the audience to see the causal relationship between the parts of the action. (*See also* **Climax, Falling action, Rising action.**)

Poetic diction Strictly speaking, *poetic diction* means any language deemed suitable for verse, but the term generally refers to elevated language intended for poetry rather than common use. Poetic diction often refers to the ornate language used in literary periods such as the Augustan age, when authors employed a highly specialized vocabulary for their verse. (*See also* **Diction.**)

Point of view The perspective from which a story is told. There are many types of point of view, including first-person narrator (a story in which the narrator is a participant in the action) and third-person narrator (a type of narration in which the narrator is a nonparticipant).

Portmanteau word An artificial word that combines parts of other words to express some combination of their qualities. Sometimes portmanteau words prove so useful that they become part of the standard language. For example, *smog* from *smoke* and *fog*; or *brunch* from *breakfast* and *lunch*.

Print culture A culture that depends primarily on the printed word—in books, magazines, and newspapers—to distribute and preserve information. In recent decades the electronic media have taken over much of this role from print.

Projective verse Charles Olson's theory that poets compose by listening to their own breathing and using it as a rhythmic guide rather than poetic meter or form. (*See also* **Open form.**)

Proscenium arch Separating the auditorium from the raised stage and the world of the play, the architectural picture frame or gateway "standing in front of the scenery" (as the word *proscenium* indicates) in traditional European theaters from the sixteenth century on.

Prose poem Poetic language printed in prose paragraphs, but displaying the careful attention to sound, imagery, and figurative language characteristic of poetry.

Prosody The study of metrical structures in poetry. (*See also* **Scansion.**)

Protagonist The central character in a literary work. The protagonist usually initiates the main action of the story, often in conflict with the antagonist. (*See also* **Antagonist.**)

Psalms Sacred songs, usually referring to the 150 Hebrew poems collected in the Old Testament.

Psychological criticism The practice of analyzing a literary work through investigating three major areas: the nature of literary genius, the psychological study of a particular artist, and the analysis of fictional characters. This methodology uses the analytical tools of psychology and psychoanalysis to understand the underlying motivations and meanings of a literary work.

Pulp fiction A type of formulaic and quickly written fiction originally produced for cheap mass circulation magazines. The term *pulp* refers to the inexpensive wood-pulp paper developed in the mid-nineteenth century on which these magazines were printed. Most pulp fiction journals printed only melodramatic genre work—westerns, science fiction, romance, horror, adventure tales, or crime stories.

Pun A play on words in which one word is substituted for another similar or identical sound, but of very different meaning.

Purgation *See* ***Katharsis.***

Quantitative meter A meter constructed on the principle of vowel length. Such quantities are difficult to hear in English, so this meter remains slightly foreign to our language. Classical Greek and Latin poetry were written in quantitative meters.

Quatrain A stanza consisting of four lines. Quatrains are the most common stanzas used in English-language poetry.

Rap A popular style of music that emerged in the 1980s in which lyrics are spoken or chanted over a steady beat, usually sampled or prerecorded. Rap lyrics are almost always rhymed and very rhythmic—syncopating a heavy metrical beat in a manner similar to jazz. Originally an African American form, rap is now international. In that way, rap can be seen as a form of popular poetry.

Reader-response criticism The practice of analyzing a literary work by describing what happens in the reader's mind while interpreting the text. Reader-response critics believe that no literary text exists independently of readers' interpretations and that there is no single fixed interpretation of any literary work.

Realism An attempt to reproduce faithfully the surface appearance of life, especially that of ordinary people in everyday situations. As a literary term, *realism* has two meanings—one general, the other historical. In a general sense, realism refers to the representation of characters, events, and settings in ways that the spectator will consider plausible, based on consistency and likeness to type. This sort of realism does not necessarily depend on elaborate factual description or documentation but more on the author's ability to draft plots and characters within a conventional framework of social, economic, and psychological reality. In a historical sense, Realism (usually capitalized) refers to a movement in nineteenth-century European literature and theater that rejected the idealism, elitism, and romanticism of earlier verse dramas and prose fiction in an attempt to represent life truthfully. Realist literature customarily focused on the middle class (and occasionally the working class) rather than the aristocracy, and it used social and economic detail to create an accurate account of human behavior. Realism began in France with Honoré de Balzac, Gustave Flaubert, and Guy de Maupassant and then moved internationally. Other major Realists include Leo Tolstoy, Henry James, Anton Chekhov, and Edith Wharton.

Recognition In tragic plotting, the moment of recognition occurs when ignorance gives way to knowledge, illusion to disillusion. In Aristotle's *Poetics*, this is usually a recognition of blood ties or kinship between the persons involved in grave actions involving suffering. According to Aristotle, the ideal moment of recognition coincides with *peripeteia* or reversal of fortune. The classic example occurs in *Oedipus* when Oedipus discovers that he had unwittingly killed his own father when defending himself at the crossroads and later married his own mother when assuming the Theban throne. (*See also* ***Hamartia, Katharsis, Peripeteia.***)

Refrain A word, phrase, line, or stanza repeated at intervals in a song or poem. The repeated chorus of a song is a refrain.

Regionalism The literary representation of a specific locale that consciously uses the particulars of geography, custom, history, folklore, or speech. In regional narratives, the locale plays a crucial role in the presentation and progression of a story that could not be moved to another setting without artistic loss. Usually, regional narratives take place at some distance from the literary capital of a culture, often in small towns or rural areas. Examples of American regionalism can be found in the writing of Willa Cather, Kate Chopin, William Faulkner, and Eudora Welty.

Resolution The final part of a narrative, the concluding action or actions that follow the climax. (*See also* **Conclusion, Dénouement.**)

Retrospect *See* **Flashback.**

Reversal *See* ***Peripeteia.***

Rhyme, Rime Two or more words that contain an identical or similar vowel sound, usually accented, with following consonant sounds (if any) identical as well: *queue* and *stew*, *prairie schooner* and *piano tuner*. (*See also* **Consonance, Exact rhyme.**)

Rhyme scheme, Rime scheme Any recurrent pattern of rhyme within an individual poem or fixed form. A rhyme scheme is usually described by using small letters to represent each end rhyme—*a* for the first rhyme, *b* for the second, and so on. The rhyme scheme of a stanza of **common meter** or hymn meter, for example, would be notated as *abab*.

Rhythm The pattern of stresses and pauses in a poem. A fixed and recurring rhythm in a poem is called **meter.**

Rising action That part of the play or narrative, including the exposition, in which events start moving toward a climax. In the rising action the protagonist usually faces the complications of the plot to reach his or her goal. In *Hamlet*, the rising action develops the conflict between Hamlet and Claudius, with Hamlet succeeding in controlling the course of events. Because the mainspring of the play's first half is the mystery of Claudius's guilt, the rising action reaches a climax when Hamlet proves the king's guilt by the device of the play within a play (3.2—the "mousetrap" scene), when Hamlet as heroic avenger has positive proof of Claudius's guilt.

Rising meter A meter whose movement rises from an unstressed syllable (or syllables) to a stressed syllable (for-*get*, De-*troit*). Iambic and anapestic are examples of rising meter.

Romance In general terms, romance is a narrative mode that employs exotic adventure and idealized emotion rather than realistic depiction of character and action. In the romantic mode—out of which most popular genre fictions develop—people, actions, and events are depicted more as we wish them to be (heroes are very brave, villains are very bad) rather than the complex ways they usually are. Medieval romances (in both prose and verse) presented chivalric tales of kings, knights, and aristocratic ladies. Modern romances, emerging in the nineteenth century, were represented by adventure novels like Sir Walter Scott's *Ivanhoe* or Nathaniel Hawthorne's *The House of the Seven Gables*, which embodied the symbolic quests and idealized characters of earlier, chivalric tales in slightly more realistic terms, a tradition carried on in contemporary popular works like the *Star Wars* and James Bond films.

Romantic comedy A form of comic drama in which the plot focuses on one or more pairs of young lovers who overcome difficulties to achieve a happy ending (usually marriage). Shakespeare's *A Midsummer Night's Dream* is a classic example of the genre.

Rondel A thirteen-line English verse form consisting of three rhymed stanzas with a refrain.

Round character A term coined by English novelist E. M. Forster to describe a complex character who is presented in depth and detail in a narrative. Round characters are those who change significantly during the course of a narrative. Most often, round characters are the central characters in a narrative. (*See also* **Flat character.**)

Run-on line A line of verse that does not end in punctuation, but carries on grammatically to the next line. Such lines are read aloud with only a slight pause at the end. A run-on line is also called *enjambment*.

Sarcasm A conspicuously bitter form of irony in which the ironic statement is designed to hurt or mock its target. (*See also* **Irony.**)

Satiric comedy A genre using derisive humor to ridicule human weakness and folly or attack political injustices and incompetence. Satiric comedy often focuses on ridiculing characters or killjoys, who resist the festive mood of comedy. Such characters, called humors, are often characterized by one dominant personality trait or ruling obsession.

Satiric poetry Poetry that blends criticism with humor to convey a message. Satire characteristically uses irony to make its points. Usually, its tone is one of detached amusement, withering contempt, and implied superiority.

Satyr play A type of Greek comic play that was performed after the tragedies at the City Dionysia, the principal civic and religious festival of Athens. The playwrights winning the right to perform their works in the festival wrote three tragedies and one satyr play to form the traditional tetralogy, or group of four. The structure of a satyr play was similar to tragedy's. Its subject matter, treated in burlesque, was drawn from myth or the epic cycles. Its chorus was composed of satyrs (half human and half horse or goat) under the leadership of Silenus, the adoptive father of Dionysius. Rascals and revelers, satyrs represented wild versions of humanity, opposing the values of civilized men. Euripides's *Cyclops* is the only complete surviving example of the genre.

Scansion A practice used to describe rhythmic patterns in a poem by separating the metrical feet, counting the syllables, marking the accents, and indicating the pauses. Scansion can be very useful in analyzing the sound of a poem and how it should be read aloud.

Scene In drama, the scene is a division of the action in an act of the play. There is no universal convention as to what constitutes a scene, and the practice differs by playwright and period. Usually, a scene represents a single dramatic action that builds to a climax (often ending in the entrance or exit of a major character). In this last sense of a vivid and unified action, the term can be applied to fiction.

Selective omniscience The point of view that sees the events of a narrative through the eyes of a single character. The selectively omniscient narrator is usually a nonparticipant narrator.

Sentimentality A usually pejorative description of the quality of a literary work that tries to convey great emotion but fails to give the reader sufficient grounds for sharing it.

Sestet A poem or stanza of six lines. *Sestet* is a term usually used when speaking of sonnets, to indicate the final six-line section of the poem, as distinct from the octave (the first eight lines). (*See also* **Sonnet.**)

Sestina A complex verse form ("song of sixes") in which six end words are repeated in a prescribed order through six stanzas. A sestina ends with an **envoy** of three lines in which all six words appear—for a total of thirty-nine lines. Originally used by French and Italian poets, the sestina has become a popular modern form in English.

Setting The time and place of a literary work. The setting may also include the climate and even the social, psychological, or spiritual state of the participants.

Shakespearean sonnet *See* **English sonnet.**

Short Story A prose narrative too brief to be published in a separate volume—as novellas and novels frequently are. The short story is usually a focused narrative that presents one or two main characters involved in a single compelling action.

Simile A comparison of two things, indicated by some connective, usually *like*, *as*, *than*, or a verb such as *resembles*. A simile usually compares two things that initially seem unlike but are shown to have a significant resemblance. "Cool as a cucumber" and "My love is like a red, red rose" are examples of similes.

Situational Irony *See* **Irony.**

Skene In classical Greek staging of the fifth century B.C., the temporary wooden stage building in which actors changed masks and costumes when changing roles. Its façade, with double center doors and possibly two side doors, served as the setting for action taking place before a palace, temple, cave, or other interior space.

Slack syllable An unstressed syllable in a line of verse.

Slant rhyme A rhyme in which the final consonant sounds are the same but the vowel sounds are different, as in letter and litter, bone and bean. Slant rhyme may also be called *near rhyme*, *off rhyme*, or *imperfect rhyme*. (*See also* **Consonance.**)

Slapstick comedy A kind of farce, featuring pratfalls, pie throwing, fisticuffs, and other violent action. It takes its name originally from the slapstick carried by the ***commedia dell'arte***'s main servant type, Harlequin.

Sociological criticism The practice of analyzing a literary work by examining the cultural, economic, and political context in which it was written or received. Sociological criticism primarily explores the relationship between the artist and society.

Soliloquy In drama, a speech by a character alone onstage in which he or she utters his or her thoughts aloud. The soliloquy is important in drama because it gives the audience insight into a character's inner life, private motivations, and uncertainties.

Sonnet From the Italian *sonnetto*: "little song." A traditional and widely used verse form, especially popular for love poetry. The sonnet is a fixed form of fourteen lines, traditionally written in iambic pentameter, usually made up of an **octave** (the first eight lines) and a concluding **sestet** (six lines). There are, however, several variations, most conspicuously the Shakespearean, or English sonnet, which consists of three quatrains and a concluding couplet. Most sonnets turn, or shift in tone or focus, after the first eight lines, although the placement may vary. (*See also* **English sonnet, Italian sonnet.**)

Spondee A metrical foot of verse containing two stressed syllables (′ ′) often substituted into a meter to create extra emphasis.

Stage business Nonverbal action that engages the attention of an audience. Expressing what cannot be said, stage business became a particularly important means of revealing the inner thoughts and feelings of a character in the development of Realism.

Stanza From the Italian, meaning "stopping-place" or "room." A recurring pattern of two or more lines of verse, poetry's equivalent to the paragraph in prose. The stanza is the basic organizational principle of most formal poetry.

Static character *See* **Flat character.**

Stock character A common or stereotypical character that occurs frequently in literature. Examples of stock characters are the mad scientist, the battle-scarred veteran, or the strong-but-silent cowboy. (*See also* **Archetype.**)

Stream of consciousness Not a specific technique, but a type of modern narration that uses various literary devices, especially interior monologue, in an attempt to duplicate the subjective and associative nature of human consciousness. Stream of consciousness often focuses on imagistic perception in order to capture the preverbal level of consciousness.

Stress An emphasis or accent placed on a syllable in speech. Clear pronunciation of polysyllabic words almost always depends on correct placement of their stress. (For instance, *de*-sert and de-*sert* are two different words and parts of speech, depending on their stress.) Stress is the basic principle of most English-language meter.

Style All the distinctive ways in which an author, genre, movement, or historical period uses language to create a literary work. An author's style depends on his or her characteristic use of diction, imagery, tone, syntax, and figurative language. Even sentence structure and punctuation can play a role in an author's style.

Subject The main topic of a poem, story, or play.

Subplot *See* **Double plot.**

Summary A brief condensation of the main idea or story of a literary work. A summary is similar to a paraphrase, but less detailed.

Surrealism A modernist movement in art and literature that tries to organize art according to the irrational dictates of the unconscious mind. Founded by the French poet André Breton, Surrealism sought to reach a higher plane of reality by abandoning logic for the seemingly absurd connections made in dreams and other unconscious mental activities.

Suspense Enjoyable anxiety created in the reader by the author's handling of plot. When the outcome of events is unclear, the author's suspension of resolution intensifies the reader's interest—particularly if the plot involves characters to whom the reader or audience is sympathetic. Suspense is also created when the fate of a character is clear to the audience, but not to the character. The suspense results from the audience's anticipation of how and when the character will meet his or her inevitable fate.

Syllabic verse A verse form in which the poet establishes a pattern of a certain number of syllables to a line. Syllabic verse is the most common meter in most Romance languages such as Italian, French, and Spanish; it is less common in English because it is difficult to hear syllable count. Syllabic verse was used by several Modernist poets, most conspicuously Marianne Moore.

Symbol A person, place, or thing in a narrative that suggests meanings beyond its literal sense. Symbol is related to allegory, but it works more complexly. In an allegory an object has a single additional significance. By contrast, a symbol usually contains multiple meanings and associations. In Herman Melville's *Moby-Dick*, for example, the great white whale does not have just a single significance but accrues powerful associations as the narrative progresses.

Symbolic act An action whose significance goes well beyond its literal meaning. In literature, symbolic acts usually involve some conscious or unconscious ritual element like rebirth, purification, forgiveness, vengeance, or initiation.

Symbolist movement An international literary movement that originated with nineteenth-century French poets such as Charles Baudelaire, Arthur Rimbaud, and Paul Verlaine. Symbolists aspired to make literature resemble music. They avoided direct statement and exposition for powerful evocation and suggestion. Symbolists also considered the poet as a seer who could look beyond the mundane aspects of the everyday world to capture visions of a higher reality.

Symbolists Members of the Symbolist movement.

Synecdoche The use of a significant part of a thing to stand for the whole of it or vice versa. To say *wheels* for *car* or *rhyme* for *poetry* are examples of synecdoche. (*See also* **Metonymy**.)

Synopsis A brief summary or outline of a story or dramatic work.

Tactile imagery A word or sequence of words that refers to the sense of touch. (*See also* **Imagery**.)

Tale A short narrative without a complex plot, the word originating from the Old English *talu*, or "speech." Tales are an ancient form of narrative found in folklore, and traditional tales often contain supernatural elements. A tale differs from a short story by its tendency toward less developed characters and linear plotting. British writer A. E. Coppard characterized the underlying difference by claiming that a story is something that is written and a tale is something that is told. The ambition of a tale is usually similar to that of a yarn: revelation of the marvelous rather than illumination of the everyday world.

Tall tale A humorous short narrative that provides a wildly exaggerated version of events. Originally an oral form, the tall tale assumes that its audience knows the narrator is distorting the events. The form is often associated with the American frontier.

Tercet A group of three lines of verse, usually all ending in the same rhyme. (*See also* ***Terza rima***.)

Terminal refrain A refrain that appears at the end of each stanza in a song or poem. (*See also* **Refrain**.)

Terza rima A verse form made up of three-line stanzas that are connected by an overlapping rhyme scheme (*aba, bcb, cdc, ded,* etc.). Dante employs *terza rima* in *The Divine Comedy*.

Tetrameter A verse meter consisting of four metrical feet, or four primary stresses, per line.

Theater of the absurd Post–World War II European genre depicting the grotesquely comic plight of human beings thrown by accident into an irrational and meaningless world. The critic Martin Esslin coined the term to characterize plays by writers such as Samuel Beckett, Jean Genet, and Eugene Ionesco. Beckett's *Waiting for Godot* (1955), considered to be the greatest example of theater of the absurd, features in two nearly identical acts two tramps waiting almost without hope on a country road for an unidentified person, Godot. "Nothing happens, nobody comes, nobody goes, it's awful," one of them cries, perhaps echoing the unspoken thoughts of an audience confronted by a play that seemingly refuses to do anything.

Theme A generally recurring subject or idea conspicuously evident in a literary work. A short didactic work like a fable may have a single obvious theme, but longer works can contain multiple themes. Not all subjects in a work can be considered themes, only the central subject or subjects.

Thesis sentence A summing-up of the one main idea or argument that an essay or critical paper will embody.

Third-person narrator A type of narration in which the narrator is a nonparticipant. In a third-person narrative the characters are referred to as "he," "she," or "they." Third-person narrators are most commonly omniscient, but the level of their knowledge may vary from total omniscience (the narrator knows everything about the characters and their lives) to limited omniscience (the narrator is limited to the perceptions of a single character).

Tone The attitude toward a subject conveyed in a literary work. No single stylistic device creates tone; it is the net result of the various elements an author brings to creating the work's feeling and manner. Tone may be playful, sarcastic, ironic, sad, solemn, or any other possible attitude. A writer's tone plays an important role in establishing the reader's relationship to the characters or ideas presented in a literary work.

Total omniscience A type of point of view in which the narrator knows everything about all of the characters and events in a story. A narrator with total omniscience can also move freely from one character to another. Generally, a totally omniscient narrative is written in the third person.

Traditional epic *See* **Folk epic.**

Tragedy The representation of serious and important actions that lead to a disastrous end for the protagonist. The final purpose of tragedy in Aristotle's formulation is to evoke ***katharsis*** by means of events involving pity and fear. A unified tragic action, from beginning to end, brings a morally good but not perfect tragic hero from happiness to unhappiness because of a mistaken act, to which he or she is led by a ***hamartia***, an error in judgment. Tragic heroes move us to pity because their misfortunes are greater than they deserve, because they are not evil, having committed the fateful deed or deeds unwittingly and involuntarily. They also move us to fear, because we recognize in ourselves similar possibilities of error. We share with the tragic hero a common world of mischance. (*See also* **Tragic flaw.**)

Tragic flaw A fatal weakness or moral flaw in the protagonist that brings him or her to a bad end, for example, Creon in *Antigonê* or Macbeth. Sometimes offered as an alternative translation of ***hamartia,*** in contrast to the idea that the tragic hero's catastrophe is caused by an error in judgment, the idea of a protagonist ruined by a tragic flaw makes more sense in relation to the Greek idea of ***hubris,*** commonly translated as "outrageous behavior," involving deliberate transgressions against moral or divine law.

Tragic irony A form of **dramatic irony** that ultimately arrives at some tragedy.

Tragicomedy A type of drama that combines elements of both tragedy and comedy. Usually, it creates potentially tragic situations that bring the protagonists to the brink of disaster but then ends happily. Tragicomedy can be traced as far back as the Renaissance (in plays likes Shakespeare's *Measure for Measure*), but it also refers to modern plays like Chekhov's *Cherry Orchard* and Beckett's *Waiting for Godot.*

Transferred epithet A figure of speech in which the poet attributes some characteristic of a thing to another thing closely associated with it. Transferred epithet is a kind of metonymy. It usually places an adjective next to a noun in which the connection is not strictly logical (Milton's phrase "blind mouths" or Hart Crane's "nimble blue plateaus") but has expressive power.

Trick ending A surprising climax that depends on a quick reversal of the situation from an unexpected source. The success of a trick ending is relative to the degree in which the reader is surprised but not left incredulous when it occurs. The American writer O. Henry popularized this type of ending.

Trimeter A verse meter consisting of three metrical feet, or three primary stresses, per line.

Triolet A short lyric form of eight rhymed lines borrowed from the French. The two opening lines are repeated according to a set pattern. Triolets are often playful, but dark lyric poems like Robert Bridge's "Triolet" demonstrate the form's flexibility.

Trochaic, trochee A metrical foot in which a stressed syllable is followed by an unstressed syllable (′ ⏑) as in the words *sum*-mer and *chor*-us. The trochaic meter is often associated with songs, chants, and magic spells in English.

Troubadours The minstrels of the late Middle Ages. Originally, troubadours were lyric poets living in southern France and northern Italy who sang to aristocratic audiences mostly of chivalry and love.

Understatement An ironic figure of speech that deliberately describes something in a way that is less than the true case.

Unities The three formal qualities recommended by Italian Renaissance literary critics to unify a plot in order to give it a cohesive and complete integrity. Traditionally, good plots honored the three unities—of action, time, and place. The action in neoclassical drama, therefore, was patterned by cause and effect to occur within a 24-hour period. The setting took place in one unchanging locale. In the *Poetics,* Aristotle urged only the requirement of unity of plot, with events patterned in a cause-and-effect relationship from beginning through middle to the end of the single action imitated.

Unreliable narrator A narrator who—intentionally or unintentionally—relates events in a subjective or distorted manner. The author usually provides some indication early on in such stories that the narrator is not to be completely trusted.

Verbal irony A statement in which the speaker or writer says the opposite of what is really meant. For example, a friend might comment, "How graceful you are!" after you trip clumsily on a stair.

Verisimilitude The quality in a literary work of appearing true to life. In fiction, verisimilitude is usually achieved by careful use of realistic detail in description, characterization, and dialogue. (*See also* **Realism.**)

Verse From the Latin *versum*, "to turn." Verse has two major meanings. First, it refers to any single line of poetry. Second, it refers to any composition in lines of more or less regular rhythm—in contrast to prose.

Vers libre *See* **Free verse.**

Villanelle A fixed form developed by French courtly poets of the Middle Ages in imitation of Italian folk song. A villanelle consists of six rhymed stanzas in which two lines are repeated in a prescribed pattern.

Visual imagery A word or sequence of words that refers to the sense of sight or presents something one may see.

Vulgate From the Latin word *vulgus*, "mob" or "common people." The lowest level of formality in language, vulgate is the diction of the common people with no pretensions at refinement or elevation. The vulgate is not necessarily vulgar in the sense of containing foul or inappropriate language; it refers simply to unschooled, everyday language.

LITERARY CREDITS

Fiction

Achebe, Chinua: "Dead Men's Path," copyright © 1972, 1973 by Chinua Achebe, from GIRLS AT WAR AND OTHER STORIES by Chinua Achebe. Used by permission of Doubleday, a division of Random House, Inc.

Alexie, Sherman: "This Is What It Means to Say Phoenix, Arizona" from THE LONE RANGER AND TONTO FISTFIGHT IN HEAVEN by Sherman Alexie. Copyright © 1993, 2005 by Sherman Alexie. Used by permission of Grove/Atlantic, Inc.

Allende, Isabel: "The Judge's Wife" reprinted with the permission of Scribner, an imprint of Simon & Schuster, Inc., from THE STORIES OF EVA LUNA by Isabel Allende, translated from the Spanish by Margaret Sayers Peden. Copyright © 1989 by Isabel Allende. English translation copyright © 1991 by Macmillan Publishing Company. All rights reserved.

Ammons, Elizabeth: "Biographical Echoes in 'The Yellow Wallpaper'" excerpted from CONFLICTING STORIES: AMERICAN WOMEN WRITERS AT THE TURN OF THE CENTURY, copyright © 1991. Reprinted by permission of Oxford University Press.

Arredondo, Inés: "The Shunammite" by Inés Arredondo as translated by Alberto Manguel. © Alberto Manguel. Reprinted by permission of Guillermo Schavelzon & Asociados, Agencia Literaria, www.schavelzon.com.

Atwood, Margaret: "Happy Endings" from GOOD BONES AND SIMPLE MURDERS by Margaret Atwood, copyright © 1983, 1992, 1994, by O.W. Toad Ltd. A Nan A. Talese Book. Used by permission of Doubleday, a division of Random House, Inc.

Baker, Houston A. and Charlotte Pierce-Baker: Excerpt from "Patches: Quilts and Community in Alice Walker's 'Everyday Use'" by Houston A. Baker and Charlotte Pierce-Baker from THE SOUTHERN REVIEW 21 (Summer 1985). Reprinted by permission of the authors.

Baldwin, James: "Sonny's Blues" © 1957 by James Baldwin was originally published in Partisan Review. Copyright renewed. Collected in GOING TO MEET THE MAN, published by Vintage Books. Reprinted by arrangement with the James Baldwin Estate.

Baldwin, James: From NOTES OF A NATIVE SON by James Baldwin. Copyright © 1955, renewed 1983, by James Baldwin. Reprinted by permission of Beacon Press, Boston.

Baraban, Elena: "The Motive for Murder in 'The Cask of Amontillado' by Edgar Allan Poe" by Elana Baraban, originally published in THE ROCKY MOUNTAIN REVIEW Vol. 58, no 2, pp. 47–62, 2004. © 2004 by the Rocky Mountain Modern Language Association. Reproduced by permission.

Baudelaire, Charles: From HISTOIRES EXTRAORDINAIRES (1856), translated from FATAL DESTINIES: THE EDGAR POE ESSAYS by Joan F. Mele. Cross Country Press, 1981.

Bidpai: "The Camel and His Friends" by Bidpai, retold in English by Arundhati Khanwalkar from THE PANCHATANTRA. (The Association of Grandparents of Indian Immigrants).

Borges, Jorge Luis: "The Gospel According to Mark" from COLLECTED FICTIONS by Jorge Luis Borges, translated by Andrew Hurley, copyright © 1998 by Maria Kodama; translation copyright © 1998 by Penguin Putnam Inc. Used by permission of Viking Penguin, a division of Penguin Group (USA) Inc.

Boyle, T. Coraghessan: "Greasy Lake", from GREASY LAKE AND OTHER STORIES by T. Coraghessan Boyle, © 1979, 1981, 1982, 1983, 1984, 1985 by T. Coraghessan Boyle. Used by permission of Viking Penguin, a division of Penguin Group (USA) Inc.

Bradbury, Ray: "A Sound of Thunder" by Ray Bradbury. Reprinted by permission of Don Congdon Associates, Inc. Copyright © 1952 by Crowell Collier Publishing Company, renewed 1980 by Ray Bradbury.

Carver, Raymond: "Cathedral," from CATHEDRAL by Raymond Carver, copyright © 1981, 1982, 1983 by Raymond Carver. Used by permission of Alfred A. Knopf, a division of Random House, Inc.

Carver, Raymond: Excerpt from "On Writing" from FIRES: Essays, Poems, Stories by Raymond Carver. Copyright © 1968, 1969, 1970, 1971, 1972, 1973, 1974, 1975, 1976, 1977, 1978, 1979, 1980, 1981, 1982, 1983 by Raymond Carver. Copyright © 1983, 1984 by the Estate of Raymond Carver. Used by permission of The Wylie Agency LLC.

Cheever, John: "The Swimmer" from THE STORIES OF JOHN CHEEVER by John Cheever, copyright © 1978 by John Cheever. Used by permission of Alfred A. Knopf, a division of Random House, Inc.

Chopin, Kate: "The Storm," from THE COMPLETE WORKS OF KATE CHOPIN, edited by Per Seyersted (Louisiana State University Press, 1969). Reprinted by permission of the publisher.

Christian, Barbara: Excerpt from the Introduction to EVERYDAY USE by Alice Walker, edited by Barbara T. Christian, from WOMEN WRITERS: TEXT AND CONTEXT SERIES. Copyright © 1994 by Rutgers, the State University. Reprinted by permission of Rutgers University Press

Cisneros, Sandra: "The House on Mango Street" from THE HOUSE ON MANGO STREET. Copyright © 1984 by Sandra Cisneros. Published by Vintage Books, a division of Random House, Inc., and in hardcover by Alfred A. Knopf in 1994. By permission of Susan Bergholz Literary Services, New York, NY and Lamy, NM. All rights reserved.

Cowan, Louise S.: From "Passing by the Dragon" by Louise S. Cowan in "REVELATION" BY FLANNERY O'CONNOR, The Trinity Forum Reading 40 (Summer 2005) (McLean, VA: The Trinity Forum, Inc., 2005). Used by permission.

Ellison, Ralph: "Battle Royal," copyright 1948 and renewed 1976 by Ralph Ellison, from INVISIBLE MAN by Ralph Ellison. Used by permission of Random House, Inc.

Evans, Rob: Lyrics from "The Donut Song" by Rob Evans. Copyright © 1982 Integrity's Hosanna! Music (ASCAP) (adm. at EMICMGPublishing.com) All rights reserved. Used by permission.

Faulkner, William: "A Rose for Emily," copyright 1930 and renewed 1958 by William Faulkner, "Barn Burning," copyright 1950 by Random House, Inc. Copyright renewed 1977 by Jill Faulkner Summers, from COLLECTED STORIES OF WILLIAM FAULKNER by William Faulkner. Used by permission of Random House, Inc.

Feeley, Kathleen: Excerpt from FLANNERY O'CONNOR: VOICE OF THE PEACOCK, 1972, by permission of Fordham University Press.

Fleenor, Juliann: "Gender and Pathology in 'The Yellow Wallpaper' " from "The Gothic Prism: Charlotte Perkins Gilman's Gothic Stories and Her Autobiography" in THE FEMALE GOTHIC by Juliann Fleenor (Montreal: Eden Press, 1983). Reprinted by permission of the author.

Flower, Dean: Excerpt from "Listening to Flannery O'Connor," reprinted by permission from THE HUDSON REVIEW, Vol. LXIII, No. 4 (Winter 2011). Copyright © 2011 by The Hudson Review, Inc.

García Márquez, Gabriel: "A Very Old Man with Enormous Wings" from LEAF STORM AND OTHER STORIES by Gabriel García Márquez. Translated by Gregory Rabassa. Copyright © 1971 by Gabriel García Márquez. Reprinted by permission of Harper Collins Publishers.

García Márquez, Gabriel: Interview with Gabriel García Márquez from WRITERS AT WORK, THE PARIS REVIEW INTERVIEWS, Sixth Series, edited by George Plimpton. Copyright © 1981 by The Paris Review, reprinted with permission of The Wylie Agency, LLC.

Gilbert, Sandra and Susan Gubar: Excerpt from THE MADWOMAN IN THE ATTIC: THE WOMAN WRITER AND THE NINETEENTH-CENTURY LITERARY IMAGINATION, pp. 85–92. Copyright © 1979 by Yale University. Copyright © 1984 by Sandra M. Gilbert and Susan Gubar. Reprinted by permission of Yale University Press.

Hemingway, Ernest: "A Clean, Well-Lighted Place," reprinted with the permission of Scribner, a Division of Simon & Schuster, Inc., from THE SHORT STORIES OF ERNEST HEMINGWAY. Copyright 1933 by Charles Scribner's Sons. Copyright renewed © 1961 by Mary Hemingway. All rights reserved.

Hemingway, Ernest: "The Direct Style" from "An Afternoon with Hemingway" by Edward Stafford, Cincinnati, OH: Writer's Digest, 1964.

Heywood, Harriet: "The Brownie Smile Song" © 1968 by Harriet F. Heywood. Used by permission of Girl Scouts of the USA.

Hoffman, Daniel: "The Father-Figure in 'The Tell-Tale Heart'" from POE POE POE POE POE POE POE. Baton Rouge: Louisiana State University Press, 1998. Copyright 1927 by Daniel Hoffman. Reprinted by permission of the author.

Jackson, Shirley: "Biography of a Story," copyright © 1960 by Shirley Jackson, from COME ALONG WITH ME by Shirley Jackson. Used by permission of Viking Penguin, a division of Penguin Group (USA) Inc.

Jackson, Shirley: "The Lottery" from THE LOTTERY by Shirley Jackson. Copyright © 1948, 1949 by Shirley Jackson. Copyright renewed 1976, 1977 by Laurence Hyman, Barry Hyman, Mrs. Sarah Webster and Mrs. Joanne Schnurer. Reprinted by permission of Farrar, Straus and Giroux, LLC.

Kafka, Franz: "Kafka's View of 'The Meta-morphosis'" by Gustav Janouch, translated by Goronwy Rees, from CONVERSATIONS WITH KAFKA, copyright © 1968 by S. Fischer Verlag GMBH, translation copyright © 1971 S. Fischer Verlag GMBH. Reprinted by permission of New Directions Publishing Corp.

Kafka, Franz: "Before the Law"and "The Metamorphosis" translated by John Siscoe. Reprinted by permission of the translator.

Kincaid, Jamaica: "Girl" from AT THE BOTTOM OF THE RIVER by Jamaica Kincaid. Copyright © 1983 by Jamaica Kincaid. Reprinted by permission of Farrar, Straus and Giroux, LLC.

Lahiri, Jhumpa: "Interpreter of Maladies" from INTERPRETER OF MALADIES by Jhumpa Lahiri. Copyright © 1999 by Jhumpa Lahiri. Reprinted by permission of Houghton Mifflin Harcourt Publishing Company. All rights reserved.

Lawrence, D. H.: "The Rocking-Horse Winner," copyright 1933 by the Estate of D. H. Lawrence, renewed © 1961 by Angelo Ravagli and C. M. Weekley, Executors of the Estate of Frieda Lawrence, from COMPLETE SHORT STORIES OF D. H. LAWRENCE by D. H. Lawrence. Used by permission of Viking Penguin, a division of Penguin Group (USA) Inc.

Le Guin, Ursula: "The Ones Who Walk Away from Omelas" copyright © 1973 by Ursula K. Le Guin; first appeared in NEW DIMENSIONS 3. Reprinted by permission of the author and the author's agent, Virginia Kidd.

Leavitt, David: "A Place I've Never Been" from COLLECTED STORIES by David Leavitt. Copyright © 2003 by David Leavitt. Reprinted by permission of Bloomsbury USA.

Mahfouz, Naguib: "The Lawsuit" from THE TIME AND THE PLACE & OTHER STORIES by Naguib Mahfouz, copyright © 1991 by the American University in Cairo Press. Used by permission of Doubleday, a division of Random House, Inc.

Mason, Bobbie Ann: "Shiloh" from SHILOH AND OTHER STORIES by Bobbie Ann Mason. Reprinted by permission of International Creative Management, Inc. Copyright © 1982 by Bobbie Ann Mason.

Maugham, W. Somerset: "An Appointment in Samarra" from SHEPPEY by W. Somerset Maugham, copyright 1933 by W. Somerset Maugham. Used by permission of Doubleday, a division of Random House, Inc.

Mowery, Carl: From "Madness in Poe's "The Fall of the House of Usher" in SHORT STORIES FOR STUDENTS. © 1997 Gale, a part of Cengage Learning, Inc. Reproduced by permission. www.cengage.com/permissions.

Munro, Alice: "How I Met My Husband" from SOMETHING I'VE BEEN MEANING TO TELL YOU by Alice Munro. Copyright © 1974 by Alice Munro. Reprinted by permission of William Morris Endeavor Entertainment, LLC on behalf of the Author.

O'Brien, Tim: "The Things They Carried" from THE THINGS THEY CARRIED by Tim O'Brien. Copyright © 1990 by Tim O'Brien. Reprinted by permission of Houghton Mifflin Harcourt Publishing Company. All rights reserved.

O'Connor, Flannery: "A Good Man Is Hard to Find" from A GOOD MAN IS HARD TO FIND AND OTHER STORIES, copyright 1953 by Flannery O'Connor and renewed 1981 by Regina O'Connor, reprinted by permission of Houghton Mifflin Harcourt Publishing Company.

O'Connor, Flannery: "Parker's Back" from THE COMPLETE STORIES by Flannery O'Connor. Copyright © 1971 by the Estate of Mary Flannery O'Connor. Reprinted with permission of Farrar, Straus & Giroux, LLC.

O'Connor, Flannery: "Revelation" from EVERYTHING THAT RISES MUST CONVERGE by Flannery O'Connor. Copyright © 1965 by the Estate of Mary Flannery O'Connor. Copyright renewed 1993 by Regina O'Connor. Reprinted with permission of Farrar, Straus & Giroux, LLC.

O'Connor, Flannery: Excerpt from letter "To 'A' " 20 July 1955 from THE HABIT OF BEING: LETTERS OF FLANNERY O'CONNOR, edited by Sally Fitzgerald. New York, NY: Farrar, Straus, & Giroux, LLC., 1979.

O'Connor, Flannery: Excerpts from "On Her Own Work" and "The Grotesque in Southern Fiction" in MYSTERY AND MANNERS by Flannery O'Connor, edited by Sally and Robert Fitzgerald. Copyright © 1969 by The Estate of Mary Flannery O'Connor. Reprinted by permission of Farrar, Straus & Giroux, LLC.

Oates, Joyce Carol: "Where Are You Going, Where Have You Been?" by Joyce Carol Oates. Copyright © 1970 ONTARIO REVIEW. Reprinted by permission of John Hawkins & Associates, Inc.

Orozco, Daniel: "Orientation" from ORIENTATION: AND OTHER STORIES by Daniel Orozco. Copyright © 2011 by Daniel Orozco. Reprinted by permission of Farrar, Straus and Giroux, LLC.

Packer, ZZ: "Brownies," from DRINKING COFFEE ELSEWHERE by ZZ Packer, copyright © 2003 by ZZ Packer. Used by permission of Riverhead Books, an imprint of Penguin Group (USA) Inc.

Porter, Katherine Anne: "The Jilting of Granny Weatherall" from FLOWERING JUDAS AND OTHER STORIES, copyright 1930 and renewed 1958 by Katherine Anne Porter, reprinted by permission of Houghton Mifflin Harcourt Publishing Company.

Schenck, Mary Jane: "Deconstructing 'A Good Man Is Hard to Find'" in AMBIGUITIES IN LITERATURE AND FILM, edited by Hans Braendlin. Florida State University Press, 1988. Courtesy of the University Press of Florida.

Showalter, Elaine: "Quilt as Metaphor in 'Everyday Use'" from SISTER'S CHOICE: TRADITION AND CHANGE IN AMERICAN WOMEN'S WRITING. Copyright © 1991 by Elaine Showalter. Reprinted by permission of Oxford University Press.

Springsteen, Bruce: From "Spirit In The Night" by Bruce Springsteen. Copyright © 1972 Bruce Springsteen, renewed © 2000 Bruce Springsteen (ASCAP). Reprinted by permission. International copyright secured. All rights reserved.

Steinbeck, John: "The Chrysanthemums," copyright 1937, renewed © 1965 by John Steinbeck, from THE LONG VALLEY by John Steinbeck. Used by permission of Viking Penguin, a division of Penguin Group (USA) Inc.

Tan, Amy: "A Pair of Tickets" from THE JOY LUCK CLUB by Amy Tan, copyright © 1989 by Amy Tan. Used by permission of G.P. Putnam's Sons, a division of Penguin Group (USA) Inc.

Tan, Amy: "Setting the Voice," excerpted from "Mother Tongue" by Amy Tan. Copyright © 1990 by Amy Tan. First appeared in THE THREEPENNY REVIEW. Reprinted by permission of the author and the Sandra Dijkstra Literary Agency.

Tate, J. O.: "A Good Source Is Not So Hard To Find" by J. O. Tate from THE FLANNERY O'CONNOR BULLETIN 9 (1980): pp. 98–103. Reprinted by permission of The Flannery O'Connor Bulletin.

Tuttleton, James: "Poe: The Quest for Supernal Beauty," excerpted from pages 34–52 of A FINE SILVER THREAD: ESSAYS ON AMERICAN WRITING AND CRITICISM. Copyright © 1998 by James W. Tuttleton, by permission of Ivan R. Dee, Publisher.

Tyler, Anne: "Teenage Wasteland" by Anne Tyler. Copyright © 1983, 2011 by Anne Tyler. Reprinted by the permission of HSG Agency as agents for the author.

Updike, John: "A & P" from PIGEON FEATHERS AND OTHER STORIES by John Updike, copyright © 1962 and renewed 1990 by John Updike. Used by permission of Alfred A. Knopf, a division of Random House, Inc.

Updike, John: "Why Write" from PICKED-UP PIECES by John Updike, copyright © 1975 by John Updike. Used by permission of Alfred A. Knopf, a division of Random House, Inc.

Vonnegut Jr., Kurt: "Harrison Bergeron" by Kurt Vonnegut, from WELCOME TO THE MONKEY HOUSE by Kurt Vonnegut, Jr., copyright © 1961 by Kurt Vonnegut, Jr. Used by permission of Dell Publishing, a division of Random House, Inc.

Vonnegut Jr., Kurt: "The Themes of Science Fiction" from MEANJIN QUARTERLY, 30, Autumn 1971. Reprinted with permission.

Walker, Alice: "Everyday Use" from IN LOVE & TROUBLE: STORIES OF BLACK WOMEN, copyright © 1973 by Alice Walker, reprinted by permission of Houghton Mifflin Harcourt Publishing Company.

Walker, Alice: "The Black Woman Writer in America" from INTERVIEWS WITH BLACK WRITERS, edited by John O'Brien, first published by Liveright Publishing Corp., © 1973 by Alice Walker. Reprinted by permission of The Wendy Weil Agency, Inc.

Walker, Alice: "I Know What the Earth Says" excerpt from an interview with William Ferris from SOUTHERN CULTURES, Spring 2004. Reprinted by permission of Southern Cultures. www.southerncultures.org.

Washington, Mary Helen: "A Postscript to My 1979 Essay on Alice Walker," previously appeared in Christian, Barbara T., ed., EVERYDAY USE; ALICE WALKER. Copyright (c) 1994 by Rutgers, The State University. Reprinted by permission of Rutgers University Press.

Welty, Eudora: "A Worn Path" from A CURTAIN OF GREEN AND OTHER STORIES, copyright 1941 and renewed 1969 by Eudora Welty, reprinted by permission of Houghton Mifflin Harcourt Publishing Company.

Wolff, Tobias: "The Rich Brother" from BACK IN THE WORLD. Copyright © 1985 by Tobias Wolff. Reprinted by permission of International Creative Management, Inc.

POETRY

Abeyta, Aaron: "thirteen ways of looking at a tortilla" from COLCHA by Aaron Abeyta. Copyright © 2000. Reprinted by permission of the University Press of Colorado.

Addonizio, Kim: "First Poem for You" from THE PHILOSOPHER'S CLUB by Kim Addonizio (BOA Editions, 1994). Reprinted by permission of the author.

Alarcón, Francisco X.: "Frontera/Border" by Francisco X. Alarcón. Copyright © 2003 by Francisco X. Alarcón. Reprinted by permission of the author.

Alarcón, Francisco X.: "The X in My Name" from NO GOLDEN GATE FOR US by Francisco X. Alarcón. Copyright © 1993 by Francisco X. Alarcón. Reprinted by permission of Pennywhistle Press, Tesuque, NM 87574.

Alexie, Sherman: "The Powwow at the End of the World" reprinted from THE SUMMER OF BLACK WIDOWS © 1996 by Sherman Alexie, by permission of Hanging Loose Press.

Ammons, A. R.: "Coward" reprinted by permission of the author.

Ashbery, John: "At North Farm" from A WAVE by John Ashbery. Copyright © 1981, 1984 by John Ashbery. Reprinted by permission of Georges Borchardt, Inc., on behalf of the author.

Atwood, Margaret: "Siren Song" from SELECTED POEMS 1965-1975 by Margaret Atwood. Copyright © 1976 by Margaret Atwood. Reprinted by permission of Houghton Mifflin Harcourt Publishing Company. All rights reserved.

Atwood, Margaret: "You fit into me" from POWER POLITICS. Copyright © 1971 by Margaret Atwood. (House of Anansi Press Ltd.) Reprinted by permission.

Auden, W. H.: "The Unknown Citizen," "Musée des Beaux Arts," "As I Walked Out One Evening," and "Funeral Blues," copyright 1940 and renewed 1968 by W. H. Auden, from COLLECTED POEMS by W. H. Auden. Used by permission of Random House, Inc.

Baca, Jimmy Santiago: "Spliced Wire" from WHAT'S HAPPENING by Jimmy Santiago Baca. Copyright © 1982 by Jimmy Santiago Baca. Reprinted by permission of Curbstone Press.

Basho, Matsuo: "Heat-lightning streak" and "In the old stone pool" translated by X. J. Kennedy. Copyright X. J. Kennedy. Reprinted by permission.

Belloc, Hilaire: "The Hippopotamus" from CAUTIONARY VERSES by Hilaire Belloc. Reprinted by permission of Peters Fraser & Dunlop.

Berryman, John: From THE FREEDOM OF THE POET by John Berryman. Copyright © 1976 renewed 1993 by Kate Berryman. Reprinted by permission of Farrar, Straus and Giroux, LLC.

Bishop, Elizabeth: "The Filling Station," "The Fish", "One Art", and "Sestina" from THE COMPLETE POEMS 1927-1979 by Elizabeth Bishop. Copyright © 1979, 1983 by Alice Helen Methfessel. Reprinted by permission of Farrar, Straus and Giroux, LLC.

Bloch, Chana: "Tired Sex" from MRS. DUMPTY by Chana Bloch. Winner of the 1998 Felix Pollak Prize in Poetry. © 1998 by the Board of Regents of the University of Wisconsin System. Reprinted by permission of The University of Wisconsin Press.

Bly, Robert: "Driving to Town Late to Mail a Letter" from SILENCE IN THE SNOW FIELDS by Robert Bly (Wesleyan University Press). Copyright © 1959, 1960, 1961, 1962, by Robert Bly. Reprinted by permission of the author.

Borges, Jorge Luis: "On His Blindness" by Jorge Luis Borges, currently collected in EL ORO DE LOS TIGRES and LOS CONJURADOS. Copyright © 1996 by Maria Kodama, used by permission of The Wylie Agency LLC.

Bridges, Lawrence: "Two Poetweets" by Lawrence Bridges, posted Jan. 25, 2011 at http://twitter.com/#!/LawrenceBridges. ©2011 Lawrence Bridges. Reprinted by permission of the author.

Brooks, Gwendolyn: "The Bean Eaters," "the mother," "We Real Cool," and "the rites for Cousin Vit" from BLACKS by Gwendolyn Brooks (Chicago: The David Company). Copyright © 1987 by Gwendolyn Brooks Blakely. Reprinted by permission of the author.

Brooks, Gwendolyn: "Speech to the Young, Speech to the Progress-Toward" from BLACKS by Gwendolyn Brooks. Copyright © 1991 by Gwendolyn Brooks Blakely. Reprinted by consent of Brooks Permissions.

Brooks, Gwendolyn: Excerpt entitled "On 'We Real Cool'" from REPORT FROM PART ONE by Gwendolyn Brooks. Reprinted by permission of the author.

Brutschy, Jennifer: "Born Again" from THE SAN FRANCISCO HAIKU ANTHOLOGY, edited by J. Ball. Reprinted by permission of the author.

Bukowski, Charles: "Dostoevsky" from BONE PALACE BALLET by Charles Bukowski. Copyright © 1997 by Linda Lee Bukowski. Reprinted by permission of HarperCollins Publishers.

Buson, Taniguchi: "On the one-ton temple bell," translated by X. J. Kennedy. Copyright X. J. Kennedy. Reprinted by permission.

Buson, Taniguchi: "The piercing chill I feel," translated by Harold G. Henderson, from AN INTRODUCTION TO HAIKU by Harold G. Henderson, copyright © 1958 by Harold G. Henderson. Used by permission of Doubleday, a division of Random House, Inc.

Buson, Taniguchi: "Moonrise on mudflats" translation by Michael Stillman. Copyright 2009 © by Michael Stillman. Reprinted with permission of the author.

Campo, Rafael: "For J.W." is reprinted with permission from the publisher of THE OTHER MAN WAS ME by Rafael Campo (©1993 Arte Público Press - University of Houston).

Cervantes, Lorna Dee: "Cannery Town in August" from EMPLUMADA by Lorna Dee Cervantes, © 1982. Reprinted by permission of the University of Pittsburgh Press.

Charles, Dorthi: "Concrete Cat" reprinted by permission of the author.

Ciardi, John: "Most Like an Arch This Marriage, copyright © 1958 by John Ciardi. Reprinted from COLLECTED POEMS by John Ciardi. Reprinted by permission of University of Arkansas Press.

Clark, Cheryl: "Convalescence," translated by Cheryl Clark Vermeulen from "Convalecencia" by Tedi López Mills, from CONNECTING LINES: NEW POETRY FROM MEXICO (Sarabande Books, 2006). Reprinted by permission of Cheryl Clark Vermeulen.

Cofer, Judith Ortiz: "Quinceañera" from TERMS OF SURVIVAL by Judith Ortiz Cofer is reprinted with permission from the publisher. (© 1987 Arte Público Press - University of Houston)

Cole, William: "On my boat on Lake Cayuga" by William Cole. Reprinted by permission.

Collins, Billy: "Care and Feeding" first appeared in FIVE POINTS, March 2003. Reprinted by permission of the author.

Collins, Billy: "Embrace" from THE APPLE THAT ASTONISHED PARIS. Copyright © 1988 by Billy Collins. Reprinted by permission of the University of Arkansas Press.

Cope, Wendy: "Lonely Hearts" from MAKING COCOA FOR KINGSLEY AMIS by Wendy Cope. Copyright © 1986 by Wendy Cope. Reprinted by permission of United Agents on behalf of Wendy Cope.

Cope, Wendy: "Variation on Belloc's 'Fatigue'" from SERIOUS CONCERNS by Wendy Cope. Copyright © 1992 by Wendy Cope. Reprinted by permission of United Agents on behalf of Wendy Cope.

Creeley, Robert: "Oh No" from THE COLLECTED POEMS OF ROBERT CREELEY,

1945-1975 by Robert Creeley. © 1982 The Regents of the University of California. Published by the University of California Press. Reprinted by permission.

Crowe, Anna: "Swallows" (English translation of "Golondrinas" by Pedro Serrano), published in MEXICAN POETRY TODAY: 20/20 VOICES. Translation © 2010 Anna Crowe. Reprinted by permission of Anna Crowe.

Cullen, Countee: "For a Lady I Know" reprinted from COLOR by Countee Cullen. Copyright 1925 by Harper & Bros, NY. Copyright renewed 1952 by Ida M. Cullen. Copyrights held by Amistad Research Center, Tulane University. Adminstered by Thompson and Thompson, Brooklyn, NY. Reprinted by permission of Thompson and Thompson.

Cummings, E. E.: "somewhere i have never travelled, gladly beyond." Copyright 1931 © 1959, 1991 by the Trustees for the E.E. Cummings Trust. Copyright © 1979 by George James Firmage, "anyone lived in a pretty how town." Copyright 1940, © 1968, 1991 by the Trustees for the E.E. Cummings Trust, "Buffalo Bill 's." Copyright 1923, 1951, © 1991 by the Trustees for the E.E. Cummings Trust. Copyright © 1976 by George James Firmage, "in Just-." Copyright 1923, 1951, © 1991 by the Trustees for the E.E. Cummings Trust. Copyright © 1976 by George James Firmage, "next to of course god america i." Copyright 1926, 1954, © 1991 by the Trustees for the E.E. Cummings Trust. Copyright © 1985 by George James Firmage, from COMPLETE POEMS: 1904-1962 by E.E. Cummings, edited by George J. Firmage. Used by permission of Liveright Publishing Corporation.

Cunningham, J.V.: "Friend, on this scaffold Thomas More lies dead" from POEMS OF J.V. CUNNINGHAM (Swallow Press/Ohio University Press, 1997). Reprinted by permission of the publisher.

de los Santos, Marisa: "Perfect Dress" from FROM THE BONES OUT by Marisa de los Santos. Reprinted by permission of the author.

Dickinson, Emily: Reprinted by permission of the publishers and the Trustees of Amherst College from THE POEMS OF EMILY DICKINSON, "Editing the Poems" from Introduction to THE POEMS OF EMILY DICKINSON, Thomas H. Johnson, ed., Cambridge, Mass.: The Belknap Press of Harvard University Press, Copyright © 1951, 1955, 1979, 1983 by the President and Fellows of Harvard College.

Dickinson, Emily: Reprinted by permission of the publishers from THE LETTERS OF EMILY DICKINSON, Thomas H. Johnson, ed., L261, Cambridge, Mass.: The Belknap Press of Harvard University Press, Copyright © 1958, 1986, The President and Fellows of Harvard College; 1914, 1924, 1932, 1942 by Martha Dickinson Bianchi; 1952 by Alfred Leete Hampson; 1960 by Mary L. Hampson.

Donoghue, Denis: From WORDS ALONE: THE POET T.S. ELIOT by Denis Donoghue. Copyright © 2000 by Denis Donoghue. Reprinted by permission of Georges Borchardt, Inc. on behalf of the author.

Dove, Rita and Marilyn Nelson: Excerpts from "A Black Rainbow: Modern Afro-American Poetry" from POETRY AFTER MODERNISM, edited by Robert McDowell. Reprinted by permission of Robert McDowell.

Dove, Rita: "Daystar" reprinted from THOMAS AND BEULAH by Rita Dove, by permission of Carnegie-Mellon University Press. Copyright © 1986 by Rita Dove.

Dylan, Bob: "The Times They Are a-Changin'" copyright © 1963 by Warner Bros. Inc. Copyright renewed 1991 by Special Rider Music. All rights reserved. International copyright secured. Reprinted by permission.

Dylan, Bob: Reprinted with the permission of Simon & Schuster Inc., from pp. 81–83, CHRONICLES, Volume I by Bob Dylan. Copyright © 2004 by Bob Dylan. All rights reserved.

Eberhart, Richard: "The Fury of Aerial Bombardment" from COLLECTED POEMS 1930–1976 by Richard Eberhart. Copyright © 1976 by Richard Eberhart. Used by permission of Oxford University Press, Inc.

Eliot, T. S.: "Virginia" and "Journey of the Magi" from COLLECTED POEMS 1909-1962 by T. S. Eliot, copyright 1936 by Harcourt, Inc., and renewed 1964 by T.S. Eliot, reprinted by permission of the publisher.

Eliot, T. S.: Excerpt from "The Music of Poetry" from ON POETRY AND POETS by T. S. Eliot. Copyright © 1957 by T. S. Eliot. Copyright renewed © 1985 by Valerie Eliot. Reprinted by permission of Farrar, Straus & Giroux, LLC.

Eliot, T. S.: Excerpted from THE USE OF POETRY AND THE USE OF CRITICISM by T. S. Eliot.

Ellman, Maud: Reprinted by permission of the publisher from THE POETICS OF IMPERSONALITY: T. S. ELIOT AND EZRA POUND by Maud Ellman, pp. 79–80, Cambridge, Mass.: Harvard University Press, Copyright © 1987 by Maud Ellman.

Espaillat, Rhina: "Bilingual / *Bilingüe*" and an excerpt from "Afterword" from WHERE HORIZONS GO by Rhina P. Espaillat, published by Truman State University Press. Copyright © 1998. Re-printed by permission of the author.

Essbaum, Jill Alexander: "The Heart" from HARLOT by Jill Alexander Essbaum, published by No Tell Books, 2007. Reprinted by permission of the author.

Farr, Judith: Reprinted by permission of the publisher from THE PASSION OF EMILY DICKINSON by Judith Farr, pp. 241–244, Cambridge, Mass.: Harvard University Press, Copyright © 1992 by the President and Fellows of Harvard College.

Fehler, Gene: "If Richard Lovelace Became a Free Agent" by Gene Fehler, reprinted by permission of the author.

Foley, Adelle: "Learning to Shave (Father Teaching Son)" copyright © 2001 by Adelle Foley. Reprinted by permission.

Frost, Robert: "Fire and Ice," "Acquainted with the Night," "Stopping by Woods on a Snowy Evening," "The Silken Tent," "Desert Places," "Design," and "The Secret Sits" from THE POETRY OF ROBERT FROST edited by Edward Connery Lathem. Copyright © 1923, 1928, 1969 by Henry Holt and Company, copyright © 1936, 1942, 1951, 1956 by Robert Frost, copyright © 1964, 1970 by Lesley Frost Ballantine. Reprinted by arrangement with Henry Holt and Company, LLC.

Frost, Robert: "The Importance of Poetic Metaphor" from "Education by Poetry." Amherst, MA, 1930.

Fulton, Alice: "What I Like" from DANCE SCRIPT WITH ELECTRIC BALLERINA: POEMS (University of Pennsylvania Press), copyright © 1983, 1982 by Alice Fulton. Reprinted by permission of the author.

Gay, Garry: "Hole in the ozone" is reprinted with permission from the author, Garry Gay.

Gilbert, Sandra and Susan Gubar: "Editors' Introduction to Emily Dickinson" from THE NORTON ANTHOLOGY OF LITERATURE BY WOMEN: THE TRADITION IN ENGLISH by Sandra M. Gilbert and Susan Gubar. Copyright © 1985 by Sandra M. Gilbert and Susan Gubar. Used by permission of W.W. Norton & Company, Inc.

Ginsberg, Allen: "A Supermarket in California" from COLLECTED POEMS 1947-1980 by Allen Ginsberg. Copyright © 1955 by Allen Ginsberg. Reprinted by permission of HarperCollins Publishers.

Gioia, Dana: "Money" from THE GODS OF WINTER by Dana Gioia. Copyright © 1991 by Dana Gioia. Reprinted with the permission of Graywolf Press, Saint Paul, Minnesota, www.graywolfpress.org.

Graves, Robert: "Counting the Beats" and "Down, Wanton, Down!" from COMPLETE POEMS IN ONE VOLUME by Robert Graves, edited by Beryl Graves and Dunstan Ward. (Carcanet Press, 2000). Reprinted by permission of Carcanet Press Limited.

Guiterman, Arthur: "On the Vanity of Earthly Greatness" from GAILY THE TROUBADOUR by Arthur Guiterman. Reprinted by permission of Richard Sclove.

Gwynn, R. S.: "Shakespearean Sonnet" copyright © 2002 by R. S. Gwynn. Reprinted by permission of the author.

H.D. (Doolittle, Hilda): "Helen" by H.D. (Hilda Doolittle), from COLLECTED POEMS, 1912-1944, copyright © 1982 by The Estate of Hilda Doolittle. Reprinted by permission of New Directions Publishing Corp.

Haaland, Tami: "Lipstick" from BREATH IN EVERY ROOM by Tami Haaland. © 2001 by Tami Haaland. Reprinted by permission of the author.

Harjo, Joy: "Mourning Song" from THE WOMAN WHO FELL FROM THE SKY by Joy Harjo. Copyright © 1994 by Joy Harjo. Used by permission of W.W. Norton & Company, Inc.

Harter, Penny: "broken bowl" from IN THE BROKEN CURVE by Penny Harter. Copyright © 1984 by Penny Harter. Reprinted by permission of Burnt Lake Press.

Hayden, Robert: "Those Winter Sundays," copyright © 1966 by Robert Hayden, "Frederick Douglass," copyright © 1966 by Robert Hayden, from COLLECTED POEMS OF ROBERT HAYDEN by Robert Hayden, edited by Frederick Glaysher. Used by permission of Liveright Publishing Corporation.

Headings, Philip R.: From T. S. ELIOT. © 1982 Gale, a part of Cengage Learning, Inc. Reproduced by permission. www.cengage.com/permissions.

Heaney, Seamus: "Digging" from OPENED GROUND: SELECTED POEMS 1966-1996 by Seamus Heaney. Copyright © 1998 by Seamus Heaney. Reprinted by permission of Farrar, Straus and Giroux, LLC.

Hecht, Anthony: "The Vow" from THE HARD HOURS by Anthony Hecht. Copyright © 1967 by Anthony Hecht. Reprinted by permission of the author.

Higginson, Thomas Wentworth: Excerpt of letter from Thomas Wentworth Higginson to Mary Channing Higginson, 16 August 1870. Courtesy of the Trustees of the Boston Public Library/Rare Books.

Hoagland, Tony: "Beauty" from DONKEY GOSPEL by Tony Hoagland. Copyright © 1998 by Tony Hoagland. Reprinted with the permission of Graywolf Press, Saint Paul, Minnesota, www.graywolfpress.org.

Hollander, John: "Swan and Shadow" from TYPES OF SHAPE by John Hollander. Copyright © 1969 by John Hollander. Reprinted by permission of the author.

Hudgins, Andrew: "Elegy for My Father, Who Is Not Dead" from THE NEVER-ENDING: NEW POEMS by Andrew Hudgins. Copyright © 1991 by Andrew Hudgins. Reprinted by permission of Houghton Mifflin Company. All rights reserved.

Hughes, Langston: "Dream Boogie," "Harlem (2) ["What happens to a dream deferred..."]," "I, Too," "Theme for English B," "Two Somewhat Different Epigrams," "Ballad of the Landlord," "Dream Variation," "Homecoming," "Nightmare Boogie," "Song for a Dark Girl," "The Weary Blues," "Prayer [2]" from THE COLLECTED POEMS OF LANGSTON HUGHES by Langston Hughes, edited by Arnold Rampersad with David Roessel, Associate Editor, copyright © 1994 by the Estate of Langston Hughes. Used by permission of Alfred A. Knopf, a division of Random House, Inc.

Hughes, Langston: "The Negro Artist and the Racial Mountain" by Langston Hughes. First published in THE NATION, June 23, 1926. Copyright 1926 by Langston Hughes. Reprinted by permission of Harold Ober Associates Incorporated.

Hughes, Langston: Excerpt from "When the Negro Was in Vogue" from THE BIG SEA by Langston Hughes. Copyright © 1940 by Langston Hughes. Copyright renewed 1968 by Arna Bontemps and George Houston Bass. Reprinted by permission of Hill and Wang, a division of Farrar, Straus & Giroux, LLC.

Hughes, Ted: "Hawk Roosting" from SELECTED POEMS 1957-1994 by Ted Hughes. Copyright © 2002 by The Estate of Ted Hughes. Reprinted by permission of Farrar, Straus, & Giroux, LLC.

Issa, Kobayashi: "Cricket" translated by Robert Bly, reprinted from TEN POEMS BY ISSA, ENGLISH VERSIONS by Robert Bly, Floating Island, 1992. Copyright © 1972, 1992 by Robert Bly. Reprinted with permission.

Issa, Kobayashi: "only one guy" translated by Cid Corman from ONE MAN'S MOON: FIFTY HAIKU (Gnomon Press, 1984). Reprinted by permission of the publisher and the author.

Jarman, Mark: "Unholy Sonnet: After the Praying" reprinted by permission of the author.

Jarrell, Randall: "The Death of the Ball Turret Gunner"" from THE COMPLETE POEMS by Randall Jarrell. Copyright © 1969, renewed 1997 by Mary von S. Jarrell. Reprinted by permission of Farrar, Straus and Giroux, LLC.

Jeffers, Robinson: "Rock and Hawk," copyright 1934 and renewed 1962 by Donnan Jeffers and Garth Jeffers, from SELECTED POETRY OF ROBINSON JEFFERS by Robinson Jeffers. Used by permission of Random House, Inc.

Jeffers, Robinson: "Hands" from THE COLLECTED POETRY OF ROBINSON JEFFERS, edited by Tim Hunt, Volume 2, 1928 - 1938. Copyright © 1938 renewed 1966 by Donnan Jeffers and Garth Jeffers. All rights reserved. Used with the permission of Stanford University Press, www.sup.org.

Jemie, Onwuchekwa: "A Dream Deferred" from LANGSTON HUGHES: AN INTRODUCTION TO POETRY by Onwuchekwa Jemie. Copyright © 1976 by Onwuchekwa Jemie. Published by Columbia University Press. Reprinted with permission.

Jin, Ha: "Missed Time" by Ha Jin originally appeared in POETRY, July 2000. Copyright © 2000 by The Modern POETRY Association. Reprinted by permission of the editor of POETRY and Ha Jin.

Justice, Donald: "Men at Forty" and "On the Death of Friends in Childhood" from COLLECTED POEMS by Donald Justice, copyright © 2004 by Donald Justice. Used by permission of Alfred A. Knopf, a division of Random House, Inc.

Kaufman, Bob: "No More Jazz at Alcatraz" from CRANIAL GUITAR by Bob Kaufman. Copyright © 1996 Eileen Kaufman. Reprinted with the permission of Coffee House Press, Minneapolis, MN.

Kees, Weldon: "For My Daughter," reprinted from THE COLLECTED POEMS OF WELDON KEES edited by Donald Justice by permission of the University of Nebraska Press. Copyright 1962, 1975 by the University of Nebraska Press. Copyright renewed 2003 by the University of Nebraska Press.

Kenyon, Jane: "The Suitor" from FROM ROOM TO ROOM. © 1978 by Jane Kenyon. Reprinted courtesy of Alice James Books, 33 Richdale Avenue, Cambridge, MA 02138.

Khayyam, Omar: "Rubai" translated by Dick Davis. Reprinted by permission.

Kim, Suji Kwock: "Occupation" from NOTES FROM A DIVIDED COUNTRY: POEMS by Suji Kwock Kim. Copyright © 2003 by Suji Kwock Kim. Reprinted by permission of Louisiana State University Press.

Kingsmill, Hugh: "What, still alive at twenty-two?" from THE BEST OF HUGH KINGSMILL. Reprinted by permission of Victor Gollancz Ltd.

Kizer, Carolyn: "Bitch" from MERMAIDS IN THE BASEMENT by Carolyn Kizer. Copyright © 1984 by Carolyn Kizer. Reprinted with the permission of Copper Canyon Press, Port Townsend, WA.

Knight, Etheridge: "Making jazz swing in" from THE ESSENTIAL ETHERIDGE KNIGHT, by Etheridge Knight, © 1986. Reprinted by permission of the University of Pittsburgh Press.

Komunyakaa, Yusef: "Facing It" from PLEASURE DOME: NEW AND COLLECTED POEMS by Yusef Komunyakaa (Wesleyan University Press, 2001). © 2001 by Yussef Komunyakaa and reprinted by permission of Wesleyan University Press.

Kooser, Ted: "Carrie" and "Abandoned Farmhouse" from SURE SIGNS: NEW AND SELECTED POEMS by Ted Kooser, © 1980. Reprinted by permission of the University of Pittsburgh Press.

Kostelanetz, Richard: "Simultaneous Translations: Three poems by Ramón Gómez de la Serna" translated by Richard Kostelanetz with Marin Zotta. First appeared in TWO LINES World Writing in Translation series, volume 7, 2000. Reprinted by permission of Richard Kostelanetz.

Larkin, Philip: "Aubade," "Poetry of Departures," and "Home is so Sad" from COLLECTED POEMS by Philip Larkin. Copyright © 1988, 2003 by the Estate of Philip Larkin. Reprinted by permission of Farrar, Straus & Giroux, LLC.

Lehman, David: "Rejection Slip" from OPERATION MEMORY by David Lehman. Copyright © 1990, all rights reserved by David Lehman.

Reprinted by permission of Writers' Representatives LLC, New York, NY, 10011.

Levertov, Denise: "Ancient Stairway" by Denise Levertov, from THIS GREAT UNKNOWING: LAST POEMS, copyright © 1999 by The Denise Levertov Literary Trust, Paul A. Lacey and Valerie Trueblood Rapport, Co-Trustees. Reprinted by permission of New Directions Publishing Corp.

Levertov, Denise: "O Taste and See" from POEMS 1960-1967, copyright © 1964 by Denise Levertov. Reprinted by permission of New Directions Publishing Corp.

Levin, Phyllis: "Brief Bio" from THE AFTERIMAGE. Reprinted by permission of Copper Beach Press.

Li Po: "Drinking Alone by Moonlight" by Li Po, translated by Arthur Waley, from THE ART OF CHINESE POETRY by James J. Y. Liu, (University of Chicago Press, 1962). Copyright © 1962 by James J. Y. Liu. Reprinted by permission of the publisher.

Lim, Shirley Geok-lin: "Learning to love America" and "Riding into California" from WHAT THE FORTUNE TELLER DIDN'T SAY by Shirley Geok-lin Lim. Copyright © 1998 by Shirley Geok-lin Lim. Reprinted with the permission of West End Press, Albuquerque, New Mexico.

Lindner, April: "Low Tide" is reprinted by permission of the author.

López Mills, Tedi: "Convalecencia" by Tedi López Mills, from CONNECTING LINES: NEW POETRY FROM MEXICO. Copyright © 2006 by Sarabande Books. Reprinted by permission of the author.

Lowell, Robert: "Skunk Hour" from LIFE STUDIES by Robert Lowell. Copyright © 1959, by Robert Lowell. Copyright renewed © 1987 by Harriet Lowell, Sheridan Lowell and Caroline Lowell. Reprinted by permission of Farrar, Straus & Giroux, LLC.

MacLeish, Archibald: "Ars Poetica" from COLLECTED POEMS, 1917-1982 by Archibald MacLeish. Copyright © 1985 by The Estate of Archibald MacLeish. Reprinted by permission of Houghton Mifflin Harcourt Publishing Company. All rights reserved.

Majmudar, Amit: "Rites to Allay the Dead" from 0°,0°: POEMS by Amit Majmudar. Copyright 2009 by Amit Majmudar. Published by TriQuarterly Books/Northwestern University Press. Reprinted by permission of the publisher.

Mann, Aimee: "Deathly" by Aimee Mann © 2000 Aimee Mann (ASCAP). Used by permission of Michael Hausman Artist Management. All Rights Reserved.

Martin, Charles: "Taken Up" from ROOM FOR ERROR (University of Georgia Press, 1978). Reprinted by permission of the author.

Mason, David: "Song of the Powers" from THE COUNTRY I REMEMBER by David Mason. Reprinted by permission of the author.

Matsushita, Suiko: "Rain shower from mountain" and "Cosmos in bloom," translated by Violet Kazue de Cristoforo, from MAY SKY: THERE IS ALWAYS TOMORROW. Reprinted by permission of Kimiko de Cristoforo.

McKuen, Rod: "Thoughts on Capital Punishment" from STANYAN STREET AND OTHER SORROWS by Rod McKuen, copyright 1954, 1960, 1961, 1962, 1963, 1964, 1965, 1966 by Rod McKuen. Used by permission of Random House, Inc.

Menashe, Samuel: "Bread" from COLLECTED POEMS by Samuel Menashe. Copyright © 1986 by Samuel Menashe. Reprinted by permission of the author.

Merwin, W. S.: "For the Anniversary of My Death" from MIGRATION by W. S. Merwin. Copyright © 1967, 2005 by W. S. Merwin, reprinted with permission of The Wylie Agency LLC.

Mezey, Robert: "On his blindness" by Jorge Luis Borges, in LOS CONJURADOS (1985), English translation by Robert Mezey. Published in Poetry Magazine, 1994. Reprinted by permission of Robert Mezey.

Millay, Edna St. Vincent: "Counting-out Rhyme" from COLLECTED POEMS, HarperCollins. Copyright © 1928, 1955 by Edna St. Vincent Millay and Norma Millay Ellis. All rights reserved. Reprinted by permission of Elizabeth Barnett, literary executor.

Momaday, N. Scott: "Simile" from ANGLE OF GEESE AND OTHER POEMS by Scott Momaday. Copyright © 1972 by Scott Momaday. Reprinted by permission of the author.

Moore, Marianne: "Silence," reprinted with the permission of Scribner, a Division of Simon & Schuster Inc., from THE COLLECTED POEMS OF MARIANNE MOORE by Marianne Moore. Copyright © 1935 by Marianne Moore, renewed © 1963 by Marianne Moore & T.S. Eliot. All rights reserved.

Moss, Howard: "Shall I Compare Thee to a Summer's Day?" from A SWIM OFF THE ROCKS. Copyright © 1976 by Howard Moss. Reprinted by permission of Richard Evans.

Mullen, Harryette: "Dim Lady" from SLEEPING WITH THE DICTIONARY by Harryette Mullen. Copyright © 2002 The Regents of the University of California. Reprinted by permission.

Nelson, Marilyn: "A Strange Beautiful Woman" from THE FIELDS OF PRAISE by Marilyn Nelson. Copyright © 1997 by Marilyn Nelson. Reprinted by permission of Louisiana State University Press.

Nemerov, Howard: "The War in the Air" from TRYING CONCLUSIONS by Howard Nemerov. Reprinted by permission of Margaret Nemerov.

Neruda, Pablo: "Muchos Somos" from EXTRAVAGARIA by Pablo Neruda. Translated by Alastair Reid. Translation copyright © 1974 by Alastair Reid. Originally published as ESTRAVAGARIO, copyright © 1958 by Editorial Losada, S.A. Buenos Aires. Reprinted by permission of Farrar, Straus & Giroux, LLC.

Niedecker, Lorine: "Popcorn-can Cover" and "Sorrow Moves in Wide Waves" from FROM THIS CONDENSERY: THE COMPLETE WRITING OF LORINE NIEDECKER, edited by Robert J. Bertolf. Copyright © Cid Corman, Literary Executor of the Lorine Niedecker Estate. Reprinted by permission.

Nims, John Frederick: "Contemplation" reprinted by permission.

Olds, Sharon: "Rite of Passage" and "The One Girl at the Boys' Party" from THE DEAD AND THE LIVING by Sharon Olds, copyright © 1987 by Sharon Olds. Used by permission of Alfred A. Knopf, a division of Random House, Inc.

Oliver, Mary: "Wild Geese" from DREAM WORK by Mary Oliver. Copyright © 1986 by Mary Oliver. Used by permission of Grove/Atlantic, Inc.

Orr, Gregory: "Two Lines from the Brothers Grimm" from NEW & SELECTED POEMS by Gregory Orr. Reprinted by permission of the author.

Ozawa, Neiji: "The war—this year," translated by Violet Kazue de Cristoforo, from MAY SKY: THERE IS ALWAYS TOMORROW. Reprinted by permission of Kimiko de Cristoforo.

Pacheco, José Emilio: "Alta Traición" from DON'T ASK ME HOW THE TIME GOES BY: POEMS 1964-1968 by José Emilio Pacheco, translated by Alastair Reid. Copyright © 1978 Columbia University Press. Reprinted with permission of the publisher.

Parker, Dorothy: "Résumé," copyright 1926, 1928, renewed 1954, © 1956 by Dorothy Parker, "Tombstones in the Starlight," from THE PORTABLE DOROTHY PARKER by Dorothy Parker, edited by Marion Meade, copyright 1928, renewed © 1956 by Dorothy Parker; copyright © 1973, 2006 by The National Assoc. for the Advancement of Colored People. Used by permission of Viking Penguin, a division of Penguin Group (USA) Inc.

Paterson, Andrea: "Because I Could Not Dump" by Andrea Paterson, originally published in THE BRAND-X ANTHOLOGY OF POETRY (1981). Reprinted by permission of Andrea Paterson.

Paz, Octavio: "With Eyes Closed" by Octavio Paz, translated by Eliot Weinberger, from THE COLLECTED POEMS 1957-1987, copyright © 1986 by Octavio Paz and Eliot Weinberger. Reprinted by permission of New Directions Publishing Corp.

Pinckney, Darryl: Excerpted from "Suitcase in Harlem" by Darryl Pinckney, from THE NEW YORK REVIEW OF BOOKS, Vol. 36, Issue 2, Feb. 16, 1989. Reprinted with permission from The New York Review of Books. Copyright © 1989 NYREV, Inc.

Pinsky, Robert: "Low Pay Piecework" by Robert Pinsky, posted on May 30, 2011 at http://twitter.com/#!/RobertPinsky. Copyright © 2011 Robert Pinsky. Reprinted by permission of the author.

Plath, Sylvia: "Daddy" and "Lady Lazarus" from ARIEL: POEMS by Sylvia Plath. Copyright © 1961, 1962, 1963, 1964, 1965, 1966 by Ted Hughes. Reprinted by permission of HarperCollins Publishers.

Plath, Sylvia: "Metaphors" from CROSSING THE WATER by Sylvia Plath. Copyright © 1960 by Ted Hughes. Reprinted by permission of HarperCollins Publishers.

Pollitt, Katha: "The Mind-Body Problem," from THE MIND-BODY PROBLEM: POEMS by Katha Pollitt, copyright © 2009 by Katha Pollitt. Used by permission of Random House, Inc.

Prufer, Kevin: "Pause, Pause" from THE FINGER BONE by Kevin Prufer. Copyright © 2002 by Kevin Prufer. Reprinted with the permission of Carnegie Mellon University Press, www.cmu.edu/universitypress.

Raffel, Burton: Excerpt from T. S. ELIOT by Burton Raffel. New York: Frederick Ungar, 1982.

Raine, Craig: "A Martian Sends a Postcard Home" from A MARTIAN SENDS A POSTCARD HOME. Reprinted by permission of David Godwin Associates.

Rampersad, Arnold: From AFRICAN AMERICAN WRITERS, 2e, edited by Valerie Smith, Lea Baechler and A. Walton Litz. © Gale, a part of Cengage Learning, Inc. Reproduced by permission. www.cengage.com/permissions.

Randall, Dudley: "Ballad of Birmingham" from CITIES BURNING. Reprinted by permission of the author.

Randall, Dudley: "A Different Image" from CITIES BURNING (Broadside Press). Copyright © 1966 by Dudley Randall. Reprinted by permission of Broadside Press.

Ransom, John Crowe: "Piazza Piece," from SELECTED POEMS, THIRD EDITION, REVISED AND ENLARGED by John Crowe Ransom, copyright 1924, 1927 by Alfred A. Knopf, Inc. and renewed 1952, 1955 by John Crowe Ransom. Used by permission of the publisher.

Reed, Henry: "Naming of Parts" from A MAP OF VERONA by Henry Reed. © 1946 The executor of the Estate of Henry Reed. Reprinted by permission of John Tydeman.

Reid, Alastair: "High Treason" from DON'T ASK ME HOW THE TIME GOES BY: POEMS 1964-1968 by José Emilio Pacheco, translated by Alastair Reid. Copyright © 1978 Columbia University Press. Reprinted with permission of the publisher.

Reid, Alastair: "Translating Neruda" from Neruda and Borges by Alastair Reid. THE NEW YORKER, 1996.

Rich, Adrienne: "Women," copyright © 1993 by Adrienne Rich. Copyright © 1969 by W.W. Norton & Company, Inc., from COLLECTED EARLY POEMS: 1950-1970 by Adrienne Rich. Used by permission of the author and W.W. Norton & Company, Inc.

Rich, Adrienne: "Aunt Jennifer's Tigers," copyright © 2002, 1951 by Adrienne Rich, "Living in Sin," copyright © 2002, 1955 by Adrienne Rich, from THE FACT OF A DOORFRAME: SELECTED POEMS 1950-2001 by Adrienne Rich. Used by permission of the author and W. W. Norton & Company, Inc.

Rich, Adrienne: Excerpt from "When We Dead Awaken": Writing as Re-Vision," from ARTS OF THE POSSIBLE: ESSAY AND CONVERSATIONS by Adrienne Rich. Copyright © 2001 by Adrienne Rich. Used by permission of the author and W.W. Norton & Company, Inc.

Ricks, Christopher: From T. S. ELIOT AND PREJUDICE by Christopher Ricks, © by Christopher Ricks. Published by the University of California Press. Reprinted by permission of the publisher.

Roethke, Theodore: "My Papa's Waltz," copyright 1942 by Hearst Magazines, Inc., "Root Cellar," copyright 1943 by Modern Poetry Association, Inc., "Elegy for Jane," copyright 1950 by Theodore Roethke, from COLLECTED POEMS OF THEODORE ROETHKE by Theodore Roethke. Used by permission of Doubleday, a division of Random House, Inc.

Rosenthal, M. L.: From "Adolescents Singing, Each to Each—When We and Eliot Were Young," OUR LIFE IN POETRY: SELECTED ESSAYS AND REVIEWS by M.L. Rosenthal. New York, NY: Persea Books, 1991.

Ryan, Kay: "Blandeur" and "Mockingbird" from SAY UNCLE by Kay Ryan, copyright © 1991 by Kay Ryan. Used by permission of Grove/Atlantic, Inc.

Ryan, Kay: "Talking with Kay Ryan." Copyright 2009 Kay Ryan. Used by permission of the author.

Ryan, Kay: "Turtle" from FLAMINGO WATCHING. Reprinted by permission of Copper Beach Press.

Sáenz, Benjamin Alire: "To the Desert" from DARK AND PERFECT ANGELS: A COLLECTION OF POEMS by Benjamin Alire Sáenz. Copyright © 1995 by Benjamin Alire Sáenz. Reprinted by permission of the author.

Satyamurti, Carole: "I Shall Paint My Nails Red" © 1990 by Carole Satyamurti. Reprinted by permission of Bloodaxe Books Ltd.

Serrano, Pedro: "Golondrinas" by Pedro Serrano, originally published in MEXICAN POETRY TODAY: 20/20 VOICES (English and Spanish Edition), published by Shearsman Books. Copyright © 2010 Pedro Serrano. Reprinted by permission of the author.

Sexton, Anne: "Cinderella" from TRANSFORMATIONS by Anne Sexton. Copyright © 1971 by Anne Sexton, renewed 1999 by Linda G. Sexton. Reprinted by permission of Houghton Mifflin Harcourt Publishing Company. All rights reserved.

Sexton, Anne: "Her Kind" from TO BEDLAM AND PART WAY BACK by Anne Sexton. Copyright © 1960 by Anne Sexton, renewed 1988 by Linda G. Sexton. Reprinted by permission of Houghton Mifflin Harcourt Publishing Company. All rights reserved.

Sexton, Anne: "Letter dated October 14, 1970" from ANNE SEXTON: A SELF-PORTRAIT IN LETTERS edited by Linda Gray Sexton and Lois Ames. Copyright © 1977 by Linda Gray Sexton and Loring Conant, Jr., executors of the will of Anne Sexton. Reprinted by permission of Houghton Mifflin Harcourt Publishing Company. All rights reserved.

Sheehan, Julie: "Hate Poem" from ORIENT POINT by Julie Sheehan. Copyright © 2006 by Julie Sheehan. Used by permission of W.W. Norton & Company, Inc.

Simic, Charles: "The Butcher Shop" from DISMANTLING THE SILENCE by Charles Simic. Copyright © 1971 by Charles Simic. Reprinted by permission of the publisher, George Braziller, Inc.

Simic, Charles: "Fork" from SOMEWHERE AMONG US A STONE IS TAKING NOTES, first published in Kayak 1969, along with "My Shoes" are from CHARLES SIMIC: SELECTED EARLY POEMS, copyright © 1999 by Charles Simic (George Braziller, Inc.). Reprinted by permission.

Simic, Charles: "The Magic Study of Happiness" by Charles Simic, reprinted by permission of the author.

Simon, Paul: "Richard Cory" by Paul Simon. Copyright © 1966 Paul Simon. Used by permission of the publisher: Paul Simon Music.

Smith, Stevie: "Not Waving But Drowning" by Stevie Smith, from COLLECTED POEMS OF STEVIE SMITH, copyright © 1957 by Stevie Smith. Reprinted by permission of New Directions Publishing Corp.

Smith, William Jay: "American Primitive" from THE WORLD BELOW THE WINDOW: POEMS 1937-1997 by William Jay Smith. © 1998 by William Jay Smith. Reprinted by permission of the author.

Snyder, Gary: "Hitch Haiku" by Gary Snyder, from THE BACK COUNTRY, copyright ©

1968 by Gary Snyder. Reprinted by permission of New Directions Publishing Corp.

Snyder, Gary: "Mid-August at Sourdough Mountain Lookout" from RIPRAP by Gary Snyder. Copyright © 1959 by Gary Snyder. Reprinted by permission of the author.

Song, Cathy: "Stamp Collecting" from FRAMELESS WINDOWS, SQUARES OF LIGHT: POEMS by Cathy Song. Copyright © 1988 by Cathy Song. Used by permission of W.W. Norton & Company, Inc.

Sor Juana: "Presente En qu el Cario Hace Regalo la Llaneza" ("A Simple Gift Made Rich by Affection") translated by Diane Thiel. Reprinted by permission.

St. John, David: "Hush" from STUDY FOR THE WORLD'S BODY: NEW AND SELECTED POEMS by David St. John. (New York: HarperCollins, 1994). Copyright © 1994, 2005 by David St. John. Reprinted by permission of the author.

Stafford, William: "Ask Me," "Traveling through the Dark," and "The Farm on the Great Plains" from THE WAY IT IS: NEW & SELECTED POEMS by William Stafford. Copyright © 1959, 1962, 1977, 1998 by the Estate of William Stafford. Reprinted with the permission of Graywolf Press, Saint Paul, Minnesota, www.graywolfpress.org.

Stafford, William: "At the Un-National Monument Along the Canadian Border" by William Stafford, reprinted by permission of the author.

Stafford, William: A paraphrase of "Ask Me," excerpted from FIFTY CONTEMPORARY POETS: The Creative Process, edited by Alberta T. Turner. Reprinted by permission of The Estate of William Stafford.

Stallings, A. E.: "First Love: A Quiz" from HAPAX by A. E. Stallings Evanston: TriQuarterly Books/Northwestern University Press, 2006, pp. 28–29. Reprinted by permission of the publisher.

Stallings, A. E.: "Sine Qua Non" first appeared in POETRY, October-November 2002. Copyright © 2002 by The Poetry Foundation. Reprinted from HAPAX by permission of A. E. Stallings (TRIQUARTERLY, 2006). "On Form and Artifice" from "Crooked Roads Without Improvement: Some Thoughts on Formal Verse," THE ALSOP REVIEW (Nov. 2000), is reprinted by permission of the author.

Stallings, A. E.: Translation by A.E. Stallings of Horace ODES Book 1, Ode XI, "A New Year's Toast." First appeared in Light. Reprinted by permission of A. E. Stallings.

Steele, Timothy: "Epitaph" from UNCERTAINTIES AND REST by Timothy Steele. Copyright © 1979. Reprinted by permission of the author.

Stevenson, Anne: "Sous-Entendu" from POEMS: 1955-2005 by Anne Stevenson (Bloodaxe Books, 2005). Reprinted by permission of Bloodaxe Books.

Stillman, Michael: "In Memoriam John Coltrane" from OCCIDENT, Fall, 1971. Copyright © 1976 by Michael Stillman. Reprinted by permission of the author.

Thiel, Diane: "The Minefield" from ECHOLOCATIONS: POEMS (Story Line Press, 2000). Reprinted by permission of the author.

Thomas, Dylan: "Fern Hill" by Dylan Thomas, from THE POEMS OF DYLAN THOMAS, copyright © 1945 by The Trustees for the Copyrights of Dylan Thomas. Reprinted by permission of New Directions Publishing Corp.

Thomas, Dylan: "In My Craft or Sullen Art" from THE POEMS OF DYLAN THOMAS, copyright © 1946 by Dylan Thomas. Reprinted by permission of New Directions Publishing Corp.

Thomas, Dylan: "Do not go gentle into that good night" by Dylan Thomas, from THE POEMS OF DYLAN THOMAS, copyright © 1952 by Dylan Thomas. Reprinted by permission of New Directions Publishing Corp.

Toomer, Jean: "Reapers" from CANE by Jean Toomer. Copyright 1923 by Boni & Liveright, renewed 1951 by Jean Toomer. Used by permission of Liveright Publishing Corporation.

Townsend, Peter: "Langston Hughes and Jazz" excerpted from JAZZ IN AMERICAN CULTURE by Peter Townsend. Copyright © 2000. Reprinted by permission of Edinburgh University Press, www.euppublishing.com.

Trethewey, Natasha: "White Lies" from DOMESTIC WORK by Natasha Trethewey. Copyright © 1998, 2000 by Natasha Trethewey. Reprinted with the permission of Graywolf Press, Saint Paul, Minnesota, www.graywolfpress.org.

Turner, Brian: "The Hurt Locker" from HERE, BULLET by Brian Turner. Copyright © 2005 by Brian Turner. Reprinted with the permission of Alice James Books, www.alicejamesbooks.org.

Updike, John: "Ex-Basketball Player" from COLLECTED POEMS 1953-1993 by John Updike, copyright © 1993 by John Updike. Used by permission of Alfred A. Knopf, a division of Random House, Inc.

Updike, John: "Recital" from TELEPHONE POLES & OTHER POEMS by John Updike, copyright © 1959 by John Updike. Used by permission of Alfred A. Knopf, a division of Random House, Inc.

Valdés, Gina: "English con Salsa" first appeared in THE AMERICAS REVIEW (Houston, TX 1993) and is reprinted by permission of the author.

Vallejo, Cesar: "Anger" by Cesar Vallejo, translated by Thomas Merton, from THE COLLECTED POEMS OF THOMAS MERTON, copyright © 1977 by Trustees of the Merton Legacy Trust. Reprinted by permission of New Directions Publishing Corp.

Wada, Hakuro: "Even the croaking of frogs," translated by Violet Kazue de Cristoforo, from MAY SKY: THERE IS ALWAYS TOMORROW. Reprinted by permission of Kimiko de Cristoforo.

Walcott, Derek: "Sea Grapes" from COLLECTED POEMS 1948-1984 by Derek Walcott. Copyright © 1986 by Derek Walcott. Reprinted by permission of Farrar, Straus and Giroux, LLC.

Walker, Margaret: "For Malcolm X" from THIS IS MY CENTURY: NEW AND COLLECTED POEMS by Margaret Walker. Copyright © 1989 by Margaret Walker Alexander. Reprinted by permission of the University of Georgia Press.

Wilbur, Richard: "Love Calls Us to the Things of this World" from THINGS OF THIS WORLD, copyright © 1956 and renewed 1984 by Richard Wilbur, reprinted by permission of Houghton Mifflin Harcourt Publishing Company.

Wilbur, Richard: "The Writer" from THE MIND-READER, copyright © 1971 by Richard Wilbur, reprinted by permission of Houghton Mifflin Harcourt Publishing Company.

Wilbur, Richard: "Concerning 'Love Calls Us to the Things of This World' " from "On My Own Work" by Richard Wilbur. Reprinted by permission of the author.

Wilbur, Richard: Excerpted from "Sumptuous Destitution" from RESPONSES: PROSE PIECES, 1953 - 1976. Reprinted by permission of the author.

Williams, William Carlos: "Spring and All: Section I," "The Red Wheelbarrow," and "This Is Just to Say" by William Carlos Williams, from THE COLLECTED POEMS: VOLUME I, 1909-1939, copyright © 1938 by New Directions Publishing Corp. Reprinted by permission of New Directions Publishing Corp.

Williams, William Carlos: "The Dance (In Brueghel's)" by William Carlos Williams, from THE COLLECTED POEMS: VOLUME II, 1939-1962, copyright © 1944 by William Carlos Williams. Reprinted by permission of New Directions Publishing Corp.

Wiman, Christian: "When the Time's Toxin" from EVERY RIVEN THING: POEMS by Christian Wiman. Copyright © 2011 by Christian Wiman. Reprinted by permission of Farrar, Straus and Giroux, LLC.

Wolff, Cynthia Griffin: Excerpts from "Emily Dickinson" by Cynthia Griffin Wolff from THE COLUMBIA HISTORY OF AMERICAN POETRY edited by Jay Parini and Brett Millier. Copyright © 1993 Columbia University Press. Reprinted with permission of the publisher.

Wright, James: "Autumn Begins in Martins Ferry, Ohio" by James Wright from THE BRANCH WILL NOT BREAK (Wesleyan University Press, 1963). © 1963 by James Wright and reprinted by permission of Wesleyan University Press.

Yeats, W. B.: "Crazy Jane Talks with the Bishop" reprinted with the permission of Scribner, a Division of Simon & Schuster, Inc., from THE COLLECTED WORKS OF W. B. YEATS, VOLUME I: THE POEMS, REVISED edited by Richard J. Finneran. Copyright © 1933 by The Macmillan Company, renewed 1961 by Bertha Georgie Yeats. All rights reserved.

Yeats, W. B.: "Sailing to Byzantium" and "Leda and the Swan," reprinted with the permission of Scribner, a Division of Simon & Schuster, Inc., from THE COLLECTED WORKS OF W. B. YEATS, VOLUME I: THE POEMS, REVISED by W. B. Yeats, edited by Richard J. Finneran. Copyright © 1928 by The Macmillan Company, renewed 1956 by Georgie Yeats. All rights reserved.

Young, Kevin: "Doo Wop" and "Late Blues" from JELLY ROLL by Kevin Young, copyright © 2003 by Kevin Young. Used by permission of Alfred A. Knopf, a division of Random House, Inc.

DRAMA

Aristotle: Excerpts from "Poetics VI, XIII-XV" from ARISTOTLE ON THE ART OF FICTION, translated by L.J. Potts, Cambridge University Press, 1968. Reprinted with the permission of Cambridge University Press.

Asquith, Clare: Excerpt from SHADOWPLAY: THE HIDDEN BELIEFS AND CODED POLITICS OF WILLIAM SHAKESPEARE by Clare Asquith. Copyright © 2005 by Clare Asquith. Reprinted by permission of PublicAffairs, a member of the Perseus Books Group; permission conveyed through Copyright Clearance Center, Inc.

Auden, W. H.: "Iago as a Triumphant Villain" from "The Joker in the Pack," THE DYER'S HAND AND OTHER ESSAYS. London: Faber and Faber, 1975.

Bamber, Linda: Excerpt from COMIC WOMEN, TRAGIC MEN by Linda Bamber (Stanford University Press). Used by permission of the publisher.

Bodkin, Maud: "Lucifer in Shakespeare's Othello" from ARCHETYPAL PATTERNS IN POETRY. London, Oxford University Press, 1934.

Burgess, Anthony: "An Asian Culture Looks at Shakespeare" excerpted from remarks on the "Importance of Translation" at a June 4, 1982 conference, as published in the Columbia University Journal Translation. Copyright © 1982 by the Estate of Anthony Burgess. Reprinted by permission.

Dodds, E. R.: "On Misunderstanding Oedipus" from "On Misunderstanding the Oedipus Rex" by E. R. Dodds. Reprinted by permission.

Fitzgerald, Robert: Excerpt from "Commentary" in OEDIPUS AT COLONUS BY SOPHOCLES by Robert Fitzgerald. Harcourt, Inc., 1941.

Greer, Germaine: "Shakespeare's 'Honest Mirth'" from SHAKESPEARE by Germaine Greer. New York: Oxford University Press, 1986.

Hwang, David Henry: "Multicultural Theater," excerpted from a June 28, 1989 interview with

David Henry Hwang. From CONTEMPORARY AUTHORS, Vol. 132 & Index 0E. © 1991 Gale, a part of Cengage Learning, Inc. Reproduced by permission. www.cengage.com/permissions.

Hwang, David Henry: THE SOUND OF A VOICE copyright © 1990 by David Henry Hwang from FOB AND OTHER PLAYS by David Henry Hwang. Reprinted by permission of Writers and Artists Group International.

Ibsen, Henrik: A DOLL'S HOUSE, translated by R. Farquharson Sharp and Eleanor Marx-Aveling, revised 2008 by Viktoria Michelsen. Copyright © 2008 by Viktoria Michelsen. Reprinted by permission.

Ives, David: SURE THING from ALL IN THE TIMING: FOURTEEN PLAYS by David Ives, copyright © 1989, 1990, 1992 by David Ives. Used by permission of Vintage Books, a division of Random House, Inc.

Ives, David: Excerpt from "The Exploding Rose" by David Ives is reprinted by permission of the author.

Kott, Jan: From SHAKESPEARE: OUR CONTEMPORARY by Jan Kott, translated by Boleslaw Taborski, copyright © 1964 by Panstwowe Wydawnictwo Naukowe and Doubleday, a division of Random House, Inc. Used by permission of Doubleday, a division of Random House, Inc.

Lee, Edward Bok: EL SANTO AMERICANO, copyright © 2001 by Edward Bok Lee. Reprinted by permission of the author.

Lee, Edward Bok: "On Being a Korean American Writer" by Edward Bok Lee. Copyright © 2006 by Edward Bok Lee. Reprinted by permission of the author.

Lines, Patricia: "Antigonê's Flaw" by Patricia Lines. Reprinted from HUMANITAS, Vol. XII, No. 1, 1999, © National Humanities Institute. Reprinted with permission.

Martin, Jane: BEAUTY by Jane Martin, reprinted by permission of Jon Jory, Trustee, P.O. Box 66, Goshen, KY 40026.

Miller, Arthur: "Tragedy and the Common Man," copyright 1949, renewed © 1977 by Arthur Miller, from THE THEATER ESSAYS OF ARTHUR MILLER by Arthur Miller, edited by Robert A. Martin. Used by permission of Viking Penguin, a division of Penguin Group (USA) Inc.

Miller, Arthur: DEATH OF A SALESMAN by Arthur Miller, copyright 1949, renewed © 1977 by Arthur Miller. Used by permission of Viking Penguin, a division of Penguin Group (USA) Inc.

Sanchez-Scott, Milcha: Introduction to "Roosters" by Milcha Sanchez-Scott from ON NEW GROUND. Copyright © 1989 by Milcha Sanchez-Scott. Published by Theatre Communications Group. Used by permission of Theatre Communications Group.

Sanchez-Scott, Milcha: THE CUBAN SWIMMER by Milcha Sanchez-Scott, copyright © 1984, 1988 by Milcha Sanchez-Scott. All rights reserved. Reprinted by permission of William Morris Endeavor Entertainment, LLC on behalf of the Author. Professionals and amateurs are hereby warned that THE CUBAN SWIMMER is subject to a royalty. It is fully protected under the copyright laws of the United States of America and of all countries covered by the International Copyright Union (including the Dominion of Canada and the rest of the British Commonwealth), the Berne Convention, the Pan-American Copyright Convention and the Universal Copyright Convention as well as all countries with which the United States has reciprocal copyright relations. All rights, including professional/amateur stage rights, motion picture, recitation, lecturing, public reading, radio broadcasting, television, video or sound recording, all other forms of mechanical or electronic reproduction, such as CD-ROM, CD-I, information storage and retrieval systems and photocopying, and the rights of translation into foreign languages, are strictly reserved. Particular emphasis is laid upon the matter of readings, permission for which must be secured from the Author's agent in writing. Inquiries concerning rights should be addressed to William Morris Endeavor Entertainment, LLC, 1325 Avenue of the Americas, New York, NY 10019.

Shakespeare, William: Notes to OTHELLO, HAMLET, and A MIDSUMMER NIGHT'S DREAM from THE COMPLETE WORKS OF SHAKESPEARE, 4th ed. by David Bevington. Copyright © 1997 by Addison-Wesley Educational Publishers, Inc. Reprinted by permission of Pearson Education, Inc.

Smith, Anna Deavere: From TWILIGHT: LOS ANGELES 1992 by Anna Deavere Smith, copyright © 1994 by Anna Deavere Smith. Used by permission of Doubleday, a division of Random House, Inc.

Sophocles: OEDIPUS REX OF SOPHOCLES: AN ENGLISH VERSION by Dudley Fitts and Robert Fitzgerald, copyright 1949 by Harcourt, Inc., and renewed 1977 by Cornelia Fitts and Robert Fitzgerald, reprinted by permission of the publisher.

Sophocles: THE ANTIGONÊ OF SOPHOCLES, AN ENGLISH VERSION by Dudley Fitts and Robert Fitzgerald, copyright 1939 by Houghton Mifflin Harcourt Publishing Company and renewed 1967 by Dudley Fitts and Robert Fitzgerald, reprinted by permission of the publisher.

Vaughan, Virginia Mason: "Black and White in Othello" from OTHELLO: A CONTEXTUAL HISTORY. Cambridge, UK: Cambridge University Press, 1994.

West, Rebecca: Excerpt from THE COURT AND THE CASTLE by Rebecca West. Copyright © 1957 Yale University. Reprinted by permission of Yale University Press.

Wiles, David: "The Chorus as Democrat" excerpt from GREEK THEATER PERFORMANCE:

AN INTRODUCTION by David Wiles. Copyright © 2000. Published by Cambridge University Press.

Williams, Tennessee: THE GLASS MENAGERIE by Tennessee Williams. Copyright © 1945, renewed 1973 The University of the South. Reprinted by permission of Georges Borchardt, Inc. for the Estate of Tennessee Williams.

Wilson, August: A LOOK INTO BLACK AMERICA, excerpted from "Interview with August Wilson" from THE ART OF THEATER NO. 14, interviewed by Bonnie Lyons and George Plimpton, published in THE PARIS REVIEW, Issue 153, Winter 1999.

Wilson, August: From FENCES by August Wilson, copyright © 1986 by August Wilson. Used by permission of Dutton Signet, a division of Penguin Group (USA) Inc.

WRITING

Barthes, Roland: Excerpt from "The Death of the Author" from IMAGE/MUSIC/TEXT, by Roland Barthes, translated by Stephen Heath. English translation copyright © 1977 by Stephen Heath. Reprinted by permission of Farrar, Straus & Giroux, LLC.

Bauerlein, Mark: "What is Cultural Studies?" excerpted from pp. 32–35 of LITERARY CRITICISM: AN AUTOPSY by Mark Bauerlein. Copyright © 1997 University of Pennsylvania Press. Reprinted with permission of the University of Pennsylvania Press.

Bloom, Harold: Excerpt from "Poetic Influence" from A MAP OF MISREADING by Harold Bloom. Copyright © 1975 by Oxford University Press. Used by permission of Oxford University Press, Inc.

Bozorth, Richard: Excerpts from "Tell Me the Truth About Love" from AUDEN'S GAMES OF KNOWLEDGE: POETRY AND THE MEANINGS OF HOMOSEXUALITY by Richard R. Bozorth. Copyright © 2001 Columbia University Press. Reprinted with permission of the publisher.

Brooks, Cleanth: Excerpts from "The Formalist Critic" copyright 1951 by Cleanth Brooks. Originally appeared in THE KENYON REVIEW. Reprinted by permission of Patricia Sue Brooks.

Clark, Michael: "James Baldwin's 'Sonny's Blues': Childhood, Light and Art" from CLA JOURNAL 29:2 (December 1985), pp. 197–205. Reprinted by permission of the College Language Association.

Colacurcio, Michael: From "Visible Sanctity and Spectar Evidence: The Tryal of G.B.," in THE PROVINCE OF PIETY, pp. 302–303. Copyright 1995, Duke University Press. All rights reserved. Used by permission of the publisher. www.dukeupress.edu.

Deane, Seamus: Excerpted from "Joyce the Irishman," pp. 34–37, THE CAMBRIDGE COMPANION TO JAMES JOYCE, 2nd Edition. © 2004 Cambridge University Press. Reprinted with the permission of Cambridge University Press.

Evans, Abbie Huston: "Wing-Spread" reprinted from COLLECTED POEMS by Abbie Huston Evans, by permission of the University of Pittsburgh Press. Copyright 1950 by Abbie Huston Evans.

Fiedler, Leslie: "The Relationship of Poet and Poem" from NO! IN THUNDER by Leslie A. Fiedler. Copyright 1960 by Leslie A. Fiedler. Reprinted by permission of Stein & Dady, a division of Madison Books, Lanham, MD 20763.

Fish, Stanley: Reprinted by permission of the publisher from IS THERE A TEXT IN THIS CLASS?: THE AUTHORITY OF INTERPRETIVE COMMUNITIES by Stanley Fish, pp. 345–347, Cambridge, Mass.: Harvard University Press, Copyright © 1980 by the President and Fellows of Harvard College.

Freud, Sigmund: "The Nature of Dreams" from NEW INTRODUCTORY LECTURES ON PSYCHOANALYSIS. New York, NY: W.W. Norton & Company, Inc., 1933.

Frye, Northrop: From ANATOMY OF CRITICISM. © 1957 Princeton University Press, 1985 renewed PUP, 2000 paperback edition. Reprinted by permission of Princeton University Press.

Hartman, Geoffrey: "On Wordsworth's "A Slumber Did My Spirit Seal' " from "Elation in Hegel and Wordsworth" in THE UNREMARKABLE WORDSWORTH by Geoffrey Hartman. Copyright © 1987 by The University of Minnesota Press. Reprinted by permission of the University of Minnesota Press.

Johnson, Barbara: "Rigorous Unreliability" from A WORLD OF DIFFERENCE. pp. 17–19. © 1987. Reprinted with permission of The Johns Hopkins University Press.

Jung, Carl: "The Collective Unconscious and Archetypes" translated by R. F. C. Hull from THE COLLECTED WORKS OF C. G. JUNG, 1931.

Kazin, Alfred: From AN AMERICAN PROCESSION by Alfred Kazin, copyright © 1984 by Alfred Kazin. Used by permission of Alfred A. Knopf, a division of Random House, Inc.

Kenner, Hugh: "Imagism" from THE POUND ERA by Hugh Kenner. Copyright © 1971 by Hugh Kenner. Reprinted by permission of the University of California Press.

Langbaum, Robert: "On Robert Browning's 'My Last Duchess'" from THE POETRY OF EXPERIENCE by Robert Langbaum. Copyright © 1957, 1986 by Robert Langbaum. Reprinted by permission of the author.

Leitch, Vincent: Excerpt from CULTURAL CRITICISM, LITERARY THEORY, POSTSTRUCTURALISM by Vincent B. Leitch.

Copyright © 1992 Columbia University Press. Reprinted with permission of the publisher.

Lukacs, Georg: "Content Determines Form" from REALISM IN OUR TIME, translated by John and Necke Mander, 1962.

Miller, Brett: "On Elizabeth Bishop's 'One Art'" copyright © 1993 by Brett C. Millier. Used by permission of the author. A fuller treatment of the subject appears in ELIZABETH BISHOP: LIFE AND THE MEMORY OF IT by Brett C. Millier (University of California Press, 1993). Lines from the first draft of "One Art" are quoted by permission of the Special Collections of the Vassar College Libraries and Elizabeth Bishop's literary executor, Alice H. Methfessell.

Paglia, Camille: Excerpted from BREAK, BLOW, BURN by Camille Paglia, copyright © 2005 by Camille Paglia. Used by permission of Pantheon Books, a division of Random House, Inc.

Scholes, Robert: "How Do We Make a Poem?" from SEMIOTICS AND INTERPRETATION by Robert Scholes, pp. 37–39. Copyright © 1982 by Yale University. Reprinted by permission of Yale University Press.

Schulz, Gretchen and R. J. R. Rockwood: "In Fairyland Without a Map: Connie's Exploration Inward in Joyce Carol Oates' 'Where Are You Going, Where Have You Been?'" by Gretchen and R. J. R. Rockwood. Copyright © 1980 by Gretchen E. Schulz and R. J. R. Rockwood. Reprinted by permission.

Seidel, Kathryn L.: Excerpts from pp. 169–173 from "The Artist in the Kitchen: The Economics of Creativity in Huston's 'Sweat'" from SWEAT, ed by Cheryl Wall. Reprinted with permission of the University Press of Florida.

Showalter, Elaine: Excerpt from "Towards a Feminist Criticism," copyright © 1979 by Elaine Showalter. From Elaine Showalter, ed. FEMINIST CRITICISM: ESSAYS ON WOMEN, LITERATURE, AND THEORY (Pantheon, 1985). Reprinted by permission of the author.

Straus, Nina: "Transformations in THE METAMORPHOSIS" from Signs: Journal of Women in Culture and Society, 14.3 (1989) pp. 651–67. Reprinted by permission of the author.

Toth, Emily: "The Source for Alcée LaBallière in 'The Storm'" adapted from KATE CHOPIN: A LIFE OF THE AUTHOR OF THE AWAKENING by Emily Toth. Reprinted by permission of the author.

Volpe, Edmond: "'Barn Burning': a Definition of Evil" from FAULKNER, THE UNAPPEASED IMAGINATION: A COLLECTION OF CRITICAL ESSAYS, edited by Glen O. Carey. Reprinted with permission.

Watkins, Daniel: Excerpt from "Labor and Religion in D. H. Lawrence's 'The Rocking-Horse Winner'" from STUDIES IN SHORT FICTION, Volume 24, No. 3, Summer, 1987. Reprinted by permission of the author.

PHOTO CREDITS

Fiction

1: Jim McHugh Photography; 2: Jim McHugh Photography; 3: Sara Krulwich/The New York Times/Redux; 8: Lebrecht Music and Arts Photo Library/Alamy; 9: Musee Conde, Chantilly, France/The Bridgeman Art Library; 12: SuperStock; 22: Bettmann/CORBIS; 31: Bettmann/CORBIS; 38: Charles Hopkinson/Camera Press/Retna Ltd.; 52: AP Photo/Associated Press; 79: Bettmann/CORBIS; 85: Everett Collection; 92: Lebrecht Music and Arts Photo Library/Alamy; 102: Lebrecht Music and Arts Photo Library/Alamy; 116: Pearson; 123: Missouri Historical Society; 127: J.E. Purdy/CORBIS; 137: Sophie Bassouls/Sygma/CORBIS; 160: Nancy Crampton; 184: Bettmann/CORBIS; 188: Time & Life Pictures/Getty Images; 195: Bettmann/CORBIS; 201: Lebrecht Music and Arts Photo Library/Alamy; 218: t14/ZUMA Press/Newscom; 230: World History Archive/Alamy; 236: Oliver Morris/Hulton Archive/Getty Images; 242: Pearson; 250: Bettmann/CORBIS; 257: Marion Wood Kolisch/Scripps Howard News Service/Newscom; 269: AP Photo/Associated Press; 280: Bettmann/CORBIS; 318: Mary Evans Picture Library/Alamy; 360: Bettmann/CORBIS; 369: INTERFOTO/Alamy; 375: Ana Segovia Camelo; 383: REUTERS/STR New; 386: APIC/Getty Images; 386: Library of Congress Prints and Photographs Division, LC-USZ62-10610; 387: Bettmann/CORBIS; 389: Everett Collection; 392: Mary Evans Picture Library/ARTHUR RACKHAM/Everett Collection (ME10004665); 398: Everett Collection; 410: Sherffius Image Courtesy of The National Endowment for The Arts; 413: Hulton Archive/Getty Images; 417: AP Photo/MTI,Bea Kallos; 419: AP Photo; 458: The Atlanta Journal Constitution; 463: The Atlanta Journal Constitution; 464: The Atlanta Journal Constitution; 472: The Granger Collection, NYC; 484: Library of Congress Prints and Photographs Division, LC-USZ62-60507; 484: Charlotte Perkins Gilman: A Biography by Cynthia Davis. Copyright 2010 by the Board of Trustees of the Leland Stanford Jr. University. All rights reserved. Used with the permission of Stanford University Press, www.sup.org.; 490: Bettmann/CORBIS; 497: AP Photo/Noah Berger, File; 499: Courtesy of Suzanne England; 506: Christie's Images/Bridgeman Art Library; 508: b17/ZUMA Press/Newscom; 511: Christopher Felver/Documentary/CORBIS; 519: Sophie Bassouls/Sygma/CORBIS; 522: The Granger Collection, NYC; 529: Nancy Crampton; 536: Lebrecht Music and Arts Photo Library/Alamy; 551: Alicia Wagner Calzada/ZUMA Press/Newscom; 553: Nancy Crampton; 563: Bettmann/CORBIS; 571: Lebrecht Music and Arts Photo Library/Alamy; 576: Neal Boenzi/New York Times/Getty Images; 577: Aurora Photos/Alamy; 592: Bettmann/CORBIS; 602: ALBERTO CRISTOFARI/A3/CONTRASTO/Redux; 613: VERNIER JEAN BERNARD/CORBIS SYGMA/CORBIS; 616: LaNelle Mason; 626: Everett Collection Inc/Alamy; 637: Peter Power/Toronto Star/ZUMA Press/Newscom; 649: Courtesy of Daniel Orozco at the University of Idaho; 653: BALTEL/SIPA/Newscom; 665: Hulton-Deutsch Collection/Historical Premium/CORBIS.

Poetry

667: Christopher Felver/CORBIS; 668: AP Photo/Steve Yeater; 669: Courtesy of Tom Roster; 684: Everett Collection; 710: Fotosearch/Getty Images; 735: Library of Congress Prints and Photographs Division, LC-USZ62-70064; 748: Bettmann/CORBIS; 764: David Lees/CORBIS; 788: Everett Collection; 807: Everett Collection; 826: AP Photo; 845: Bettmann/CORBIS; 867: John Psarolpoulos; 876: Erich Lessing/Art Resource, NY; 889: CORBIS; 904: Culver Pictures, Inc.; 922: Bettmann/CORBIS; 946: Rhina P. Espaiilat; 960: Pamela Chandler/TopFoto/The Image Works; 964: The Art Gallery Collection/Alamy; 965: (c)RDA/Hulton Archive/Getty Images; 967: Charles H. Phillips//Time Life Pictures/Getty Images; 968: AP Photo/Mary Kent; 970: Schalkwijk/Art Resource, NY; 994: Pearson; 1000: The Everett Collection; 1000 Amherst College Archives and Special Collections; 1007: Visions of America, LLC/Alamy; 1008: Warren Picture History/Newscom; 1017: MPI/Stringer/Archive Photos/Getty Images; 1025: Hulton Archive/Getty Images; 1027: Underwood & Underwood/CORBIS; 1036: By permission of the Houghton Library, Harvard University; 1037: Mary Evans Picture Library/Alamy; 1043: National Poetry Foundation; 1046: CSU Archives/Everett Collection; 1049: Keystone Pictures USA/Alamy; 1063: Sophie Bassouls/Sygma/CORBIS; 1064: CORBIS; 1066: Scala/Art Resource, NY; 1067: Everett Collection; 1068: Lebrecht Music and Arts Photo Library/Alamy;

1069: The British Lbry/Heritage/The Image Works; 1070: Bettmann/CORBIS; 1074: MAGNOLIA PICTURES/MONTFORT, MICHAEL/Album/Newscom; 1078: Christopher Felver/CORBIS; 1079: Library of Congress Prints and Reproductions Division; 1080: Luigi Ciuffetelli; 1081: CORBIS; 1083: Christopher Felver/Documentary/CORBIS; 1087: Eric Schaal/Time Life Pictures/Getty Images; 1091: Archive Pics/Alamy; 1093: Topham/The Image Works; 1099: Hulton Archive/Getty Images; 1100: Reuters/CORBIS; 1103: GL Archive/Alamy; 1106: Mirrorpix/Lebrecht Authors; 1107: Christopher Felver/CORBIS; 1108: Shirley Geok-Lin Lim; 1111: Underwood & Underwood/CORBIS; 1113: Beowulf Sheehan/ZUMA Press/CORBIS; 1114: Gail and Bonnie Roub/Courtesy of the Hoard Historical Museum; 1115: ON CREDIT REQUIRED: Thomas Victor/Harriet Spurlin; 1116: Bettmann/CORBIS; 1120: Reproduced by permission of the Dudley Randall Literary Estate; 1124: Pictorial Press Ltd/Alamy; 1129: Photograph of Cathy Song from School Figures, by Cathy Song, O 1994. Reprinted by permission of the University of Pittsburgh Près.; 1131: Bettmann/CORBIS; 1134: Sueddeutsche Zeitung Photo/The Image Works; 1136: Reuters/CORBIS; 1138: Library of Congress Prints and Reproductions Division; 1140: Hulton Archive/Getty Images; 1141: Classic Image/Alamy; 1144: Lebrecht Music and Arts Photo Library/Alamy.

Drama

1147: JM11 WENN Photos/Newscom; 1148: AP Photo/Frank Franklin II; 1149: Damon Winter/The New York Times/Redux Pictures; 1161: Ellen Locy, Echo Theatre; 1168: AP Photo; 1179: Utah Shakespearean Festival; 1184: The Granger Collection, NYC; 1187: T. Charles Erickson Photography; 1196: Janette Pellegrini/WireImage/Getty Images; 1199: The Granger Collection, NYC; 1202: Bettmann/CORBIS; 1205: Bettmann/CORBIS; 1206: Merlyn Severn/Stringer/Hulton Archive/Getty Images; 1245: Martha Swope Studio/The New York Public Library; 1284: Oli Scarff/Getty Images; 1285: Andrea Pistolesi/The Image Bank/Getty Images; 1286: Georgios Kollidas/Alamy; 1287: Martha Swope Studio/The New York Public Library; 1288-1460: T. Charles Erickson Photography; 1485: Tate, London/Art Resource, NY; 1488-1503: T. Charles Erickson Photography; 1509: Photofest; 1510-1575: Utah Shakespeare Festival; 1577: Donald Cooper/Photostage; 1588: Classic Image/Alamy; 1600: Geraint Lewis/Alamy; 1601: Harvard Theatre Collection; 1651: Hulton-Deutsch Collection/CORBIS; 1654: The Everett Collection; 1655: Cineplex-Odeon Pictures/Courtesy of Everett Collection; 1700: Bettmann/CORBIS; 1705: Mark Garvin; 1721: Jay Thompson/Center Theatre Group; 1725: Jay Thompson/Center Theatre Group; 1727: Joe Kohen/WireImage; 1738: Richard Feldman/American Repertory Theater; 1753: Adam Rountree/Getty Images; 1758: Jeff Wheeler/ZUMA Press/Newscom; 1764: AF archive/Alamy; 1765: AF archive/Alamy; 1831: Bettmann/CORBIS; 1834: JM11 WENN Photos/Newscom; 1835: 1987 Ron Scherl/StageImage/The Image Works; 1883: RICH SUGG/KRT/Newscom.

Writing

1885: The New York Public Library Photographic Services/Art Resource, NY; 1970: Scala/Art Resource, NY.

INDEX OF MAJOR THEMES

If you prefer to study by theme or want to research possible subjects for an essay, here is a listing of stories, poems, and plays arranged into fifteen major themes.

Art, Language, and Imagination

Stories

BALDWIN, Sonny's Blues, 58
BORGES, The Gospel According to Mark, 360
BRADBURY, A Sound of Thunder, 137
CARVER, Cathedral, 105
CHEEVER, The Swimmer, 249
GARCÍA MÁRQUEZ, A Very Old Man with Enormous Wings, 364
GILMAN, The Yellow Wallpaper, 473
LE GUIN, The Ones Who Walk Away from Omelas, 257
O'CONNOR, Parker's Back, 445
PORTER, The Jilting of Granny Weatherall, 85
WALKER, Everyday Use, 491
WOOLF, A Haunted House, 665

Poems

AUDEN, Musée des Beaux Arts, 1065
BLAKE, The Tyger, 1068
BRADSTREET, The Author to Her Book, 689
BUKOWSKI, Dostoevsky, 1074
CARROLL, Jabberwocky, 734
DICKINSON, After great pain, a formal feeling comes, 1004
DICKINSON, Tell all the Truth but tell it slant, 1006
DICKINSON, There is no Frigate Like a Book, 1006
FULTON, What I Like, 889
HEANEY, Digging, 1092
HUGHES, My People, 1018
HUGHES, Theme for English B, 1022
JEFFERS, Hands, 780
KAUFMAN, No More Jazz at Alcatraz, 820
KEATS, Ode on a Grecian Urn, 1101
KEATS, Ode to a Nightingale, 986
LEHMAN, Rejection Slip, 708
MACLEISH, Ars Poetica, 996
MOORE, Poetry, 1112
POPE, True Ease in Writing comes from Art, not Chance, 811
RAINE, A Martian Sends a Postcard Home, 777
SÁENZ, To the Desert, 691
SHAKESPEARE, My mistress' eyes, 1126
SIMIC, The Butcher Shop, 1126
STEVENS, Anecdote of the Jar, 903
STILLMAN, In Memoriam John Coltrane, 824
THOMAS, In My Craft or Sullen Art, 990
VALDÉS, English con Salsa, 733
WALCOTT, Sea Grapes, 1136
WILBUR, The Writer, 1139
WILLIAMS, The Dance, 875
YEATS, Sailing to Byzantium, 981
YOUNG, Doo Wop, 825

Plays

SHAKESPEARE, A Midusmmer Night's Dream, 1512
WILLIAMS, The Glass Menagerie, 1653

Childhood and Adolescence

Stories

ALEXIE, This Is What It Means to Say Phoenix, Arizona, 511
BAMBARA, The Lesson, 2000
CATHER, Paul's Case, 536
CISNEROS, The House on Mango Street, 551
ELLISON, Battle Royal, 552
JOYCE, Araby, 571
KINCAID, Girl, 576
LAWRENCE, The Rocking-Horse Winner, 592
MUNRO, How I Met My Husband, 218
OATES, Where Are You Going, Where Have You Been?, 626
PACKER, Brownies, 38

Poems

BISHOP, Sestina, 865
BLAKE, The Chimney Sweeper, 706
BROOKS, Speech to the Young. Speech to the Progress-Toward, 692
CLEGHORN, The Golf Links, 705
COFER, Quinceañera, 935
CUMMINGS, in Just-, 886
ESPAILLAT, Bilingual / *Bilingüe*, 932
FROST, Birches, 1085
HAYDEN, Those Winter Sundays, 677
HOUSMAN, When I was one-and-twenty, 842
JUSTICE, On the Death of Friends in Childhood, 1101
LAWRENCE, Piano, 1107
OLDS, The One Girl at the Boys' Party, 1115
OLDS, Rite of Passage, 703
ORR, Two Lines from the Brothers Grimm, 916
PRUFER, Pause, Pause, 763
ROETHKE, My Papa's Waltz, 687

SIMIC, The Magic Study of Happiness, 881
SMITH, American Primitive, 707
THIEL, The Minefield, 745
THOMAS, Fern Hill, 1134
TRETHEWEY, White Lies, 693

Plays
WILLIAMS, The Glass Menagerie, 1653

Comedy and Satire

Stories
ATWOOD, Happy Endings, 519
CHUANG TZU, Independence, 11
KINCAID, Girl, 576
MUNRO, How I Met My Husband, 218
OROZCO, Orientation, 649
PACKER, Brownies, 38
TYLER, Teenage Wasteland, 188
VONNEGUT, Harrison Bergeron, 232

Poems
ABEYTA, thirteen ways of looking at a tortilla, 958
AMMONS, Coward, 786
ANONYMOUS, Carnation Milk, 733
ANONYMOUS, Dog Haiku, 696
ATWOOD, Siren Song, 1063
AUDEN, The Unknown Citizen, 702
BLOCH, Tired Sex, 762
R. BROWNING, Soliloquy of the Spanish Cloister, 1072
CLEGHORN, The Golf Links, 705
COPE, Lonely Hearts, 728
CULLEN, For a Lady I Know, 688
DONNE, The Flea, 1081
FEHLER, If Richard Lovelace Became a Free Agent, 958
GRAVES, Down, Wanton, Down!, 718
HARDY, The Ruined Maid, 727
HOUSMAN, When I was one-and-twenty, 842
HUGHES, Dream Boogie, 844
KINGSMILL, What, still alive at twenty-two?, 956
MARVELL, To His Coy Mistress, 1110
MOSS, Shall I Compare Thee to a Summer's Day?, 772
MULLEN, Dim Lady, 957
PARKER, The Actress, 862
PARKER, Résumé, 835
POLLITT, Mind-Body Problem, 943
SHAKESPEARE, My mistress' eyes, 1126
SHEEHAN, Hate Poem, 704
YEATS, Crazy Jane Talks with the Bishop, 1144

Plays
IVES, Sure Thing, 1186
MARTIN, Beauty, 1759
SHAKESPEARE, A Midsummer Night's Dream, 1512

Death

Stories
ACHEBE, Dead Men's Path, 508
ALEXIE, This Is What It Means to Say Phoenix, Arizona, 511
ARREDONDO, The Shunammite, 375
BIERCE, An Occurrence at Owl Creek Bridge, 522
BORGES, The Gospel According to Mark, 360
CRANE, The Open Boat, 201
FAULKNER, A Rose for Emily, 31
GARCÍA MÁRQUEZ, A Very Old Man with Enormous Wings, 364
GRIMM, Godfather Death, 12
HURSTON, Sweat, 562
LONDON, To Build a Fire, 127
MAUGHAM, The Appointment in Samarra, 6
O'CONNOR, A Good Man Is Hard to Find, 420
POE, The Cask of Amontillado, 391
POE, The Fall of the House of Usher, 397
POE, The Tell-Tale Heart, 387
PORTER, The Jilting of Granny Weatherall, 85
TOLSTOY, The Death of Ivan Ilych, 280
WOOLF, A Haunted House, 665

Poems
ANONYMOUS, The Three Ravens, 1060
ASHBERY, At North Farm, 1062
AUDEN, Funeral Blues, 802
BROOKS, the mother, 1070
BROOKS, the rites for Cousin Vit, 1071
COLLINS, The Names, 730
DICKINSON, Because I could not stop for Death, 1005
DICKINSON, I heard a Fly buzz – when I died, 1005
DONNE, Death be not proud, 1081
FROST, "Out, Out—," 680
FROST, Birches, 1085
HARJO, Mourning Song, 881
HECHT, The Vow, 1093
HOUSMAN, To an Athlete Dying Young, 1098
JONSON, On My First Son, 1100
JUSTICE, On the Death of Friends in Childhood, 1101
KEATS, Ode to a Nightingale, 986
KEATS, This living hand, now warm and capable, 850
KEATS, When I have fears that I may cease to be, 1103
LARKIN, Aubade, 944
MAJMUDAR, Rites to Allay the Dead, 860
MERWIN, For the Anniversary of my Death, 874
OWEN, Anthem for Doomed Youth, 1115
PLATH, Lady Lazarus, 929
POE, Annabel Lee, 993
ROBINSON, Luke Havergal, 695
ROETHKE, Elegy for Jane, 1124
ROSSETTI, Uphill, 900
SHAKESPEARE, Fear no more the heat o' the sun, 794
SMITH, American Primitive, 707
STEVENS, The Emperor of Ice-Cream, 1131
STILLMAN, In Memoriam John Coltrane, 824
TENNYSON, Break, Break, Break, 834
TENNYSON, Tears, Idle Tears, 746
THOMAS, Do not go gentle into that good night, 864
WHITMAN, O Captain! My Captain!, 989

WIMAN, When the Time's Toxins, 732
WORDSWORTH, A Slumber Did My Spirit Seal, 814
YOUNG, Late Blues, 803

Plays
GLASPELL, Trifles, 1153
HWANG, The Sound of a Voice, 1738
MILLER, Death of a Salesman, 1764
SHAKESPEARE, Hamlet, 1396
SHAKESPEARE, Othello, 1290
SOPHOCLES, Antigonê, 1245

Faith, Doubt, and Religious Vision

Stories
ALEXIE, This Is What It Means to Say Phoenix, Arizona, 511
BORGES, The Gospel According to Mark, 360
GARCÍA MÁRQUEZ, A Very Old Man with Enormous Wings, 364
HAWTHORNE, Young Goodman Brown, 92
LUKE, The Parable of the Prodigal Son, 230
O'CONNOR, A Good Man Is Hard to Find, 420
O'CONNOR, Parker's Back, 445
O'CONNOR, Revelation, 431

Poems
ARNOLD, Dover Beach, 1061
BORGES, On his blindness, 968
BRUTSCHY, Born Again, 760
S. CRANE, The Wayfarer, 876
DICKINSON, Because I could not stop for Death, 1005
DICKINSON, Some keep the Sabbath going to Church, 1003
DONNE, Batter my heart, three-personed God, 719
DONNE, Death be not proud, 1081
ELIOT, Journey of the Magi, 1084
FROST, Fire and Ice, 744
HARDY, Hap, 1092
HECHT, The Vow, 1093
HERBERT, Easter Wings, 882
HERBERT, Love, 1094
HERBERT, Redemption, 897
HOPKINS, God's Grandeur, 822
HOPKINS, Pied Beauty, 757
HOPKINS, The Windhover, 1097
JARMAN, Unholy Sonnet, 859
LARKIN, Aubade, 944
LEVERTOV, O Taste and See, 1107
MATTHEW, The Parable of the Good Seed, 896
MENASHE, Bread, 723
MILTON, When I consider how my light is spent, 1111
OLIVER, Wild Geese, 901
ROSSETTI, Uphill, 900
SÁENZ, To the Desert, 691
WILBUR, Love Calls Us to the Things of This World, 746
WORDSWORTH, The World Is Too Much with Us, 909
YEATS, The Magi, 1144
YEATS, The Second Coming, 915

Plays
MARLOWE, Doctor Faustus, 1178
SANCHEZ-SCOTT, The Cuban Swimmer, 1703

Families/Parents and Children

Stories
ALEXIE, This Is What It Means to Say Phoenix, Arizona, 511
ARREDONDO, The Shunammite, 375
CHEEVER, The Swimmer, 249
CHOPIN, The Storm, 123
CISNEROS, The House on Mango Street, 551
FAULKNER, Barn Burning, 170
KAFKA, The Metamorphosis, 318
KINCAID, Girl, 576
LAHIRI, Interpreter of Maladies, 577
LAWRENCE, The Rocking-Horse Winner, 592
LUKE, The Parable of the Prodigal Son, 230
MAHFOUZ, The Lawsuit, 612
O'CONNOR, A Good Man Is Hard to Find, 420
PORTER, The Jilting of Granny Weatherall, 85
TAN, A Pair of Tickets, 146
TYLER, Teenage Wasteland, 188
WALKER, Everyday Use, 491
WELTY, A Worn Path, 52
WOLFF, The Rich Brother, 653

Poems
BROOKS, Speech to the Young. Speech to the Progress-Toward, 692
H. CRANE, My Grandmother's Love Letters, 1078
DOVE, Daystar, 1083
ESPAILLAT, Bilingual / *Bilingüe*, 932
HAYDEN, Those Winter Sundays, 677
HEANEY, Digging, 1092
HECHT, The Vow, 1093
HUDGINS, Elegy for my Father, Who Is Not Dead, 944
KEES, For My Daughter, 692
LARKIN, Home is so Sad, 1105
LAWRENCE, Piano, 1107
NIEDECKER, Sorrow Moves in Wide Waves, 1114
OLDS, Rite of Passage, 703
ORR, Two Lines from the Brothers Grimm, 916
PLATH, Daddy, 1116
ROETHKE, My Papa's Waltz, 687
ST. JOHN, Hush, 888
STALLINGS, Sine Qua Non, 860
THIEL, The Minefield, 745
WILBUR, The Writer, 1139

Plays
MILLER, Death of a Salesman, 1764
SANCHEZ-SCOTT, The Cuban Swimmer, 1703
SHAKESPEARE, Hamlet, 1396
SOPHOCLES, Oedipus, 1207
WILLIAMS, The Glass Menagerie, 1653
WILSON, Fences, 1833

Immigration and Assimilation

Stories
CISNEROS, The House on Mango Street, 551
LAHIRI, Interpreter of Maladies, 577
TAN, A Pair of Tickets, 146

Poems
ABEYTA, thirteen ways of looking at a tortilla, 958
ALARCÓN, Frontera / Border, 887
ALARCÓN, The X in My Name, 935
COFER, Quinceañera, 935
ESPAILLAT, Bilingual / *Bilingüe*, 932
LAZARUS, The New Colossus, 992
LIM, Learning to love America, 1108
LIM, Riding into California, 934
MATSUSHITA, Rain shower from mountain, 759
OZAWA, The war—this year, 759
RAINE, A Martian Sends a Postcard Home, 777
THIEL, The Minefield, 745
VALDÉS, English con Salsa, 733
WADA, Even the croaking of frogs, 759

Plays
SANCHEZ-SCOTT, The Cuban Swimmer, 1703
SMITH, Twilight: Los Angeles, 1992, 1717

Individual Versus Society

Stories
ACHEBE, Dead Men's Path, 508
ALEXIE, This Is What It Means to Say Phoenix, Arizona, 511
CATHER, Paul's Case, 536
CHEEVER, The Swimmer, 249
CHUANG TZU, Independence, 11
ELLISON, Battle Royal, 552
FAULKNER, Barn Burning, 170
FAULKNER, A Rose for Emily, 31
GARCÍA MÁRQUEZ, A Very Old Man with Enormous Wings, 364
HAWTHORNE, Young Goodman Brown, 92
JACKSON, The Lottery, 262
LE GUIN, The Ones Who Walk Away from Omelas, 257
UPDIKE, A & P, 17
VONNEGUT, Harrison Bergeron, 232
WOLFF, The Rich Brother, 653

Poems
ALEXIE, The Powwow at the End of the World, 936
AUDEN, Musée des Beaux Arts, 1065
AUDEN, The Unknown Citizen, 702
BLAKE, London, 741
BLAKE, The Sick Rose, 1069
BROOKS, We Real Cool, 833
BUKOWSKI, Dostoevsky, 1074
CUMMINGS, anyone lived in a pretty how town, 729
CUMMINGS, next to of course god america i, 744
DICKINSON, I'm Nobody! Who are you?, 1003
DICKINSON, Much madness Is Divinest Sense, 1004
DICKINSON, Some keep the Sabbath going to Church, 1003
DICKINSON, The Soul selects her own Society, 1003
DYLAN, The Times They Are a-Changin', 804
ELIOT, The Love Song of J. Alfred Prufrock, 1038
FROST, Acquainted with the Night, 858
FROST, Mending Wall, 1087
FROST, Stopping by Woods on a Snowy Evening, 1088
HAYDEN, Frederick Douglass, 985
HUGHES, I, Too, 1019
HUGHES, Theme for English B, 1022
MACHADO, The Traveler, 900
MCKAY, America, 933
MILTON, When I consider how my light is spent, 1111
NERUDA, Muchos Somos / We Are Many, 966
STEVENS, Disillusionment of Ten O'Clock, 742

Plays
GLASPELL, Trifles, 1153
IBSEN, A Doll's House, 1598
MILLER, Death of a Salesman, 1764
SANCHEZ-SCOTT, The Cuban Swimmer, 1703
SMITH, Twilight: Los Angeles, 1992, 1717
WILLIAMS, The Glass Menagerie, 1653
WILSON, Fences, 1833

Loneliness and Alienation

Stories
ALEXIE, This Is What It Means to Say Phoenix, Arizona, 511
ARREDONDO, The Shunammite, 375
CATHER, Paul's Case, 536
CHEEVER, The Swimmer, 249
ELLISON, Battle Royal, 552
GILMAN, The Yellow Wallpaper, 473
HEMINGWAY, A Clean, Well-Lighted Place, 167
JOYCE, Araby, 571
KAFKA, The Metamorphosis, 318
MANSFIELD, Miss Brill, 102
MUNRO, How I Met My Husband, 218
OROZCO, Orientation, 649
STEINBECK, The Chrysanthemums, 244

Poems
BOGAN, Medusa, 912
COLLINS, Embrace, 762
DICKINSON, After great pain, a formal feeling comes, 1004
DICKINSON, I felt a Funeral, in my Brain, 1002
DICKINSON, I'm Nobody! Who are you?, 1003
DICKINSON, The Soul selects her own Society, 1003
DICKINSON, Success is counted sweetest, 1001
DOVE, Daystar, 1083
ELIOT, The Love Song of J. Alfred Prufrock, 1038
ELIOT, The winter evening settles down, 753
FROST, Acquainted with the Night, 858
FROST, Desert Places, 822
GINSBERG, A Supermarket in California, 1088
HUGHES, Homecoming, 1024

JOHNSON, Sence You Went Away, 793
JONSON, Slow, slow, fresh fount, 834
KOOSER, Abandoned Farmhouse, 1104
LARKIN, Home is so Sad, 1105
LARKIN, Poetry of Departures, 1106
LI PO, Drinking Alone Beneath the Moon, 951
LOWELL, Skunk Hour, 1108
MANN, Deathly, 805
MILLAY, What lips my lips have kissed, 857
NELSON, A Strange Beautiful Woman, 1113
OLIVER, Wild Geese, 901
POE, A Dream within a Dream, 1118
RANSOM, Piazza Piece, 1121
ROBINSON, Luke Havergal, 695
SHAKESPEARE, When to the sessions of sweet silent thought, 1125
SIMIC, My Shoes, 784
STAFFORD, The Farm on the Great Plains, 1130
STEVENS, The Snow Man, 903
WILLIAMS, El Hombre, 761
WILLIAMS, Smell!, 843

Plays
GLASPELL, Trifles, 1153
IBSEN, A Doll's House, 1598
LEE, El Santo Americano, 1754
MILLER, Death of a Salesman, 1764
WILLIAMS, The Glass Menagerie, 1653

Love and Desire

Stories
ARREDONDO, The Shunammite, 375
ATWOOD, Happy Endings, 519
CHOPIN, The Storm, 123
CHOPIN, The Story of an Hour, 549
FAULKNER, A Rose for Emily, 31
JOYCE, Araby, 571
LAHIRI, Interpreter of Maladies, 577
LEAVITT, A Place I've Never Been, 602
MAHFOUZ, The Lawsuit, 612
MASON, Shiloh, 616
MUNRO, How I Met My Husband, 218
O'CONNOR, Parker's Back, 445
PORTER, The Jilting of Granny Weatherall, 85
STEINBECK, The Chrysanthemums, 242
UPDIKE, A & P, 17
WOOLF, A Haunted House, 665

Poems
ADDONIZIO, First Poem for You, 859
ANONYMOUS, Bonny Barbara Allen, 797
ARNOLD, Dover Beach, 1061
AUDEN, As I Walked Out One Evening, 1064
BACA, Spliced Wire, 1066
BLOCH, Tired Sex, 762
BRIDGES, Triolet, 865
BURNS, Oh, my love is like a red, red rose, 787
CAMPO, For J. W., 940
CHAUCER, Merciless Beauty, 1075
COPE, Lonely Hearts, 728
CUMMINGS, somewhere i have never travelled, gladly beyond, 1079
DICKINSON, The Soul selects her own Society, 1003
DICKINSON, Wild Nights – Wild Nights!, 1002
DONNE, The Flea, 1081
DONNE, A Valediction: Forbidding Mourning, 1082
DRAYTON, Since there's no help, come let us kiss and part, 857
ESSBAUM, The Heart, 776
FROST, The Silken Tent, 785
FULTON, What I Like, 889
GRAVES, Counting the Beats, 852
GRAVES, Down, Wanton, Down!, 718
H.D., Oread, 761
HARDY, Neutral Tones, 895
HAYDEN, Those Winter Sundays, 677
HOAGLAND, Beauty, 1095
HOUSMAN, When I was one-and-twenty, 842
JOHNSON, Sence You Went Away, 793
JONSON, To Celia, 792
KEATS, La Belle Dame sans Merci, 912
MARVELL, To His Coy Mistress, 1110
MILLAY, What lips my lips have kissed, 857
POE, Annabel Lee, 993
POE, To Helen, 910
POUND, The River Merchant's Wife: A Letter, 1119
SEXTON, Cinderella, 919
SHAKESPEARE, My mistress' eyes, 1126
SHAKESPEARE, Shall I compare thee to a summer's day?, 771
SHEEHAN, Hate Poem, 704
STALLINGS, First Love: A Quiz, 918
STEVENSON, Sous-entendu, 938
THOMAS, In My Craft or Sullen Art, 990
WALLER, Go, Lovely Rose, 1137
WILLIAMS, Queen-Anne's-Lace, 1141
WYATT, They flee from me, 1143
YEATS, Crazy Jane Talks with the Bishop, 1144
YEATS, When You Are Old, 1145

Plays
HWANG, The Sound of a Voice, 1738
IBSEN, A Doll's House, 1598
IVES, Sure Thing, 1186
SHAKESPEARE, A Midsummer Night's Dream, 1512
SHAKESPEARE, Othello, 1290

Men and Women/Marriage

Stories
ARREDONDO, The Shunammite, 375
ATWOOD, Happy Endings, 519
CARVER, Cathedral, 105
CHEEVER, The Swimmer, 249
CHOPIN, The Storm, 123
GILMAN, The Yellow Wallpaper, 473
HENRY, The Gift of the Magi, 184
HURSTON, Sweat, 562
LAHIRI, Interpreter of Maladies, 577
MAHFOUZ, The Lawsuit, 612

MASON, Shiloh, 616
STEINBECK, The Chrysanthemums, 242
UPDIKE, A & P, 17
WOOLF, A Haunted House, 665

Poems
E. BROWNING, How Do I Love Thee?, 1071
R. BROWNING, My Last Duchess, 682
CIARDI, Most Like an Arch This Marriage, 1076
DONNE, A Valediction: Forbidding Mourning, 1082
DOVE, Daystar, 1083
ELIOT, The Love Song of J. Alfred Prufrock, 1038
HARDY, The Workbox, 705
HERRICK, To the Virgins, to make much of time, 1095
JUSTICE, Men at Forty, 941
LOVELACE, To Lucasta, 709
MARVELL, To His Coy Mistress, 1110
POUND, The Garden, 877
POUND, The River-Merchant's Wife: a Letter, 1119
RICH, Living in Sin, 1122
SEXTON, Cinderella, 919
SHAKESPEARE, Let me not to the marriage of true minds, 856
STEVENSON, Sous-entendu, 938
WILLIAMS, The Young Housewife, 901

Plays
GLASPELL, Trifles, 1153
HWANG, The Sound of a Voice, 1738
IBSEN, A Doll's House, 1598
IVES, Sure Thing, 1186
LEE, El Santo Americano, 1754
SHAKESPEARE, A Midsummer Night's Dream, 1512
SHAKESPEARE, Othello, 1290
WILLIAMS, The Glass Menagerie, 1653
WILSON, Fences, 1833

Nature

Stories
BRADBURY, A Sound of Thunder, 137
CHOPIN, The Storm, 123
CRANE, The Open Boat, 201
LONDON, To Build a Fire, 127

Poems
ALEXIE, The Powwow at the End of the World, 936
BISHOP, The Fish, 754
BLAKE, The Tyger, 1068
BLAKE, To see a world in a grain of sand, 775
BUSON, Moonrise on mudflats, 758
DICKINSON, The Lightning is a yellow Fork, 894
DICKINSON, A Route of Evanescence, 756
FROST, Desert Places, 822
H.D., Oread, 761
H.D., Storm, 745
HARDY, The Darkling Thrush, 1091
HOLLANDER, Swan and Shadow, 883
HOPKINS, Pied Beauty, 757
HOPKINS, Spring and Fall, 1097
HOPKINS, The Windhover, 1097
HOUSMAN, Loveliest of trees, the cherry now, 1098
T. HUGHES, Hawk Roosting, 696
JEFFERS, Rock and Hawk, 1099
KEATS, Ode to a Nightingale, 986
KEATS, To Autumn, 1103
KOSTELANETZ, Simultaneous Translations, 884
LEVIN, Brief Bio, 855
MATSUSHITA, Cosmos in Bloom, 759
OLIVER, Wild Geese, 901
ROETHKE, Root Cellar, 753
RYAN, Blandeur, 726
RYAN, Mockingbird, 721
RYAN, Turtle, 786
SÁENZ, To the Desert, 691
SANDBURG, Fog, 784
SMART, For I will consider my Cat Jeoffry, 1127
STAFFORD, Traveling Through the Dark, 980
STEPHENS, The Wind, 779
STEVENS, Anecdote of the Jar, 903
STEVENS, The Snow Man, 903
STEVENS, Thirteen Ways of Looking at a Blackbird, 878
TENNYSON, The Eagle, 771
TENNYSON, Flower in the Crannied Wall, 775
WILLIAMS, Spring and All, 1140
WORDSWORTH, I Wandered Lonely as a Cloud, 697
YEATS, Lake Isle of Innisfree, 675

Plays
SANCHEZ-SCOTT, The Cuban Swimmer, 1703

Race, Class, and Culture

Stories
ACHEBE, Dead Men's Path, 508
ALEXIE, This Is What It Means to Say Phoenix, Arizona, 511
ALLENDE, The Judge's Wife, 369
ARREDONDO, The Shunammite, 375
BALDWIN, Sonny's Blues, 58
BAMBARA, The Lesson, 2000
CHUANG TZU, Independence, 11
CISNEROS, The House on Mango Street, 551
ELLISON, Battle Royal, 552
FAULKNER, Barn Burning, 170
HURSTON, Sweat, 562
MAHFOUZ, The Lawsuit, 612
O'CONNOR, Revelation, 431
PACKER, Brownies, 38
TAN, A Pair of Tickets, 146
WALKER, Everyday Use, 491
WELTY, A Worn Path, 52

Poems
ALARCÓN, The X in My Name, 935
BLAKE, The Chimney Sweeper, 706
BROOKS, The Bean Eaters, 743
BROOKS, the mother, 1070
BROOKS, Speech to the Young. Speech to the Progress-Toward, 692

BROOKS, We Real Cool, 833
CERVANTES, Cannery Town in August, 1075
CLEGHORN, The Golf Links, 705
COFER, Quinceañera, 935
CULLEN, For a Lady I Know, 688
DUNBAR, We Wear the Mask, 992
HARJO, Mourning Song, 881
HAYDEN, Frederick Douglass, 985
HAYDEN, Those Winter Sundays, 677
HUGHES, Dream Boogie, 844
HUGHES, Harlem [Dream Deferred], 1024
HUGHES, I, Too, 1019
HUGHES, My People, 1018
HUGHES, The Negro Speaks of Rivers, 1017
HUGHES, Nightmare Boogie, 1023
HUGHES, Song for a Dark Girl, 1021
HUGHES, Theme for English B, 1022
LIM, Learning to Love America, 1108
MCKAY, America, 933
RANDALL, Ballad of Birmingham, 800
RANDALL, A Different Image, 1120
SEXTON, Her Kind, 699
B. SMITH, Jailhouse Blues, 802
SONG, Stamp Collecting, 1129
STILLMAN, In Memoriam John Coltrane, 824
TOOMER, Reapers, 756
TRETHEWEY, White Lies, 693
VALDÉS, English con Salsa, 733
WALKER, For Malcolm X, 1137

Plays
HWANG, The Sound of a Voice, 1738
SANCHEZ-SCOTT, The Cuban Swimmer, 1703
SMITH, Twilight: Los Angeles, 1992, 1717
WILSON, Fences, 1833

War, Murder, and Violence

Stories
ALLENDE, The Judge's Wife, 369
BIERCE, An Occurrence at Owl Creek Bridge, 522
BORGES, The Gospel According to Mark, 360
BOYLE, Greasy Lake, 529
BRADBURY, A Sound of Thunder, 137
ELLISON, Battle Royal, 552
FAULKNER, A Rose for Emily, 31
HURSTON, Sweat, 562
OATES, Where Are You Going, Where Have You Been?, 626
O'BRIEN, The Things They Carried, 637
O'CONNOR, A Good Man Is Hard to Find, 420
POE, The Cask of Amontillado, 391
POE, The Fall of the House of Usher, 397
POE, The Tell-Tale Heart, 387

Poems
ARNOLD, Dover Beach, 1061
EBERHART, The Fury of Aerial Bombardment, 728
HUGHES, Song for a Dark Girl, 1021
JARRELL, The Death of the Ball Turret Gunner, 1099
KEES, For My Daughter, 692
KIM, Occupation, 898
KOMUNYAKAA, Facing It, 937
LOVELACE, To Lucasta, 709
NEMEROV, The War in the Air, 1113
OWEN, Anthem for Doomed Youth, 1115
OWEN, Dulce et Decorum Est, 709
OZAWA, The war—this year, 759
RANDALL, Ballad of Birmingham, 800
REED, Naming of Parts, 1121
SANDBURG, Grass, 723
STAFFORD, At the Un-National Monument Along the Canadian Border, 708
THIEL, The Minefield, 745
TURNER, The Hurt Locker, 942
WHITMAN, Beat! Beat! Drums!, 843
WHITMAN, Cavalry Crossing a Ford, 876
YEATS, Leda and the Swan, 821

Plays
GLASPELL, Trifles, 1153
LEE, El Santo Americano, 1754
SHAKESPEARE, Hamlet, 1396
SHAKESPEARE, Othello, 1290
SMITH, Twilight: Los Angeles, 1992, 1717
SOPHOCLES, Antigonê, 1245
SOPHOCLES, Oedipus, 1207

Woman's Identity

Stories
ARREDONDO, The Shunammite, 375
MASON, Shiloh, 616
GILMAN, The Yellow Wallpaper, 473
STEINBECK, The Chrysanthemums, 242

Poems
BROOKS, the mother, 1070
BROOKS, the rites for Cousin Vit, 1071
COFER, Quinceañera, 935
DE LOS SANTOS, Perfect Dress, 1080
DICKINSON, My Life had stood – a Loaded Gun, 774
DOVE, Daystar, 1083
HAALAND, Lipstick 902
HOAGLAND, Beauty, 1095
KIZER, Bitch, 939
NELSON, A Strange Beautiful Woman, 1113
NIEDECKER, Sorrow Moves in Wide Waves, 1114
OLDS, The One Girl at the Boys' Party, 1115
PLATH, Daddy, 1116
POLLITT, Mind-Body Problem, 943
RICH, Aunt Jennifer's Tigers, 678
RICH, Women, 941
SATYAMURTI, I Shall Paint My Nails Red, 887
SEXTON, Cinderella, 919
SEXTON, Her Kind, 699
STALLINGS, First Love: A Quiz, 918
WILLIAMS, The Young Housewife, 901

Plays
GLASPELL, Trifles, 1153
IBSEN, A Doll's House, 1598
IVES, Sure Thing, 1186
MARTIN, Beauty, 1759

INDEX OF FIRST LINES OF POETRY

A Book of Verses underneath the Bough, 954
A cup of wine, under the flowering trees, 951
A cold coming we had of it, 1084
A Dying Tiger – moaned for Drink –, 977
A line in long array where they wind betwixt green islands, 876
A *little Learning* is a dang'rous Thing, 1119
A man is haunted by his father's ghost, 861
A nick on the jaw, 760
A poem should be palpable and mute, 996
A Route of Evanescence, 756
A slumber did my spirit seal, 814
A strange beautiful woman, 1113
A sudden blow: the great wings beating still, 821
A telephone line goes cold, 1130
Abortions will not let you forget, 1070
About suffering they were never wrong, 1065
After great pain, a formal feeling comes –, 1004
After the praying, after the hymn-singing, 859
After weeks of watching the roof leak, 760
Ah Love! Could you and I with Him conspire, 955
Al cabo de los años me rodea, 968
All day I hear the noise of waters, 816
All Greece hates, 910
All night it humps the air, 1075
All the friends, 863
All you violated ones with gentle hearts, 1137
Allons! the road is before us!, 1138
Although she feeds me bread of bitterness, 933
among twenty different tortillas, 958
Among twenty snowy mountains, 878
Anger which breaks a man into children, 971
anyone lived in a pretty how town, 729
As I walked out one evening, 1064
As the guests arrive at my son's party, 703
As virtuous men pass mildly away, 1082
At ten A.M. the young housewife, 901
Aunt Jennifer's tigers prance across a screen, 678

Batter my heart, three-personed God, for You, 719
Bearer of no news, 855
Beat! beat! drums!—blow! bugles! blow!, 843
Because a bit of color is a public service, 887
Because I could not Dump the Trash –, 957
Because I could not stop for Death –, 1005
Because I will turn 420 tomorrow, 1078
because it has no pure products, 1108
Bent double, like old beggars under sacks, 709
Between my finger and my thumb, 1092
Black reapers with the sound of steel on stones, 756
Blanche—don't ask—it isn't right for us to know what ends, 953
Born Again, 760
Bravery runs in my family, 786
Break, break, break, 834
Bright star, would I were steadfast as thou art—, 760
broken bowl, 760
Buffalo Bill 's, 874
By the road to the contagious hospital, 1140

Call the roller of big cigars, 1131
Caminante, son tus huellas, 900
Can someone make my simple wish come true?, 728
Carnation Milk is the best in the land, 733
Carried her unprotesting out the door, 1071
Caxtons are mechanical birds with many wings, 777
Come, fill the Cup, and in the fire of Spring, 954
Come gather 'round people, 804
Con los ojos cerrados, 969
Cosmos in bloom, 759
Cricket, be, 759

De tantos hombres que soy, 966
Death be not proud, though some have callèd thee, 1081
Do not ask, Leuconoë—to know is not permitted—, 952
Do not go gentle into that good night, 864
Does the road wind uphill all the way?, 900
Don't think, 938
Dostoevsky against the wall, the firing squad ready, 1074
Down valley a smoke haze, 762
Down, wanton, down! Have you no shame, 718
Dream-singers, 1018
Drink to me only with thine eyes, 792
Droning a drowsy syncopated tune, 1020
Dusk, 883

Earth has not anything to show more fair, 1141
el rasguño de esta fiebre, 973
Enganchadas al cable como pinzas de ropa, 972
Eskimos in Manitoba, 814
Even the croaking of frogs, 759
Every year without knowing it I have passed the day, 874

Farewell, my younger brother!, 1061
Farewell, thou child of my right hand, and joy, 1100
Fear no more the heat o' the sun, 794
Flower in the crannied wall, 775
Footsteps like water hollow, 870
For a saving grace, we didn't see our dead, 1113
For I will consider my Cat Jeoffry, 1127
Four simple chambers, 776
Friend, on this scaffold Thomas More lies dead, 723
Friend—the face I wallow toward, 889
From my mother's sleep I fell into the State, 1099

Gather up, 1021
Gather ye rose-buds while ye may, 1095
Glory be to God for dappled things—, 757
Go, lovely rose, 1137
Go and catch a falling star, 854
Go to the western gate, Luke Havergal, 695
Good morning, daddy!, 844
Gr-r-r—there go, my heart's abhorrence!, 1072

Had we but world enough, and time, 1110
Hark, hark, the lark at heaven's gate sings, 825
Having been tenant long to a rich Lord, 897
He came up to me, 918
He clasps the crag with crooked hands, 771
He drew a circle that shut me out—, 898
He stood, and heard the steeple, 816
He was a big man, says the size of his shoes, 1104
He was found by the Bureau of Statistics to be, 702
He was running with his friend from town to town, 745
Heat-lightning streak—, 758
Helen, thy beauty is to me, 910
Her body is not so white as, 1141
Her name, cut clear upon this marble cross, 862
Here is a symbol in which, 1099
Here lies Sir Tact, a diplomatic fellow, 744
Hole in the ozone, 760
Home is so sad. It stays as it was left, 1105
Honey baby, 825
How do I love thee? Let me count the ways, 1071

I, too, sing America, 1019
I am a gentleman in a dustcoat trying, 1121
I am told by many of you that I must forgive and so I shall, 936
I came to you one rainless August night, 691
I caught a tremendous fish, 754
I caught this morning morning's minion, king-, 1097
I do not love my country. Its abstract lustre, 972
I felt a Funeral, in my Brain, 1002
I filled your house with light, 1066
I had a dream, 1023
I had come to the house, in a cave of trees, 912
I hardly ever tire of love or rhyme—, 862
I hate you truly. Truly I do, 704
I have been one acquainted with the night, 858
I have done it again, 929
I have eaten, 716
I have gone out, a possessed witch, 699
I hear America singing, the varied carols I hear, 1138
I heard a Fly buzz – when I died –, 1005
I know exactly what I want to say, 940
I leant upon a coppice gate, 1091
I like to see it lap the Miles –, 690
I like to touch your tattoos in complete, 859
I met a traveler from an antique land, 984
I met the Bishop on the road, 1144
I need a bare sufficiency—red wine, 954
I placed a jar in Tennessee, 903
I pray you not, Leuconoë, to pore, 952
I remember the neckcurls, limp and damp as tendrils, 1124
I shoot the Hippopotamus, 820
I sit in the top of the wood, my eyes closed, 696
I taste a liquor never brewed –, 1002
I too, dislike it: there are things that are important beyond all this fiddle, 1112
I wander through each chartered street, 741
I wandered lonely as a cloud, 697
I want a jug of ruby wine and a book of poems, 954
I went back in the alley, 1024
I will arise and go now, and go to Innisfree, 675
I wonder how they do it, those women, 902
I work all day, and get half-drunk at night, 944
If but some vengeful god would call to me, 1092
If I die, 803
If it please God, 726
If you come to a land with no ancestors, 934
If you wander far enough, 701
I'm a riddle in nine syllables, 775
"I'm Mark's alone!" you swore. Given cause to doubt you, 862
I'm Nobody! Who are you?, 1003
I'm tired of Love: I'm still more tired of Rhyme, 862
In a solitude of the sea, 1089
In Brueghel's great picture, The Kermess, 875
In her room at the prow of the house, 1139
in Just-, 886
In my craft or sullen art, 990
In the fullness of the years, like it or not, 968
In the old stone pool, 758
In the Shreve High football stadium, 1142
In the smallest theater in the world, 881
In the third month, a sudden flow of blood, 1093
In this strange labyrinth how shall I turn?, 1142
In Xanadu did Kubla Khan, 1076
Inside a cave in a narrow canyon near Tassajara, 780
It dropped so low – in my Regard –, 776
It is a cold and snowy night. The main street is deserted, 762
It is dangerous to see more stars than there are, 884
It is never enough to close their door, 860
It little profits that an idle king, 1132
It was in and about the Martinmas time, 797
It was many and many a year ago, 993
It's a strange courage, 761
It's early evening here in the small world, 881
It's here in a student's journal, a blue confession, 1080
I've known rivers, 1017

Julius Caesar, 852

La cólera que quiebra al hombre en niños, 971
Landlord, landlord, 1021
Let me not to the marriage of true minds, 856
Let us go then, you and I, 1038
Like a skein of loose silk blown against a wall, 877
Listen to the coal, 824
Look at him there in his stovepipe hat, 707
Looking into my daughter's eyes I read, 692
Lord, who createdst man in wealth and store, 882
Love bade me welcome; yet my soul drew back, 1094
Love is like the wild rose-briar, 787
Loveliest of trees, the cherry now, 1098
Lysi, I give to your divine hand, 965
Lysi: a tus manos divinas, 965

Make me thy lyre, even as the forest is, 852
Making jazz swing in, 760
Márgarét, áre you gríeving, 1097
Mark but this flea, and mark in this, 1081
Men at forty, 941
Mine, said the stone, 844
Miniver Cheevy, child of scorn, 1123
Money, the long green, 783
Moonrise on mudflats, 758
More tease than strip, the surf slips back, 786
Most like an arch—an entrance which upholds, 1076
Mother dear, may I go downtown, 800
Much Madness is divinest Sense –, 1004
My black face fades, 937
My dolls have been put away like dead, 935
My father liked them separate, one there, 932
My father used to say, 718
My heart aches, and a drowsy numbness pains, 986
My honeybunch's peepers are nothing like neon, 957
My Life had stood – a Loaded Gun –, 774
My mistress' eyes are nothing like the sun, 1126
My notebook has remained blank for months, 1100
My three sisters are sitting, 941

Nature's first green is gold, 909
Nautilus Island's hermit, 1108
next to of course god america i, 744
ninguna, 887
no, 887
No amo mi Patria. Su fulgor abstracto, 972
No More Jazz, 820
Nobody heard him, the dead man, 763
Not like the brazen giant of Greek fame, 992
Nothing but the hurt left here, 942
Nothing whole, 721
Nothing would sleep in that cellar, dank as a ditch, 753
Now, when he and I meet, after all these years, 939
Now as at all times I can see in the mind's eye, 1144
Now as I was young and easy under the apple boughs, 1134
Now hardly here and there an hackney-coach, 1131
Now that I've met you, 805
Now we must get up quickly, 916

O Captain! my Captain! our fearful trip is done, 989
O 'Melia, my dear, this does everything crown!, 727
O Moon, when I gaze on thy beautiful face, 976
O Rose, thou art sick!, 1069
O what can ail thee, knight at arms, 912
O where ha you been, Lord Randal, my son?, 1059
Of the many men who I am, who we are, 966
Oh, but it is dirty!, 1067
Oh, God of dust and rainbows, help us see, 862
Oh, how glad I am that she, 708
Oh, my love is like a red, red rose, 787
Oh strong-ridged and deeply hollowed, 843
On a flat road runs the well-train'd runner, 761
On my boat on Lake Cayuga, 818
On the one-ton temple bell, 758
One day I'll lift the telephone, 944
One must have a mind of winter, 903
only one guy and, 759

Pearl Avenue runs past the high-school lot, 1135
Peligroso es ver mas estrellas de las que hay, 884
Pile the bodies high at Austerlitz and Waterloo, 723
Pinned to the wire like clothes-pegs, 973
Popcorn-can cover, 903
Praise to the empty schoolroom, when the folders, 763
Praise ye the Lord, 872

Quinquireme of Nineveh from distant Ophir, 740

Rain shower from mountain, 759
Razors pain you, 835
Red river, red river, 826

Safe upon the solid rock the ugly houses stand, 705
Say to them, 692
Season of mists and mellow fruitfulness, 1103
See, here's the workbox, little wife, 705
Seems lak to me de stars don't shine so bright, 793
September rain falls on the house, 865
Shall I compare thee to a summer's day?, 771
She even thinks that up in heaven, 688
She had thought the studio would keep itself, 1122
She is as in a field a silken tent, 785
She wanted a little room for thinking, 1083
Shoes, secret face of my inner life, 784
Silver bark of beech, and sallow, 841
Since there's no help, come let us kiss and part, 857
Slow, slow, fresh fount, keep time with my salt tears, 834
Snow falling and night falling fast, oh, fast, 822
Snow on every field, 863
so much depends, 700
Softly, in the dusk, a woman is singing to me, 1107

Some for the Glories of This World, 955
Some keep the Sabbath going to Church –, 1003
Some say the world will end in fire, 744
Some time when the river is ice ask me, 685
Something there is that doesn't love a wall, 1087
Sometimes walking late at night, 1126
Sometimes you hear, fifth-hand, 1106
somewhere i have never travelled,gladly beyond, 1079
Somewhere someone is traveling furiously toward you, 1062
Sorrow moves in wide waves, 1114
Stop all the clocks, cut off the telephone, 802
Success is counted sweetest, 1001
Sundays too my father got up early, 677

Take this kiss upon the brow!, 1118
Tears, idle tears, I know not what they mean, 746
Tell all the Truth but tell it slant –, 1006
Tell me not, fans, I am unkind, 958
Tell me not, Sweet, I am unkind, 709
That is no country for old men. The young, 981
That sail which leans on light, 1136
That time of year thou mayst in me behold, 1125
That's my last Duchess painted on the wall, 682
The age, 1120
The apparition of these faces in the crowd, 751
The art of losing isn't hard to master, 985
The buzz-saw snarled and rattled in the yard, 680
The eyes open to a cry of pulleys, 746
The falling flower, 757
The fifth-grade teacher and her followers—, 863
The fog comes, 784
The golf links lie so near the mill, 705
The houses are haunted, 742
The instructor said, 1022
The king sits in Dumferling toune, 679
The kingdom of heaven is likened unto a man which sowed good seed in his field, 896
The lanky hank of a she in the inn over there, 699
The lies I could tell, 693
The Lightning is a yellow Fork, 894
The Moving Finger writes, 955
The piercing chill I feel, 751
the poor, 935
The poorest countries, 1129
The readers of the *Boston Evening Transcript*, 893
The sea is calm to-night, 1061
The soldiers, 898
The Soul selects her own Society –, 1003
The splendor falls on castle walls, 817
The time you won your town the race, 1098
The tusks that clashed in mighty brawls, 983
The war—this year, 759
The way a tired Chippewa woman, 888
The wayfarer, 876
The whiskey on your breath, 687
The wind stood up, and gave a shout, 779
The winter evening settles down, 753
The world is, 1107
The world is charged with the grandeur of God, 822
The world is too much with us; late and soon, 909
Thee for my recitative, 690
There are no stars tonight, 1078
There is no Frigate like a Book, 1006
There ought to be capital punishment for cars, 979
There were three ravens sat on a tree, 1060
There's never an end to dust, 901
They eat beans mostly, this old yellow pair, 743
They flee from me that sometime did me sekë, 1143
They say that Richard Cory owns, 796
Thirty days hath September, 673
Thirty days in jail with my back turned to the wall, 802
this feverish scratch, 973
This is my letter to the World, 1004
This is the field where the battle did not happen, 708
This is the one song everyone, 1063
This living hand, now warm and capable, 850
This strange thing must have crept, 756
Thou ill-formed offspring of my feeble brain, 689
Thou still unravished bride of quietness, 1101
Thy Friendship oft has made my heart to ache, 861
Thy will be done, 723
Tired of earth, they dwindled on their hill, 917
To fling my arms wide, 1019
To see a world in a grain of sand, 775
Today I sniffed, 696
Today we have naming of parts. Yesterday, 1121
Tongi-ye may-e la'l kh'aham o divani, 954
Traveler, your footsteps are, 900
Traveling through the dark I found a deer, 980
Treason doth never prosper; what's the reason?, 861
True Ease in Writing comes from Art, not Chance, 811
Tu ne quaesieris—scire nefas—quem mihi, quem tibi, 952
Turning and turning in the widening gyre, 915
Twas brillig, and the slithy toves, 734
Two roads diverged in a yellow wood, 899
Tyger! Tyger! burning bright, 1068

Way Down South in Dixie, 1021
We dance round in a ring and suppose, 786
We four lads from Liverpool are—, 956
We lie back to back. Curtains, 785
We real cool. We, 833
We shall not ever meet them bearded in heaven, 1101
We stood by a pond that winter day, 895
We wear the mask that grins and lies, 992
We were very tired, we were very merry—, 1111
Welcome to ESL 100, English Surely Latinized, 733
Well, son, I'll tell you, 1018
We're trying to strike a match in a matchbook, 762
What, still alive at twenty-two, 956
What did we say to each other, 776
What happens to a dream deferred?, 1024
What lips my lips have kissed, and where, and why, 857
What passing-bells for these who die as cattle?, 1115

What thoughts I have of you tonight, Walt Whitman, 1088
When, in disgrace with Fortune and men's eyes, 1124
When first we met we did not guess, 865
When God at first made man, 782
When I consider how my light is spent, 1111
When I have fears that I may cease to be, 1103
When I see birches bend to left and right, 1085
When I take my girl to the swimming party, 1115
When I think of my youth I feel sorry not for myself, 943
When I was one-and-twenty, 842
When it is finally ours, this freedom, this liberty, this beautiful, 985
When maidens are young, and in their spring, 814
When my mother died I was very young, 706
When the medication she was taking, 1095
When the summer fields are mown, 721
When the time's toxins, 732
When to the sessions of sweet silent thought, 1125
When you are old and grey and full of sleep, 1145
Whenas in silks my Julia goes, 725
Whenever Richard Cory went down town, 795
While my hair was still cut straight across my forehead, 1119
Whirl up, sea—, 761
Who says you're like one of the dog days?, 772
Who will go drive with Fergus now, 813
Who would be a turtle who could help it?, 786
Whose woods these are I think I know, 1088
What are you staring at, mariner man, 842
Wild Nights – Wild Nights!, 1002
With eyes closed, 969

Yesterday, I lay awake in the palm of the night, 730
You, love, and I, 852
You always read about it, 919
You crash over the trees, 745
You do not do, you do not do, 1116
You do not have to be good, 901
you fit into me, 782
You know the parlor trick, 762
You would think the fury of aerial bombardment, 728
Your absence, father, is nothing. It is naught—, 860
Your ÿen two wol slee me sodenly, 1075

INDEX OF AUTHORS AND TITLES

Every page number immediately following a writer's name indicates a quotation from or reference to that writer. A number in **bold** refers you to the page on which you will find the author's biography.

A & P, 17
Abandoned Farmhouse, 1104
ABEYTA, AARON
thirteen ways of looking at a tortilla, 958
ACHEBE, CHINUA, **508**, 1177
Dead Men's Path, 508
Acquainted with the Night, 858
Actress, The, 862
ADAMS, RICHARD, 83
ADDONIZIO, KIM
First Poem for You, 859
Adolescents Singing, 1057
AESCHYLUS, 1176, 1200, 1205
AESOP, **7**, 199
Fox and the Grapes, The, 7
After great pain, a formal feeling comes, 1004
After weeks of watching the roof leak, 760
Aftermath, 721
AIKEN, CONRAD, 1044
ALARCÓN, FRANCISCO X., 933
Frontera / Border, 887
X in My Name, The, 935
ALDRICH, THOMAS BAILEY, 4
ALEXIE, SHERMAN, **511**
Powwow at the End of the World, The, 936
This Is What It Means to Say Phoenix, Arizona, 511
All day I hear, 816
ALLENDE, ISABEL, 359, **369**
Judge's Wife, The, 369
Alta Traición, 972
ALVAREZ, JULIA, 821
America, 933
American Primitive, 707
AMMONS, A. R.
Coward, 786
AMMONS, ELIZABETH
Biographical Echoes in "The Yellow Wallpaper," 490
Ancient Stairway, 870
ANDERSEN, HANS CHRISTIAN, 12
Anecdote of the Jar, 903
ANGELOU, MAYA, 791
Anger, 971
Annabel Lee, 993
ANONYMOUS
Bonny Barbara Allan, 797
Carnation Milk, 733
Dog Haiku, 696
Last Words of the Prophet, 1061
Little Poem Regarding Computer Spell-Checkers, A, 1907
Lord Randall, 1059
O Moon, when I gaze on thy beautiful face, 976
Sir Patrick Spence, 679
Three Ravens, The, 1060
We four lads from Liverpool are, 956
ANOUILH, JEAN, 1176
Anthem for Doomed Youth, 1115
Antigonê, 1245
anyone lived in a pretty how town, 729
Appointment in Samarra, The, 6
AQUINAS, THOMAS, 983
Araby, 571
ARISTOPHANES, 1185
ARISTOTLE, 1167, 1176, 1177, 1203-05, 1595, 1701
Defining Tragedy, 1274
ARMSTRONG, LOUIS, 670
ARNOLD, MATTHEW
Dover Beach, 1061
ARREDONDO, INÉS, 359, **375**
Shunammite, The, 375
Ars Poetica, 996
As I Walked Out One Evening, 1064
ASHBERY, JOHN
At North Farm, 1062
Asian Culture Looks at Shakespeare, An, 1577
Ask Me, 685
ASQUITH, CLARE
Shakespeare's Language as a Hidden Political Code, 1585
ASTURIAS, MIGUEL ÁNGEL, 357
At North Farm, 1062
At the Un-National Monument Along the Canadian Border, 708
ATWOOD, MARGARET, 83, 196, **519**
Happy Endings, 519
Siren Song, 1063
You fit into me, 782
Aubade, 944
AUDEN, W. H., 351, 819, 961, 997, 1887, 1970, 2035–36
As I Walked Out One Evening, 1064
Funeral Blues, 802
Iago as a Triumphant Villain, 1578
Musée des Beaux Arts, 1065
Unknown Citizen, The, 702
AUGUSTINE, 748

Aunt Jennifer's Tigers, 678
AUSTEN, JANE, 280
Author to Her Book, The, 689
Autumn Begins in Martins Ferry, Ohio, 1142

BACA, JIMMY SANTIAGO
Spliced Wire, 1066
BAKER, HOUSTON A.
Stylish vs. Sacred in "Everyday Use," 503
BALDWIN, JAMES, **58**, 2008-9
Race and the African American Writer, 79
Sonny's Blues, 58
Ballad of Birmingham, 800
Ballad of the Landlord, 1021
BALZAC, HONORÉ DE, 16, 84, 120
BAMBARA, TONI CADE, **2000**
Lesson, The, 2000
BAMBER, LINDA
Female Power in *A Midsummer Night's Dream*, 1587
BARABAN, ELENA V.
Motive for Murder in "The Cask of Amontillado," The, 414
Barn Burning, 170
BARTHES, ROLAND, 2041
Death of the Author, The, 2042
BASHO, MATSUO, 758, 759
Heat-lightning streak, 758
In the old stone pool, 758
Batter my heart, three-personed God, for You, 719
Battle Royal, 552
BAUDELAIRE, CHARLES
Poe's Characters, 416
BAUERLEIN, MARK
What Is Cultural Studies?, 2047
Bean Eaters, The, 743
Beat! Beat! Drums!, 843
BEATTIE, ANN, 165
Beauty (*Hoagland*), 1095
Beauty (*Martin*), 1759
BEAUVOIR, SIMONE DE, 2033
Because I Could Not Dump, 957
Because I could not stop for Death, 1005
BECKETT, SAMUEL, 1702
BEHN, APHRA
When maidens are young, 814
Being a Bilingual Writer, 946
BELLOC, HILAIRE
Fatigue, 862
Hippopotamus, The, 820
BERENDT, JOHN, 278
BERGSON, HENRI, 1184
BERRYMAN, JOHN
Prufrock's Dilemma, 1054
BETTELHEIM, BRUNO, 2021, 2023
BIBLE, 10, 239, 855, 872, 897, 908
Parable of the Good Seed, The, 896
Parable of the Prodigal Son, The, 230
BIDPAI, **8**
Camel and His Friends, The, 8
BIERCE, AMBROSE, 276, **522**
Occurrence at Owl Creek Bridge, An, 522
Bilingual/*Bilingüe*, 932
Biographical Echoes in "The Yellow Wallpaper," 490
Biography of a Story, 269
Birches, 1085
BISHOP, ELIZABETH, 720, 766-69, 931, 961, 998, 2013-14
Filling Station, 1067
Fish, The, 754
One Art, 985
Sestina, 865
Bitch, 939
Black and White in *Othello*, 1579
Black Identity in Langston Hughes, 1031
Black Woman Writer in America, The, 497
BLAKE, WILLIAM, 694, 741-42, 749, 818, 824, 832, 837, 914, 2015, 2049-50
Chimney Sweeper, The, 706
London, 741
Sick Rose, The, 1069
To H—, 861
To see a world in a grain of sand, 775
Tyger, The, 1068
Blandeur, 726
BLOCH, CHANA
Tired Sex, 762
BLOOM, HAROLD
Poetic Influence, 2024
BLY, ROBERT, 765, 858, 908, 2033
Cricket (*translation*), 759
Driving to Town Late to Mail a Letter, 762
BODKIN, MAUD
Lucifer in Shakespeare's *Othello*, 1579
BOGAN, LOUISE, 1036
Medusa, 912
Bonny Barbara Allan, 797
Book of Verses underneath the Bough, A, 954
BORGES, JORGE LUIS, 17, 196, 357, 359, **360**, 928, 964, **967**
Gospel According to Mark, The, 360
On his blindness, 968
Born Again, 760
Boston Evening Transcript, The, 893
BOSWELL, JAMES, 724
BOTTOME, PHYLLIS, 117
BOWLES, PAUL, 29
BOYLE, T. CORAGHESSAN, **529**
Greasy Lake, 529
BOZORTH, RICHARD R.
"Tell Me the Truth About Love," 2035
BRADBURY, RAY, **137**
Sound of Thunder, A, 137
BRADLEY, A. C.
Hamlet's Melancholy, 1580
BRADSTREET, ANNE, 689-90, 693
Author to Her Book, The, 689
Bread, 723
Break, Break, Break, 834
BRETON, ANDRÉ, 969
BRIDGES, LAWRENCE, 863
Two Poetweets, 863

BRIDGES, ROBERT
Triolet, 865
Brief Bio, 855
Bright Star, would I were steadfast as thou art, 760
broken bowl, 760
BRONTË, EMILY
Love and Friendship, 787
BROOKS, CLEANTH
Formalist Critic, The, 2006
BROOKS, GWENDOLYN, 975
Bean Eaters, The, 743
Hearing "We Real Cool," 845
mother, the, 1070
rites for Cousin Vit, the, 1071
Speech to the Young. Speech to the Progress-Toward, 692
We Real Cool, 833
BROOKS, MEL, 1735
Brownies, 38
BROWNING, ELIZABETH BARRETT
How Do I Love Thee? Let Me Count the Ways, 1071
BROWNING, ROBERT, 676, 681, 700, 831, 833, 839, 975, 2003, 2009-11
My Last Duchess, 682
Soliloquy of the Spanish Cloister, 1072
BRUEGEL, PIETER, 876, 1066, 1970
BRUTSCHY, JENNIFER
Born Again, 760
Buffalo Bill 's, 874
BUKOWSKI, CHARLES
Dostoevsky, 1074
BUNYAN, JOHN, 240, 897, 899
BURGESS, ANTHONY
Asian Culture Looks at Shakespeare, An, 1577
BURGON, JOHN, 780
BURNS, ROBERT, 789, 795, 819
Oh, my love is like a red, red rose, 787
BURROUGHS, WILLIAM, 280
BUSON, TANIGUCHI, 751-52, 758, 895
Moonrise on mudflats, 758
On the one-ton temple bell, 758
piercing chill I feel, The, 751
Butcher Shop, 1126
BYNNER, WITTER, 815
BYRON, GEORGE GORDON, LORD, 819, 836, 841, 978

Call to the Community, A, 1727
CALVINO, ITALO, 167
Camel and His Friends, The, 8
CAMERON, JAMES, 121
CAMP, JAMES, 956
CAMPBELL, JOSEPH, 2025
CAMPION, THOMAS, 794
CAMPO, RAFAEL
For J. W., 940
CAMUS, ALBERT, 85
Cannery Town in August, 1075
CAPOTE, TRUMAN, 278
Care and Feeding, 1078
Cargoes, 740
CARLYLE, THOMAS, 895
Carnation Milk, 733
"Carpe Diem" Ode, 952
CARPENTIER, ALEJO, 358
Carrie, 901
CARROLL, LEWIS [CHARLES LUTWIDGE DODGSON]
Humpty Dumpty Explicates "Jabberwocky," 735
Jabberwocky, 734
CARVER, RAYMOND, **105**, 165
Cathedral, 105
Commonplace but Precise Language, 116
Cask of Amontillado, The, 391
Cathedral, 105
CATHER, WILLA, 122, **536**
Paul's Case, 536
Cavalry Crossing a Ford, 876
CERVANTES, LORNA DEE
Cannery Town in August, 1075
Character of Mrs. Turpin in "Revelation," The, 467
CHARLES, DORTHI
Concrete Cat, 885
CHAUCER, GEOFFREY
Merciless Beauty, 1075
CHEEVER, JOHN, **249**, 2012
Swimmer, The, 249
CHEKHOV, ANTON, 16, 163-64, 895, 1595
CHESTERFIELD, PHILIP STANHOPE, LORD, 1595
CHESTERTON, G. K., 770, 781
CHILD, FRANCIS J., 797
Chimney Sweeper, The, 706
CHOPIN, KATE, 122, **123**, 196, 2014-15
Storm, The, 123
Story of an Hour, The, 549
Chorus as Democrat, The, 1278
CHRISTIAN, BARBARA T.
"Everyday Use" and the Black Power Movement, 499
Chrysanthemums, The, 242
CHUANG TZU, **11**
Independence, 11
CHURCHILL, CARYL, 1703
CIARDI, JOHN, 892, 933
Most Like an Arch This Marriage, 1076
CINDERELLA, 919
CINTHIO, GIRALDI, 1287
CISNEROS, SANDRA, **551**
House on Mango Street, The, 551
CLANCY, LAURIE, 236-37
CLARK, CHERYL
Convalescence (*translation*), 973
CLARK, MICHAEL
Light and Darkness in "Sonny's Blues," 2008
Clean, Well-Lighted Place, A, 167
CLEGHORN, SARAH N.
Golf Links, The, 705
CLIFTON, LUCILLE, 998
COFER, JUDITH ORTIZ
Quinceañera, 935

COLACURCIO, MICHAEL J.
End of Young Goodman Brown, The, 2040
COLE, WILLIAM
On my boat on Lake Cayuga, 818
COLERIDGE, SAMUEL, 673, 676, 724, 726, 779, 840, 997
Kubla Khan, 1076
Collective Unconscious and Archetypes, The, 2025
COLLINS, BILLY
Care and Feeding, 1078
Embrace, 762
Names, The, 730
COLLINS, WILLIAM, 779
Commonplace but Precise Language, 116
Composed upon Westminster Bridge, 1141
Con los ojos cerrados, 969
Concerning "Love Calls Us to the Things of This World," 748
Concrete Cat, 885
CONNOLLY, CYRIL, 276
CONRAD, JOSEPH, 164, 240
Contemplation, 862
Content Determines Form, 2030
Convalecencia, 973
Convalescence, 973
Convergence of the Twain, The, 1089
COOGLER, J. GORDON, 977
COPE, WENDY
Lonely Hearts, 728
Variation on Belloc's "Fatigue," 862
CORMAN, CID
only one guy (*translation*), 759
Correspondence on the Final Scene of *A Doll's House*, 1651
CORTÁZAR, JULIO, 358
Cosmos in bloom, 759
Costume in "The Cask of Amontillado," 414
Counting-out Rhyme, 841
Counting the Beats, 852
COWAN, LOUISE S.
Character of Mrs. Turpin in "Revelation," The, 467
Coward, 786
CRABBE, GEORGE, 851
CRANE, HART, 716
My Grandmother's Love Letters, 1078
CRANE, STEPHEN, 5, 122, **201**, 237, 276-77, 278
Open Boat, The, 201
Wayfarer, The, 876
Crazy Jane Talks with the Bishop, 1144
Creating *Trifles*, 1168
CREELEY, ROBERT, 701, 873
Oh No, 701
Cricket, 759
CROWE, ANNA
Swallows (*translation*), 973
Cuban Swimmer, The, 1703
CULLEN, COUNTEE, 934
For a Lady I Know, 688
CUMMINGS, E. E., 724, 781-82, 815, 1649
anyone lived in a pretty how town, 729
Buffalo Bill 's, 874
in Just-, 886
next to of course god america i, 744
somewhere i have never travelled,gladly beyond, 1079
CUNNINGHAM, J. V.
Friend, on this scaffold Thomas More lies dead, 723
Daddy, 1116
Dance, The, 875
DANTE (DANTE ALIGHIERI), 240, 852, 896, 997, 1177
Darkling Thrush, The, 1091
DAVIDSON, JOHN, 773-74
DAVIS, DICK
I Need a Bare Sufficiency (*translation*), 954
Daystar, 1083
DE CRISTOFORO, VIOLET KAZUE
Cosmos in bloom (*translation*), 759
Even the croaking of frogs (*translation*), 759
Rain shower from mountain (*translation*), 759
war—this year (*translation*), The, 759
DE LOS SANTOS, MARISA
Perfect Dress, 1080
DE MAN, PAUL, 2041
DE VRIES, PETER, 1933
Dead Men's Path, 508
DEANE, SEAMUS
Joyce's Vision of Dublin, 2017
Death be not proud, 1081
Death of a Salesman, 1764
Death of Ivan Ilych, The, 280
Death of the Author, The, 2042
Death of the Ball Turret Gunner, The, 1099
Deathly, 805
Deconstructing "A Good Man Is Hard to Find," 466
Defining Tragedy, 1274
DEFOE, DANIEL, 5, 277
DEGAS, EDGAR, 716
DENHAM, JOHN, 851
DERRIDA, JACQUES, 2042
Description of the Morning, A, 1131
Desert Places, 822
Design, 1934
Destiny of Oedipus, The, 1275
DEUTSCH, BABETTE, 1045
falling flower (*translation*), The, 757
DICK, PHILIP K., 280
DICKENS, CHARLES, 83, 84
DICKINSON, EMILY, 698, 778, 799, 812, 836, 895, 957, 997, 1000, **1001**, 1008-16, 2029
After great pain, a formal feeling comes, 1004
Because I could not stop for Death, 1005
Dying Tiger – moaned for Drink, A, 977
I felt a Funeral, in my Brain, 1002
I heard a Fly buzz – when I died, 1005
I like to see it lap the Miles, 690
I taste a liquor never brewed, 1002
I'm Nobody! Who are you?, 1003
It dropped so low – in my Regard, 776

Lightning is a yellow Fork, The, 894
Much Madness is divinest Sense, 1004
My Life had stood – a Loaded Gun, 774
Recognizing Poetry, 1006
Route of Evanescence, A, 756
Self-Description, 1007
Some keep the Sabbath going to Church, 1003
Soul selects her own Society, The, 1003
Success is counted sweetest, 1001
Tell all the Truth but tell it slant, 1006
There is no Frigate like a Book, 1006
This is my letter to the World, 1004
Wild Nights – Wild Nights!, 1002
Dickinson and Death, 1012
Different Image, A, 1120
Difficulty of Poetry, The, 1047
Digging, 1092
Dim Lady, 957
DINESEN, ISAK, 810-11
Direct Style, The, 195
DISCH, M. THOMAS, 280
Discovery of Emily Dickinson's Manuscripts, The, 1010
Discussing *The Metamorphosis*, 348
Disillusionment of Ten O'Clock, 742
Do not go gentle into that good night, 864
Doctor Faustus, 1178
DODDS, E. R.
On Misunderstanding Oedipus, 1276
Dog Haiku, 696
Doll's House, A, 1598
DONNE, JOHN, 830, 837
Batter my heart, three-personed God, for You, 719
Death be not proud, 1081
Flea, The, 1081
Song, 854
Valediction: Forbidding Mourning, A, 1082
DONOGHUE, DENIS
One of the Irrefutable Poets, 1049
DONOSO, JOSÉ, 358
Doo Wop, 825
DOOLITTLE, HILDA. *See* H.D.
Dostoevsky, 1074
DOVE, RITA
Daystar, 1083
Voices in Langston Hughes, The, 1029
Dover Beach, 1061
Down, Wanton, Down!, 718
DRAYTON, MICHAEL
Since there's no help, come let us kiss and part, 857
Dream Boogie, 844
Dream Deferred. *See* Harlem
Dream Variations, 1019
Dream within a Dream, A, 1118
DREISER, THEODORE, 122, 278
DREW, ELIZABETH, 1995
Drinking Alone Beneath the Moon, 951
Drinking Alone by Moonlight, 951
Driving to Town Late to Mail a Letter, 762
DRURY, JOHN, 904
DRYDEN, JOHN, 841, 852, 978
Dulce et Decorum Est, 709
DUNBAR, PAUL LAURENCE, 677
We Wear the Mask, 992
DYER, JOHN, 683-84, 781, 979
Dying Tiger – moaned for Drink, A, 977
DYLAN, BOB, 795
Term "Protest Singer" Didn't Exist, The, 807
Times They Are a-Changin', The, 804

Eagle, The, 771
Easter Wings, 882
EASTHOPE, ANTHONY, 2046
EBERHART, RICHARD
Fury of Aerial Bombardment, The, 728
Economics of Zora Neale Hurston's "Sweat," The, 2019
Eight O'Clock, 816
EISLER, RACHEL, 831
El Hombre, 761
El Santo Americano, 1754
Elegy, 2038
Elegy for Jane, 1124
Elegy for My Father, Who Is Not Dead, 944
ELIOT, GEORGE, 163, 276
ELIOT, T. S., 674, 681, 689, 718, 722, 726, 795, 873, 893, 908, 914, 916, 997, **1037**, 1042-46, 1049-57, 1993-94
Boston Evening Transcript, The, 893
Difficulty of Poetry, The, 1047
Journey of the Magi, 1084
Love Song of J. Alfred Prufrock, The, 1038
Music of Poetry, The, 826
Objective Correlative, The, 1047
Poetry and Emotion, 1046
Virginia, 826
winter evening settles down, The, 753
ELLINGTON, DUKE, 840
ELLISON, RALPH, **552**
Battle Royal, 552
ELLMANN, MAUD
Will There Be Time?, 1052
Embrace, 762
EMERSON, RALPH WALDO, 5, 720
Emperor of Ice-Cream, The, 1131
End of Young Goodman Brown, The, 2040
English con Salsa, 733
Epitaph, 744
Eskimo "A Rose for Emily," An, 2037
ESPAILLAT, RHINA, 932, 933
Being a Bilingual Writer, 946
Bilingual/*Bilingüe*, 932
ESSBAUM, JILL ALEXANDER
Heart, The, 776
EURIPIDES, 1176, 1203, 1205
EVANS, ABBIE HUSTON, 1948-50
Wing-Spread, 1948
Even the croaking of frogs, 759
Everyday Use, 491
"Everyday Use" and the Black Power Movement, 499
"Everyday Use" as a Portrait of the Artist, 502

Ex-Basketball Player, 1135
Excerpt from "On Her Own Work": Insights into "A Good Man Is Hard to Find," 458
Excerpt from "The Grotesque in Southern Fiction": The Serious Writer and the Tired Reader, 461

Facing It, 937
Fairy Tale Motifs in "Where Are You Going, Where Have You Been?," 2022
Fall of the House of Usher, The, 397
falling flower, The, 757
Farm on the Great Plains, The, 1130
FARR, JUDITH
  Reading of "My Life had stood – a Loaded Gun," A, 1014
Father-Figure in "The Tell-Tale Heart," The, 412
Fatigue, 862
FAULKNER, WILLIAM, 16, 29, 30, **31**, 84, 121, 122, 165, 166, 170, 196, 200, 240, 241, 895, 1925-27, 2027-29, 2037
  Barn Burning, 170
  Rose for Emily, A, 31
Fear no more the heat o' the sun, 794
FEELEY, KATHLEEN
  Mystery of Divine Direction: "Parker's Back," The, 469
FEHLER, GENE
  If Richard Lovelace Became a Free Agent, 958
Female Power in *A Midsummer Night's Dream*, 1587
Fences, 1833
Fern Hill, 1134
FERRIS, WILLIAM R., 499
FEYDEAU, GEORGES, 1186
FIEDLER, LESLIE
  Relationship of Poet and Poem, The, 2012
FIELDING, HENRY, 84, 279
FIELDS, W. C., 117
Filling Station, 1067
FINCH, ANNIE, 832
Fire and Ice, 744
First Love: A Quiz, 918
First Poem for You, 859
FISH, STANLEY
  Eskimo "A Rose for Emily," An, 2037
Fish, The, 754
FITTS, DUDLEY
  Antigonê (*translation*), 1245
  Oedipus the King (*translation*), 1207
FITZGERALD, EDWARD, 953, 954
  Book of Verses underneath the Bough (*translation*), A, 954
  Rubaiyat (*translation*), 954
FITZGERALD, F. SCOTT, 28, 239, 1176, 2012
FITZGERALD, ROBERT
  Antigonê (*translation*), 1245
  Oedipus the King (*translation*), 1207
  Translating Sophocles into English, 1281
FLAUBERT, GUSTAVE, 27, 999
Flea, The, 1081
FLEENOR, JULIANN
  Gender and Pathology in "The Yellow Wallpaper," 486
FLOWER, DEAN
  Listening to Flannery O'Connor, 470
Flower in the Crannied Wall, 775
Fog, 784
FOLEY, ADELLE
  Learning to Shave, 760
FOLEY, JACK, 874
For a Lady I Know, 688
For I will consider my Cat Jeoffry, 1127
For J. W., 940
For Malcolm X, 1137
For My Daughter, 692
For the Anniversary of My Death, 874
Fork, 756
Formalist Critic, The, 2007
FORSTER, E. M., 84, 279
FOUCAULT, MICHEL, 2041
FOWLES, JOHN, 716
Fox and the Grapes, The, 7
FRAYN, MICHAEL, 1185, 1717
FRAZER, SIR JAMES, 908
Frederick Douglass, 985
Freedom of Emily Dickinson, The, 1015
FREUD, SIGMUND, 85, 905, 907, 2021-22
  Destiny of Oedipus, The, 1275
  Nature of Dreams, The, 2022
FREYTAG, GUSTAV, 1167
FRIEDMAN, ALBERT B., 799
Friend, on this scaffold Thomas More lies dead, 723
Frontera / Border, 887
FROST, ROBERT, 670, 780, 824, 836, 839, 847, 849, 871, 917, 949, 996, 997, 1890-93, 1896-97, 1903-05, 1936-38, 1942-45, 1946-47, 1948-50
  Acquainted with the Night, 858
  Birches, 1085
  Desert Places, 822
  Design, 1934
  Fire and Ice, 744
  Importance of Poetic Metaphor, The, 788
  In White, 1953
  Mending Wall, 1087
  Nothing Gold Can Stay, 909, 1888
  "Out, Out—," 680
  Road Not Taken, The, 899
  Secret Sits, The, 786
  Silken Tent, The, 785
  Stopping by Woods on a Snowy Evening, 1088
FRY, CHRISTOPHER, 998
FRYE, NORTHROP, 911, 2025
  Mythic Archetypes, 2026
FUENTES, CARLOS, 358
FULTON, ALICE
  What I Like, 889
Funeral Blues, 802
Fury of Aerial Bombardment, The, 728
FUSSELL, PAUL, 840

García Márquez, Gabriel, 17, 358, 359, **364**
My Beginnings as a Writer, 383
Very Old Man with Enormous Wings, A, 364
Garden, The, 877
Garnett, Constance
Death of Ivan Ilych (*translation*), The, 280
Gascoigne, George, 720
Gass, William, 84
Gay, Garry
Hole in the ozone, 760
Gay, John, 795
Gender and Pathology in "The Yellow Wallpaper," 486
Gift of the Magi, The, 184
Gilbert, Sandra M., 2033
Freedom of Emily Dickinson, The, 1015
Imprisonment and Escape: The Psychology of Confinement, 488
Giles, Herbert
Independence (*translation*), 11
Gilgamesh, 678
Gilman, Charlotte Perkins, **472**, 486-90
Nervous Breakdown of Women, The, 485
Whatever Is, 485
Why I Wrote "The Yellow Wallpaper," 484
Yellow Wallpaper, The, 473
Gilman, Richard, 1703
Ginsberg, Allen, 873
Supermarket in California, A, 1088
Gioia, Dana
Godfather Death (*translation*), 12
Money, 783
Girl, 576
Glaspell, Susan, **1153**, 1164-68, 1170-75, 1885, 1956, 1959-60, 1962
Creating *Trifles*, 1168
Trifles, 1153
Glass Menagerie, The, 1649
Glass of Beer, A, 699
Go, Lovely Rose, 1137
Godfather Death, 12
God's Grandeur, 822
Goethe, Johann Wolfgang von, 278, 687
Hamlet as a Hero Unfit for his Destiny, 1584
Gogol, Nikolai, 358
Golf Links, The, 705
Golondrinas, 972
Gómez de la Serna, Ramón, 884
Simultaneous Translations, 884
Good Man Is Hard to Find, A, 387
Good Source Is Not So Hard to Find: The Real Life Misfit, A, 463
Gorky, Maxim, 1595
Gospel According to Mark, The, 360
Gosse, Sir Edmund, 976
Grass, 723
Graves, Robert, 121, 278, 915
Counting the Beats, 852
Down, Wanton, Down!, 718
Gray, Thomas, 839
Greasy Lake, 529
Greer, Germaine
Shakespeare's "Honest Mirth," 1586
Grigson, Geoffrey, 955
Grimm, Jakob and Wilhelm, **12**, 14-16, 27, 29
Godfather Death, 12
Grosholz, Emily, 778
Guare, John, 1185
Gubar, Susan
Freedom of Emily Dickinson, The, 1015
Imprisonment and Escape: The Psychology of Confinement, 488
Guest, Edgar A., 978
Guiterman, Arthur
On the Vanity of Earthly Greatness, 983
Gwynn, R. S., 821
Shakespearean Sonnet, 861
Gylys, Beth, 778

H.D. [Hilda Doolittle], 758, 924-27
Helen, 910
Oread, 761
Storm, 745
Haaland, Tami
Lipstick, 902
Hadas, Rachel, 818
Haigh, A. E.
Irony of Sophocles, The, 1277
Hamilton, Edith, 908, 1199
Hamlet, Prince of Denmark, 1396
Hamlet and Ophelia, 1581
Hamlet as a Fictional Character, 1584
Hamlet as a Hero Unfit for his Destiny, 1584
Hamlet's Melancholy, 1580
Hammett, Dashiell, 29
Hands, 780
Hansen, Ron, 121
Hap, 1092
Happy Endings, 519
Hardy, Thomas, 183, 681, 701, 978, 997
Convergence of the Twain, The, 1089
Darkling Thrush, The, 1091
Hap, 1092
Neutral Tones, 895
Ruined Maid, The, 727
Workbox, The, 705
Harjo, Joy, 998
Mourning Song, 881
Hark, hark, the lark, 825
Harlem [Dream Deferred], 1024
Harlem Renaissance, The, 1026
Harrington, Sir John
Of Treason, 861
Harrison Bergeron, 231
Harter, Penny
broken bowl, 760
Hartman, Geoffrey
On Wordsworth's "A Slumber Did My Spirit Seal," 2043
Hate Poem, 704
Haunted House, A, 665
Hawk Roosting, 696

HAWTHORNE, NATHANIEL, **92**, 120, 239, 276, 278, 2040-41
Young Goodman Brown, 92
HAYDEN, ROBERT, 934, 984
Frederick Douglass, 985
Those Winter Sundays, 677
HEADINGS, PHILIP R.
Pronouns in the Poem: "One," "You," and "I," The, 1051
HEANEY, SEAMUS
Digging, 1092
Hearing "We Real Cool," 845
Heart, The, 776
HEATH, STEPHEN
Death of the Author (*translation*), The, 2042
Heat-lightning streak, 758
HECHT, ANTHONY
Vow, The, 1093
Helen, 910
HELPRIN, MARK, 358
HEMINGWAY, ERNEST, 166, **167**, 183, 196, 199-200, 240, 276
Clean, Well-Lighted Place, A, 167
Direct Style, The, 195
HENDERSON, HAROLD G.
piercing chill I feel (*translation*), The, 751
HENLEY, BETH, 1702
HENRY, O. [WILLIAM SYDNEY PORTER], **184**
Gift of the Magi, The, 184
Her Kind, 699
HERBERT, GEORGE, 882, 892
Easter Wings, 882
Love, 1094
Pulley, The, 782
Redemption, 897
HERRICK, ROBERT, 725, 793, 818
To the Virgins, to Make Much of Time, 1095
Upon Julia's Clothes, 725
HERSEY, JOHN, 278
HIGGINSON, THOMAS WENTWORTH
Meeting Emily Dickinson, 1008
High Treason, 972
HILMI, ALI, 979
Hippopotamus, The, 820
HITCHCOCK, ALFRED, 831, 1150
HOAGLAND, TONY
Beauty, 1095
HOFFMAN, DANIEL
Father-Figure in "The Tell-Tale Heart," The, 412
Hole in the ozone, 760
HOLLANDER, JOHN
Swan and Shadow, 883
Home is so Sad, 1105
Homecoming, 1024
HOMER, 84, 275, 678
HOOD, THOMAS, 781, 820, 838
HOPKINS, GERARD MANLEY, 673, 677, 724, 981, 997
God's Grandeur, 822
Pied Beauty, 757
Spring and Fall, 1097
Windhover, The, 1097
HORACE, 952-53, 997
"Carpe Diem" Ode, 952
Horace to Leuconoë, 952
New Year's Toast, A, 953
Horace to Leuconoë, 952
House on Mango Street, The, 551
HOUSMAN, A. E., 687, 799, 956
Eight O'Clock, 816
Loveliest of trees, the cherry now, 1098
To an Athlete Dying Young, 1098
When I was one-and-twenty, 842
How Do I Love Thee? Let Me Count the Ways, 1071
"How Do We Make a Poem?," 2038
How I Met My Husband, 218
How to Stage *The Glass Menagerie*, 1700
HOWE, TINA, 1185, 1703
HUDGINS, ANDREW
Elegy for My Father, Who Is Not Dead, 944
HUGHES, LANGSTON, 934, 1000, **1017**, 1028-35
Ballad of the Landlord, 1021
Dream Boogie, 844
Dream Variations, 1019
Dream Deferred. *See* Harlem
Harlem [Dream Deferred], 1024
Harlem Renaissance, The, 1026
Homecoming, 1024
I, Too, 1019
Mother to Son, 1018
My People, 1018
Negro Artist and the Racial Mountain, The, 1025
Negro Speaks of Rivers, The, 1017
Nightmare Boogie, 1023
Prayer ("Gather up"), 1021
Song for a Dark Girl, 1021
Theme for English B, 1022
Two Somewhat Different Epigrams, 862
Weary Blues, The, 1020
HUGHES, TED, 928
Hawk Roosting, 696
Hughes as an Experimentalist, 1028
HULL, R. F. C.
Collective Unconscious and Archetypes (*translation*), The, 2025
Humpty Dumpty Explicates "Jabberwocky," 735
HURLEY, ANDREW
Gospel According to Mark (*translation*), The, 360
HURSTON, ZORA NEALE, 200, 497-98, **562**, 2019-21
Sweat, 562
Hurt Locker, The, 942
Hush, 888
HWANG, DAVID HENRY, 1703, **1738**
Multicultural Theater, 1752
Sound of a Voice, The, 1738

I, Too, 1019
I felt a Funeral, in my Brain, 1002
I Hear America Singing, 1138
I heard a Fly buzz – when I died, 1005
I like to see it lap the Miles, 690

I Need a Bare Sufficiency, 954
I Shall Paint My Nails Red, 887
I taste a liquor never brewed, 1002
I Wandered Lonely as a Cloud, 697
Iago as a Triumphant Villain, 1578
IBSEN, HENRIK, 1152, 1165, 1595, 1596, **1598**, 1729, 1730-32
  Correspondence on the Final Scene of *A Doll's House*, 1651
  Doll's House, A, 1598
If Richard Lovelace Became a Free Agent, 958
I'm Nobody! Who are you?, 1003
Image, The, 764
Imagism, 2016
Importance of Poetic Metaphor, The, 788
Imprisonment and Escape: The Psychology of Confinement, 488
In a Station of the Metro, 751, 2016
in Just-, 886
In Memoriam John Coltrane, 824
In My Craft or Sullen Art, 990
In the old stone pool, 758
In this strange labyrinth, 1142
In White, 1953
Independence, 11
"Indeterminacy" in Eliot's Poetry, 1053
INNAURATO, ALBERT, 1702
Interpreter of Maladies, 577
IONESCO, EUGÈNE, 1702, 1735
Irony of Sophocles, The, 1277
ISOU, ISIDORE, 811
ISSA, KOBAYASHI, 758
  Cricket, 759
  only one guy, 759
It dropped so low – in my Regard, 776
IVES, DAVID, 1147-49, **1186**
  On the One-Act Play, 1196
  Sure Thing, 1186
  Talking With David Ives, 1148

Jabberwocky, 734
JACKSON, SHIRLEY, 200, **262**
  Biography of a Story, 269
  Lottery, The, 262
Jailhouse Blues, 802
JAMES, HENRY, 31, 239, 280, 895
JAMES, WILLIAM, 30
JARMAN, MARK, 821
  Unholy Sonnet: After the Praying, 859
JARRELL, RANDALL, 1944-45
  Death of the Ball Turret Gunner, The, 1099
JEFFERS, ROBINSON
  Hands, 780
  Rock and Hawk, 1099
JEMIE, ONWUCHEKWA
  Reading of "Dream Deferred," A, 1033
Jilting of Granny Weatherall, The, 85
JIN, HA
  Missed Time, 1100
JOHNSON, BARBARA
  Rigorous Unreliability, 2042
JOHNSON, JAMES WELDON, 801, 813, 934
  Sence You Went Away, 793
JOHNSON, SAMUEL, 683, 724, 781, 881, 997
JOHNSON, THOMAS H.
  Discovery of Emily Dickinson's Manuscripts, The, 1010
JOHNSON-DAVIES, DENYS
  Lawsuit (*translation*), The, 612
JONES, V. S. VERNON
  Fox and the Grapes (*translation*), The, 7
JONSON, BEN, 791-92
  On His Friend and Rival William Shakespeare, 1588
  On My First Son, 1100
  Slow, slow, fresh fount, keep time with my salt tears, 834
  To Celia, 792
JOSEPH, CHIEF, 998-99
Journal Entry, 698
Journey of the Magi, 1084
JOYCE, JAMES, 16, 30, 84, 122, 200, 240, 278, **571**, 2017-19
  All day I hear, 816
  Araby, 571
Joyce's Vision of Dublin, 2017
Judge's Wife, The, 369
JUNG, CARL, 907, 911, 2021, 2025
  Collective Unconscious and Archetypes, The, 2025
JUSTICE, DONALD
  Men at Forty, 941
  On the Death of Friends in Childhood, 1101

KAFKA, FRANZ, 85, 276, **318**, 348-53, 357, 2034-35
  Discussing *The Metamorphosis*, 348
  Metamorphosis, The, 318
KAHLO, FRIDA, 964, 970
  Two Fridas, The, 970
KAUFMAN, BOB
  No More Jazz at Alcatraz, 820
KAZIN, ALFRED
  Walt Whitman and Abraham Lincoln, 2032
KEATS, JOHN, 752, 779, 799, 836
  Bright Star, would I were steadfast as thou art, 760
  La Belle Dame sans Merci, 912
  Ode on a Grecian Urn, 1101
  Ode to a Nightingale, 986
  This living hand, now warm and capable, 850
  To Autumn, 1103
  When I have fears that I may cease to be, 1103
KEELER, GREG, 831
KEES, WELDON, 1978-79, 2011, 2015-16
  For My Daughter, 692
KENNEDY, X. J.
  Heat-lightning streak (*translation*), 758
  In the old stone pool (*translation*), 758
  On the one-ton temple bell (*translation*), 758
  To the Muse, 672
KENNER, HUGH
  Imagism, 2016

KENYON, JANE
Suitor, The, 785
KHANWALKAR, ARUNDHATI
Camel and His Friends (*translation*), The, 8
KHAYYAM, OMAR, 953-54
Book of Verses underneath the Bough, A, 954
I Need a Bare Sufficiency, 954
Rubai XII, 954
Rubaiyat, 954
KIM, SUJI KWOCK
Occupation, 898
KINCAID, JAMAICA, **576**
Girl, 576
KINGSMILL, HUGH
What, still alive at twenty-two?, 956
KIPLING, RUDYARD, 804, 836
KIZER, CAROLYN
Bitch, 939
KNIGHT, ETHERIDGE
Making jazz swing in, 760
KOCH, KENNETH, 873
KOMUNYAKAA, YUSEF
Facing It, 937
KOOSER, TED
Abandoned Farmhouse, 1104
Carrie, 901
KOSTELANETZ, RICHARD, 884
Simultaneous Translations, 884
KOTT, JAN
Producing *Hamlet*, 1582
Kubla Khan, 1076
KUSHNER, TONY, 1703
KYD, THOMAS, 1393

La Belle Dame sans Merci, 912
La cólera que quiebra al hombre en niños, 971
Lady Lazarus, 929
LAHIRI, JHUMPA, 240, **577**
Interpreter of Maladies, 577
LAKE, PAUL, 821
Lake Isle of Innisfree, The, 675
LANGBAUM, ROBERT
On Robert Browning's "My Last Duchess," 2009
Langston Hughes and Jazz, 1032
LARKIN, PHILIP, 778
Aubade, 944
Home is so Sad, 1105
Poetry of Departures, 1106
Last Words of the Prophet, 1061
Late Blues, 803
LAWRENCE, D. H., 275, **592**, 2030-31
Piano, 1107
Rocking-Horse Winner, The, 592
Lawsuit, The, 612
LAZARUS, EMMA
New Colossus, The, 992
LE GUIN, URSULA K., **257**
Ones Who Walk Away from Omelas, The, 257
LEAR, EDWARD, 815, 862
Learning to love America, 1108
Learning to Shave, 760
LEAVIS, F. R., 358
LEAVITT, DAVID, **602**
Place I've Never Been, A, 602
Leda and the Swan, 821
LEE, EDWARD BOK, **1754**
El Santo Americano, 1754
On Being a Korean American Writer, 1758
LEECH, CLIFFORD, 1204
LEHMAN, DAVID, 2041
Rejection Slip, 708
LEITCH, VINCENT B.
Poststructuralist Cultural Critique, 2046
LEMAITRE, GEORGE, 773
LESSING, DORIS, 907
Lesson, The, 2000
Let me not to the marriage of true minds, 856
LEVERTOV, DENISE, 870-71, 998, 1991
Ancient Stairway, 870
O Taste and See, 1107
LEVIN, PHILLIS
Brief Bio, 855
LI PO, 950-51
Drinking Alone Beneath the Moon, 950-51
Light and Darkness in "Sonny's Blues," 2008
LIGHTMAN, ALAN, 773
Lightning is a yellow Fork, The, 894
LIM, SHIRLEY GEOK-LIN, 933
Learning to love America, 1108
Riding Into California, 934
LINCOLN, ABRAHAM, 872, 2032
LINDNER, APRIL
Low Tide, 786
LINES, PATRICIA M.
What Is Antigonê's Tragic Flaw?, 1278
Lipstick, 902
Listening to Flannery O'Connor, 470
little Learning is a dang'rous Thing, A, 1119
Little Poem Regarding Computer Spell-Checkers, A, 1907
Living in Sin, 1122
LLOSA, MARIO VARGAS, 358
London, 741
LONDON, JACK, 122, **127**, 183, 276, 2029
To Build a Fire, 127
Lonely Hearts, 728
Long Poem Does Not Exist, A, 994
LONGFELLOW, HENRY WADSWORTH, 678, 778, 837
Aftermath, 721
Look Into Black America, A, 1883
Lord Randall, 1059
Lottery, The, 262
Love, 1094
Love and Friendship, 787
Love Calls Us to the Things of This World, 746
Love Song of J. Alfred Prufrock, The, 1038
LOVELACE, RICHARD, 955, 958
To Lucasta, 709
Loveliest of trees, the cherry now, 1098
Low Pay Piecework, 863
Low Tide, 786
LOWELL, JAMES RUSSELL, 1887

LOWELL, ROBERT, 929, 949
Skunk Hour, 1108
LOWES, JOHN LIVINGSTON, 976
LOY, MINA, 997
LUCAS, GEORGE, 916
Lucifer in Shakespeare's *Othello*, 1579
LUCRETIUS, 683
LUKACS, GEORG, 2029
Content Determines Form, 2030
LUKE, **230**
Parable of the Prodigal Son, The, 230
Luke Havergal, 695

MACDONALD, DWIGHT, 740, 955
MACHADO, ANTONIO, 973
Traveler, 900
MACLEISH, ARCHIBALD, 997
Ars Poetica, 996
Madness in Poe's "The Fall of the House of Usher," 418
MAETERLINCK, MAURICE, 1597
Magi, The, 1144
Magic Study of Happiness, The, 881
MAHFOUZ, NAGUIB, **612**
Lawsuit, The, 612
MAILER, NORMAN, 278
MAJMUDAR, AMIT
Rites to Allay the Dead, 860
Making jazz swing in, 760
MALLARMÉ, STÉPHANE, 716, 739
MAMET, DAVID, 1702
MANGUEL, ALBERTO
Shunammite (*translation*), The, 375
MANN, AIMEE
Deathly, 805
MANN, THOMAS, 1966
MANSFIELD, KATHERINE, **102**, 1925-27
Miss Brill, 102
Mariner Man, 842
MARKHAM, EDWIN
Outwitted, 898
MARLOWE, CHRISTOPHER, 832-33, 839, 984, **1178**
Doctor Faustus, 1178
MÁRQUEZ, GABRIEL GARCÍA. *See* GARCÍA MÁRQUEZ, GABRIEL
Martian Sends a Postcard Home, A, 777
MARTIN, CHARLES, 821
Taken Up, 917
MARTIN, JANE, **1759**
Beauty, 1759
MARVELL, ANDREW, 689, 720, 780, 836
To His Coy Mistress, 1110
MARX, GROUCHO, 1185
MASEFIELD, JOHN, 740-41
Cargoes, 740
MASON, BOBBIE ANN, 165, **616**
Shiloh, 616
MASON, DAVID
Song of the Powers, 844
MATSUSHITA, SUIKO
Cosmos in bloom, 759
Rain shower from mountain, 759
MATTHEW
Parable of the Good Seed, The, 896
MATTHEWS, WASHINGTON
Last Words of the Prophet (*translation*), 1061
MAUGHAM, W. SOMERSET, 7, 122, 183
Appointment in Samarra, The, 6
MAUPASSANT, GUY DE, 16
MCEWAN, IAN, 121
MCINERNEY, JAY, 30
MCKAY, CLAUDE, 933, 934
America, 933
MCKUEN, ROD
Thoughts on Capital Punishment, 979
Medusa, 912
Meeting Emily Dickinson, 1008
MELVILLE, HERMAN, 84-85, 199, 239, 241, 781, 892, 895
Men at Forty, 941
MENASHE, SAMUEL
Bread, 723
Mending Wall, 1087
Merciless Beauty, 1075
MERTON, THOMAS
Anger (*translation*), 971
MERWIN, W. S., 2038-40
Elegy, 2038
For the Anniversary of My Death, 874
Metamorphosis, The, 318
Metaphors, 775
Method of Translation, The, 960
MEZEY, ROBERT
On His Blindness (*translation*), 968
MICHENER, JAMES A., 277
Mid-August at Sourdough Mountain, 762
MIDDLEBROOK, DIANE, 2021
Midsummer Night's Dream, A, 1512
MILES, JOSEPHINE, 2011
MILLAY, EDNA ST. VINCENT, 928
Counting-out Rhyme, 841
Recuerdo, 1111
Second Fig, 705
What lips my lips have kissed, and where, and why, 857
MILLER, ARTHUR, 1596, **1764**
Death of a Salesman, 1764
Tragedy and the Common Man, 1831
MILLETT, KATE, 2033
MILLIER, BRETT C.
On Elizabeth Bishop's "One Art," 2013
MILLS, TEDI LÓPEZ
Convalecencia, 973
MILTON, JOHN, 684, 726, 781, 811, 815, 850, 858, 895, 975, 984
When I consider how my light is spent, 1111
Mind-Body Problem, 943
Minefield, The, 745
Miniver Cheevy, 1123
Miss Brill, 102
Missed Time, 1100
Mockingbird, 721
MOLIÈRE (JEAN-BAPTISTE POQUELIN), 681

MOMADAY, N. SCOTT
Simile, 776
Money, 783
Money and Labor in "The Rocking-Horse Winner," 2030
Moonrise on mudflats, 758
MOORE, MARIANNE, 770, 1045
Poetry, 1112
Silence, 718
MOORE, THOMAS, 823
MORITAKE, ARAKIDA
falling flower, The, 757
MOSS, HOWARD
Shall I Compare Thee to a Summer's Day?, 772
Most Like an Arch This Marriage, 1076
mother, the, 1070
MOTHER GOOSE, 830, 837, 840
Mother to Son, 1018
Motive for Murder in "The Cask of Amontillado," The, 414
Mourning Song, 881
MOWERY, CARL
Madness in Poe's "The Fall of the House of Usher," 418
Much Madness is divinest Sense, 1004
Muchos Somos, 966
MULLEN, HARRYETTE
Dim Lady, 957
Multicultural Theater, 1752
MUNRO, ALICE, **218**
How I Met My Husband, 218
Musée des Beaux Arts, 1065
Music of Poetry, The, 826
My Beginnings as a Writer, 383
My Grandmother's Love Letters, 1078
My Last Duchess, 682
My Life had stood – a Loaded Gun, 774
My mistress' eyes are nothing like the sun, 1126
My Papa's Waltz, 687
My People, 1018
My Shoes, 784
Mystery of Divine Direction: "Parker's Back," The, 469
Myth in Faulkner's "Barn Burning," 2027
Mythic Archetypes, 2026

NABOKOV, VLADIMIR, 933
Names, The, 730
Naming of Parts, 1121
NASHE, THOMAS, 717
Nature of Dreams, The, 2022
Negro Artist and the Racial Mountain, The, 1025
Negro Speaks of Rivers, The, 1017
NELSON, MARILYN, 821
Strange Beautiful Woman, A, 1113
Voices in Langston Hughes, The, 1029
NEMEROV, HOWARD
War in the Air, The, 1113
NERUDA, PABLO, 964, **965**, 974
Muchos Somos, 966
Nervous Breakdown of Women, The, 485
Neutral Tones, 895
New Colossus, The, 992
New Year's Toast, A, 953
NEWTON, JOHN, 799
next to of course god america i, 744
NIEDECKER, LORINE
Popcorn-can cover, 903
Sorrow Moves in Wide Ways, 1114
Nightmare Boogie, 1023
NIMS, JOHN FREDERICK, 866
Contemplation, 862
No More Jazz at Alcatraz, 820
NORMAN, MARSHA, 1703
Not Waving but Drowning, 763
Nothing Gold Can Stay, 909, 1888

O Captain! My Captain!, 989
O Moon, when I gaze on thy beautiful face, 976
O Taste and See, 1107
OATES, JOYCE CAROL, 16, **626**, 1973-74, 1975, 2022-24
Where Are You Going, Where Have You Been?, 626
Objective Correlative, The, 1047
O'BRIEN, JOHN, 497
O'BRIEN, TIM, **637**, 1929-30
Things They Carried, The, 637
Occupation, 898
Occurrence at Owl Creek Bridge, An, 522
O'CONNOR, FLANNERY, **419**, 463-70, 1997-98
Excerpt from "On Her Own Work": Insights into "A Good Man Is Hard to Find," 458
Excerpt from "The Grotesque in Southern Fiction": The Serious Writer and the Tired Reader, 461
Good Man Is Hard to Find, A, 420
On Her Catholic Faith, 460
Parker's Back, 445
Revelation, 431
Ode to a Nightingale, 986
Ode on a Grecian Urn, 1101
Oedipus the King, 1207
Of Treason, 861
O'FAOLAIN, SEAN, 84
Oh, my love is like a red, red rose, 787
Oh No, 701
OLDS, SHARON
One Girl at the Boys' Party, The, 1115
Rite of Passage, 703
OLIVER, MARY
Wild Geese, 901
OLSON, CHARLES, 871
On Being a Korean American Writer, 1758
On Elizabeth Bishop's "One Art," 2013
On Form and Artifice, 867
On Her Catholic Faith, 460
On his blindness (*Borges*), 968
On His Blindness (*Mezey*), 968
On His Friend and Rival William Shakespeare, 1588
On Imagination, 411

On Misunderstanding Oedipus, 1276
On my boat on Lake Cayuga, 818
On My First Son, 1100
On Robert Browning's "My Last Duchess," 2009
On the Death of Friends in Childhood, 1101
On the One-Act Play, 1196
On the one-ton temple bell, 758
On the Vanity of Earthly Greatness, 983
On Wordsworth's "A Slumber Did My Spirit Seal," 2043
One Art, 985
One Girl at the Boys' Party, The, 1115
One of the Irrefutable Poets, 1049
O'NEILL, EUGENE, 953, 1596, 1597
Ones Who Walk Away from Omelas, The, 257
only one guy, 759
Open Boat, The, 201
Oread, 761
Orientation, 649
OROZCO, DANIEL, **649**
  Orientation, 649
ORR, GREGORY
  Two Lines from the Brothers Grimm, 916
ORTIZ, MICHAEL
  Traveler (*translation*), 900
ORWELL, GEORGE, 240, 976
Othello, the Moor of Venice, 1290
"Out, Out—", 680
Outwitted, 898
OVID, 683, 907
OWEN, WILFRED, **710**, 819, 928
  Anthem for Doomed Youth, 1115
  Dulce et Decorum Est, 709
  War Poetry, 711
OZAWA, NEIJI
  war—this year, The, 759
Ozymandias, 984

PACHECO, JOSÉ EMILIO, 933, 964
  Alta Traición, 972
PACKER, ZZ, **38**
  Brownies, 38
PAGLIA, CAMILLE
  Reading of William Blake's "The Chimney Sweeper," A, 2049
Pair of Tickets, A, 146
Parable of the Good Seed, The, 896
Parable of the Prodigal Son, The, 230
Paraphrase of "Ask Me," A, 685
PARKER, DOROTHY, 812
  Actress, The, 862
  Résumé, 835
Parker's Back, 445
PATERSON, ANDREA
  Because I Could Not Dump, 957
Paul's Case, 536
Pause, Pause, 763
PAZ, OCTAVIO, 358, 359, 963, **968**, 970, 998
  Con los ojos cerrados, 969
PEDEN, MARGARET SAYERS
  Judge's Wife (*translation*), The, 369
Perfect Dress, 1080
PETRARCH, 856, 984
Philosophy of Composition, The, 411
Piano, 1107
Piazza Piece, 1121
Pied Beauty, 757
PIERCE-BAKER, CHARLOTTE
  Stylish vs. Sacred in "Everyday Use," 503
piercing chill I feel, The, 751
PINCKNEY, DARRYL
  Black Identity in Langston Hughes, 1031
PINSKY, ROBERT
  Low Pay Piecework, 863
Place I've Never Been, A, 602
PLATH, SYLVIA, 928, 938, 2011
  Daddy, 1116
  Lady Lazarus, 929
  Metaphors, 775
PLAUTUS, 1701
POE, EDGAR ALLAN, 121, 241, **387**, 412-19, 722, 829, 831, 837, 892, 895, 999, 1909, 1910-12, 1917-21, 1920-22, 1923-24
  Annabel Lee, 993
  Cask of Amontillado, The, 391
  Dream within a Dream, A, 1118
  Fall of the House of Usher, The, 397
  Hamlet as a Fictional Character, 1584
  Long Poem Does Not Exist, A, 994
  On Imagination, 411
  Philosophy of Composition, The, 411
  Tale and Its Effect, The, 410
  Tell-Tale Heart, The, 387
  To Helen, 910
Poe's Characters, 416
Poe's Protagonists and the Ideal World, 417
Poetic Influence, 2024
Poetic Symbols, 904
Poetry, 1112
Poetry and Emotion, 1046
Poetry of Departures, 1106
Poetry of the Future, The, 889
POLLITT, KATHA
  Mind-Body Problem, 943
Popcorn-can cover, 903
POPE, ALEXANDER, 810, 811-12, 815, 817-18, 824, 832, 841, 851, 983
  little Learning is a dang'rous Thing, A, 1119
  True Ease in Writing comes from Art, not Chance, 811
PORTER, KATHERINE ANNE, **85**
  Jilting of Granny Weatherall, The, 85
PORTER, WILLIAM. *See* HENRY, O.
Poststructuralist Cultural Critique, 2046
POTTS, L. J.
  Defining Tragedy (*translation*), 1274
POUND, EZRA, 718, 751, 752, 758, 795, 821, 871, 873, 883, 949, 983, 990, 1042-43, 2016-17
  Garden, The, 877
  Image, The, 764
  In a Station of the Metro, 751, 2016
  River-Merchant's Wife: A Letter, The, 1119
POWELL, JAMES HENRY, 978

Powwow at the End of the World, The, 936
Prayer, 1021
Presente en que el Cariño Hace Regalo la Llaneza, 965
PRITCHETT, V. S., 508
Producing *Hamlet*, 1582
Pronouns in the Poem: "One," "You," and "I," The, 1051
PRUFER, KEVIN
Pause, Pause, 763
Prufrock's Dilemma, 1054
Pulley, The, 782

Queen-Anne's-Lace, 1141
Quilt as Metaphor in "Everyday Use," 505
Quinceañera, 935

RABASSA, GREGORY
Very Old Man with Enormous Wings (*translation*), A, 364
Race and the African American Writer, 79
RAFFEL, BURTON
"Indeterminacy" in Eliot's Poetry, 1053
Rain shower from mountain, 759
RAINE, CRAIG
Martian Sends a Postcard Home, A, 777
RAMPERSAD, ARNOLD
Hughes as an Experimentalist, 1028
RANDALL, DUDLEY
Ballad of Birmingham, 800
Different Image, A, 1120
RANSOM, JOHN CROWE, 812
Piazza Piece, 1121
RATUSHINSKAYA, IRINA, 670
Reading of "Dream Deferred," A, 1033
Reading of "My Life had stood – a Loaded Gun," A, 1014
Reading of William Blake's "The Chimney Sweeper," A, 2049
Reapers, 756
Recalling "Aunt Jennifer's Tigers," 684
Recital, 814
Recognizing Poetry, 1006
Recuerdo, 1111
Red Wheelbarrow, The, 700
Redemption, 897
REED, HENRY
Naming of Parts, 1121
REEVE, CLARA, 275
Reflections on Writing and Women's Lives, 499
REID, ALASTAIR
High Treason, 972
Translating Neruda, 974
We Are Many (*translation*), 966
Rejection Slip, 708
Relationship of Poet and Poem, The, 2012
Résumé, 835
Revelation, 431
RICH, ADRIENNE
Aunt Jennifer's Tigers, 678
Living in Sin, 1122
Recalling "Aunt Jennifer's Tigers," 684
Women, 941
Rich Brother, The, 653
Richard Cory (*Robinson*), 795
Richard Cory (*Simon*), 796
RICHARDSON, SAMUEL, 277
RICKS, CHRISTOPHER
What's in a Name?, 1050
Riding Into California, 934
Rigorous Unreliability, 2042
Rite of Passage, 703
rites for Cousin Vit, the, 1071
Rites to Allay the Dead, 860
River-Merchant's Wife: A Letter, The, 1119
Road Not Taken, The, 899
ROBBE-GRILLET, ALAIN, 85
ROBINSON, EDWIN ARLINGTON, 694, 702
Horace to Leuconoë (*translation*), 952
Luke Havergal, 695
Miniver Cheevy, 1123
Richard Cory, 795
Rock and Hawk, 1099
Rocking-Horse Winner, The, 592
ROCKWOOD, R. J. R.
Fairy Tale Motifs in "Where Are You Going, Where Have You Been?," 2022
ROETHKE, THEODORE, 677, 688, 712-14, 938
Elegy for Jane, 1124
My Papa's Waltz, 687
Root Cellar, 753
ROOSEVELT, THEODORE, 694
Root Cellar, 753
Rose for Emily, A , 31
ROSENTHAL, M. L.
Adolescents Singing, 1057
ROSSETTI, CHRISTINA
Uphill, 900
Route of Evanescence, A, 756
Rubai XII, 954
Rubaiyat, 954
Ruined Maid, The, 727
Runner, The, 761
RUSHDIE, SALMAN, 358
RYAN, KAY, 667-69
Blandeur, 726
Mockingbird, 721
Talking With Kay Ryan, 668
Turtle, 786

SÁENZ, BENJAMIN ALIRE
To the Desert, 691
Sailing to Byzantium, 981
SALTUS, FRANCIS SALTUS, 978
SANCHEZ-SCOTT, MILCHA, **1703**
Cuban Swimmer, The, 1703
Writing The Cuban Swimmer, 1712
SANDBURG, CARL
Fog, 784
Grass, 723
SATYAMURTI, CAROLE
I Shall Paint My Nails Red, 887
SCHENCK, MARY JANE

Deconstructing "A Good Man Is Hard to Find," 466
SCHOLES, ROBERT
"How Do We Make a Poem?," 2038
SCHULZ, GRETCHEN
Fairy Tale Motifs in "Where Are You Going, Where Have You Been?," 2022
SCOTT, RIDLEY, 121
SCOTT, SIR WALTER, 276, 797, 1999
SCOTT, WILBUR, 2029
Sea Grapes, 1136
Second Coming, The, 915
Second Fig, 705
Secret Sits, The, 786
SEIDEL, KATHRYN LEE
Economics of Zora Neale Hurston's "Sweat," The, 2019
Self-Description, 1007
Sence You Went Away, 793
SENECA, 163
SERRANO, PEDRO
Golondrinas, 972
SERVICE, ROBERT, 830-31
Sestina, 865
Setting the Voice, 160
SEXTON, ANNE, 819, 929, 2021
Cinderella, 919
Her Kind, 699
Transforming Fairy Tales, 922
SHAKESPEARE, WILLIAM, 673, 681, 701, 752, 770, 778, 779, 782, 832, 836, 837, 838, 850, 928, 957, 1151, 1165, 1185, 1186, 1197, 1204, 1284-87, **1286**, 1393, 1508-89, 1577-93, 1702, 2021, 2025, 2029
Fear no more the heat o' the sun, 794
Hamlet, Prince of Denmark, 1396
Hark, hark, the lark, 825
Let me not to the marriage of true minds, 856
Midsummer Night's Dream, A, 1512
My mistress' eyes are nothing like the sun, 1126
Othello, the Moor of Venice, 1290
Shall I compare thee to a summer's day?, 771
That time of year thou mayst in me behold, 1125
When, in disgrace with Fortune and men's eyes, 1124
When to the sessions of sweet silent thought, 1125
Shakespearean Sonnet, 861
Shakespeare's "Honest Mirth," 1586
Shakespeare's Language as a Hidden Political Code, 1585
Shall I Compare Thee to a Summer's Day? (*Moss*), 772
Shall I compare thee to a summer's day? (*Shakespeare*), 771
SHARP, R. FARQUHARSON
Doll's House (*translation*), A, 1598
SHAW, GEORGE BERNARD, 1185
SHEEHAN, JULIE
Hate Poem, 704
SHELLEY, PERCY BYSSHE, 772, 852, 975
Ozymandias, 984
SHEPARD, SAM, 1703
Shiloh, 616
SHOWALTER, ELAINE
Quilt as Metaphor in "Everyday Use," 505
Toward a Feminist Poetics, 2033
Shunammite, The, 375
Sick Rose, The, 1069
Silence, 718
Silken Tent, The, 785
SILVERSTEIN, SHEL, 1703
SIMIC, CHARLES, 998
Butcher Shop, 1126
Fork, 756
Magic Study of Happiness, The, 881
My Shoes, 784
Simile, 776
SIMON, PAUL, 795
Richard Cory, 796
Simple Gift Made Rich by Affection, A, 965
Simultaneous Translations, 884
Since there's no help, come let us kiss and part, 857
SINCLAIR, MAY, 1045
Sine Qua Non, 860
SINGER, ISAAC BASHEVIS, 182
Sir Patrick Spence, 679
Siren Song, 1063
SISCOE, JOHN
Metamorphosis (*translation*), The, 318
SITWELL, EDITH
Mariner Man, 842
Skunk Hour, 1108
Slow, slow, fresh fount, keep time with my salt tears, 834
Slumber Did My Spirit Seal, A, 814
SMART, CHRISTOPHER
For I will consider my Cat Jeoffry, 1127
Smell!, 843
SMITH, ANNA DEAVERE, **1717**
Call to the Community, A, 1727
Twilight: Los Angeles, 1992, 1717
SMITH, BESSIE
Jailhouse Blues, 802
SMITH, STEVIE, 928
Not Waving but Drowning, 763
SMITH, WILLIAM JAY
American Primitive, 707
SNODGRASS, W. D., 780, 929
Snow Man, The, 903
SNYDER, GARY, 874
After weeks of watching the roof leak, 760
Mid-August at Sourdough Mountain, 762
SOCRATES, 671
Soliloquy of the Spanish Cloister, 1072
Some keep the Sabbath going to Church, 1003
somewhere i have never travelled,gladly beyond, 1079
Song, 854
SONG, CATHY
Stamp Collecting, 1129

Song for a Dark Girl, 1021
Song of the Open Road, 1138
Song of the Powers, 844
Sonny's Blues, 58
SOPHOCLES, 182-83, 701, 1152, 1167, 1176, 1184, 1200-1206, **1205**, 1274-80, 1282, 1729, 2022
  Antigonê, 1245
  Oedipus the King, 1207
SOR JUANA, 963, **964**
  Presente en que el Cariño Hace Regalo la Llaneza, 965
Sorrow Moves in Wide Waves, 1114
Soul selects her own Society, The, 1003
Sound of a Voice, The, 1738
Sound of Thunder, A, 137
Source for Alcée Laballière in "The Storm," The, 2014
Sous-entendu, 938
Speech to the Young. Speech to the Progress-Toward, 692
SPENSER, EDMUND, 816
SPIELBERG, STEVEN, 916
splendor falls on castle walls, The, 817
Spliced Wire, 1066
Spring and All, 1140
Spring and Fall, 1097
ST. JOHN, DAVID
  Hush, 888
STAFFORD, WILLIAM
  Ask Me, 685
  At the Un-National Monument Along the Canadian Border, 708
  Farm on the Great Plains, The, 1130
  Paraphrase of "Ask Me", A, 685
  Traveling Through the Dark, 980
STALLINGS, A. E., 821
  First Love: A Quiz, 918
  New Year's Toast (*translation*), A, 953
  On Form and Artifice, 867
  Sine Qua Non, 860
Stamp Collecting, 1129
STANDISH, DAVID, 236-37
STANISLAVSKY, CONSTANTIN, 1596
STAVANS, ILAN, 357
STEELE, TIMOTHY, 821
  Epitaph, 744
STEINBECK, JOHN, 15, 122, **242**, 272-73
  Chrysanthemums, The, 242
STEINER, GEORGE, 2006
STEPHENS, JAMES
  Glass of Beer, A, 699
  Wind, The, 779
STEVENS, WALLACE, 749, 819, 841, 870, 878, 958, 997
  Anecdote of the Jar, 903
  Disillusionment of Ten O'Clock, 742
  Emperor of Ice-Cream, The, 1131
  Snow Man, The, 903
  Thirteen Ways of Looking at a Blackbird, 878
STEVENSON, ANNE
  Sous-entendu, 938
STEVENSON, ROBERT LOUIS, 1908
  Costume in "The Cask of Amontillado," 414
STEWART, GEORGE, 83
STILLMAN, MICHAEL
  In Memoriam John Coltrane, 824
  Moonrise on mudflats (*translation*), 758
STOPPARD, TOM, 1185, 1738
Stopping by Woods on a Snowy Evening, 1088
Storm (*H.D.*), 745
Storm (*Chopin*), The, 123
Story of an Hour, The, 549
STRACHEY, JAMES
  Destiny of Oedipus (*translation*), The, 1275
Strange Beautiful Woman, A, 1113
STRAUS, NINA PELIKAN
  Transformations in The Metamorphosis, 2033
STRINDBERG, AUGUST, 1596, 1597
STUDENT PAPERS
  Analysis of the Symbolism in Steinbeck's "The Chrysanthemums," An, 272
  Bonds Between Love and Hatred in H.D.'s "Helen," The, 924
  By Lantern Light: An Explication of a Passage in Poe's "The Tell-Tale Heart," 1917
  Card Report: "The Tell-Tale Heart," 1923
  Card Report: *Trifles*, 1959
  Design of Robert Frost's "Design," The, 1946
  Faded Beauty: Bishop's Use of Imagery in "The Fish," 766
  Hearer of the Tell-Tale Heart, The, 1920
  Helmer vs. Helmer, 1730
  Kafka's Greatness, 350
  Lost Innocence in Robert Frost's "Nothing Gold Can Stay," 1903
  Othello: Tragedy or Soap Opera?, 1590
  Outside *Trifles*, 1170
  "Perfect Balance and Perfect Posture": Reflecting on "The Things They Carried," 1929
  Successful Adaptation in "A Rose for Emily" and "Miss Brill," 1926
  Trifles Scores Mixed Success in Monday Player's Production, 1962
  Unfolding of Robert Frost's "Design," An, 1942
  "Wing-Spread" Does a Dip, 1948
  Word Choice, Tone, and Point of View in Roethke's "My Papa's Waltz," 712
Stylish vs. Sacred in "Everyday Use," 503
Success is counted sweetest, 1001
SUGARHILL GANG, 803
Suitor, The, 785
Supermarket in California, A, 1088
Sure Thing, 1186
Swallows, 973
Swan and Shadow, 883
Sweat, 562
SWIFT, JONATHAN, 275, 358, 700
  Description of the Morning, A, 1131
Swimmer, The, 249
SWINBURNE, ALGERNON, 778, 855
SYNGE, JOHN MILLINGTON, 949

Taken Up, 917
Tale and Its Effect, The, 410
Talking With Amy Tan, 2
Talking With David Ives, 1148
Talking With Kay Ryan, 668
TAN, AMY, 1-3 **146**, 196, 276
  Pair of Tickets, A, 146
  Setting the Voice, 160
  Talking With Amy Tan, 2
TANNEN, DEBORAH, 938
TATE, ALLEN, 2029
TATE, J. O.
  Good Source Is Not So Hard to Find: The Real Life Misfit, A, 463
Tears, Idle Tears, 746
Teenage Wasteland, 188
Tell all the Truth but tell it slant, 1006
"Tell Me the Truth About Love," 2035
Tell-Tale Heart, The, 387
TENNYSON, ALFRED, LORD, 678, 749, 771, 811, 812, 846, 850, 853, 976, 977
  Break, Break, Break, 834
  Eagle, The, 771
  Flower in the Crannied Wall, 775
  splendor falls on castle walls, The, 817
  Tears, Idle Tears, 746
  Ulysses, 1132
Term "Protest Singer" Didn't Exist, The, 807
That time of year thou mayst in me behold, 1125
Theme for English B, 1022
Themes of Science Fiction, The, 236
There is no Frigate like a Book, 1006
They flee from me that sometime did me sekë, 1143
THIEL, DIANE
  Minefield, The, 745
  Simple Gift Made Rich by Affection (*translation*), A, 965
Things They Carried, The, 637
Thirteen Ways of Looking at a Blackbird, 878
thirteen ways of looking at a tortilla, 958
This Is Just to Say, 716
This is my letter to the World, 1004
This Is What It Means to Say Phoenix, Arizona, 511
This living hand, now warm and capable, 850
THOMAS, DYLAN, 779, 812, 854
  Do not go gentle into that good night, 864
  Fern Hill, 1134
  In My Craft or Sullen Art, 990
Those Winter Sundays, 677
Thoughts on Capital Punishment, 979
Three Privations of Emily Dickinson, The, 1011
Three Ravens, The, 1060
Times They Are a-Changin', The, 804
Tired Sex, 762
To a Locomotive in Winter, 690
To an Athlete Dying Young, 1098
To Autumn, 1103
To Build a Fire, 127
To Celia, 792
To H—, 861
To Helen, 910
To His Coy Mistress, 1110
To Lucasta, 709
To see a world in a grain of sand, 775
To the Desert, 691
To the Muse, 672
To the Virgins, to Make Much of Time, 1095
TOLKIEN, J. R. R., 276, 916
TOLSTOY, LEO, 28, **280**
  Death of Ivan Ilych, The, 280
TOOMER, JEAN, 934
  Reapers, 756
TOTH, EMILY
  Source for Alcée Laballière in "The Storm," The, 2014
Toward a Feminist Poetics, 2033
TOWNSEND, PETER
  Langston Hughes and Jazz, 1032
Tragedy and the Common Man, 1831
Transformations in *The Metamorphosis*, 2034
Transforming Fairy Tales, 922
Translating Neruda, 974
Translating Sophocles into English, 1281
Traveler, 900
Traveling Through the Dark, 980
TRETHEWEY, NATASHA, 694
  White Lies, 693
TREVOR, WILLIAM, 984
Trifles, 1153
Triolet, 865
TROLLOPE, ANTHONY, 163
True Ease in Writing comes from Art, not Chance, 811
Turtle, 786
TURNER, BRIAN
  Hurt Locker, The, 942
TUTTLETON, JAMES
  Poe's Protagonists and the Ideal World, 417
TWAIN, MARK, 16, 27, 30, 279, 780, 849
Twilight: Los Angeles, 1992, 1717
Two Fridas, The, 970
Two Lines from the Brothers Grimm, 916
Two Poetweets, 863
Two Somewhat Different Epigrams, 862
Tyger, The, 1068
TYLER, ANNE, 183, **188**
  Teenage Wasteland, 188

Ulysses, 1132
Unholy Sonnet: After the Praying, 859
Unknown Citizen, The, 702
UPDIKE, JOHN, **17**, 164, 183
  A & P, 17
  Ex-Basketball Player, 1135
  Recital, 814
  Why Write?, 22
Uphill, 900
Upon Julia's Clothes, 725

VALDÉS, GINA
  English con Salsa, 733
Valediction: Forbidding Mourning, A, 1082

VALÉRY, PAUL, 998
VALLEJO, CÉSAR, 964, 967
La cólera que quiebra al hombre en niños, 971
Variation on Belloc's "Fatigue," 862
VAUGHAN, VIRGINIA MASON
Black and White in *Othello*, 1579
Very Old Man with Enormous Wings, A, 364
VILLA, JOSÉ GARCIA, 997
Virginia, 826
Voices in Langston Hughes, The, 1029
VOLPE, EDMOND
Myth in Faulkner's "Barn Burning," 2027
VONNEGUT, KURT, JR., **231**
Harrison Bergeron, 231
Themes of Science Fiction, The, 236
Vow, The, 1093

WADA, HAKURO
Even the croaking of frogs, 759
WALCOTT, DEREK, 933
Sea Grapes, 1136
WALDROP, KEITH, 979
WALEY, ARTHUR
Drinking Alone by Moonlight (*translation*), 951
Method of Translation, The, 960
WALKER, ALICE, 275, **490**, 499-507
Black Woman Writer in America, The, 497
Everyday Use, 491
Reflections on Writing and Women's Lives, 499
WALKER, MARGARET
For Malcolm X, 1137
WALLER, EDMUND
Go, Lovely Rose, 1137
WALPOLE, HORACE, 1176
Walt Whitman and Abraham Lincoln, 2032
War in the Air, The, 1113
War Poetry, 711
war—this year, The, 759
WARREN, AUSTIN, 2007
WARREN, ROBERT PENN, 2007
WASHINGTON, MARY HELEN
"Everyday Use" as a Portrait of the Artist, 502
WASSERSTEIN, WENDY, 1703
WATKINS, DANIEL P.
Money and Labor in "The Rocking-Horse Winner," 2030
Wayfarer, The, 876
We Are Many, 966
We four lads from Liverpool are, 956
We Real Cool, 833
We Wear the Mask, 992
Weary Blues, The, 1020
WEBSTER, JOHN, 832
WEINBERGER, ELIOT
With eyes closed (*translation*), 969
WELLEK, RENÉ, 2007
WELLES, ORSON, 1177
WELTY, EUDORA, **52**, 892
Worn Path, A, 52
WEST, REBECCA
Hamlet and Ophelia, 1581
What, still alive at twenty-two?, 956
What I Like, 889
What Is Antigonê's Tragic Flaw?, 1278
What Is Cultural Studies?, 2047
What lips my lips have kissed, and where, and why, 857
Whatever Is, 483
What's in a Name?, 1050
When, in disgrace with Fortune and men's eyes, 1124
When I consider how my light is spent, 1111
When I have fears that I may cease to be, 1103
When I was one-and-twenty, 842
When maidens are young, 814
When the Time's Toxins, 732
When to the sessions of sweet silent thought, 1125
When You Are Old, 1145
Where Are You Going, Where Have You Been?, 626
White Lies, 693
WHITMAN, WALT, 795, 821, 872-73, 956, 975, 989, 2032
Beat! Beat! Drums!, 843
Cavalry Crossing a Ford, 876
I Hear America Singing, 1138
O Captain! My Captain!, 989
Poetry of the Future, The, 889
Runner, The, 761
Song of the Open Road, 1138
To a Locomotive in Winter, 690
Who Goes with Fergus?, 813
Why I Wrote "The Yellow Wallpaper," 484
Why Write?, 22
WILBUR, RICHARD, 840, 850, 975
Concerning "Love Calls Us to the Things of This World," 748
Love Calls Us to the Things of This World, 746
Three Privations of Emily Dickinson, The, 1011
Writer, The, 1139
Wild Geese, 901
Wild Nights – Wild Nights!, 1002
WILDE, OSCAR, 861, 1151, 1185, 1955, 2037
WILDER, THORNTON, 121, 1597
WILES, DAVID
Chorus as Democrat, The, 1278
Will There Be Time?, 1052
WILLIAMS, CLARENCE
Jailhouse Blues, 802
WILLIAMS, MILLER, 673
WILLIAMS, RAYMOND, 2045
WILLIAMS, TENNESSEE, 239, 1597-98, **1649**
How to Stage The Glass Menagerie, 1700
Glass Menagerie, The, 1649
WILLIAMS, WILLIAM CARLOS, 717, 758, 821, 869, 871, 883, 2024
Dance, The, 875
El Hombre, 761
Queen-Anne's-Lace, 1141
Red Wheelbarrow, The, 700
Smell!, 843

Spring and All, 1140
This Is Just to Say, 716
Young Housewife, The, 901
WILSON, AUGUST, 1703, **1833**
Fences, 1833
Look Into Black America, A, 1883
WILSON, WOODROW, 863
WIMAN, CHRISTIAN
When the Time's Toxins, 732
Wind, The, 779
Windhover, The, 1097
Wing-Spread, 1948
winter evening settles down, The, 753
With eyes closed, 969
WOLFF, CYNTHIA GRIFFIN
Dickinson and Death, 1012
WOLFF, TOBIAS, 278, **653**
Rich Brother, The, 653
Women, 941
WOODWORTH, SAMUEL, 979
WOOLF, VIRGINIA, 29, 30, **665**
Haunted House, A, 665
WORDSWORTH, DOROTHY
Journal Entry, 698
WORDSWORTH, WILLIAM, 697-98, 724, 779, 819, 975, 989, 997, 2043-45
Composed upon Westminster Bridge, 1141
I Wandered Lonely as a Cloud, 697
Slumber Did My Spirit Seal, A, 814
world is too much with us, The, 909
Workbox, The, 705
world is too much with us, The, 909
Worn Path, A, 52
WRIGHT, JAMES
Autumn Begins in Martins Ferry, Ohio, 1142
WRIGHT, RICHARD, 278
Writer, The, 1139
Writing *The Cuban Swimmer*, 1712
WROTH, MARY SIDNEY
In this strange labyrinth, 1142
WYATT, SIR THOMAS
They flee from me that sometime did me sekë, 1143

X in My Name, The, 935

YEATS, WILLIAM BUTLER, 675, 676, 677, 717, 752, 830, 838, 849, 894, 914, 982-83, 990, 999, 1597
Crazy Jane Talks with the Bishop, 1144
Lake Isle of Inninsfree, The, 675
Leda and the Swan, 821
Magi, The, 1144
Poetic Symbols, 904
Sailing to Byzantium, 981
Second Coming, The, 915
When You Are Old, 1145
Who Goes with Fergus?, 813
Yellow Wallpaper, The, 473
You fit into me, 782
YOUNG, KEVIN
Doo Wop, 825
Late Blues, 803
Young Goodman Brown, 92
Young Housewife, The, 901

ZAR, JERROLD H., 1907
ZOLA, ÉMILE, 1596

INDEX OF LITERARY TERMS

Page numbers indicate discussion of terms in anthology. A page number in **bold** indicates entry in the Glossary of Literary Terms. n following a page number indicates entry in a note.

abstract diction, 717, 738, **2052**
accent, 829, 848, **2052**
accentual meter, 840, 848, **2052**
acrostic, 855, **2052**
allegory, 239, 274, 896, 906, **2052**
alliteration, 815, 828, **2052**
all-knowing narrator, 28, 29, 81, **2052**
allusion, 84, 722, 738, **2052**
analysis, 1919, 1945, 1957, **2052**
anapest, anapestic, 836, 848, **2052**
antagonist, 15, 25, **2053**
anticlimax, **2053**
antihero, 84, 1702, 1734, **2053**
antithesis, 851, **2053**
apostrophe, 779, 790, **2053**
apprenticeship novel, 278, 356, **2053**
archetype, 911, 927, 2025, **2053**
aside, 1152, 1175, **2053**
assonance, 816, 828, **2053**
atmosphere 121, 162, **2053**
auditory imagery, 751, **2053**

ballad, 686, 797, 809, **2053**
ballad stanza, 799, 809, **2054**
bathos, 979, 995, **2054**
Bildungsroman, 278, 356, **2054**
biographical criticism, 2011, 2051, **2054**
biography, 2012, **2054**
blank verse, 850, 869, **2054**
blues, 801, 809, **2054**
box set, 1596, 1734, **2054**
broadside ballad, **2054**
burlesque, 1185, 1198, **2054**

cacophony, 811, 828, **2054**
card report, 1922, 1957
carpe diem, **2055**
catharsis. *See katharsis*
central intelligence, **2055**
cesura, caesura, 832, 848, **2055**
character, 83, **2055**
character description, 119
character development, 119, **2055**
characterization, 119, **2055**
Child ballad, 797, **2055**
clerihew, **2055**
climax, 15, 25, 1166, 1174, **2055**
closed couplet, 851, 869, **2055**
closed dénouement, **2055**
closed form, 849, 869, **2055**
close reading, 2007, **2055**
colloquial English, 724, 738, **2056**
comedy, 1184, 1198, **2056**
comedy of manners, 1185, 1198, **2056**
comic relief, 1702, 1734, **2056**
coming-of-age story, 25, **2056**
commedia dell'arte, 1185, **2056**
common meter, 799, 809, **2056**
comparison, 1924, 1947, 1957, **2056**
complication, 15, 25, **2056**
conceit, 984, 995, **2057**
conclusion, 15, 26, 1167, **2057**
concrete diction, 717, 738, **2057**
concrete poetry, 884, 891, **2057**
Confessional poetry, 929, **2057**
conflict, 15, 25, 1164, 1174, **2057**
connotation, 739, 750, **2057**
consonance, 819, 828, **2057**
contrast, 1925, 1947, 1957, **2057**
convention, 856, 984, 995, 1152, **2057**
conventional symbol, 274, 892, 906, **2057**
cosmic irony, 183, 198, 701, 715, **2057**
cothurni, 1201, 1283, **2058**
couplet, 851, 869, **2058**
cowboy poetry, **2058**
crisis, 15, 25, 1166, 1174, **2058**
cultural studies, 2045, 2051, **2058**

dactyl, dactylic, 837, 848, **2058**
deconstructionist criticism, 2041, 2051, **2058**
decorum, 724, **2058**
denotation, 739, 750, **2058**
dénouement, 15, 26, 1167, **2058**
deus ex machina, 1200, 1283, **2058**
dialect, 725, 738, **2059**
dialogue, 1150, **2059**
diction, 165, 198, 717, 738, **2059**
didactic fiction, didactic poetry, 683, 686, **2059**
dimeter, 838, **2059**
doggerel, **2059**
double plot, 1165, 1174, **2059**
drama, **2059**
dramatic irony, 182, 198, 701, 715, **2059**
dramatic monologue, 681, 686, **2059**
dramatic poetry, 681, **2059**
dramatic point of view, **2060**
dramatic question, 1166, **2060**
dramatic situation, 15, **2060**
dumb show, **2060**
dynamic character, 84, **2060**

echo verse, **2060**
editorial omniscience, 29, 81, **2060**
editorial point of view, **2060**
"El Boom," 357, 385
elegy, **2060**
endnote, **2060**
end rime, 819, 828, **2060**
end-stopped line, 832, 848, **2060**
English sonnet, 856, 869, **2060**
envoy, 866n, **2060**
epic, 686, 850, 869, **2061**
epigram, 861, 869, 1185, **2061**
epigraph, **2061**
epiphany, 16, 26, **2061**
episode, 1201, **2061**
episodic plot, **2061**
epistolary novel, 277, 356, **2061**
euphony, 811, 828, **2061**
evaluate, 1735
exact rime, 818, 828, **2061**
éxodos, 1202
explication, 1916, 1941, 1957, **2061**
exposition, 15, 25, 1165, 1174, **2061**
Expressionism, 1597, 1733, **2061**
eye rime, 821, 828, **2061**

fable, 6, 25, **2062**
fairy tale, 12, 25, **2062**
falling action, 1167, **2062**
falling meter, 838, **2062**
fantasy, **2062**
farce, 1185, 1198, **2062**
feminine rime, 819, 828, **2062**
feminist criticism, **2062**
feminist theater, 1702
fiction, 5, **2062**
figure of speech, 770, **2062**
first-person narrator, 81, **2062**
fixed form, 856, 869, **2063**
flashback, 16, 26, **2063**
flat character, 84, 119, **2063**
folk ballad, 797, 809, **2063**
folk epic, **2063**
folklore, **2063**
folktale, 25, **2063**
foot, 836, 848, **2063**
footnote, **2063**
foreshadowing, 16, 26, 1165, 1174, **2063**
form, 849, 869, **2063**
formal English, 725, 738, **2063**
formalist criticism, 2007, 2051, **2064**
found poetry, **2064**
free verse 869, 871, 891, **2064**

gender criticism, 2033, 2051, **2064**
general English, 724, 738, **2064**
genre, **2064**
Gothic fiction, **2064**

haiku, 757, 769, **2064**
hamartia, 1203, 1283, **2064**
heptameter, 838, **2065**
hero, 15, 84, **2065**
heroic couplet, 851, 869, **2065**
hexameter, 838, **2065**
hidden alliteration, 815
high comedy, 1185, 1198, **2065**
historical criticism, 2015, 2051, **2065**
historical fiction, historical novel, 121, 278, 356, **2065**
hubris, 1204, 1283, **2065**

hyperbole, 780, 790, **2065**

iamb, iambic, 836, 848, **2065**
iambic meter, **2065**
iambic pentameter, 838, 848, **2065**
image, 751, 769, **2065**
imagery, 752, 769, **2065**
impartial omniscience, 29, 81, **2065**
imperfect rime, 818
implied metaphor, 772, 790, **2066**
in medias res, 16, 26, **2066**
initial alliteration, 815, 828
initiation story, 16, 25, **2066**
innocent narrator, 30, 82, **2066**
interior monologue, 30, 82, **2066**
internal alliteration, 815, 828, **2066**
internal refrain, 793, **2066**
internal rime, 819, 828, **2066**
ironic point of view, 183, 700, **2066**
irony, 182, 198, 700, 715, **2066**
irony of fate, 183, 198, 701, 715, **2066**
Italian sonnet, 857, 869, **2067**

katharsis, 1204, 1283, **2067**

legend, **2067**
levels of diction, 724, **2067**
limerick, 862, **2067**
limited omniscience, 28, 81, **2067**
literary ballad, 799, 809, **2067**
literary epic, **2067**
literary genre, **2067**
literary theory, 2006, **2067**
local color, **2067**
locale, 120, 162, **2067**
low comedy, 1185, 1198, **2067**
lyric poem, 677, 686, **2067**

madrigal, 794, **2068**
magic (or magical) realism, 358, 385, **2068**
masculine rime, 819, 828, **2068**
masks, 1200, 1283, **2068**
melodrama, **2068**
metafiction, **2068**
metaphor, 772, 790, **2068**
meter, 830, 835, **2068**
metonymy, 781, 790, **2068**
minimalist fiction, 165, **2068**
mixed metaphor, 773, 790, **2068**
monologue, **2069**
monometer, 838, **2069**
monosyllabic foot, 838, **2069**
moral, 7, **2069**
motif, **2069**
motivation, 83, 119, **2069**
myth, 907, 927, **2069**
mythological criticism, 2025, 2051, **2069**
mythology, 907

naive narrator, 30, 82, **2069**
narrative poem, 678, 686, **2069**
narrator, 27, **2069**
naturalism, 122, 162, 1596, 1733, **2069**
near rime, 818
New Formalism, 821, **2070**
new naturalism, **2070**
nonfiction novel, 278, 356, **2070**
nonparticipant narrator, 28, 82, **2070**
novel, 275, 356, **2070**
novelette, 279
novella, 279, 356, **2070**

objective point of view, 29, 81, **2070**
observer, 28, 81, **2070**
octameter, 838, **2070**
ode, 1201
octave, 857, 869, **2070**
off rime, 818, **2070**
omniscient narrator, 28, 29, 81, **2070**
onomatopoeia, 812, 828, **2070**
open dénouement, **2071**
open form, 849, 869, 870, 891, **2071**
oral tradition, **2071**
orchestra, 1200, 1283, **2071**
overstatement, 780, 790, **2071**

parable, 10, 25, **2071**
paradox, 781, 790, **2071**
parallel, parallelism, 851, **2071**
paraphrase, 674, 686, **2071**
párodos, 1201
parody, 955, **2071**
participant narrator, 28, 81, **2071**
pentameter, 838, **2071**
peripeteia, peripety, 1204, 1283, **2071**
persona, 694, 715, **2071**
personification, 779, 790, **2072**
Petrarchan sonnet, 857, 869, **2072**
picaresque, 278, 356, **2072**
picture-frame stage, 1596, 1734, **2072**
play, 1150
play review, 1960, **2072**
plot, 15, 1165, **2072**
poetic diction, 724, 738, **2072**
poetic inversion, 975, 995
poetweet, 863
point of view, 28, **2072**
portmanteau word, 736n, **2072**
print culture, **2072**
projective verse, 871, **2073**
prologue, 1201
proscenium arch, 1596, 1734, **2073**
prose poem, 880, 891, **2073**

prosody, 835, 848, **2073**
protagonist, 15, 25, 1165, **2073**
psalms, 872, **2073**
psychological criticism, 2021, 2051, **2073**
pulp fiction, **2073**
pun, 781, **2073**
purgation, 1204, **2073**

quantitative meter, **2073**
quatrain, 852, 869, **2073**

rap, 803, 809, **2073**
reader-response criticism, 2036, 2051, **2073**
realism, 162, 1595, 1733, **2073**
recognition, 1204, 1283, **2074**
refrain, 793, 809, **2074**
regional writer, 122
regionalism, 162, **2074**
resolution, 15, 26, 1167, 1175, **2074**
response paper, 1928
retrospect, 16, **2074**
reversal, 1204
rhyme, rime, 817, 828, **2074**
rhythm, 829, 848, **2074**
rime, rhyme, 817, 828, **2074**
rime scheme, 793, 809, **2074**
rising action, 1167, **2074**
rising meter, 838, **2075**
romance, 278, 356, **2075**
romantic comedy, 1186, 1198, **2075**
rondel, roundel, 1075n, **2075**
round character, 84, 119, **2075**
run-on line, 833, 848, **2075**

sarcasm, 182, 198, 701, 715, **2075**
satiric comedy, 1184, 1198, **2075**
satiric poetry, 688, 715, **2075**
satyr play, 1200, **2075**
scansion, 835, 848, **2076**
scene, 16, **2076**
selective omniscience, 29, 81, **2076**
sentimentality, 979, 995, **2076**
sestet, 857, 869, **2076**
sestina, 866n, **2076**
setting, 120, 162, **2076**
Shakespearean sonnet, 856, 869, **2076**
short novel, 279
short story, 16, 25, **2076**
simile, 772, 790, **2076**
situational irony, **2076**
skene, 1200, 1283, **2076**
slack syllable, 830, 848, **2076**
slant rime, 818, 828, **2076**
slapstick comedy, 1186, 1198, **2076**
sociological criticism, 2029, 2051, **2076**
soliloquy, 1152, 1175, **2077**
sonnet, 856, 869, **2077**
spondee, 838, 848, **2077**
stage business, 1167, 1175, **2077**

stanza, 793, 809, **2077**
static character, 84, **2077**
stock character, 83, 119, **2077**
story of initiation, 16, 25
stream of consciousness, 30, 82, **2077**
stress, 829, 848, **2077**
style, 164, 198, **2077**
subject, 676, 686, **2077**
subplot, 1165, 1174
summary, 16, 199, 238, 674, 686, **2077**
Surrealism, 969, **2077**
suspense, 15, 1167, **2077**
syllabic verse, 854, **2078**
symbol, 239, 274, 892, 906, 1168, **2078**
symbolic act, 241, 274, 895, 906, **2078**
symbolist drama, 1733
Symbolist movement, 894, 1597, **2078**
synecdoche, 781, 790, **2078**
synopsis, **2078**

tactile imagery, 751, **2078**
tale, 11, 25, **2078**
tall tale, 12, 25, **2078**
tercet, 852, **2078**
terminal refrain, 793, **2078**
terza rima, 852, **2079**
tetrameter, 838, **2079**
theater of the absurd, 1702, 1733, **2079**
theme, 199, 238, 676, 686, 1152, **2079**
thesis sentence, **2079**
third-person narrator, 82, **2079**
tone, 164, 198, 687, 715, **2079**
total omniscience, 29, 81, **2079**
traditional epic, **2079**
tragedy, 1176, 1198, **2079**
tragic flaw, 1177, 1203, 1283, **2079**
tragic irony, **2080**
tragicomedy, 1701, 1734, **2080**
transferred epithet, **2080**
trick ending, **2080**
trimeter, 838, **2080**
triolet, 865n, **2080**
trochaic, trochee, 837, 848, **2080**
troubadour, 795, **2080**

understatement, 780, 790, **2080**
unities, 1167, 1175, **2080**
unreliable narrator, 30, 82, **2080**

verbal irony, 182, 198, 700, 715, **2080**
verisimilitude, **2081**
verse, 673, 686, 793, **2081**
vers libre, 871, 891, **2081**
villanelle, 729n, 864n, **2081**
visual imagery, 751, **2081**
vulgate, 724, 738, **2081**